Bertrand de Margerie, S.J.

WITHDRAWN

An Introduction to the
History of Exegesis

I
The Greek Fathers

Preface by Ignace de la Potterie, S.J.
Translated from French by Leonard Maluf

SAINT BEDE'S PUBLICATIONS
PETERSHAM, MASSACHUSETTS

Saint Bede's Publications
271 North Main Street
Petersham, MA 01366-0545

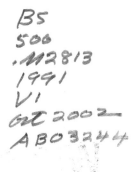

Imprimi potest   H. Madelin, S.J.
                   Provincial, French Province
                   September 24, 1979

Imprimatur   + P. Faynel, v.é
                   Paris, November 4, 1979

The *Imprimi potest* and *Imprimatur* are official declarations that a book or
pamphlet is free of doctrinal and moral error. No implication is contained herein that those granting the *Imprimi potest* or *Imprimatur* agree
with the content, opinions or statements expressed.

LIBRARY OF CONGRESS CATALOGING-IN-PUBLICATION DATA
Margerie, Bertrand de.
    [Introduction à l'histroire de l'exégèges. English]
    An introduction to the history of exegesis / Bertrand de Margerie.
        p.   cm.
    Includes bibliographical references and index.
    Contents: 1. The Greek fathers.
    ISBN 1-879007-05-3 (v. 1) : $19.95
    1. Bible—Criticism, interpretation, etc.—History. I. Title.
BS500.M2813   1994
220.6'09—dc20
                                            94-31340
                                            CIP

Contents

List of Abbreviations of Periodicals and Collections Used in the Work

AH	*Adversus Hæreses*, St. Irenæus
BAC	Biblioteca de Autores Christianios, (Madrid)
CSCO	*Corpus Scriptorum Christianorum Orientalium*, (Louvain)
DBS	*Supplément du Dioctionnaire de la Bible*, (Paris)
DS	Denzinger-Schönmetzer, *Enchiridion Symbolorum*, Ed. XXXII, Herder, Freiburg-im-Brisgau, 1963
DSAM	*Dictionnaire de Spiritualité ascétique et mystique*, (Paris)
DTC	*Dictionnaire de Théologie catholique*, (Paris)
EC	*Ecriture et Culture philosophique dans la pensée de Grégoire de Nysse*, Actes du Colloque de Chevtogne, 1969, M. Harl., ed., (Leiden, 1971)
Eph. Theol. Lovan.	*Ephemerides Theologicæ Lovanienses*, (Louvain)
GNO	*Gregori Nyssenii Opera Omnia*, (Berlin, Leiden)
Hex.	*In Hexæmeron S. Gregorii Nyssenii.*
LTK	*Lexicon für Theologie und Kirche*, (Herder, Freiburg
Nouv. Rev. Théol.	*Nouvelle Revue Théologique*, (Louvain)
Or. Christ. Per.	*Orientalia Christiana Periodica*, (Rome)
PG	*Patrologia Græca*, J.-P. Migne, (Paris, 1857-1866)
PL	*Patrologia Latina*, J.-P. Migne, (Paris, 1878-1890)
Rech. Sc. Re.	*Recherches de Science Religieuse*, (Paris)
RB	*Revue Biblique*, (Paris)
RHE	*Revue d'Histoire ecclésiastique*, (Louvain)
SC	*Sources Chrétiennes*, (Paris)
SCAT	*Sens chrétien de l'Ancien Testament*, P. Grelot, (Tournai, 1962)

TU	*Texte und Untersuchungen zur Geschichte der altchristlichen Literatur*, (Berlin)
Vig. Christ.	*Vigiliæ Christianæ*, (Amsterdam)

Preface

Here is a book whose hour has come. In order better to grasp its importance, a few reflections on the present situation in the field of exegesis should be made.

Since the end of the last century, Catholic exegesis can be said to have traversed two great periods. In the climate of the modernist crisis, the historical-critical method was looked upon in the Church with suspicion. With the perspective of time, these apprehensions can be assessed more equitably. In the preceding age an excessively radical separation between history and dogma had taken hold.

Under the influence of the prevailing rationalism, theology all too often fell into a certain extrinsecism, was often cut off from history. The introduction of critical and historical methods into exegesis was a novelty. Unfortunately, and this was indeed one of the reasons for the crisis, these methods were not always practiced with the necessary discernment. Some of those who were applying them were infected with a dangerous penchant toward historicism. This accounts for the distrust of the Church authorities toward the new methods in those first decades of the twentieth century. It was not until 1943, with the encyclical *Divino Afflante Spiritu*, that the use of the critical methods was officially recognized as legitimate.

The publication of this papal document was a liberation. In the period that followed, things changed very rapidly. Continuing the work of pioneers like Father Lagrange, contemporary Catholic exegesis has since made enormous progress, and has succeeded to a very large degree in catching up in the scientific study of the Bible. So much is this the case that today the most qualified work in exegesis is as often Catholic as it is

Protestant. The universal use of the historical-critical method is hence-forth taken for granted.

But now a completely different problem is appearing. The histori-cal-critical method, which some celebrate—perhaps with excessive emphasis—as the only valid method of exegesis, is more and more revealing its narrowness and its limitations. Indeed, from various quar-ters, much serious criticism is being leveled against it. To be sure, this criticism itself is at times excessive and unjust, for one cannot renounce the objective of the method. It will always be indispensable to make a critical examination of the texts and to go on to a study of the milieu from which they arose. But for the genuine interpretation of a text, this perspective is proving to be too narrow. With its essential focus on the past as such, the historical-critical method often shows itself insensitive to the vital dynamic of the text itself, to the profound movement that animates it and which, as in a living organism, tends inexorably toward growth and toward more explicit expression. Now, as Paul Ricœur has very well shown, the study of this latent dynamism in a given textual unity (for us, that of the biblical text) constitutes one of the fundamental tasks of interpretation. In contrast to that of the preceding method, this dimension of hermeneutics is directed toward the future. Hence, what Ricœur called "the conflict of interpretations" is inevitable.

It is important to take full account of the entire range of contempo-rary reflection on the interpretative process. To avoid one-sidedness, the act of interpreting must be developed along two fundamental dimen-sions. This first is that of "archeological" interpretation, whose nature it is to trace a text back to its *arche*, to its historical genesis, to its pre-text. This we call the historical-critical method. Quite different is the dimension of the "teleological" interpretation: with its focus on the future, it looks to the telos of the text, to the after-text. The interest brought to this second dimension is one of the major characteristics of the philosophical herme-neutics of our time (cf. Hegel, Heidegger, Ricœur, Gadamer, Pareyson). For Heidegger, for example, "to ex-plain" (*aus-legen*) a text is "to say the non-said," to make explicit what is implicit; it is "to bring to light the possibilities that it conceals," to develop its harmonics. It is this that he calls, with an apparently ill-suited term, "to repeat" or "to conserve" a problem, not in the static sense of the simple repetition of the already known, but in the sense of a constant effort to "liberate and safeguard the inner force [*inneren Kräften*]" of the text. To discover this dynamism of a text is an integral part of the search for its truth (cf. Hegel). We must agree with L. Pareyson that truth is accessible only in the very act of interpretation, and therefore in the successive formulations which one gives to it, in the re-readings and the applications one makes of it in the course of history.

It is here, precisely, that the role of tradition comes in. Contrary to the view of the *Aufklärung*, the Enlightenment, for which tradition was nothing more than a dead weight inherited from the past, a "horrible gulf" (Lessing) separating us from our origins, many thinkers today see tradition as one of the essential principles of hermeneutics. The vital milieu of tradition, says H. G. Gadamer, is "the well of truth"; it is like a bridge that enables us to accomplish "the fusion of horizons" between the past and ourselves. This was already the great idea of M. Blondel at the beginning of this century, when he said that to escape not only from the extrinsecism of a rigid sclerotic theology but also from the historicism toward which the critical methods were leaning, only the living tradition i.e., the collective consciousness and experience of the Church, offers us the means of "effecting the synthesis of history and dogma"; only tradition can give us the "sense of historical continuity," "the sense of the unity of life and of thought" between Christian origins, Christian dogma, and Christian life. These reflections of M. Blondel, in his celebrated study *Histoire et Dogme. Les lacunes philosophiques de l'exégèse moderne*, retain a burning relevance.

What does all this mean for the practice of exegesis today? Through an all-too-exclusive use of the historical-critical method, contemporary exegesis is in danger of becoming isolated from the other theological disciplines, or reaching an impasse, and of becoming doomed to sterility at the ecclesial or pastoral level. All to often, it limits itself to the study of the origin and composition of texts. It is often more interested in the historical event itself than in its meaning. It is more interested in philological and literary problems or in the structure of a literary unit than in its theological and religious import. In the work of interpretation, it almost completely ignores the contribution of medieval and patristic exegesis, the living tradition of the Church, and the resonance of Scripture in the life of believers. Exegesis is thus in danger of becoming a science reserved to specialists, that is, that "separated exegesis" so feared by M. Blondel.

Today the time has come—and this, it seems will be an important task for the exegetes of tomorrow—to effect a new synthesis between the two fundamental exigencies of interpretation, and to achieve a continuity between exegesis properly so-called and hermeneutics. It is our task to bring out more clearly the unity between the Bible, theology, spirituality, and Christian life, that is, between Scripture and the living Tradition of the Church. On the one hand, we must fully retain the considerable accomplishments of modern exegesis due to the employment of the historical-critical method. On the other hand, we must rediscover the great idea of the ancient tradition, namely, that Scripture must be interpreted *in Ecclesia*, and hence also *ex fide in fidem*. We must therefore effect a unity between critical exegesis and believing exegesis. We must integrate philological and historical analysis with our theological study, and we must move beyond the literal sense of the texts to discover their spiritual meaning. We will have to strike a balance between the rigorous use of the analytical methods of the moderns and the directly religious approach of Scripture, so characteristic of the exegesis of the ancients.

It should now be clear why anyone studying and interpreting Scripture should develop renewed interest in the exegesis of the Fathers: not in order simply to resume, in a mechanical way, their hermeneutical methods, which are to a great extent superseded and which all too often led them into allegorism, to discover, above their methods, the spirit that animated them and the profound vital principle that inspired their exegesis. We must learn from them how to interpret Scripture, not only from a historical and critical point of view, but also "in Church" and "for the Church."

This should help us to understand how much the work of Bertrand de Margerie that we are introducing here has to offer. As he himself explains in his introduction, he is not attempting to give us a complete and detailed history of the exegesis of the Fathers. Such a project would be premature. What he is offering us is at the same time more simple and more important: his is giving us an introduction to that history. He is explaining, synthetically, how the Scriptures were viewed by some of the most prestigious representatives of the Greek and Oriental Fathers: Irenæus, Origen, Athanasius, John Chrysostom, Cyril of Alexandria, and a few others. He is also very honest in pointing out the limitations of their views, which stimulates us, as modern commentators, to pursue our own reflection and to rethink the problem for the benefit of our time.

By way of illustration of what the thinking of the Fathers can contribute to our exegesis, we could describe a few of their fundamental principles that are presented in this work. For Irenæus and for Cyril of Alexandria, John 1:14, which speaks of "the Word made flesh" concerns not only the mystery of Christ; it likewise contains an important norm for the interpretation of Scripture. The reality of the Incarnation carries into and unfolds in ecclesial exegesis: in Christ, we must see both the "flesh" and the divinity, the son of man and the Son of God. In an analogous way, the Church teaches us to see in Scripture a series of profoundly human events, and the providential design of revelation and of salvation, the progressive unveiling of God's love for men. The Bible presents us at once both a human history and a divine mystery. This implies that the historical method alone is insufficient to give us a true understanding of its message.

Another principle that often appears in the Fathers is expressed in the aphorism: "one and the same" (*heis kai hautos*). It is employed in various controversies as a sovereign norm against the divisions and partial "choices" (*hairesis*) of the heretics. So for example, Irenæus in his fight against gnosticism. According to the felicitous formula of J. Guitton, the fundamental principle of gnostic thought is "the law of dissociation." It consists "in never accepting the idea that, in temporal existence, form mixes with matter, the pure with the impure, the eternal with time." This is obviously to "render the Incarnation unthinkable." Like the antichrists combated by St. John, the Gnostics were intent on "dividing Jesus" (1 John 4:3). Against this deviation, Irenæus forcefully affirms that the Logos, the Only-begotten, the Son of God, Jesus, Who took on flesh like our own, is "one and the same." Cyril of Alexandria expresses himself in similar terms against the Nestorians (cf. his treatise *Quod unus sit Christus*). The formula reappears in the celebrated definition of Chalcedon against monophysitism, and it is again taken up by Maximus the Confessor and the Lateran Council (649) against Byzantine monothelitism: "In Christ [Son] of God, there are two wills, the divine will and the human will; but Christ is one and the same." It would be entirely in line with this spirit of the Fathers to apply this principle to the two channels through which we receive the one Gospel of Jesus Christ: Scripture and tradition. For Irenæus, Christian truth dwells in the theandric Person of Christ, preached by the Apostles and then by the Church. However, he says, the Christian communities are numerous and their languages are different, but "the strength of tradition is one and the same"; everywhere and always, in the whole Church, there is "one and the same faith, one and the same doctrine." Scripture must then be read in the Church, in close conjunction with tradition. The indivisible unity between the two is well expressed in a concise formula that appears often in Cyril of Alexandria: *hoi Pateres kai hê Graphê*, "the Fathers and Scripture."

These are some reflections that came to us in reading this important work of B. de Margerie. One will find in it many other principles and many other examples. But it is obvious that some important questions remain open, especially regarding method. The task of resolving these questions falls mainly on the exegetes, since it is they who have received in the Church the mission of interpreting Scripture. The present moment is particularly propitious. Modern reflection on hermeneutics and the very numerous works on patristic and medieval exegesis are opening up enormous possibilities. These works challenge us not to limit ourselves to the technical study of the texts, but to investigate their theological and spiritual sense as well. Another stimulant comes to us from the contemporary orientation of exegesis. With the work of *Formgeschichte* and of *Redaktionsgeschichte*, it has become obvious that the text of the Bible itself not only recounts facts, but also points to their meaning; it gives us already in outline a first theological and religious vision of history. One could even say, without falling into paradoxical exaggeration, that the literal sense of Scripture is already the spiritual sense, at least incipiently. Broad perspectives, then, are opening before us to help us achieve a much-needed synthesis between critical exegesis and spiritual exegesis. Hans Urs von Balthasar recently made the perceptive observation that,

> The four senses of Scripture are enjoying today, in the most up-to-date Protestant theology, a secret renaissance. The "literal sense" is that which results from historical-critical investigation; the "spiritual sense" appears in the kerygmatic sense; the "tropological sense" (or moral sense) corresponds to the existential sense; the "anagogical sense" reappears in the eschatological sense.

Every exegete who attempts to orient his work in this way, but who also seeks to grasp more profoundly the theological and religious sense of the texts of the Bible by listening to their resonance in the Church's tradition, makes the delightful and surprising discovery of the unsuspected riches of the Word of God. It is then that he comes in his turn to the great realization so often described in the Fathers: that of the *mira profunditas* of Holy Scripture.

I. de La Potterie, S.J.
Professor of New Testament Exegesis
at the Biblical Institute of Rome
Louvain, August 28, 1980
Feast of St. Augustine

Introduction

The limits and scope of the project. The method followed.
Jewish Antecedents and biblical foundations of the exegesis of the Fathers.
Its evaluation by the Magisterium of the Church.

It is generally acknowledged that we do not have at our disposal today, in any language, a history of patristic exegesis. We have many monographs on the exegesis of this or that Father, even of this or that school (Antioch, Alexandria), or on the history of the patristic and post-patristic exegesis of a particular verse of Scripture or of a particular psalm, or even of a particular Gospel, that of John for example. But there exists no general work presenting the principal traits and characteristics of the exegesis practiced by each of the great Fathers of the Church, taken one at a time and in order. This is a regrettable lack.

The volume introduced here is intended to partially fill this lacuna at least in what pertains to Greek and oriental patristic exegesis. I hope later, if this volume meets the approval of God and men, to complement it with another treating the exegesis of the Latin Fathers.

A. The Project

The project is at the same time limited and ambitious.

It is limited in that the reader will find nothing in this introductory work on Gregory Nazianzen, Basil, Cyril of Jerusalem, Maximus the Confessor, John Damascene. Neither will he find anything on other important writers of the patristic period such as Melito of Sardis, nor certain later writers such as Diodore of Tarsus and Theodoret of Cyrus in

Antioch or Isidore of Pelusium in Alexandria.[1] At most, a passing reference will be made to one or another of these writers.

The project is limited also for another reason: it would be possible to
dedicate a whole volume, indeed, more than a volume, to each of the
Fathers to whom we have devoted only a single chapter. We are aware
of having passed over certain treasures and certain truly great minds.
But our intention was, specifically, to offer only an introduction to a
wider study which others will be able to undertake.

Nevertheless, the project is ambitious. We would like to bring out the
enduring theological importance that the exegesis of the Fathers retains,
especially in view of contemporary unbelief. This exegesis is assembled
and epitomized in the doctrinal work of the great Trinitarian and Christological councils of the fourth and fifth centuries. Their permanent value
is recognized by all the communities and churches that continue to
invoke these great councils at Geneva, at Canterbury, at Moscow, at
Constantinople, and at Rome. Not only Catholic and orthodox theologians, but even such Protestant thinkers as Barth, Pannenberg, André
Benoît[2] vie with one another in insisting that the theologian, in his
reflection on the Scriptures, cannot ignore the Fathers. In view of their
declarations, one would even be inclined to revive St. Jerome's celebrated expression cited by Vatican II as follows: ignorance of the Fathers
is ignorance of the Scriptures and of Christ.[3]

Is it not possible that an in-depth study of the exegesis of the Fathers,
undertaken in common by the different ecclesial communities and

---

[1]On the other hand, some authors, such as Origen, who strictly speaking are not
Fathers of the Church, will be treated. They were in fact sources on which the Fathers and
Doctors drew, and this is undoubtedly the reason why they are abundantly cited in the
recent and official *Liturgy of the Hours*. Among these, we note especially Theodore of Mop-
suestia. It would be good to recall, with S. Otto (*Encyclopédie de la Foi*, vol. 3, article
"Patristique," [Paris, 1966]) that "the designation 'Father of the Church' is an honorary title
whose attribution is contingent on dogmatic considerations. Already in the language of
Scripture, the term 'father' means 'doctor' (1 Cor 4:15). The bishop is in a special sense
father of his particular church because he is its authorized doctor, or teacher (Eusebius,
Ecclesiastical History, 7, 7, 4). Bishops who have died are simply the 'Fathers,' since by their
doctrinal ministry they witness to the Church's tradition (Basil, *Ep.* 140, 2)." Subsequently,
the marks by which a Father of the Church is recognized are as follows: 1) orthodox science; 2) sanctity of life; 3) recognition and approval by the Church (at least indirectly); 4)
membership in the early Church (*ibid.* p. 339). It is to Augustine that we owe this extension
of the notion of "Father" (*Contra Jul.*, I, 34). See below, note 56, how Leo XIII views the
question.
[2]See especially André Benoît, *Actualité des Pères*, pp. 65 ff. and the *indices* of the volumes
of Karl Barth's *Dogmatics*.
[3]Saint Jerome, *Comm. in Is.*, Prol.; *PL* 24, 18; Vatican II Constitution *Dei Verbum*, 25.

churches, would facilitate the common profession of the Creed of the Fathers? Could the ecumenical importance of this project be better underscored than by this single observation?

Does it follow that this project has importance only for believers, or at least only for Christians? Not at all. Many an unbeliever has made a useful contribution to the development of patristic studies and will no doubt continue to do so. One may be passionately fond of studying the history of patristic exegesis or theology without necessarily being a believer. An atheist or an agnostic could well engage in this sort of work, with the effect of helping believers themselves to better understand the Fathers.

This is not meant to imply that our own work here presented and developed is no more than patristic exegesis. On the contrary, it is the work of a believer whose conscious intention is to present, considering the episcopal magisterium of the Fathers (nearly all of them bishops) and the constant and still relevant teachings of the universal Church, a history of the charisms given by the Spirit to the Church of the Fathers in the domain of biblical interpretation. In other words, this is the history of those gratuitous gifts, which surpass human effort, by means of which the Spirit of Truth willed unceasingly to lead the Church to the Truth in its entirety. The project presented here should be seen then as an introduction to a theological history of patristic exegesis.

Theological, in this sense, the work here presented is so from another perspective as well. It is not possible to dissociate the exegesis of a Father from his understanding of the role of the Scriptures in the economy of salvation. The particular exegesis of a particular Father is always situated within his comprehensive vision of how the written word of God functions within the economy of salvation. The execution of this project could not overlook this fact. A history of patristic exegesis necessarily includes then a history (present at least in summary) of the views of the Fathers— or of some among them—on the way the divine Scriptures tie in with the Mystery of Salvation, of which they are an integral part.[4]

Such is the project, at once limited and ambitious.

Can it be realized?

---

[4]A theme developed in my study: "La diffusion de la Bible et l'économie du salut," *Esprit et Vie*, 22 janvier 1976. This study was reprinted in my book, *Vers la plénitude de la communion*, (Paris: Tequi, 1980). The Second Vatican Council presented Scripture as one of the "elements and endowments which together go to build up and give life to the Church" (*Unitatis Redintegratio*, 3), following Karl Rahner among others.

B. *The Method*

1. THE METHOD FOLLOWED IN THIS WORK

An eminent patrologist told me quite plainly that for any author such an enterprise would simply exceed human efforts.

One would seem to be compelled to accept this opinion, in view of the vast amount of material the project covers, even taking into account the limits I have proposed. Who would be capable, given the demands of original research, to treat with equal competence the weighty exegetical works of an Irenæus, a Gregory of Nyssa, a Cyril of Alexandria?

In view of such an impossible task, it was essential to work out a method suited to the subject. The solution immediately presented itself. Since I was scarcely claiming to write a definitive book on the subject, I would content myself with an introduction aimed at facilitating the work of future researchers. I would merely "clear the ground." I would limit my work here to synthesizing some of the acquired results others have offered through various articles or monographs on the exegesis of individual Fathers. My work would be to set forth what seemed to be the unique contribution or contributions, of each Father, while providing concrete examples in each case of his exegesis. This would not, of course, exclude our making an occasional new contribution.[5]

In summary, I have followed, *mutatis mutandis*, a historico-systematic method analogous to that employed, a short time ago, in my work: *The Christian Trinity in History* (Petersham, MA: St. Bede's Publications, 1982). Since that book was well received by the public and has even been viewed as "a veritable compendium, revealing a personal knowledge of the Fathers from the sources," it is perhaps not too much to hope that the present volume, filling a more obvious lacuna, will be no less favorably received.[6]

2. THE METHOD OF THE FATHERS

Having thus answered the legitimate questions of the reader concerning the scope and the method of our work, it seems fitting, before discussing in detail the particular exegesis of each of the Fathers examined,

---

[5] For example, what we say on the significance of the confession of Justin Martyr; on Eve and Mary in Irenæus, with respect to the Pastoral Epistles; on the mystery of the Incarnation as the basis of Chrysostom's exegesis, etc.

[6] G. Ferraro, *Civ. Cattolica* 128, IV (1977), pp. 200-201.

to present the reader with a global exposition of the method common to the Fathers in their reading of Scripture, a method that transcends that of Jewish exegesis while being in continuity with it.

Of course, as Pierre Grelot has insisted,[7] there were in the New Testament period a number of distinct currents in Jewish exegesis. The exegesis of the Essenes is not that of Pharisaic rabbinism,[8] nor is the latter that of the Sadducees, which is still less known; all of these currents differ markedly from that of Alexandrian Judaism, which alone seems to have exercised a major influence on the hermeneutics of the Fathers. It is true that the procedure of the Fathers reminds one rather of the eschatological actualization typical of the interpretations of the Essene *pesherim*.[9] However, the major influence, at least on the Alexandrian school, was undoubtedly that of Philo.

One point moreover is common to all these currents: the tendency to engage in a re-reading of texts with a view to unveiling the meaning they can have for today and the light they shed on the vital problems of the present, in function of a revelation that forms a whole and which grows with time. By comparing these texts one with another, by reading them from a new perspective, whether historical or theological, one discovers in them a more profound meaning and an enduring validity.

For example, since there was no longer any king in Jerusalem, the royal psalms preserved in the cult begin to serve as a prophetic proclamation in song of the future Messiah: a developing exegesis that illustrates the later flowering of messianic ideas, only seminally present at the time when those psalms were composed. The term midrash, the meaning of which is strongly disputed, has sometimes been applied to such an exegetical procedure.[10] But with Philo, Jewish exegesis of this heightening tendency joins with the allegorical method derived from Greek thought. This Alexandrian Jew, a contemporary of Jesus of Nazareth, attempted to apply to the Old Testament-rigorously, but transforming it in the process-a method that the Greeks were using to interpret their

---

[7]Cf. Pierre Grelot, *La Bible, parole de Dieu*, (Paris, 1965), pp. 182ff.

[8]See especially, J. Bonsirven, *Exégèse rabbinque et exégèse paulinienne*, (Paris, 1939), and with regard to the influence of rabbinical exegesis on Ephraem, Jerome and medieval exegesis, R. Loewe, *The Jewish Midrashim and Patristic and Scholastic Exegesis of the Bible*, TU 63, pp. 492-514.

[9]See the bibliography relative to these different currents in P. Grelot.

[10]Cf. P. Grelot, p. 183; R. Bloch, "Midrash," *DBS* vol. 5, col. 1263ff.; and A. Feuillet, *Jesus and His Mother*, (Petersham, Mass.: St. Bede's Publications, 1984), p. 145: "The term [midrash] applies to paraphrases of Scripture aimed at edifying the faithful" and p. 146: "Midrash has its point of departure in ancient texts which it seeks to make relevant."

mythological legends, while the Stoics found that it could be employed to reconcile the myths with the exigencies of their doctrines. Firmly devoted to the observance of the Law, Philo seeks through the allegorical method to bring out the interior and profound meaning of the external Law.

Thus his allegorical commentary on Genesis contains a moral history of the human soul, from its heavenly origin to its final moral purification.

The allegorical method allows Philo to find all of Greek philosophy in the Old Testament. In his view, the wise men of Greece neither said nor taught anything that the inspired writers had not already said or taught better than they. Philo thus sees himself as a citizen of the world. Instead of being confined within the narrow limits of his race and of his religion, he lives in communion with all the wise men of all time. As he describes it, Judaism becomes the spiritual religion of mankind.[11]

In reading Philo, one could have the impression that he is reducing the biblical drama to a moral allegory of the interior drama of the human soul, not without toning down the personal character of the God of Israel and the historicity of the Bible, to replace it with a Greek outlook, abstract and non-historical. This impression is heightened by his language. Almost every line of his writings contains expressions deriving from Greek philosophy.

Nevertheless, as R. Arnaldez brings out, Philo never denies either the letter of the prescriptions of the Law or the historical reality of the events narrated by the Bible. In their materiality, the commandments are addressed to the body. Now it is through his body that man lives in history. Philo never reduces spiritual realities to abstract ideas; his thought is incarnate. In Philo, it is not a question of the originality of the Jews— the true discoverers of history—being lost through contact with Greek thought. Rather, the opposite is true. Greek ideas become enriched with all the traits of the personality incarnating them.[12] Thus Greek contemplation becomes Moses. It is not a question of Plato re-animating the

---

[11]G. Bardy, "Philon," *DTC* XII, 1 (1933), 1444.

[12]R. Arnaldez, "Philon," VI, *DBS* vol. VII, (1966), col. 1312. A point of view that challenges that of Jean Daniélou, *Philon*, (Paris, 1958), p. 119: "[Philo] is totally devoid of a sense of history... Instead of showing how Old Testament events prefigure eschatological events, as was done by the apocalypses of the same period, he views them rather as the visible reflection of a timeless intelligible world." The point of view expressed by Arnaldez amounts to saying that for Philo, in his view, Greek culture plays the same role with respect to the Old Testament that the latter plays, for a Christian, with respect to the New Testament.

images of the Bible, which were losing their vitality for some; rather it is Moses conferring on Platonism all the richness of embodied reality.[13]

Even when Philo makes material use of the procedures he learned from Stoic allegory, his exegetical intention is original. His aim is not to rationalize myths, but to rediscover a revealed truth, subject to the inadequacies of human language that is always symbolic. To hear is less perfect than to see. God speaks then to allow men to hear what he himself sees; such is the dynamic of allegory. By a radical transposition, Philo has profoundly integrated the allegorical method of the Greeks into his thought as a believing Jew.[14]

Thus it is—although the matter may be beyond the range of proof—that Philo was able to influence the authors of the New Testament at the moment when they were preoccupied with presenting the message of Christ to the Greek world and in the Greek language. Thus it is above all—and here we may speak with certainty—that Philo exercised a decisive influence on the Fathers of the School of Alexandria and on their exegetical method. So true is this that a Christian legend attempted to make Philo, if not a Father of the Church, in any case a prophet. In the Cathedral of Le Puy, France, an old fresco represents him together with Isaiah, Hosea and Jeremiah, around a crucifixion.[15]

A contemporary exegete, André Feuillet, thinks that Paul drew directly from Philo in a text immediately preceding the passage that constitutes one of the decisive biblical foundations for the typological exegesis of the Fathers.[16] We are referring to the identification of the Wisdom of God with the Rock of Exodus, an identification formally made by Philo on which the Apostle drew in 1 Cor 10:1-5 immediately before announcing his great principle: "These things happened to them to serve as an example, and they were written down to instruct us, on whom the ends of the ages have come" (1 Cor 10:11; cf. 10:6).

Such a principle, set forth so broadly and without limitation, constitutes the inspired basis of patristic exegesis, even if the latter occasionally abused it. This in substance is the insight recognized and developed by another contemporary exegete, Pierre Grelot.[17] We could hold with him to the essential thrust of the Pauline idea.

---

[13]R. Arnaldez, col. 1318-1320.

[14]*Ibid.*, col. 1320-1322.

[15]Cf. C. Mondésert, "Philon d'Alexandrie," *DBS* vol. VII, (1966), col. 1289.

[16]André Feuillet, *ibid.*, col. 1349.

[17]Pierre Grelot, *Sense chrétien de l'Ancien Testament*, (henceforth referred to as *SCAT*), (Tournai, 1962), pp. 25-26.

Although in setting forth this principle, Paul immediately draws from it certain moralizing applications (10:6-10), the principle itself provides the moral examples with a deep foundation. The personalities and the events of earlier times (Moses, the passing through the Red Sea, the manna, the water from the rock to which the preceding context alluded: 10:1-4) possessed a signfication in relation to the eschatological future, to the last times into which we have entered (10:11), that is to say, in relation to the mystery of Christ and to the sacraments of the New Covenant. Indeed, to say they possessed a signification is to say too little. For those prophetic figures also embodied a hidden presence of the future mystery, they implied a mysterious participation in its reality. Hence the qualifying term "spiritual" attached to the manna, to the rock, and to the water from the rock—spiritual food, spiritual drink, spiritual rock (10:3).

This principle is not restricted to the events of the Exodus itself. Theoretically, it could be applied, not, of course, to every detail of the Old Law, but at least to the great historical events that the Old Testament describes in relation to the Exodus.[18]

The only other explicit mention St. Paul makes of this principle—outside 1 Cor 10—is about Adam, "type of the one who was to come" (Rom 5:14; cf. 1 Cor 15:45-49). But it is, for example, the presupposition of the *allegory* (Gal 4:22-30) built on the two wives and the two sons of Abraham who are, i.e., who represent, the two covenants, the two Jerusalems, the two peoples, because Isaac, the child of the promise, prefigured us (cf. note 65).

A figure (*typos*, Rom 5:14; 1 Cor 10:10) can be defined as a symbol, inscribed within the fabric of sacred history, announcing eschatological realities. Conversely, the eschatological realities (Christ, the Church and the sacraments, the final consummation of the mystery of salvation[19]) corresponding to the biblical *types* can be characterized as *anti-types* (*antitypoi*, 1 Pt 3:21 concerning baptism). Paradoxically, these terms are used by the Letter to the Hebrews in a diametrically opposite sense.[20] There the *typos*, i.e., the model or archetype, of the worship of the Old Testament with its holy place, its priests and its rites, is discovered in the sacrifice of Christ who enters by way of his ascension into the heavenly

---

[18]With the addition of a nuance, we are borrowing a statement of the same author (*ibid.*, p. 26: 'This principle could theoretically extend to the whole Old Testament'). It will become clearer to the reader below why we have added this nuance which, moreover, is doubtless consistent with the thinking of P. Grelot.

[19]*Ibid.*, pp. 26 and 447.

[20]*Ibid.*, pp. 26 ff.; C. Spicq, *Epître aux Hébreux*, vol. I, pp. 74-75 and 346.

sanctuary (8:5). Christian worship embodies the substantial image of this heavenly reality that is to come, of this truth (8:5; 9:11; 10:1). It contains its "icon" (*eikon*, 10:1) as opposed to the old worship, which possessed but a replica, an antitype (*antitypos*, 9:24), a copy (*hypodeigma*, 8:5; 9:23), a symbol and a parable in its institutions or events (9:9; 11:19), no more than a shadow (8:5; 10:1), nonetheless real, already a hidden presence of the New Testament in the Old, within the profound unity of the divine plan in two stages.[21]

Moreover, the significance of the Old Testament as figure still subsists in the New, even after the abrogation of its provisional injunctions which were connected with the pedagogical role of the law. The Scriptures of the Old Covenant can therefore still instruct us and so they are in this sense, and always remain, the sacred Scriptures of the New Covenant.[22] But it appears, in the light of the Letter to the Hebrews, that the figures of the Old Covenant point toward a single reality in three stages: Christ and his already passed history, Christ in his present Church (image), Christ in his future manifestation or reality.[23]

Christ thus appears as both the eternal and prior *archetype*, and the final *teleotype* illuminating our present and historical experience in the Church.

This complex phenomenon becomes clear in the light of another problematic which was relatively simple at the time of the New Testament, but which history has seen fit to confuse for us today, that of the letter and the spirit. For Paul, on whom the Fathers of the Church drew, the letter designates the Scripture interpreted after the manner of the Jews and not in the light of Christ, while the spirit of Scripture, likewise for Paul, is the meaning which the revelation of the mystery of Christ has given to it, the interpretation of the texts of the Old Testament in the light of Christ:[24] the letter kills the spirit gives life (2 Cor 3:6; cf. Rom 2:29;

---

[21]*SCAT*, p. 27. We should add here with Divo Barsotti, that "it is the exegesis of symbolism, not typological exegesis, that comes first. Before Abraham, man lived in a certain communion with God by living in communion with things: trees, the moon, animals, mountains. Such is the language of the first chapters of Genesis: the serpent, the tree, the garden, the rainbow. This is still now the language through which man knows God: (*Ruth, La parole et l'ésprit*, [Paris, 1977], pp. 151-152; the treatise *La parole et l'Esprit* is a treatise on spiritual exegesis). See also K. J. Woollcombe, "Le sense de *type* chez les Pères," *Suppl. de la Vie Spir.* 4, (1951), pp. 85-100.

[22]*SCAT*, p. 27

[23]We will insist below on this triple spiritual sense, in the light of the Fathers. Our intention here was to bring out the foundation in the Letter to the Hebrews of the triple spiritual sense of the Old Testament.

[24]*SCAT*, pp. 444 and 446.

7:6). Hence we have the expression *spiritual* sense and, by way of opposition, that of the *literal* or *corporal* or *historical* sense.

Today, with obvious differences and nuances, "the distinction between the literal sense and the *sensus plenior* practically corresponds to the distinction between the spirit and the letter, such as St. Paul understands it," observes P. Grelot.[25] In the modern age, the term literal sense is employed to denote the sense the human author had in mind. This literal sense is always related to the mystery of salvation. In the case of prophetic oracles, then, the literal sense already would refer directly to the mystery of Christ, the fullness of salvation. According to this definition, the literal sense includes everything toward which Paul's "letter" is oriented. "Letter," of course, carried in Paul a negative nuance that we cannot attach to the literal sense, as long as it remains open to a Christian reading. On the contrary, if the spiritual sense of the biblical texts is defined in function of the Pauline *spirit*, it becomes the exact equivalent of the *sensus plenior*, since the latter consists in going beyond the letter so as to find in the texts the life-giving presence of Christ,[26] by placing the sense of a particular text within the global context of the whole divine plan of salvation. This *sensus plenior* goes beyond the horizon of a human author, but not beyond that of God, who had it in mind from the moment he inspired the composition of the text.[27]

Thus, for example, Psalm 22 was only one individual lament among others, expressing the prayer of a pious Israelite overwhelmed by trial. But from the moment it was recited by Christ on the cross to express his own situation, there has emerged from its literal sense a *sensus plenior* with a direct relation to the mystery of the Passion—a meaning which God had in mind at the time he inspired the human author.

Let us take a closer look at what we just said about typology, letter and spirit in Paul and try to unravel its implications. It is clear that for the Apostle the events of the Old Testament have several senses: an immediate and historical sense—we could call this the literal sense—and a derived, Christological, spiritual sense—the spiritual sense or *sensus plenior*. The spiritual sense, according to the line of thought indicated by the Letter to the Hebrews is itself twofold: earthly and heavenly. It

---

[25]*Ibid.*, p. 452.

[26]*Ibid.*

[27]R. E. Brown, *CBQ* 25 (1963), p. 278. An extract from an article, "The *sensus plenior* in the Last Ten Years." Regarding the discussion in the recent past on the literal sense and the *sensus plenior*, the article of J. Coppens, *Concilium*, vol. 30 (1967), is still a useful reference; C. H. Giblin, "As is Written," *CBQ* 1958, pp. 327-353 and 477-498; *SCAT*, pp. 449-455.

concerns Christ both in his historical existence, and in his existence that endures—now, in the Church, and eternally in the future, in the heavenly Jerusalem of the consummated Kingdom. With Paul, the events of the Old Law and even those earlier events of the times of the promise and of the first creation suggest the idea of material cause with relation to Christ, while, in the Letter to the Hebrews, the Pascal mystery of Christ is equivalent to a final cause of the first Adam and of the Old Covenant.

It is as if Paul had been trying consciously to unite, in the service of Christ and of the Revelation of the New Covenant, on the one hand rabbinical techniques of exegesis[28] and on the other a "typological conception which distinguishes him most profoundly from Jewish homilists"[29] and which he received from Philo, not without re-thinking the whole thing through the light of Christ. While Philo put this typological thinking at the service of Old Covenant revelation, Paul employs it for his part to focus on that New Covenant toward which the Old was tending.

It is important to underline that such an integration, which was already anticipated by Deutero-Isaiah,[30] took place under the inspiration of the Holy Spirit. Through Paul, it is the Spirit of God who is proposing to us a specific reading of the Old Testament.

These brief remarks, perhaps not entirely free from oversimplification (and for this we beg the pardon of the specialists), generally justify, at the level of the New Testament itself, the way in which the Fathers read the Old. We say generally. The point is not, of course, to canonize every application of detail, nor to sanction the dangerous

---

[28]"Homiletic elaboration, distributive exegeses, philological considerations, expressed or sub-intended arguments linking the text invoked with the statement to be justified, historical analyses, parabolic exegesis, the use of a scriptural maxim to illustrate or confirm an idea—some of these procedures Paul derives from his rabbinical formation... However, even when he argues in a rabbinical manner, the Apostle never falls into arbitrariness" (Bonsirven, p. 234).

[29]*Ibid*. This "typological conception" leads Paul into "figurative accommodations" which by no means amount to an "accommodating sense":

> The latter takes the words in a purely material way and injects a new soul into them—often with no relation at all to the old. In the other form of interpretation, what the inspired commentator sees above all is an image, a sign, a presentiment of the various realities that go to make up the Christian mystery.... This relationship is not arbitrary or imaginary: the shadows by which the Old Testament manifests the New are real, albeit often faint (*ibid.*, p. 330).

[30]Cf. Louis Bouyer, "Liturgie et Exégèse spirituelle," *Maison-Dieu* 7 (1946), pp. 27-50; Jean Daniélou, *Sacramentum Futuri*, (Paris, 1950), pp. 131-132; Henri de Lubac, *Exégèse Médiévale I*, I, (Paris: Aubier, 1959), p. 313.

allegorizing tendency of the Alexandrian Fathers.[31] Although it may not fully satisfy us today, a Thomist presentation of the meaning of Scripture re-assumes and luminously synthesizes the method that the Fathers practiced and that has its foundation in the Pauline writings: "What is said *literally* of Christ our Head can be interpreted *allegorically* by referring it to his Mystical Body, *morally* by referring it to our acts which should be remodelled according to his example, and *anagogically*, in as much as the path of glory is shown to us in the person of Christ."[32]

The two-fold merit of this statement of Thomas Aquinas should be noted. On the one hand, the saint in no way claimed that every line of the Old Testament was susceptible to such a reading. On the other hand, what he says also applies to the Gospels and is in harmony with their own presentation of the deeds and sayings of Christ in his earthly life.

We may remark in passing that modern exegesis also recognizes a plurality of senses in the New Testament, plurality already intended by the inspired authors. Thus, by the very fact that they transmit to us what the Lord had said and done in the light of Easter and of Pentecost, "in a manner adapted to the situation of the Churches"—to use the very terms of the Second Vatican Council[33]—the Evangelists are implicitly telling us that the same word, or the same deed, is to be understood at distinct and successive levels, namely, that corresponding to Jesus' own intention, that of the understanding proper to the community hearing and transmitting the deed or the word in question, and finally, the level of what they themselves intended to communicate through these words and deeds by the act of recording them in writing. Moreover, we know how modern exegetes have stressed the inseparably ecclesial, ethical, and sacramental meaning of the Johannine signs.[34] So our own principles of interpretation have come a long way from a one-time fashionable, false literalism and are coming nearer to allowing the rich plurality of

---

[31]Cf. *SCAT*, pp. 79, note 3; p. 216, note 3; p. 445, note 4; Pius XII *Divino Afflante Spiritu*, DS 3828 *sub fine*.

[32]Saint Thomas Aquinas, *Quodlibet* 7, a. 15, ad 3m. The subtitle of de Lubac's book *Exégèse Médiévale: les quatre sens de l'Ecriture* is borrowed from this method, and the existence of this book inspired the last two chapters of the book by M. Van Esbroeck cited below (note 47).

[33]*Dei Verbum*, 19. Cf. the instruction of the Pontifical Biblical Commission on the exegesis of the Gospels: *AAS* 56 (1964), 715.

[34]In the Gospel of John, the "sign" is a miracle of Jesus that prefigures the sacrament of Baptism or the Eucharist and solicits the faith of the person who understands it. Lagrange (*Evangile selon Jean*, 1925[2], pp. 59-60) is therefore right in bringing out the difference of nuance that distinguishes the Johannine use of the word "sign" from that of the Synoptics.

meanings—sometimes explicit, sometimes implicit[35]—that the Fathers gave to so many biblical texts!

Thus it seems that, in certain quarters, and often without knowing it,[36] modern exegetes are rediscovering the horizons of a patristic exegesis which, in spite of its many limitations, can help them in their present research.

There are, in fact, exegetical theses defended at the Biblical Institute in Rome today which, in reference to a particular verse of Scripture, will take the trouble to review not only modern commentaries on it, but first of all, and in a methodical way, that of the Fathers.[37] In Jerusalem, the professors of the Franciscan Biblical Institute require systematic study of the ante-Nicene patristic commentary on a particular verse of Scripture.

C. The Interest in Patristic Exegesis

There are several reasons for this renewed interest in patristic exegesis. We shall attempt to enumerate the principal ones.

First of all, modern exegetes are beginning to suspect they could learn much from the Fathers on particular points and that they might discover in them certain leads for solutions to still pending problems.[38]

Furthermore, many were impressed by the depth with which Henri de Lubac presented the exegetical undertaking of the Fathers. For one thing, he succeeded in showing how well the Fathers grasped the fact that the literal sense and the spiritual sense make up the very fabric of the Old and New Testaments, two Economies, two dispensations, two Covenants that gave birth to two peoples, to two regimes established in succession by God to regulate man's relationships with himself.[39] But above all, with an astounding wealth of erudition, de Lubac brings us back to the vision of the Fathers who view Christ as both the exegete (cf. Lk 24:44-45; Jn 1:18) and the exegesis of Scripture, not primarily a verbal

---

[35]P. Grelot (*SCAT*, p. 446) writes with regard to the literal sense: "There is no way that it could be plural, unless the author in question was being intentionally ambiguous." We think that the human author of a biblical book, in a number of cases, did in fact intend just such a plurality of senses. Semantic plurality is not a monopoly of the divine author. St. Augustine, in his *Confessions*, treated this highly disputed point in some depth.

[36]It frequently happens that an exegete will propose an interpretation, thinking it new, that he is unaware has already been proposed by one or another Father of the Church.

[37]So Vellanickal in his recent thesis on adoptive filiation in the Gospel of John: *Divine Adoptive Sonship in Johannine Writings, An. Bib.* 72, (Rome, 1977).

[38]Such as the meaning of John the Baptist's expression "I am not worthy to untie the thong of his sandals" (Lk 3:16).

[39]Henri de Lubac, p. 309, (n. 30).

exegesis, but one in act. Christ's exegesis is Act.[40] It would be helpful here to quote Henri de Lubac at some length:

> Before explaining to his disciples, on the eve of the Pasch, how the old Scriptures bear witness to the New Testament and so find themselves transformed in it, Jesus himself effects this transformation.... Jesus is the Exegete of the Scripture *par excellence* in the act by which he accomplishes his mission, at that solemn hour for which he came, namely, in the act of his sacrifice, at the hour of his death on the cross. It is then that he says in substance: *Ecce nova facio omnia*, see, I am making all things new (Rv 21:5). It is then that he destroys in their letter the shadows and the image and that he reveals their spirit, which will nourish his faithful.... In pronouncing the *consummatum est* (Jn 19:30) on the gibbet which symbolically represents the last letter of the Hebrew alphabet, Jesus gives to all of Scripture its consummation,[41] revealing thereby the whole mystery of man's redemption hidden in the twenty-two books of the Old Testament. His cross is the one and only universal key.[42] By this sacrament of the cross, he unites the two Testaments into a single body of doctrine, joining the ancient precepts to evangelical grace. As Lion of Juda, he achieves by his death the victory that opens the book with the sevenfold seal.[43] (...) The blow of the centurion's lance accomplished in truth what Moses' rod striking the rock had accomplished in figure. From the side pierced by the lance gushed forth the fountains of the New Testament. "If Jesus had not been struck, if the water and blood had not flowed from his side, we would all still be thirsting for the Word of God."[44] (...) As he leaves the sepulchre, Christ moves aside the rock that conceals it, that rock of the letter which until then was an obstacle to spiritual understanding, that rock which he had already prophetically removed from Lazarus' tomb.[45]

In other words, the new regard of the exegetes for the Fathers and for their hermeneutics is connected with the importance they attach to the problem of the relationship between the two Testaments, the problem of messianism and that of Christology in general.

Finally, many are beginning to feel that a partial and nuanced return—adapted to the more recent technical advances—to the exegesis

---

[40]*Ibid.*, pp. 322-323. In a note, the author cites Martin Heidegger who says in *Essays and Conferences* that *logos* is both the *legein* and the *legomenon*, the saying and the said.

[41]Cf. St. Chromatius of Aquilea, *In Matthæum*, tr. VI, c. 1, n. 2: *CCL* IX, 409.

[42]Augustine, *In Ps. 45*, n. 1, *PL* 36, 1378. Cf. M. Pontet, *L'exégèse de saint Augustin prédicateur*, pp. 373-374.

[43]Gregory the Great, *In Ezech.*, II.4, 19; *PL* 76, 984 A.

[44]Origen, *In Exod.*, h. 11, n. 254.

[45]St. Augustine, *Tract. in Johan.*, XLIX, 22; *CCL* 36, 430. We took this entire passage from the above-mentioned work of Henri de Lubac, pp. 324-327.

of the Fathers and to their method could help them as exegetes in the direction of a synthetic unification of the exegetical act and as preachers in their service of the Word of God. It is clear that many of the works produced by contemporary exegetes lead to a kind of atomization in the reading of Scripture and to a technical virtuosity that pulverizes the text, leaving the reader bewildered. We have today at our disposal more accurate and more numerous scientific tools for discovering the spiritual sense of the Scriptures,[46] but many of our present works of exegesis are scarcely oriented, as were those of the Fathers, toward the disclosure of the anagogical sense, toward man's return to God, through the practice of the virtues and through the sacraments, through the reading of Scriptures. Whence the crisis in pastoral homiletics, and more radically, the crisis of faith, not of the Church, but within the Church.

There exists today a keen awareness of how much the patristic theory of the four senses of Scripture can contribute to doctrinal-kerygmatic expression and to missionary impetus. Within this context, some writers are proposing[47] a highly attractive comparison and integration between these four "marks of Scripture"[48] and the classical four marks of the Church found in the Credo of the Fathers. We give here an exposition of this relationship in our terms.

Scripture is unique and so is the Church to which it belongs and the humanity which it addresses. The unity of Scripture is a factor of the unity of the Church,[49] and the holiness of this sanctifying Scripture makes her holy. The apostolic Church receives from the Apostles a coherent overall explanation of the Old Testament in the light of the mystery of Christ. She also receives from them a comprehensive insight into all cultures as preparations for the Gospel. By the fact that it is thus universally accepted, Scripture contributes to the catholicity of the Church whose growth will continue until the return of Christ, toward which this same Scripture is directing us, by way of its anagogical sense.

Thus, within the norms presently recognized by sound exegesis and by the magisterium of the Church, the concrete, measured, but ever faithful exercise of the patristic method of interpretation would provide

---

[46]See in this sense the judicious observations of Walter Burghardt, "Early Christian Exegesis," *Theological Studies* 11 (1950), pp. 78-116.

[47]M. Van Esbroeck, *Herméneutique, Structuralisme et Exégèse*, (Paris, 1968), *passim* and especially p. 197.

[48]In terms of the four senses just mentioned, one could say that Scripture is historical, parenetic, Christocentric and eschatological in the sense that one who reads it with good will is led to his final end.

[49]See above, note 4.

the decisive impetus in helping us avoid rigid compartmentalizing and the ruptures between reading of Scripture, sacramental life, ethical endeavor, and ecclesial action. Integration would be achieved through the tension of a common focus on the attainment of the final end. It is in this way that human and Christian life, reunited about the Word of God, would cause the inadmissible unity of the one Church of the one God to shine forth with a new splendor.

Our thesis is this: the Fathers would be able today to render us the service we have just described if we were ourselves inspired by their fundamental preoccupation, while remaining with them "faithful to the rule of Christ's heavenly Church (*ekklesia ouranios*[50]), a rule that has come down to us through apostolic succession." In the last century, this norm of Origen[51] was commented on in a brilliant way by J. A. Moehler:

> Scripture must be interpreted according to the Spirit, for it is the work of the Holy Spirit. This Spirit is given to us by the Church of Jesus, which has come down to us in perfect continuity. Whatever contradicts her must be regarded as erroneous.... When we say the Scripture is to be interpreted spiritually, we mean that nothing can be found in Scripture that would be in contradiction with the conviction of the Church.... It belongs to the Catholic Church to expound the Scripture.... There is something great, something sublime, something truly divine in the way a Catholic reads Holy Scripture. He reads it as part of the totality of the faithful with whom he is united by the same spirit without distinction of time. It is as if all were assembled in a holy temple in which the same Spirit breathes, penetrating all. It is as if all formed but one living organism-as if a whole family were reading together the affectionate letter of a loving and beloved father.... This is the *consensus unanimis*[52] of the Council of Trent, the image of a unity in complete freedom.[53]

---

[50]As J. A. Moehler rightly observes (*L'Unité dans l'Eglise*, [Paris, 1938], p. 264), "as is shown by the predicate *according to the succession of the Apostles*, it is a question of the Church ever visible and ever in perfect spiritual continuity—the Church of Jesus Christ who came from heaven."

[51]Origen, *De Principiis*, IV, 9; PG 11, 360.

[52]On the exact meaning of this Tridentine formula, see G. Geenan, O.P., *Maria in Sancta Scriptura*, (Rome, 1967), t. III, pp. 63-140, especially p. 132: the Council of Trent wished to indicate a method of preaching, not to place limits on the efforts of exegetes.

Other authors, however, complement the above remark by emphasizing the subtle nuance in the way Vatican I chose to clarify the sense of Trent: for Vatican I (*DS 3007*), it is because exegetes (like other Christians) ought to adhere to the judgment of the Church concerning the true sense and interpretation of the Scriptures that they should also (*ideo*) never interpret anything contrary to the unanimous consent of the Fathers. This suggests that the accord of the Fathers in these matters is one of the forms under which the

constantly.[64] Such usage can, however, occasion abuse, and it is certain that some of the Fathers seem "to have presented clearly metaphorical interpretations of Holy Scripture as its authentic meaning," a practice against which the pope of *Divino Afflante Spiritu* put exegetes on guard.[65]

Pius XII further notes that many biblical problems remained "impenetrable" for the Fathers (the first chapters of Genesis, the literal sense of the Psalms, he himself specifies) who lacked the equipment to fully understand them.[66]

The Church is then in no way advocating a return pure and simple to patristic exegesis, especially not to that of the Alexandrian School. She wishes to encourage the search for the spiritual sense only when this is founded on thorough preliminary examination of the literal sense and never in contradiction to it. The exegesis of the spiritual sense must not be anti-literal, but "postliteral" and "transliteral." This is clearly the meaning of what Pius XII teaches in his *Humani Generis* of 1950.[67]

The Church must then *go beyond* the exegesis of the Fathers in all its elements that have since been superseded as a result of new discoveries.

---

[64]*Ibid.*, *AAS* 35 (1943), 311; *DS* 3828.

[65]*Ibid.* However Pius concedes—and this justifies the primarily homiletic exegesis of the Fathers—that "in the ministry of preaching especially, broader and more metaphoric use of the sacred text can be useful for clarifying and substantiating certain points of faith and morals, as long as this is done with moderation and discretion.... This usage of the words of Sacred Scripture is, as it were, extrinsic and adventitious"; he ends by pointing out the dangers of such a usage today.

Allegory in Origen is not the same as a metaphorical signification: he does not deny the reality of facts of the Bible in their historical sense. Although Origen uses the word allegory in different senses, his work as a whole takes its inspiration from one principal sense, derived from Paul, namely the "spiritual" interpretation. Nevertheless, neither Origen nor the Christian writers really managed to limit the use of the term "allegory," in any strict way, to its Pauline signification alone, i.e., to the discerning of the figures in Israel which were announcing Christ, within the context of an opposition between figure and truth, letter and spirit, old and new. Henri de Lubac makes this point in his "Typologie et Allégorisme," *Rech. Sc. Rel.* 34, 1947, 185-209. The rejection of Alexandrian allegorism does not imply the rejection of this Christo-ecclesial dimension of the spiritual sense. Whereas pagan allegorism tends toward myth, Christian allegory is rooted in history (cf. Henri de Lubac, "A propos de l'allégorie chrétienne," *Rech. Sc. Rel.* 47, 1959, pp. 5-43, especially pp. 28ff., where he refutes J. Pépin on this point).

[66]Pius XII, *Divino Afflante Spiritu*, p. 249.

[67]Pius XII, *Humani Generis*, *AAS* 42 (1950) 570; *DS* 3888. The passage here cited does not condemn the sound search for the spiritual and symbolic sense praised by *Divino Afflante Spiritu* seven years earlier, but rather the kind of interpretative endeavor that ignores the literal sense altogether or holds it in contempt. Thus understood, this passage is not inconsistent with the view that the Old Testament to a certain extent remains a closed book within the Church today, since many are insensitive to its spiritual sense even in passages where such a sense is to be found.

But this "going beyond" must remain in the line of the Fathers' exegesis itself. With this latter and in its light, modern exegesis must remain fundamentally a search for the spiritual and doctrinal meaning of the biblical texts.

But it was Vatican II, in its dogmatic constitution on divine revelation, *Dei Verbum*, that assembled the insistent appeals of earlier pontiffs and made it clear why exegesis would be condemning itself to superficiality were it to ignore the Fathers.

We quote the decisive text:[68]

> The spouse of the incarnate Word, which is the Church, is taught by the Holy Spirit. She strives to reach day by day a more profound understanding of the sacred Scriptures, in order to provide her children with food from the divine words. For this reason also she duly fosters the study of the Fathers, both Eastern and Western, and of the sacred liturgies.

One is struck by the relationship of causality that here unites the study of the Fathers and the Liturgies on the one hand with that of the Scriptures on the other. Precisely because she encourages the study and the ever deeper understanding of the Scriptures, the Church also promotes the study of the Fathers. The latter is presented as an appropriate means to attaining an "ever deeper understanding of the Scriptures," which is the goal in view. May we not then conclude that ignorance of the Fathers would result in ignorance of the deeper aspects of Scripture, or in the superficiality of biblical research, especially regarding the *doctrine*[69] of the Scriptures?

Moreover, does not ignorance of patristic exegesis inevitably entail ignorance of the type of exegesis employed by the liturgy, or, better by the liturgies whose origins are often, most often, contemporary with the patristic era? Was not that exegesis in fact largely conditioned by patristic exegesis? This would have all the more serious consequences in that, according to the explicit teaching of Vatican II in the same solemn document, it is "above all in the sacred Liturgy that the Church continuously takes the bread of life from the table of the word of God and offers it to the faithful" together with the Body of Christ.[70]

---

[68]*Dei Verbum*, 23. It seems that the allusion to the Fathers and to their importance for exegesis was a last minute addition to the text of the constitution, which shows both how much patristic exegesis had been forgotten and, in reaction, how strongly the Council wished to endorse it.

[69]Cf. note 61 and *Dei Verbum* 23-24.

[70]*Ibid.*, 21; cf. below note 73 and the reference there to the article of Montague.

The conciliar declaration on the importance of the study of the Fathers in view of acquiring an ever deeper understanding of the Holy Scriptures may be elucidated by reading it in the light of earlier statements (nos. 12 and 16) of the same constitution *Dei Verbum*, which it illuminates in its turn. It is indeed above all the Fathers who help us to seek and to discover not only what the human authors of the Scriptures intended, but also what their sole supreme Author, God, "intended to communicate to us and to channel through their words...by directing our attention to the unity of Scripture as a whole, with attention to the living Tradition of the whole Church and to the analogy of faith" (no. 12). It is the Fathers too who help us to see that "the books of the Old Testament, integrally resumed in the evangelical message, acquire and reveal their full signification in the New Testament" alone (no. 16).

While some modern exegesis is excessively analytical to the point of atomizing the sacred text, the Church of Vatican II wishes—and the passages we have just quoted make this sufficiently evident—to help us regain within the contexts of our faith, of our liturgical and Eucharistic life, and of our spiritual contemplation,[71] a unified and Christocentric understanding of those Scriptures which are threatened with profanation and which she continues to qualify emphatically as "holy" and "divine," even underlining their analogy to the Incarnation, in the weakness of human flesh and of human language, of the Eternal Father's only Word (*ibid.*, no. 13).

This also explains the explicit call, in the post-conciliar documents on the liturgical reform,[72] for a return to daily preaching which can hardly fail to stimulate the study of the Fathers and of their continuous commentaries on Scripture. Indeed, their exegesis is very largely a "homiletic exegesis," in the course of which, moreover, it remains in perfect harmony with the documents it is expounding. And was it not a contemporary exegete who noted that the majority of biblical texts were originally

---

[71]*Dei Verbum*, 7: "This sacred tradition, then, and the sacred Scripture of both Testaments, are like a mirror, in which the Church, during its pilgrim journey here on earth, contemplates God, from whom she received everything, until such time as she is brought to see him face to face as he really is." It is noteworthy that the same text specifies that the Old Testament forms part of that mirror.

[72]*Institutio Generalis Missalis Romani*, 42, (Vatican City, 1970). Cf. H. von Campenhausen, *Les Pères Grecs*, (Paris, 1970), p. 165: "A conscientious exegesis is ultimately at the service of preaching...it is there that it finds its raison d'être and its purpose."

writings intended for liturgical celebration and that their meaning cannot be completely grasped except within the context of a ritual celebration?[73]

In spite of its imperfections and its limitations, we hope that the work here introduced will allow some insight into the fascinating character of patristic exegesis, which begins and ends in the sacramental, liturgical dimension of the presence among us of the Incarnate Word, Exegete of the Father.

It is no doubt by virtue of this synthetic, global, existential approach that the "ancient Christian exegesis" so successfully "brings out the prodigious newness of the Christian reality. It employs a subtle dialectic of the before and the after; it defines the relationship between historical reality and spiritual reality…. It organizes the whole of revelation around a concrete center: the cross of Jesus Christ. It is itself a dogmatic and a spirituality, complete and thoroughly integrated," wrote Henri de Lubac in 1959.[74]

Yes, the ancient Christian exegesis is not just a system of dogmatics and a spirituality; it is the perfect integration of the two as well. It treats dogma under the aspect of its spiritual potentialities, and it gives full attention to the dogmatic aspects inherent in a spiritual life whose ecclesial character is securely established. It is precisely for this reason that the exegesis of the Fathers is of such incalculable value even for today. It meets a need which present-day exegesis, though in many ways better equipped, often fails to satisfy. We await the day when exegetes, returning to the school of the Fathers, will be able to go beyond them and to rediscover, in the Church, the integral sense of their theological and pastoral vocation.[75]

The irreplaceable character of recourse to patristic exegesis has been stressed more recently by Yves Congar in these terms:

> The spirituality of the Fathers is indistinguishable from their dogmatic contemplation, which is itself tied to their meditation on the Holy Scriptures. The Fathers have shaped the life of the Church…taking as their starting point the Holy Scriptures and the experience of Christian reality, the two conditioning and illuminating each other mutually…. Our faith in the Holy Trinity…in Jesus

---

[73]G. T. Montague, "Hermeneutics and the Teaching of Scripture," *Catholic Biblical Quarterly*, 41 (1979), p. 16.

[74]Henri de Lubac, pp. 16-17. From the perspective here sustained by de Lubac, one can only be delighted to see the great wealth of patristic texts (including biblical commentaries of the Father) now made available for the official prayer of the people of God in the new *Liturgy of the Hours*.

[75]Cf. notes 69 and 61.

Christ true God and true man, in grace, in the Eucharist, in the Virgin Mary, in the Church and Her priesthood is, in its entirety, thoroughly biblical and thoroughly patristic.[76]

We hope therefore that this Introduction to the history of the Greek and Eastern Fathers will be useful, not only to exegetes and to theologians, but also to preachers and catechists.

---

[76]Yves Congar, *Tradition and traditions*, (New York: MacMillan, 1967), p. 445.

Chapter I
Saint Justin, Exegete of the Presence of the Word-Messiah in the Law and the Prophets

Born in Palestine to a Greek and pagan family, Justin was converted to Christ after having gone through the complete (or nearly complete) cycle of all the philosophical positions possible in the first half of the second century: Stoicism, Aristotelianism, Platonism, the school of Pythagoras. He retained the mantle of the philosopher and dedicated himself, as a simple layman, to the defense of the faith. Whence his *Apologies* addressed to emperors, and his *Dialogue with Trypho*, a Rabbi who died about 134. It is particularly in this last work that we find numerous examples of the exegesis of this "philosopher and martyr" (as Tertullian called him[1]) who gave his life for Christ in Rome, about the year 165.

Justin was one of the first Christian exegetes. The interest aroused by his works has not lost ground during recent years. Careful studies have

---

[1]Tertullian, *Adv. Valent.*, 5. A number of scholars, however, such as E. R. Goodenough (*The Theology of Justin Martyr*, [Jena, 1923], p. 292), believe that Justin was in no sense a true philosopher, and they bolster this position with a number of arguments. In his book on St. Justin (Paris, 1914, ch. V), M. J. Lagrange had already dealt with this question.

been devoted both to his exegesis[2] and to his way of conceiving the relationship between philosophy and Christianity.[3]

His exegesis is situated within the context of a dialogue (one of the first which is extant in the post-New Testament period) between a Jew and a Christian.

Justin's dialogue with Trypho will hardly be viewed by our contemporaries as a model of ecumenism. But it does manifest his charisms as an interpreter of the Old Testament, the care he took in collecting the fruits of Judeo-Christian exegesis, and the genuine openness he maintained before his interlocutor and toward pagans as well. In the cultural reality of the world, Justin sees the reflected rays of the Logos that enlightens every man.

Today more than ever, the relationship between the Old and the New Testaments is commanding the serious attention of Christian exegetes and theologians[4] within the various confessions. It is in this context that we present a number of Justin's views on the presence of the Messiah Jesus in the Law and in the Prophets: the typology of Christ in the Law of Moses, the verbal announcement of Christ by the Prophets.

In presenting things in this way, we are moreover following the very order of the works studied. The dialogue with Trypho includes an initial section that establishes "the nullity of the Old Law" and its typological character. The later sections comprise a demonstration through prophecies of the truth of Christianity. Justin distinguishes clearly between the *typoi*, or events fashioned by the Holy Spirit, and the *logoi*, inspired words.[5]

Next we shall examine the methods Justin applied in his biblical exegesis and how its results are to be evaluated.

---

[2]See especially W. A. Shotwell, *The Biblical Exegesis of Justin Martyr*, (London, 1965); P. Prigent, *Justin et l'Ancien Testament*, (Paris, 1964); J. Daniélou, *Message évangélique et culture hellénistique aux IIe et IIIe siécles*, (Paris, 1961), pp. 199-220. The last is the principle source on which I have drawn here. Other references include: *DTC*, Tables, "Justin," bibliography; C. Kannengiesser, *DSAM* 8 (1974), 1642-1643 on Justin's exegesis.

[3]See especially J. C. M. Van Winden, *An Early Christian Philosopher*, (Leiden, 1971), a methodical commentary on the nine first chapters of the *Dialogue with Trypho*; L. W. Barnard, *Justin Martyr, His Life and Thoughts*, (Cambridge, 1967); and the books mentioned in note 1.

[4]As is attested to by the following declaration of the International Commission of Theology: "The unity-in-duality of the Old and New Testaments, as the fundamental historical expression of the Christian faith, offers a concrete starting point for the unity-in-duality of that same Faith" (*DC*, 70, 1973, 459).

[5]*Dialogue*, XC, 2; CXIV, 1; F. M. Sagnard, "Y a-t-il un plan du Dialogue avec Tryphon," *Mél. Joseph de Ghellinck*, vol. I, (Gembloux, 1951), pp. 171-182.

A. The Law of Moses Manifests the Presence of the Messiah in its Types

By Law of Moses we understand here the Pentateuch, including the Book of Genesis, the description of the Creation, the Fall, the Flood, everything leading up to the entrance into the Promised Land. Justin sees the Tree of Life as a figure of Christ. Adam's temptation by the Serpent prefigures that of Christ by Satan. The philosopher-martyr is in fact the first to point out the parallel between Eve and Mary: "Eve was a virgin, without corruption. By conceiving through the word of the serpent, she gave birth to disobedience and death. The virgin Mary conceived faith and joy, when the angel Gabriel announced to her the good news."[6] We shall see in the next chapter how Irenæus resumed this theme and developed it in greater depth. With Justin, it constitutes an extension of the parallel between Adam and Christ which Paul expounded in his letter to the Romans (ch. 5). Indeed, the Apostle says explicitly (Rom 5:14) that Adam was the type, meaning the real but imperfect figure, of Christ.[7]

For Justin, the Flood prefigures at once the eschatological Judgment and the new flood that came with the new Noah, Christ.

In presenting the Flood as a figure of the last judgment, Justin remains in the line of both the Old and the New Testaments (cf. Mt 24:37; 2 Pt 3:10).[8] Justin expresses this idea as follows: If God reconsiders the catastrophe that is to overturn the universe and annihilate bad angels, demons, and sinners, he does so for the sake of the Christian people. Were it not for this, the fire of judgment would come down and wreak universal destruction, as the Flood once did. The theme is then connected to that of God's patience (cf. 2 Pt 3:5-10).[9]

The typology of the new Noah is even more specifically Christian:

At the flood the mystery of the world's salvation was at work. The just man Noah, together with the other flood personages, namely, his wife, his three sons and their wives, made eight in number thereby symbolizing the eighth day on which our Christ was raised from the dead, that day being always implicitly the first. Christ, the first-born of all creation, has become in a new

---

[6]*Dial.*, LXXXVI, 1 (the tree of life); CIII, 6 (the temptation of Adam); C, 4-5 (Eve and Mary).

[7]See the note on Rom 5:14 in the *New Jerusalem Bible* (New York: Doubleday, 1992).

[8]Cf. J. Daniélou, *From Shadows to Reality*, (Westminster, MD: The Newman Press, 1960), pp. 74-78; book II of this work is generally devoted to Noah and the flood.

[9]Cf. Hans Küng, *Justification*, (New York: Thomas Nelson & Sons, 1964), pp. 197ff.: the preservation of the universe is a merciful non-annihilation, due to the merits of Christ. The text of Justin cited here is taken from II *Apol.* VII.

sense the head of another race, regenerated by Him, through water, through faith, and through the wood which contained the mystery of the cross, just as Noah was saved through the wood of the Ark, carried by the waters of the flood.... And I mean here that those who receive preparation through water, faith, and wood escape the judgment of God that is to come.[10]

As Jean Daniélou suggests,[11] we have here an ideal specimen of typological exegesis with the help of which we may distinguish its different levels.

The fundamental datum is the biblical *theologoumenon* of the flood that we may state briefly as follows: the world is under sin; the chastisement of God strikes the sinful world; a remnant is spared to become the principle of a new humanity.

Justin portrays this *theologoumenon* as realized on three levels. The first is Christ himself, who has made himself one with the sinful world, bears with it the chastisement for sin, but is spared, in the mystery of his resurrection, to become the principle of a new humanity. The second level is that of the eschatological judgment; and finally baptism, which is a sacramental representation of the judgment. In baptism, sinful man is destroyed and the new man created. One who has undergone this rite will escape the judgment to come.

Here again, Justin's typological exegesis carries forward and explicates an exegesis that the New Testament itself had inaugurated. St. Peter (1 Pt 3:18-21) and the author of the Letter to the Hebrews (11:7) had already highlighted the correspondence between flood and baptism.

Everything we have dealt with so far concerns the types of Christ and of his Church present in the human race before the establishment of the chosen people, and of the Old Covenant. Next we must ask what the Law, the Sabbath, circumcision, and sacrifices represent for Justin.

---

[10]*Dial.*, CXXXVIII, 1-3. We have in this text a first inkling of the distinction made by the later tradition, within the spiritual sense, between the tropological sense (pertaining to the Christian mystery) and the anagogical sense (regarding the hereafter).

[11]Daniélou, *Message évangélique et culture hellénistique* (cited in note 2), pp. 191ff. We should also note, with Henry Chadwick, *Early Christian Thought and the Classical Tradition*, (Oxford, 1966), p. 11, Justin's sensitivity to stoicism and its cosmology, according to which the world is subject to periodic catastrophes by way of floods and conflagrations; however, Justin rejects (II *Apol.* VII, 2) the Stoic idea of a destruction of the world through the mutual absorption of beings. But ultimately this comparison is misleading. Justin did not betray the biblical atmosphere at all. He notes that this conflagration is not periodic and its fire is the hell-fire reserved for the impious at the end of the world (I *Apol.* LVII, 1). Justin makes it clear that this will not take place in accordance with fate, but rather in accordance with the deserts of free choice (II *Apol.*, VII, 3-4), as is noted by M. Spanneut in *Le stoïcisme des Pères de l'Eglise*, (Paris, 1957), p. 359.

Within the Law, Justin distinguishes prescriptions of natural morality, which are immutable, from the ceremonial and ritual prescriptions that are of their nature contingent.

"Before Moses and Abraham, the just were not circumcised and they did not observe the Sabbath. Why did God not teach them these practices," which were even observed by certain pagan peoples?[12] Why did God only later enjoin them upon his people?

Contrary to Barnabas, who affirmed that God never really intended the Sabbath and circumcision to be practiced,[13] Justin believes that God purposely imposed them on the Jews, but did so because of their hardness of heart. Finding them incapable of keeping a spiritual Law, God gave them an exterior Law. This comprises Temple, sacrifices, and Sabbath.

> He does not accept[14] sacrifices from you. If He ordained them for you in earlier times, it was not because He has any need of them, but because of your sins. The Temple also, which is referred to as the Temple of Jerusalem, He did not call His house because He has any need of it. Rather it too was for you, so that you might remain devoted to Him and not commit idolatries…. It is because men have sinned that He Who is Himself always the same prescribed these and other like ordinances.[15]

Thus, the observances are in no way a glory for the Jews, but rather a sign of their iniquity.[16]

It should be noted that this reason for establishing observances would not be limited to the Old Covenant, since the whole Christian and sacramental economy of the New Covenant is also a medicinal dispensation aimed at healing and saving sinners.[17] But is this the only motivation operative here?

No. Clearly for Justin the gift of an exterior Law to the Jews had another reason beyond that occasioned by their hardness of heart. It also served to prefigure the future realities of the New Covenant in Christ and to prepare men's minds for those realities. "The mystery of the Lamb that God ordained to be immolated as a Pasch was a type of the Anointed Christ…. The offering of wheat was the type of the bread of

---

[12]*Dial.*, XXVII, 5; XXVIII, 3.

[13]Cf. P. Prigent, *L'Epître de Barnabé I-XVI et ses sources*, (Paris, 1961), p. 35; Bourgeault, *Décalogue et Morale Chrétienne*, (Paris, 1971), p. 140.

[14]*Today* is here implied.

[15]*Dial.* XXII, 11—XXIII, 2.

[16]*Ibid.*, XXI, 1.

[17]Cf. 1 Tm 1:9-10; Mt 9:13; Lk 15, etc.

the thanksgiving…. Taking them one by one, I could show that all of Moses' other prescriptions are types (*typoi*), symbols, annunciations of what is to come to pass in Christ."[18]

The words used to designate the typical sense of the law of Moses are diverse, as we see: type, symbol, annunciation. Justin defines the term type thus: "Sometimes the Holy Spirit caused the visible appearance of something which was a figure (*typos*) of the future."[19] This term appears in Justin as the technical term designating the historical correspondence. Its use seems to depend on Paul (Rom 5:14).

It is noteworthy that Justin never employs the term *allegoria* that will make its appearance with the Alexandrians, even though it was used by Paul to signify the same reality as *typos* (Gal 4:23-24). Justin does not want to allegorize the entire text of Scripture, as Philo did. With Justin the domain of figures is confined to a limited number of episodes or institutions which earlier tradition had already interpreted as having a relation to the New Testament, notably circumcision and the Sabbath.[20]

In Justin's view, as in that of Paul, circumcision is a figure of baptism. "For us, who are going to God, it is not this circumcision according to the flesh that we receive, but that spiritual one which Enoch and those like him observed. As for us, by God's mercy, we have received this baptism."Circumcision on the eighth day is "a figure of the true circumcision given in the name of Him Who was raised on the eighth day."[21] As for the Sabbath, the observance of which contributes nothing to man's justification,[22] it prefigures the cessation of sin.[23]

Other figures emerge in the Moses cycle: the Pasch, Joshua's victory over Amalek.

"The Pasch saved those who were in Egypt; likewise, the Blood of Christ will preserve those who believe in him."[24]

---

[18]*Dial.*, XL, 1; XLII, 4; see the detailed study of Shotwell on Justin's typological vocabulary as a whole (pp. 13-20). In XLIV, 2, Justin speaks clearly of the plurality of motives of the Old Testament.

[19]*Dial.*, CIV, 1; cf. Daniélou, p. 189.

[20]*Ibid.* However, in 1965, four years later, Shotwell (pp. 20-23) will contradict this view of Daniélou—apparently, at least—by endeavoring to show, in the light of *Dial.* XCIV, that Justin's real motive in allegorizing Scripture was to reconcile data that he believed to be otherwise irreconcilable: for example, the law against making images, reported by Moses, and the order given to Moses to make a brazen serpent.

[21]*Dial.*, XLIII, 2; XLI, 4.

[22]*Ibid.*, *Dial.* XLVI, 7; cf. Shotwell, pp. 9-11.

[23]*Ibid.*, XIV, 2..

[24]*Ibid.*, CXI, 3.

In the episode of the victory over Amalek, Christ is prefigured by the stone on which Moses leans, by the sign of the cross described by his outstretched arms (an event already exploited by Judaism, not as a sign of the cross, but as a work of God's power), and by Joshua's name that is equivalent to Jesus, a combat title.[25]

The name of Joshua is a figure of the name of Jesus. Just as Joshua led the people into the Holy Land, so also "Jesus will bring about the return of the Diaspora of the people and will distribute the good land to each." Joshua stopped the sun; but Jesus, the eternal light, is to shine in Jerusalem. Joshua circumcised the people with a second circumcision; but that circumcision is a figure of the one Jesus effects in hearts and it is he who is the rock of the true circumcision (*Dial.* CXIII, 1-7). Joshua's victory over Amalek is a figure of Jesus' enduring victory over the forces of evil (XLIX, 8). The salvation granted to Rahab because of the scarlet cord is a symbol of the salvation granted to sinners through the blood of Christ (CXI, 4).

Is this typology original with Justin? We find these figures already in the New Testament or in Barnabas. They are part of a common and universal tradition. Justin's only originality consists in extending the parallel to one or another detail. Such is the case with the circumcision of the eighth day. But the procedure follows a Jewish line already operative in the New Testament, for example, in John the parallel between the unbroken bones of the Paschal Lamb and Christ's unbroken limbs.

Despite this limited character of Justin's originality, his *Dialogue with Trypho*, holds a central place in the history of typology.

For one thing, it constitutes the corpus of the principal figures, which existed before him, but not all in one place. In contrast to the prophecies, these had not yet, it seems, been made into collections (*testimonia*). These figures will be taken up again by Irenæus, who depends directly on Justin. Indeed, they will soon be encountered everywhere. They will come to constitute the typological tradition of the whole Church

Then too, this typology appears in Justin in all its purity. It has almost completely broken with the exegetical methods of Judaism,[26] though it

---

[25]*Ibid.*, XC, 4; cf. Daniélou, p. 194.

[26]Justin very strongly criticizes the purely literal exegesis of the Jews: "Your commentators, one and all, are content to explain why there are only female camels [in Gn 32:15] or why there are so many measures of grain in the offerings. Their explanations are contemptible and quite earthy, and, as for the important points, which would really merit investigation, they never dare to bring them up or to explain them" (*Dial.*, CXII, 4). Cf. Daniélou, pp. 188 and 195.

retains the latter's tendency to drawn out detailed comparisons. It is not yet contaminated by Hellenistic allegorism.

What Justin has not completely worked out is the theology of history presupposed by this typology.[27] This will be the work of Irenæus. However, for Justin, the events of the Old Testament form part of God's design and of his Christ-oriented economy, insofar as they are already a kind of first draft of what will be accomplished in Christ. Thus the marriages of the patriarchs prefigure the union of Christ and the Church: "a prediction, a certain economy was at work in the marriages of Jacob" (CXXXIV, 2). The link between typology and salvation history is already marked.

At a deeper level, for Justin, it is the Law as such that prefigures Christ: "We have now been given Christ, the eternal and definitive law, the guaranteed pact after which there is no more law, nor precepts, nor commandments" (*Dial.* XI, 2).[28] Christ, Law and Logos, had prophesied the abrogation of the Old Testament in its very own prophecies. Justin expressed his most fundamental thesis as follows:

I have read that there would be a final law and the most important covenant of all; it is this law that all men who lay claim to God's heritage must now keep. The law of Horeb is already the old law, and it is for yourselves alone; this law is for all without exception. But a law that counters another law abrogates that which precedes it, and a covenant concluded after another likewise annuls the former (*ibid.*).

These manifest allusions to Pauline theology (Heb 7:18) have already brought us from the Christ signified by the types of the Old Law to the Christ announced by his prophets, acting under his Spirit, in the context of the same Old Law. This is a decisive point in Justin's theology.

B. The Prophets of the Old Covenant Announced Christ by their Words

We are indeed touching here the center at which Justin's personal life and thought meet perfectly. Converted to Christ through the testimony of the prophets as explained to him by an elderly Christian man, he knew their power through personal experience. As a Christian coming from the pagan aristocracy but led to Christ by the Jewish prophets, what could he more naturally desire than to make use of the converging

---

[27]Daniélou, *ibid.*, p. 195. A little earlier (p. 147), Daniélou recognizes that Justin had laid its foundations (pp. 147-149).

[28]A point clearly brought out by G. Bourgeault, p. 195.

testimony of these prophets to lead not only Trypho, but all his Jewish and pagan readers as well, to Jesus, Son of David?

It seems that scholars have so far not sufficiently remarked the intimate link that unites Justin's conversion with his own witness, the identity of Justin the disciple of the prophets and Justin the apologist of their immortal prophecies, the continuity between the conversion and the exegesis of this philosopher-martyr. To help us grasp this connection, we cite the following magnificent passage, that implicitly contains a whole biblical theology of prophecy and of the role God assigned to it in the economy of salvation:

> There were men in times past, more ancient than these supposed philosophers, favored, just, and beloved of God, who spoke by the Holy Spirit and who uttered oracles which have now been fulfilled. These men are called prophets. They alone[29] saw and announced the truth to men, fearlessly and without respect of persons. They were not moved by the desire for glory, but would declare only what they had heard and seen, being filled with the Holy Spirit. Their writings have survived to this day and whoever reads them can, if he has faith in them, derive from them all kinds of profit, regarding first principles[30] and the final end, in short, regarding everything the philosopher is supposed to know. They did not employ demonstration in their speech; beyond all demonstration they were worthy witnesses of the truth. The events themselves of the past and of the present compel one to adhere to what they said. The miracles they performed made them worthy of belief, when they glorified God the Father, the Author of the universe, and when they announced his Son, the Christ, who comes from him. The false prophets filled with the spirit of error and impurity did not do this, and do not do it now. On the contrary, they have the audacity to perform prodigies so as to strike men with stupor, and they glorify the spirits of error and the demons. But you, pray above all that the doors of light may be opened to you, for no one can see or understand unless God and His Christ give him to understand.[31]

For Justin, the prophets—as stated clearly in this text—are at once those who speak in the name of God and who announced realities to come, those who announced Christ in advance. Unlike the philosophers, they speak without fear, without desire for human glory, and not as

---

[29]Justin wishes to emphasize that the prophets and not the philosophers (who, in his view, derived many truths from the prophets) saw and announced Christ, who is *the Truth* par excellence: cf. Jn 14:6. This idea of borrowing by the philosophers was explicitly affirmed by Justin, *I Apol*, 44, 9.

[30]An allusion to the creation, taught by Moses (Gn 1:1).

[31]*Dialogue*, VII, 1.

using the style of demonstration. Rather, they point out in advance the one who is to come. Miracles are added to their words to make of them a demonstration of spirit and of power (cf. 1 Cor 2:4). Their true miracles are contrasted with the false miracles of the false prophets, who were instruments of the demons. Justin already hints at the struggle between the two cities, that conflict under the two standards which Augustine and Ignatius of Loyola will later develop and expound. In this astonishing passage, which could well be analyzed at greater length[32] in view of its great synthetic richness, we even find a pneumatological and trinitarian structure which is perfectly faithful both to the Johannine gospel and the preparation in the prophets of the trinitarian revelation: through the prophets, the Holy Spirit glorifies and announces, helps us to see and to understand, in and through the prayer of petition, the Father, the Author of the universe and Christ his Son.[33] It is "this action of the Holy Spirit which opens the portals of light."[34]

Justin is wholly taken with this idea. When the old man had departed, he tells us, "a fire was suddenly kindled in my soul. I was taken with love for the prophets and for these men who were friends of Christ. Through interior reflection on all these words, I found that this was the only certain and useful philosophy."[35]

From this reflection was born Justin's whole apologetic method, which is essentially based on the prophetic argument.

What exactly is Justin's idea of scriptural prophecy?

Every scriptural prophecy comprises a sign, consisting of words or of actions, and a meaning, which is Christ himself, announced or prefigured by these words or actions. Such a definition applies at least to the prophecies of the Old Testament, with which St. Justin was normally concerned.

Thus he tells us in his *Dialogue* (84):

What is truly a sign and ground of faith for the human race is the fact that from a virginal womb the first-born of all creatures becomes truly flesh, is born an infant, and the fact that, knowing all this in advance, he had foretold it

---

[32]As does J. C. M. Van den Winden, pp. 111ff.

[33]Cf. J.-P. Martin, *El Espiritu Santo en los origenes del Cristianismo*, (Zürich, 1971), pp. 299-300. The author here distinguishes between two different presentations in Justin of the Trinitarian mystery, one in a Jewish context, the other in a Greek context; following Harnack, he thinks that the converging developments of the Old Testament views on the Messiah-Christ, on the Spirit, and on God are at the origin of Trinitarian doctrine. Cf. pp. 340-348.

[34]An expression of Lagrange, p. 19.

[35]*Dialogue*, VIII, 1.

through the Prophetic Spirit...so that when the event would take place, one might know that it took place through the power and through the will of the Creator of the universe.

One will remark the complexity of the very notion of prophecy in St. Justin's view: it is the eternal Word himself who, through his Spirit and through a human instrument, announces in advance the mystery which he will himself accomplish later in time. Christ is at once both the supreme Prophet and the reality prophesied: the supreme Prophet as eternal *Logos*, the reality prophesied as *incarnate* Logos. He gives in prophecy a sign that makes it possible for one to recognize him when the prophecy is fulfilled. When it is as it were reduplicated in and by its fulfillment, the sign becomes fully effective as sign: its truth is proven (cf. L. Thoré, *DSAM* IV, 1, [1960], 143). Such is the prophetic argument in its essence.

Moreover, Justin took pains to recapitulate the broad outline of this prophetic argument:

In the books of the prophets we find it announced in writing that Jesus, our Christ, is to come, that he will be born of a Virgin, that he will grow to mature manhood, that he will heal all maladies and all infirmities, that he will raise the dead; we read that he will be misunderstood and persecuted, that he will be crucified, that he will die, that he will rise and ascend to Heaven; we read that he is and is called Son of God, that he will send men to announce these things in the whole world and that it will be the Gentiles above all who will believe in him. The prophecies were made five thousand, three thousand, two thousand, one thousand, eight hundred years before his coming, for the prophets followed one another from generation to generation.[36]

If we gather the scattered prophetic arguments, not now in the *Apologia*, (cf. the preceding text) but in the *Dialogue*, we obtain the following synthesis:[37]

Jesus was to descend from David, for this had been announced by Isaiah, and to be born in Bethlehem, which was indicated by Micah. The virginal conception was affirmed by Isaiah, hinted at in Genesis through mysterious expressions like the blood of the vine of Judah. We find the adoration of the Magi in Isaiah, the flight into Egypt in Malachi. David had said in advance in the name of God: "You are my Son." Isaiah has spoken of Jesus' miracles but especially of his sufferings; the dying Jacob and Zechariah of his entrance into Jerusalem

---

[36]*I Apol.*, XXXI, 1, 7-8.
[37]Following the synthesis proposed by Fr. Feder, S.J., in his work *Justins des Märtyrers Lehre von Jesus Christus*, (Freiburg, 1906), pp. 69ff. Cf. Lagrange, p. 46.

riding on an ass. The psalmist had spoken of his prayers, of his sufferings, of his arrest; Zechariah of the dispersion and flight of his disciples. Also in the psalms we read of the gathering of the Sanhedrin, of Jesus' silence before the Roman procurator, of the Jews' complicity with Herod and Pilate, of Jesus' appearance before Herod, of his pierced hands and his feet, his robe drawn by lot, the jeering of the Jews, the dying Christ's last cry commending his soul to his Father. Having been placed in the tomb, as Isaiah had foretold, Jesus had been raised in accordance with the prophecy of Isaiah, and also of David, who had further predicted his apparitions and his ascension.

It will be noted that many of the Old Testament texts which Justin considers prophetic are precisely those which the New Testament regards and presents as such. Justin's prophetic argument is thus undeniably in the line of the exegesis of the inspired authors of the New Testament.

Justin's work represents an important constitutive moment in the development of the *Testimonia* or dossier of biblical witnesses (at least insofar as the historian can affirm the existence of such a dossier[38]). That certain prophetic references did in fact belong to some such collection is especially apparent in the existence of composite citations: thus Numbers 24:17 (star of Jacob), Isaiah 11:1 (flower sprouting from the stem of Jesse) and 11:10 are combined in a single quotation attributed to Isaiah (I *Apol.* XXXII, 12). This dossier was already present at Qumram.[39]

But in the use of these texts, Justin exhibits certain characteristics of his own. Going beyond the catechetical demonstration on which the dossiers of the *Testimonia* were centered, Justin's thought moves in the direction of a Christian commentary on Scripture, such as might be presented in preaching, and of which we have a specimen in Luke.

Justin's *Dialogue with Trypho* thus contains a number of Old Testament passages that we find here applied to Christ and to the Church for the first time, though we cannot know for certain if he is the first to have used them in this way.

---

[38] A. Benoît, *Saint Irénée, Introduction à l'étude de sa théologie*, (Paris, 1960), p. 101: "Various elements, in the *Adversus Hæreses*, lead one to believe that Irenæus is using collections of *Testimonia*; no absolute demonstration of this can be made on the basis of this work, and we do not have total certainty...Daniélou states this opinion as an acquired fact and without seeking to justify it: *Rech. Sc. Rel.*, 42, (1954), pp. 192-203." Perhaps the same should be said about Justin.

[39] I Q Ben. V, 24, 28. Cf. Jean Daniélou, *Message évangélique*, p. 196. Likewise, "L'étoile de Jacob et la mission chrétienne à Damas," *VC*, 11, (1957), pp. 124-127; M. A. Chevallier, *L'Esprit et le Messie dans le Bas-Judaïsme et le N.T.*, (Paris, 1958), pp. 32-41.

Thus it is for the first time in Justin that we find Isaiah 33:16 applied to Christ's birth in Bethlehem with an allusion to the cave that is not from the Gospel: "He will live on the heights; his refuge will be the fortresses of rocks."[40] There appears also in Justin, for the first time in reference to the Nativity, the text of Isaiah 1:3-4 which will later enjoy such fortune in the history of the Christmas crib: "The ox knows its owner, and the donkey its master's crib; but Israel does not know, my people do not understand" (*I Apol.* XXXVII, 1).

In contrast to Clement of Alexandria and Origen, who will stress the spiritual content of the realities foretold, Justin lays the stress on the historical fulfillment of the prophecies. He notes tangible facts, which may be verified as historical. He then goes on to show that these events had been foretold by the prophets. He concludes from this that the latter are not mere episodes devoid of signification, but rather the realization of the Savior God's eternal design. In his view, this gives demonstrative force to the prophecies, even for the pagans.[41] For Justin, as Daniélou remarks, "the prophetic argument constitutes the essential appeal, the final resort of the Gospel demonstration." This explains why it occupies the major part not only of the *Dialogue* addressed to the Jews, but also of the *Apology* offered to the pagans.[42] In Justin, the prophetic argument does not appear within the context of an allegorization which would dissolve history into myth. On the contrary, he sees the pagan mysteries as a distortion of the prophecies, under the influence of demons, whose effect is to dissolve into myths what in reality had a historical meaning, brought to fulfillment in Jesus.[43] Justin sees the prophecies and their fulfillment as the sign of the fact that the history of humanity is a history of salvation, the history of mankind's salvation accomplished by an all-powerful and good God, whose eternity rules time.

Justin's attention is not confined to the two past levels, the second of which—that of Christ's earthly life and of his Pasch—fulfills the promises

---

[40]Cf. *Dial.* LXXVIII, 6. Cf. A. Guilding, *The Fourth Gospel and Jewish Worship*, (1960), p. 103: Is 32–33 formed part of the readings for the Feast of Tabernacles, which is the period in which the birth of Jesus has been set with some probability.

[41]Daniélou, *Message évangelique*, p. 197.

[42]*Ibid.*, p. 196.

[43]*Ibid.*, p. 198. We note, however, that Shotwell (p. 99), after a long and very detailed comparison between the exegesis of Philo and that of Justin, concludes by insisting that both authors were using the two exegetical methods of literal interpretation and allegorical interpretation—the latter, whenever it suited their purposes! We could say, by way of synthesizing the conclusions of Shotwell and Daniélou, that Justin is sometimes concerned to put allegory at the service of history.

contained in the first, when God was addressing Israel. His interest extends also to the ecclesial present. He shows us the prophecies still being realized here and now in the actual events of Christian expansion. This type of demonstration based on evangelical expansion anticipates the work of Augustine. A few examples would illustrate this approach.

For the apologist, Isaiah's prophecy announcing that all the nations will come flowing like a great stream toward Jerusalem, will turn their swords into plowshares and their spears into pruning hooks[44] is being fulfilled before the very eyes of his contemporaries:

> These words have been fulfilled, you may be certain. Twelve men went out from Jerusalem to conquer the world. We who, before, knew only how to kill one another, not only do not fight anymore with our enemies, but, rather than lie to our judge, we joyfully profess Christ and go to our deaths (*I Apol.* XXXIX, 3).

Likewise for Psalm 18:3-6: "There is absolutely no people, barbarian or Greek among which, in the name of the crucified Jesus, prayers and thanksgiving are not offered up to God the Father of the universe" (*Dial.* CXVII, 3).[45]

This, in broad outline, is the prophetic argument in support of Christ's Gospel found in Justin's writings—an argument of extraordinary breadth, offered not only to the Jews but also to the pagans, and related first of all, to the past and to the present, but also to the future. Every human person will have to render to God an account of the reception he gives to the words of the prophets that come down to him through the memories of the Apostles[46] and through the testimony of the Church. And he is formally notified that he will be condemned to eternal perdition should he disregard the prophets, the Apostles, and the Church.[47]

How did Trypho take this argument?

On the one hand, the rabbi affirms that certain prophecies were fulfilled in Jewish history. Thus he applies Isaiah 7:14 (the virgin[48] will give

---

[44]Is 2:3-4.

[45]We note in passing the Hellenistic character of the expression *Father of the Universe*, commonly employed by the non-Christian authors of the period.

[46]Cf. Lagrange, pp. 120ff.

[47]*I Apol.* VIII, XVIII, XLVI and XVII: "You and all those who hate us without cause, if you do not repent, will be destined to the eternal fire" (XLVI).

[48]Trypho does not read *parthenos* (virgin) with the Septuagint, but *neanis* (young girl) with Aquila. Cf. Justin, *Dialogue*, XLIII, 7; LXVII, 1; CXX, 1. In the first of these three texts, Justin brings out an important aspect of prophecy, "That in the family of Abraham according to the flesh no one was ever born and no one was ever said to have been born of a virgin, except our Christ, is evident to all." Justin insists on this again in LXVI. A little

birth) and Psalm 109 to King Hezekiah, Psalms 23 and 71 to Solomon.[49] It should be noted that this position will be partially resumed by the school of Antioch (cf. VII), and no doubt under the influence of Jewish exegesis. With a significant difference, however: for the school of Antioch, the messianic prophecies received only an initial fulfillment in the Old Testament; it is only in the Mystery of Christ and of his Church that they are completely fulfilled.

On the other hand—and this is an objection still made today—Trypho shows surprise that Justin should present him with a suffering Messiah, whereas the prophets announce a glorious Messiah.[50] Justin responds by distinguishing the two comings of the Messiah: he appeared the first time in humiliation and in suffering, but he will appear the second time in glory.[51] So strong are the texts (especially Isaiah 53) which acclaim a servant of God, suffering and expiating the sins of men, that Trypho surrenders on this point. He himself attests that belief in a suffering Messiah was alive in the Judaism of his time,[52] but he refuses to recognize him in Jesus of Nazareth. For Trypho, the Messiah's victory would have to have come in his lifetime.

---

earlier (LXIII), Justin presented in a very original way the implications of the virginal conception for the twofold generation of Christ by his Father, the human and the divine: "God the Father of the universe must have begotten him ages ago and through a human womb," thus implying that God the Father is also the Father of Christ according to his humanity. The centuries have not ceased to ponder the mysterious prophecy of Is 7:14, which we will meet again in the analysis of Irenæus in the following chapter and of which Bossuet spoke with such depth and originality in three letters, all written in 1703 (October 1, October 26 and November 8) to M. de Valincour (*Œuvres complètes*, [Paris: Lachat, 1863], vol. II, pp. 244-163). On Justin and Is 7:14, see J. A. de Aldama, *Maria en la Patristica*, (Madrid, 1970), *passim*.

[49]See especially on Psalm 109 *Dialogue*, XXXIII, 1; LXXXIII, 1; cf. Daniélou, *Message évangélique...*, p. 201. Justin would have been quite surprised if he could have known that two centuries after his time the views of Trypho would again be partially maintained, this time by the school of Antioch, though not, it should be noted, regarding Is 7:14. We will show in the following chapter that no Father ever entertained a partial fulfillment of this prophecy in the Old Testament.

[50]Cf. Lagrange, chapter 2, "Controverse avec les Juifs," p. 47.

[51]*Ibid.*, p. 48. Cf. *Dialogue*, XXX–XXXIV and XXXVI–XLI; CX, 2: "I have shown by all the Scriptures that there are two Parousias foretold in his regard, one in which it is foretold that he will suffer, be crucified, the other in which he is to appear from heaven on high, in glory."

[52]*Dialogue*, LXVIII, 9; LXXXIX, 1; XC, 1; Shotwell, p. 76, calls attention to a commentary on Zec 9:9 dating from about the ninth century A.D. which some believe to be the most ancient historical testimony (from the Jewish side, and discounting that placed by Justin on the lips of Trypho) to a suffering Messiah. I refer to the *Pesiqta Rabbathi*.

The man chiefly responsible for the renewal of Catholic exegesis in the twentieth century, Father Lagrange, had a remarkable grasp of the extent to which the dialogue between Trypho and Justin is tied to the issue of the cross of Jesus. He summarizes their positions, as well as the perpetual relevance of the debate as follows:[53]

> Trypho did not yet comprehend the true character of the Messiah's victories. We too find it difficult to accept this law of suffering. As decisive as the solution of the two comings is, the second remains for us an object rather than a motive of belief. We need assurance that already Jesus is victor. And if we will only open our eyes, that assurance is easy for us to find, simply by going through the already long history of the Catholic Church.... It is enough for us to interpret the victories dreamed of by the Jews as victories of the grace of Jesus over sin and over the evil desires that lead to sin. Now this is what St. Justin brought clearly to light already in the second century: "We can see clearly that it is by the name of the Crucified himself, Jesus Christ, that men renounce idols and all iniquity, that they go toward God, and that they persevere until death in the profession of their piety. By his works, by the power that accompanied him, all men can understand that it is he who is the new law, the New Covenant, the hope of those who, in all the nations, await the blessings of God. For the true, spiritual Israelite race...are we, we whom this crucified Christ has led toward God.[54]

As Justin sees it then, the Church that he has before his eyes is evidence of the victory of the Cross. This already present triumph directed the attention of the Christian philosopher toward the even more manifest triumph of His glorious coming. As Lagrange so well puts it: "one believed in it [his glorious coming] because it had been foretold by the prophets, and the authority of the prophets had been guaranteed by the fulfillment of the prophecies regarding Christ's humility and sufferings."[55]

This is how the crucified Lord's divinity was manifested for Justin. The proof of Christ's divine mission based on prophecies embraces then both the past and the future, both Christ's sorrows and his glories. All of this is the fruit of a twofold research, one in the sacred book, and one in history. No one but God could have traced this design in advance. And if he toward whom everything is converging is also announced as King and as Judge of the living and the dead, if these same ancient oracles

---

[53]Lagrange, pp. 48-49.
[54]*Dialogue*, XII.
[55]Lagrange, p. 122.

announced his birth from a virgin, if they name him Son of God: "You are my son; today I have begotten you" can anyone refuse to recognize Jesus Christ as the Son of God and as God? To prove that this suffering was willed by God, since it was foretold, and that it was the prelude to an eternal triumph was but to respond to the anxious questioning of souls.[56] Through the combined impact of all these various strands of evidence the prophetic argument acquires a decisive force:

> How should we believe, in fact, that a crucified man is the first-born of the unbegotten God, and that he will judge the whole human race, if we did not see all the prophecies made concerning him before His incarnation fulfilled point by point: the devastation of Judea, men of all nations embracing the teaching of his Apostles, renouncing the ancient customs in which they had gone astray, and if on the other hand we did not see ourselves, and this multitude of Gentiles, Christians more numerous and more sincere than those who are of Jewish or Samaritan origin?[57]

There is still more: for Justin, the prophetic argument was all the more decisive since in his view "Christ was the Word, he who is in everything, who predicts the future through the prophets and who personally takes on our nature in order to instruct us." (*II Apol.* 10:8). In the view of the apologist, Christ as Word is then both the Prophet and the prophesied Messiah, the Prophet who prophesies himself and who then fulfills his prophetic promises, in an initial fulfillment which is the pledge of their final and total fulfillment.

C. Critique: Methods and Net Results of Justin's Exegesis

We have just mentioned the Word, the Prophet announcing himself in prophecy. This idea is the foundation of Justin's theology, which unfortunately we cannot here discuss in depth, since our primary objective concerns exegesis. The subject moreover, has been adequately treated elsewhere.[58]

How are we to assess today the net results of the philosopher-martyr's exegesis? What is to be said of its limitations, of its method, of its advantages?

---

[56]*Ibid.*, pp. 122-127.

[57]*I Apol.*, LIII.

[58]Cf. Lagrange, chapter VI, on Justin as theologian and his doctrine on the Word; Cf. pp. 50-54. Like other Fathers, Justin wished to show the divinity of the Word from certain texts of the Old Testament, but Augustine and the exegetes of our time have shown the futility of such attempts (cf. Augustine, *The City of God*, XVI, 29).

Justin, we must acknowledge, was occasionally wrong. He mistakenly considered biblical a number of texts that are not so, and he reproached the Jews for having removed these from the Scriptures. A case in point is the narrative of Isaiah's martyrdom. The work is one of the Christian *midrashim*. On this point Trypho was right and Justin wrong.[59]

Likewise, because of his Christologization of the *Testimonia* of the Old Testament, Justin did not always read the Scriptures of the Old Testament correctly. Thus he wrongly reproached the Jews for having left out of Psalm 96 "from the wood" (i.e., the cross) (*Dial.* LXXIII, 1). Here again Trypho was right. It may at least be said in his favor that here Justin's error occurs within the context of a living transmission, of a tradition of an Old Testament read in the Church, in the light of Christ,[60] with a clear awareness of the fact that the Word was himself the one and total supreme author of all the books of the Old and of the New Testaments. In other words, his error was the exaggeration of a truth, anticipating a tendency later characteristic of the Alexandrian school. That the Word is speaking throughout the Bible does not mean he is speaking at every moment of himself.

This is what Lagrange pointed out, already in 1914, as the root of Justin's exegetical errors:

If he was mistaken, along with so many other great minds, in the exegesis of certain texts, it was because Holy Scripture appealed to him only insofar as the Person of the Incarnate Word, whether distinctly or under the veil of symbols, could be discovered therein. Once he had given his faith to Christ and was disposed to give him even his life, he saw him everywhere—with God at the creation, conversing with the patriarchs—indeed, he is convinced he hears Christ's voice beneath the oaks of Mambre, in the burning bush, and amid the dramatic thunderbolts of Sinai.[61]

While the Word as God may have been present in these incidents, the Old Testament itself does not enable us to distinguish between the Word and his Father.

By way of summary it may be said that, in a number of cases, Justin does not give enough consideration to the literal sense of the Old Testament scriptures. Annoyed by the literalism of Jewish exegesis,

---

[59]Cf. Jean Daniélou, *Théologie du Judéo-Christianisme*, (Paris, 1958), pp. 115-116; *Message évangelique...*, p. 199.
[60]*Ibid.* Cf. Vatican II, *Dei Verbum*, 16 (see note 74 below).
[61]Lagrange, pp. 54-55.

perhaps because he failed to understand clearly enough the historical sense of the Bible, its precise value in its own day and subsequently down the ages until it should reach its term, the Messiah, Justin does not allow that God could ever have been concerned with things sometimes so low, or at least not without having invested these things with a more exalted and spiritual meaning suitable for our instruction. His was a fault of excess—St. Augustine qualified it thus—but an excess of a Christian overflow, inundating the present, while still looking back to the past. [62]

In certain respects then, Justin's exegesis does not sufficiently value history, or the peculiar content and immediate sense of Old Testament data. At the same time, like his Jewish contemporaries he is exposed to other errors in the reading of texts universally recognized as inspired. These errors may be traced to the limited knowledge of the bible in his time or to the simplistic application of certain methodological principles not altogether lacking in validity.[63] We have already alluded to these principles in passing. We state them here with greater precision:

1. *Apparent contradictions* point to a hidden sense. For example, God forbade Moses to make images. If He then orders him to raise up a brazen serpent, this brazen serpent must be a figure of Christ.[64]

2. The *reduplication* of expressions is significant. Thus we are able to discover the "second God, the Logos" in Gn 19:24.

3. Likewise, *omissions* have a meaning. If the Scripture does not say that Enoch received circumcision according to the flesh, it is because he observed a spiritual circumcision (*Dial.* XLIII, 1).

4. Words have a *fixed allegorical meaning*. For example, if the "day of the Lord" corresponds to "a thousand" in one passage, it has the same sense elsewhere.

These are four of the nine principles of allegorical exegesis which C. Siegfried in 1875 considered operative in the writings both of Philo and of Justin. According to him—and the later research of Shotwell[65] tends in the same direction—these principles would derive from Palestinian and rabbinical usage.

---

[62]*Ibid.*, p. 54. Cf. p. 124: "Not every speculative mind has been endowed with a historical sense. It is notably lacking in Justin."

[63]Cf. C. Siegfried, *Philo von Alexandria als Ausleger des Alten Testaments*, (Jena, 1875), pp. 337-340; R. M. Grant, *The Letter and the Spirit*, (London, 1957), pp. 76-77; Shotwell, p. 41, 43.

[64]Cf. *Dialogue*, XCI, 4; cf. Daniélou, *Message évangélique*, p. 194.

[65]Cf. Shotwell, chapters 2 and 4.

We thought it necessary to indicate here these personal imperfections of Justin as well as those which he reveals in common with his contemporaries. Having noted this, one can only feel more at ease in rendering homage to the "very serious and substantial value of his *Apologies*" and of his *Dialogue*, as was done already in 1914 by a great exegete, M. J. Lagrange.

His well chosen texts, inadequate (despite Justin's opinion) to the task of demonstrating Christ's divinity, do however show him to be the Messiah, the envoy of God, the one whom all Israel was awaiting and who was also destined to instruct the Gentiles and to reconcile them with God. Isaiah supplies the majority of his texts, which announced the virginity of the Mother of the Messiah, the sufferings and humiliation of the man of sorrows, his exaltation and his triumph (Isaiah 7 and 53). These are the very texts that Christians, since the time of the New Testament, have always cited as proof that Jesus is the promised and announced Messiah.[66] The fact that one can affirm and demonstrate in detail that the life of Jesus of Nazareth, his passion, his death, and his glorification correspond, in a synthetic and living unity, to the multiplicity of all these different prophecies constitutes a further confirmation, a supplementary and irrefutable proof of his messianic sending.[67]

To be sure, the impressive advances realized in the course of the last century in the various disciplines that affect exegesis help us to perceive the urgency of a return to the "Gospel demonstration" through the prophecies, with a view to perfecting it and purifying it. Today, are we not often tempted to think that "only the latest parts of the Old Testament—and this applies as well to the prophetic books—are predictions in the strict sense"?[68]

In our time, the demonstration of the Messiahship of Jesus by way of seeing in his person a living synthesis of prophetic fulfillment goes on under the guise of the "Christological concentration" that modern studies offer us. In the three-phase existence of the one Jesus of Nazareth, all the types of mediation, which appear to include contradictory features, come together, according to the New Testament. Jesus is the ideal and total mediator of salvation. He is at once royal (Son

---

[66]Lagrange, p. 125.

[67]Cf. Freppel, *Les Apologistes chrétiens au IIe siècle, saint Justin*, (Paris, 1860), p. 390, and note 69 below.

[68]N. Füglister, *Mysterium Salutis*, vol. IX, French translation, (Paris, 1973), p. 321; cf. p. 162 in the same sense, a view that is at odds with the teaching of Vatican II (cf. notes 72-74 below) as well as the tradition of the Fathers.

of David), priestly (high priest and new temple), prophetic (Servant of God, second Moses), and heavenly (Son of Man, Wisdom of God)—in short, the absolute Mediator.[69]

Justin is of great interest today because he offers us, already in the second century—in a still imperfect, of course non-technical, but nevertheless suggestive way—a foretaste of that Christological concentration that is inseparable from the fulfillment of the prophecies. The following is an example of this taken from the *Dialogue* (XXXIV, 2):

> Christ was announced to us as king, priest, God, Lord, angel, man, supreme head, rock, little child by his birth, as a being of sorrow at first, then as one ascending to heaven, returning in glory as eternal king, as I can substantiate from all the Scriptures.

In other words, Justin's prophetic proof is not only analytic, but synthetic as well. It is because of this very union of elements that his proof remains impressive.

It constitutes a rather early link in that integrating reading of the Scriptures that was begun by the risen Christ himself (Lk 24:27, 44-47) and which the Church will never cease to pursue during her history.

It lays the early groundwork for the reaction of Constantinople II, in 553, against a Nestorian reading of the Old Testament,[70] and above all it anticipates the declaration of Vatican I and II:

> So that the homage of our faith might be in conformity with reason (Romans 12:1), God willed that the internal helps of the Holy Spirit be accompanied by external proofs of his revelation, namely, the divine deeds and especially the miracles and prophecies which, being a marvelous exhibition of the infinite omnipotence and infinite wisdom of God, are very sure signs of revelation, adapted to the understanding of all.[71]

---

[69]*Ibid.*, p. 324. See in the same sense Louis Bouyer, *Le Fils éternel*, (Paris, 1974), several chapters; P. Grelot, *SCAT*, (Tournai, 1963), *passim*, and especially p. 40. On the theological problems posed by the argument from prophecy, see G. de Broglie, *Les signes de crédibilité de la Révélation chrétienne*, (Paris, 1964), chapters 22-25, pp. 136ff, etc.

[70]Cf. below, chapter VII.

[71]Vatican I, *DS* 3009. Cf. this extract of the anti-modernist oath prescribed by Pius X: "I admit and acknowledge the external proofs of revelation, that is to say, divine deeds, particularly miracles and prophecies, as *very certain signs* of the divine origin of Christian revelation; and I hold that they are *fully adapted to the minds of all times and of all human beings, even those of today.*" This important qualification (*DS* 3539) shows us the enduring relevancy of the apologetic method of St. Justin. Cf. G. de Broglie, p. 152: prophecy is even more adapted to the modern mind than are miracles; to acknowledge the sign of the Messianic prophecies is also to acknowledge more completely the sign of the Church that is

The principal purpose of the economy of the Old Covenant was to prepare for the coming both of Christ, the universal Redeemer, and of the messianic kingdom, to announce this coming by prophecy (cf. Lk 24:44; Jn 5:39; 1 Pt 1:10) and to indicate its meaning through various types (*ut Christi adventum praepararet, prophetice nuntiaret et variis typis significaret*).[72]

If we must acknowledge that Justin did not sufficiently understand, study, and present the lesser purpose of the Old Testament, he did nevertheless perceive, long before Vatican II, its Christocentric orientation and the inseparable connection and interplay in its message between verbal prophecy and real sign or type: *logoi, typoi*.[73]

The permanent value of his message is confirmed and actually surpassed by Vatican II in this declaration: "The books of the Old Testament integrally embodied in the message of the Gospel, acquire and reveal their complete signification in the New Testament (cf. Mt 5:17; Lk 24:27; Rom. 16:25-26; 2 Cor 3:14-16) and in turn shed light on it and explain it."[74]

In its dialogues with the Tryphos of our time, the Christian world today cannot but repeat to them, without employing the aggressiveness that Justin sometimes displayed, the impossibility of grasping perfectly the full meaning of the Old Testament while refusing to accept the illumination that the crucified and risen Jesus gives to it.

---

divine even in her coming to be. See also the decisions of the Biblical Commission on the prophecies contained in the book of Isaiah (*DS* 3505ff.) and in the psalms (*DS* 3528: in the text of 1910, the commission insists on the unanimous consent of the Fathers and on that of the Jewish authors); and especially *DS* 3506, where the commission stresses the unanimous consent of the Fathers when they affirm that the prophets knew the events foretold long before they happened.

It is interesting to note that, in the view of the Biblical Commission, the existence of Messianic psalms as containing prophetic predictions was one of the cases where that unanimous consent of the Fathers, which Pius XII was to declare quite rare (*Divino Afflante Spiritu, DS* 3831), does come into play.

[72]Vatican II, *Dei Verbum*, 15, our emphasis. Christian exegetes who today would be inclined to minimize in fact, if not in theory, this fundamental orientation of the Old Testament toward Christ and toward the Church, his Messianic Kingdom (*oeconomia ad hoc potissimum disposita...*) are not in harmony with the teaching of the Church. See also *Lumen Gentium* 55, regarding the Mother of the Messiah in the Old Testament.

[73]Cf. the notion of revelation proposed by Vatican II, *Dei Verbum*, 2 and 4: "The works performed by God in the history of salvation show forth and bear out the doctrine and realities signified by the words; the words, for their part, proclaim the works, and bring to light the mystery they contain." Is there not perfect harmony and continuity between this doctrine of Revelation and that of Justin on the *typoi* and *logoi*?

[74]Vatican II, *Dei Verbum*, 16.

Justin's exegesis, with its center in the prophetic argument, thus seems itself to be prophetic[75] and all the more so in that it was consciously situated by him within the context of a Church that was subject as well as object of prophecy, a Church which enjoyed an abundance of certain prophetic charisms which once again appear to be more markedly present in the Church of our time: "Even to this day, we retain possession of prophetic charisms, which should cause you to see for yourselves that those charisms which your race used to possess have been transferred to us" (*Dial.* LXXXII, 1).

Justin's exegesis is the prophetically ecclesial exegesis of one who is himself a prophet, an exegesis that recapitulates the utterances of all those who prophesied He who is the Prophet par excellence. We can still view his exegesis as a very high attainment, one that parallels that of his Master. It is an exegesis sealed by his personal witness and by his martyr's blood; the exegesis that brought him to his sacramental baptism in the Blood of Christ and that ultimately gave meaning to the baptism of blood that was his own death.

The last testimony rendered by Justin to the testimony of the Prophets and, with and through them, to Jesus, the supreme Prophet, is the following, contained in his response to a question of Rusticus, Prefect of Rome:

> This is the doctrine that Christians follow religiously: ...to profess Jesus Christ, Son of God, *foretold in ancient times by the Prophets*, future judge of the human race, messenger of salvation.... As a feeble human being, I am too weak to speak worthily of his infinite divinity. That is the *work of the Prophets*. For centuries, by inspiration from Above, they announced the coming into the world of him whom I have called the Son of God.[76]

---

[75]Not only in the sense that it anticipates what would be the constant exegesis of the Church, but also because Justin, as charismatically enlightened interpreter of the Scriptures, can and should be called a prophet in the sense that St. John Chrysostom (Hom. 1 on the obscurity of the prophecies, *PG* 56, 171 and Hom. 2, *PG* 56, 176) would give to that term: prophecy is a charismatic exposition of the Sacred Scriptures, notably of the Old Testament, in the light of Christ. Cf. S. Tromp, *Corpus Christi quod est Ecclesia*, vol. III, *De Spiritu Christi Anima*, (Rome, 1960), p. 322. It would make perfect sense to imagine that Justin himself, when alluding to the prophetic charisms which are at work in the Church of his time (*Dial.*, LXXXII, 1; we will cite this text shortly) does not exclude himself and that he shows an awareness of being a prophet of the New Covenant in the very importance he ascribes to the prophets of the Old.

[76]Note that the statements mentioned, relative to Christ, follow a first article that pertained to the Father: "To believe in God Creator of all things, visible and invisible." This also confirms our interpretation according to which the confession of Justin intended to

We cannot emphasize too much the Trinitarian character of this final profession of faith, which echoes in this way the Trinitarian description of his conversion by Justin.

In fact, the original Greek text, imperfectly translated by Lagrange, contains an explicit allusion to the "prophetic power" (*prophetiken tina dynamin*) which confesses Jesus Christ, and which Lagrange renders: "C'est l'œuvre des prophetes" (that is the work of the prophets). Now, in Justin's language, the Spirit is seen as a *Dynamis* proper to the Messiah, who was already giving it to the prophets of the Old Covenant and who is giving it now to his anointed one.[77]

Justin is here borrowing for his purposes a fairly common formulation of the Apostle's Creed. This second century formulation we find attested also in Irenæus. Here, the third article of the Creed, relative to the Holy Spirit, is seen in the context of the testimony of the prophets: "The Holy Spirit, through whom the prophets prophesied."[78]

Justin thinks and proclaims that both his own testimony and that of the prophets, whose predictions are so important to his argument, are channels through which the prophetic power of the Holy Spirit rendered and renders testimony to the only Son of God and to his infinite divinity as well as to him who sends him, the Father and Creator, by means of types[79] and words.

The reading of the prophets helped Justin to bear a witness culminating in martyrdom. His death as a martyr invites the unbeliever to search the prophets and in them to find Christ.

---

evoke the Holy Spirit through the mention of the prophetic power. The original Greek text of the acts of the martyrdom of St. Justin may be found in the edition of D. Ruiz Bueno, *Acta de los martires*, BAC, (Madrid, 1968), pp. 311-312; and also in *PG* 6, 1568: more specifically, the paragraph we are translating and studying here. A comparison with *I Apol.* 31 confirms our interpretation.

[77]We are drawing here on J.-P. Martin (cited in note 33) and on the conclusions he comes to on p. 195.

[78]St. Irenæus, *Démonstration de la Prédication Apostolique*, 6, SC, (Paris, 1954), p. 40. Cf. *Adv. Hær.* I, 10.2; and the observation of Fr. J. Lebreton: "If, in Irenæus and already in Justin, the mysteries of Christ's life are put forth in the Creed as fulfillment of prophecies, and are thus intimately linked to the third article (that of the Holy Spirit), one must clearly recognize here the influence of the apologetics of the time. The argument from prophecy was the preferred argument at the time; thus, it was natural to set forth the life of Christ to the neophytes under this formality: everything in this story—incarnation, virgin birth, passion, death, resurrection, ascension—is fulfillment of prophecy" (*Histoire du dogme de la Trinité*, vol. II, [Paris, 1928], p. 156).

[79]Cf. the texts cited in notes 5 and 19 above.

Chapter II
Saint Irenæus, Ecclesial Exegete of Christocentric Recapitulation

With Irenæus, who was the beneficiary of Justin's work, we do not yet find a methodical commentary on the biblical texts. We do find in his writings an extremely rich ensemble of sporadic exegeses within the context of a highly developed biblical theology. This exegesis often has the appearance of a homogeneous outgrowth of the sacred text. It is both apologetic and doctrinal, and not always immune to the dangers of the systematic approach.

Irenæus lived and wrote in the second century.[1] He was the Bishop of Lyons, a disciple of Polycarp, and through him, of the Apostle John. His two main works that have come down to us, and by way of which we can form some idea of his exegesis, are his *Demonstration of the Apostolic Preaching* and his *Adversus Hæreses*, whose full title is *Detection and Refutation of Claimed Knowledge*, or of false gnosis.[2]

In this latter, the more important of the two, Irenæus is fighting against the "gnosis" of Valentinus and of others. These gnostic heresies, which in part condition Irenæus' exegesis, had two things in common:

---

[1]The dates of the birth and death of Irenæus are unknown: cf. M. Jourjon, *Catholicisme*, vol. VI (1967), co. 81ff., article "Irénée."

[2]Cf. Louis Bouyer, *Dictionary of Theology*, (Tournai: Desclée, 1963), pp. 180-181: "At this time the terms *gnosis* and *gnostic* were the common prrperty of Christians and of the Jews from whom they had taken them. In fact, orthodox authors who endeavor to refute those who today are referred to as Gnostics, as though this were their distinctive trait, will usually emphasis that, in their view, these heretics are really pseudo-Gnostics (the formula is found in the very title of the work written against them by St. Irenæus).

on the one hand, the affirmation of a radical dualism between matter and spirit; on the other, the supposed revelation of a series of emanations and combinations which, from a good God (spirit) and an evil principle (matter), are supposed to have produced the world as we know it.[3] It was against this background that Valentinus and the false gnostics interpreted the Scriptures, especially the Gospel of John. In the name of Christianity, they attempted to establish the law of the cultural experience of their time as the valid criterion of truth and meaning, even, if necessary, when this conflicted with the Scriptures.[4] A tendency, by the way, that exists today as well.[5]

It was in this context that Irenæus began to work out rules of exegesis and to apply them—within the framework of the entirely Pauline doctrine of the Christocentric recapitulation of salvation history—to the mystery of Mary, the new Eve, and to the Gospel parables, particularly that of the Good Samaritan. These are the points we shall examine briefly in this chapter.

A) *The Rules of Irenæan Exegesis*

Confronted with the false gnoses and their polytheistic tendencies—which denied to the supreme God the inspiration of the Old Testament—Irenæus' entire effort consists in showing that the Old Testament comes from the same God, through the agency of the same Word and the same Spirit who have now been fully manifested in Christ. Also, the accusations of hypocrisy and falsification[6] of the false gnostics regarding the teaching of the Apostles help us to understand Irenæus' formulation of the rules for exegesis.

The exegesis of Scripture must always be ecclesial. In his *Adversus Hæreses*, we find Irenæus employing the expression *rule of the truth*[7] a dozen times. The expression refers to the doctrine itself, rather than

---

[3]*Ibid.*, p. 283.

[4]Cf. M. J. Le Guillou, O.P., *Le mystère du Père, Foi des Apôtres, Gnoses actuelles*, (Paris, 1973), pp. 31ff.

[5]*Ibid.*, p. 26: the author here denounces, in the writings of certain thinkers who call themselves Christian, a "servile attitude with respect to a variety of theses taken from Marx, Nietzsche, Freud, sometimes according to a narrow interpretation amounting almost to caricature."

[6]Irenæus, *Adversus Hæreses* (hereafter referred to as *AH*), III, 5.1.

[7]D. Van Den Eynde, *Les Normes de l'enseignement chrétien dans la littérature patristique des trois premiers siècles*, (Paris, 1933), citing *AH* I, 1; I, 15; II, 40; III, 2; III, 11; III, 12; III, 15; IV, 57. See also the whole of chapter VII of this book, devoted to "the rule of truth."

designating any particular doctrinal norm. The rule is at once object of revelation, of Scripture, of the tradition of the Apostles, of Church preaching and catechesis. Nevertheless, in specifying that the rule is received with and through Baptism, Irenæus seems to suggest that, when he uses this expression, he is thinking primarily of the living doctrine of the churches which is communicated to neophytes by those whose mission it is to incorporate them into the body of the faithful.[8]

For example, at the beginning of his denunciation of the false gnosis, Irenæus presents the truth as a body whose members are formed by the different doctrines that are thus "the members of the truth." Then he adds that

> he who possesses within himself the immutable canon of the truth that he received through Baptism will surely recognize [in the writings of the heretics] terms, expressions, and parables taken from the Scriptures. But he will not recognize the subject they originally treated…. On the contrary, if he will restore each of the texts to its respective place and fit them all to the body of the truth, he will expose [the fiction of the heretics] and demonstrate its inconsistency,

not without enumerating the different points of that faith "which the Church received from the Apostles and their disciples."[9] He will read "the Scriptures attentively with the presbyters who are in the Church, since it is with them that the doctrine of the Apostles is to be found (*AH* IV, 32.1).

What is involved here then is the search for a criterion that will enable one to distinguish the false interpretations of Scripture from the true,[10] a criterion that is (only initially[11]) exterior to Scripture itself. We could even say that the immutable rule of the truth consists for Irenæus in the fundamental truths that the Church has received from the Apostles and their disciples and which were being taught already in his time, before the celebration of Baptism. (This explains moreover, the

---

[8]*Ibid.*, p. 291.

[9]*AH* I, 9.4.

[10]Cf. (commenting on this text of Irenæus) S. Herrera, *Saint Irénée de Lyon exégète*, (Paris, 1920), pp. 124-126. The author rightly brings out (p. 126, note 3) the fact that "biblical exegesis in conformity with the rule of truth is simply that which we call *juxta analogiam fidei*," in accordance with the analogy of faith, on which the Second Vatican Council has since insisted (*Dei Verbum*, 12. In order to uncover the exact meaning of the sacred texts, attention must be paid to the content and unity of the whole of Scripture, taking into account the living tradition of the whole Church and the analogy of faith).

[11]In reality, the Church is internal to Scripture, which is itself an element of the divine constitution of the Church, as the Second Vatican Council underscores in the decree *Unitatis Redintegratio*, 3, 2.

Trinitarian character of this immutable rule of truth in Irenæus' writings.[12]) Useful not only in helping us perceive the falseness of the heretics' teachings,[13] this rule also clearly shows us that the true interpretation of the Holy Scriptures cannot be in contradiction with the fundamental truths of the faith transmitted by the Church.

The *second rule*, that of Tradition, differs from the first, though it is in some sense an extension of it. Since the false gnostics were claiming to interpret the Scriptures in the light of a tradition which was supposedly transmitted to them orally, and without relying on the Apostles who had supposedly added the dispositions of the law to the words of the Savior, what means should be employed to safeguard the truth and to guarantee the purity of teaching?

What judge will be the ultimate arbiter regarding the legitimacy of doctrine? According to Irenæus, it will be the teaching of the bishops who hold uninterrupted succession in the churches founded by the Apostles, from the time of these latter right down to our own. The preceding rule referred us to the apostolic preaching itself; this one specifies for us its organ of transmission. Let us cite rather Irenæus' words on this subject:

> It is not necessary to seek elsewhere the truth we can easily receive from the Church, for the Apostles amassed in Her, in the fullest possible way, as in a rich cellar, everything connected with the truth, so that whoever so desires may drink here of the potion of life. For She it is indeed who gives access to life. All others are thieves and robbers [cf. Jn 10:8]. This is why we must reject them, loving instead, with utmost zeal, what comes from the Church and laying hold of the Tradition of the truth.... If a controversy should arise, is it not our duty to have recourse to the most ancient Churches, those in which the Apostles themselves lived, to receive from them the correct doctrine concerning the disputed question? (*AH* III, 4.1)

The universal Church through which Irenæus receives the apostolic preaching is not however an amorphous Church. It is a structured Church, an episcopal Church centered about a privileged bishop who presides over the universal charity that unites all the bishops:

> The Tradition of the Apostles that has been made known in the whole world can be perceived in every Church by anyone who wants to see the truth. And we could enumerate the bishops who were established by the Apostles in the

---

[12]Cf. *AH*, I, 15, and D. Farkasfalvy, "The Theology of Scripture in S. Irenæus," *Revue Bénédictine*, 78 (1968), pp. 318-333, especially pp. 324-327.

[13]A point emphasized by S. Herrera, p. 126.

Churches and their successors down to us…. But since it would be too long in a work like this to enumerate the successions of all the Churches, we will take only one of them, the very great, very ancient Church, known by all, which the two glorious Apostles Peter and Paul founded and established at Rome…for with that Church, by reason of its most excellent origin, all Churches, that is, the faithful everywhere, must necessarily agree—that Church in which the Tradition that comes from the Apostles has always been preserved for the benefit of these peoples everywhere.

These famous texts, especially the last,[14] have long captured the attention of interpreters. What interests us here is the fact that for Irenæus the uninterrupted succession of bishops, especially in the Roman Church headed by the successors of Peter and Paul, constitutes a sufficient and perfect guarantee of the pure and certain transmission of the teaching of the Apostles,[15] and, consequently, of a correct interpretation of the Scriptures, particularly of the New Testament of which those Apostles themselves were authors.

All the more so because, with their succession in the episcopate, the bishops have received "a certain charism of truth, according to the good pleasure of the Father" (*AH* IV, 26.2). It is then "from them that we must learn the truth, for it is they who expound the Scriptures to us without danger of error" (*AH* IV, 26.5). By shunning the judgments of the heretics and fleeing for refuge to the Church, a paradise in this world, we will be able there to eat of the fruit of all the trees of this paradise, that is, the fruit of all the Lord's Scriptures (*AH* V, 20.2).

These two fundamental rules are supplemented by three others that are more difficult to tie together logically.

These three other rules are concerned with the unity of the Scriptures and their inner harmony, the explication of obscure passages, and respect for the transcendence of the divine Author.

The *third rule* can be formulated thus: an interpretation has a chance of being correct if one can prove its "consonance" and its harmony with other texts of Scripture. The verb *consonare*, used repeatedly by Irenæus in an exegetical context, takes on a technical character in Irenæus' lan-

---

[14]*AH* III, 3.2. On the interpretation of this text, see D. Van den Eynde, pp. 171-179; Irenæus of Lyons, *Contre les Hérésies*, III, critical edition, SC 210, (Paris, 1974), vol. I, pp. 224-236, with the interpretation of Dom Rousseau and P. Doutreleau and the bibliography supplied on p. 236; one might add too the article of Dom Lanne. *Irénikon*, (1976), pp. 275-322 entitled "L'Eglise de Rome et le martyre de Pierre et Paul chez Irénée."
It is particularly remarkable that in this famous text Irenæus makes no explicit allusion to the thre great Petrine passages of the Gospels: Mt 16, Lk 22 and Jn 21.
[15]S. Herrera, p. 133.

guage and exegesis. He regards as one of the principal aims of his exegesis that the perfect mutual harmony of the Scriptures be brought out. The Scriptures are in "symphony."[16]

This rule has a double foundation. On the one hand, all the Scriptures have the same God, his Word, and his Spirit as their Author. Now God cannot contradict himself. Therefore, there can be no contradiction between them. On the other hand, since the Old Testament itself has the Word for its author[17] and Christ for its meaning, the history of Revelation, as Irenæus understands it, obliges the Christian exegete to move constantly from one Testament to the other, clarifying the one by means of the other.

The *fourth rule* would have us interpret *obscure passages*, not by recourse to other equally obscure passages, but with the help of texts that are more clear and more explicit than they. "One should not resolve an enigma by another still greater than the first, nor a doubt by means of another, rather, doubts and enigmas should be resolved in the light of what is manifest and in harmony."[18] There is no point in making a "new knot in our efforts to untie the first" (*AH* II, 10.2). If the interpreter of Scripture observes this method and this rule of clarity, there will be no danger of his giving erroneous explanations. Rather, he will be safeguarding the body of the truth that will remain unshaken in all its parts (*AH* III, 27.1).[19] This rule, like the preceding one, is aimed particularly at the methods of the false gnostics. This will again be the case with the last.

The *fifth rule* affirms that we must never abandon certain and indubitable truths to go looking for solutions to questions that are either useless or beyond the range of our understanding. We should leave such questions to God. Many created realities escape our understanding. What harm is there then if we resolve some scriptural difficulties thanks to God's grace and leave the others to God, so that man may always learn what is clearly from God and what God is always teaching (*AH* II, 28.3).

For example—and Irenæus insisted on this against the false gnosis—who knows what God was doing before the creation of the world? Who

---

[16]*AH* I, 3.87; II, 58.2; II, 115; II, 48; III, 25.1; III, 2.11; cf. Farkasfalvy, p. 328. The author cites especially this text of *AH* II, 41.4: "Omnis scriptura a Deo nobis data *consonans* [symphonos] invenietur"; I, p. 352.

[17]Cf. *AH* II, 41.1; I, 349; IV, 3.1; cf. D. Farkasfalvy, pp. 325-327; his opinions will be nuanced at some points in the light of the more in-depth study of Herrera, pp. 70-88.

[18]*AH* II, 10.1.

[19]Cf. Herrara, 120-123.

knows how the eternal generations of the Word took place (*AH* II, 28.3.6)?[20]

We might observe that these rules, excepting of course the fourth, primarily assist the interpreter of Scripture in discovering with certainty the exegeses that are to be excluded and the fundamental truths that the divine book contains, rather than helping him interpret specific points. They are nonetheless valuable for all that, for much has already been gained if we can avoid the "false gnosis" of understanding of Scripture, and if we can extract its fundamental message more easily.

In short, these rules crystallize the exegesis that Irenæus himself practiced and that enabled him to place the accent on Christ the Recapitulator.

B) *Irenæus, the Exegete and Teacher of Christocentric Recapitulation*

In Irenæus' work, a particular Pauline verse takes on decisive importance. We are referring to Ephesians 1:10, God's "purpose that he set forth in Christ as a plan for the fullness of time, to unite all things in him, things in heaven and things on earth." We can regard the following passage[21] of Irenæus as both a commentary and a development of the Pauline verse:

> There is but one God the Father and but one Christ Jesus our Lord Who came by way of a whole divine economy and Who has everything recapitulated in Himself. That everything also included man, that piece of work fashioned by God; He has then recapitulated man too in Him, who being invisible became visible, being incomprehensible, being incapable of suffering, became a man of sorrows, being Word became man. He has recapitulated everything in Himself so that, just as the Word of God holds the primacy over all the spiritual and invisible beings above the heavens, He should rule likewise over all visible and corporal beings, and so that, by assuming that primacy in Himself and giving Himself as Head to the Church, He might draw everything to Himself at the opportune moment.

Irenæus stresses here, in the idea of recapitulation, the Father's plan to place everything, including the angels, under Christ. He does so by commenting on this Pauline verse from Ephesians in the light of the

---

[20]One may be allowed to think that on this point the response of Irenæus to the "Gnostic" theologians was not adequate; cf. Bertrand de Margerie, *The Christian Trinity in History*, (Petersham, MA: St. Bede's Publications, 1982), pp.68-72.

[21]*AH* III, 16.6.

prologue of the Letter to the Colossians. The recapitulation is not merely one of men, but extends as well to the angels and to the entire universe, an idea that is perfectly in harmony with Pauline thought. The meaning is clearly cosmic.

A second sense is more soteriological. Recapitulation is renewal (as the particle *ana*, in the Greek *anakephalaiosis*, implies). It is a new beginning. For the humanity that Christ has reassembled had fallen into the power of the demon. The Word is taking back from Satan what the latter had stolen. "The Word has recapitulated the long history of humanity so that we might recover in Jesus Christ what we had lost in Adam, namely, our being in the image and likeness of God" (*AH* III, 18.1). Recapitulation implies a special relationship with Adam, insofar as it is restoration of what had been compromised by him.

Irenæus' interpretation of recapitulation is then best understood in the context of Paul's theology of the two Adams:

> This is why Luke presents a genealogy going back from the birth of Our Lord to Adam and comprising seventy-two generations. For he thus links the end to the beginning and suggests that it is the Lord Who recapitulates in Himself all the nations dispersed from the time of Adam, all the languages and all the generations of men, including Adam himself. It is also for this reason that Paul calls Adam himself the "figure of Him Who was to come" [Rom 5:14]. For the Word, the artisan of the universe, had begun to trace out in Adam the future "economy" of the humanity which the Son of God would take on, God having established first the physical man so that, in plain logic, he might be saved by the spiritual Man. In fact, since the Savior already existed, it was fitting that the saved also come into existence, so that the Savior not remain without *raison d'être* (*AH* III, 22.3).

Here, the recapitulation of Eph 1:10 is seen in the double context of a reaction against the false gnosis that denied the creation of the first Adam by a good God, and of an elucidation provided by the Letter to the Romans. As in the passage quoted earlier, Irenæus' exegesis consists in placing a key verse within the total context of Pauline thought, demonstrating thereby the "consonance" and the "symphony" that results from this procedure.

Having considered the cosmic and soteriological sense, if indeed one may legitimately dissect an idea as pregnant as that of Irenæus: recapitulation of the race of Adam which He reclaims means not only that the Word epitomizes this race by fathering the totality of its aspects into his single Person (*AH* II, 22.4; 20.8; V, 14.2), but above all the term points to the installation of the glorious Christ as head of the Church and as principle of all spiritual life. Recapitulation is conclusion, goal, crowning.

This meaning, besides harmonizing well with the two theologies of Paul and of Irenæus, respects perfectly the meaning of the Greek word *kephalaion* from which our word recapitulate derives its root. Now this word has the various meanings of head, chief and summary. Therefore, to recapitulate means to embrace in a comprehensive way, to summarize-in-fullness, to bring to perfection and to consummate. Such an eschatological meaning includes and synthesizes the cosmic and soteriological senses, while going beyond time. What is here involved is the resumption by the Creator himself, without rupture of continuity, of his creative action, the full flowering of what was already present in seed at the beginning, the crowning moment that concludes the long preparations.[22]

This triple and unique sense (cosmic, soteriological, eschatological) of recapitulation is magnificently present in these two extracts from the *Adversus Hæreses*: "Our Lord has come to us in the end times, recapitulating everything in Himself (...) He became flesh and hung on the wood so as to recapitulate everything in Himself" (IV, 38.1; V, 18.3).

Finally, in "consonance" with another Pauline text (1 Cor 11:3), recapitulation assumes, in Irenæus' view, a Trinitarian nuance:

> Above everything there is the Father and He is the Head of Christ; through everything there is the Word and He is the Head of the Church; in everything there is the Spirit and He is the fountain of living water.... He (Christ) has recapitulated the spiritual things in the heavens and the things that are on earth, namely, the disposition concerning man, uniting man with the Spirit and causing the Spirit to dwell within man, becoming Himself the Head of the Spirit and giving the Spirit to be the head of man. For it is by this Spirit that we see, hear, and speak (*AH* V, 18.2; 20.2).

This is indeed a magnificent perspective.[23] Christ, recapitulated by his Head, the Father, is himself Head and recapitulator in the gift of his Spirit to men, the One who brings together heaven and earth, angels and men. The Word sends the Spirit to men for their salvation; it is in

---

[22]We have drawn here on Jean Daniélou, *Message évangélique et culture hellénistique*, (Tournai, 1961), pp. 156-169 and especially on J.-M. Dufort, "La récapitulation paulinienne dans l'exégèse des Pères," *Sciences ecclésiastiques*, 12 (1960), pp. 24-27.

[23]We are here reproducing some observations made in our book *Christ for the World*, (Chicago: Franciscan Herald Press, 1975). We showed there how, particularly in *Gaudium et Spes*, on the Church in the modern world, the Second Vatican Council effectively adopted Irenæus' notion of recapitulation.

giving them his Spirit that Christ is Head both of the Spirit and of the Church. It is by the Spirit that we see, with the eyes of faith, Christ our Head, that we speak of Christ, when that Spirit speaks of him through us, as he spoke of him through the prophets of the Old Testament. To see, to listen, to speak, etc., are activities that can and must be attributed both to Christ the Head and to the Spirit, who is both Head and Soul of the Church, which will retain rather this latter image.[24] It is in and by the Spirit that Christ assembles his Church and makes of it his Body, to offer her then, in homage of filial adoration, to his Head and recapitulator, the Father (cf. 1 Cor 15:24-28).

We see then how in Irenæus, biblical exegesis and biblical theology remain inseparably tied together. For him, to interpret Scripture means, with a particular theme in mind, to tie together numerous—not to say all—of the mysteries it offers us. As it strives to work out the idea of recapitulation such as St. Paul understands it, Irenæus' exegesis itself recapitulates all and everything. It is essentially a synthetic interpretive approach rather than an analytical one. While not disregarding distinctions, Irenæus is much more inclined, in his reading of the Scriptures, to the work of reducing the many to unity. Whatever the precise subject, Irenæus seems always to be engaged in a kind of recapitulation.

Thus, Irenæus reduces what we today would be tempted to call the written Gospels to a single four-faceted Gospel, through which the one Church proclaims one only God, one only Christ, one only Spirit.[25] "The Word, Maker of the universe, He Who is seated above the Cherubim and Who sustains the whole universe, after having been manifested to men, gave us the four-faceted Gospel, a Gospel, however, sustained by one only Spirit," as the bishop of Lyons so magnificently put it (*AH* III, 11.8; II, 7).

For Irenæus, there are not four distinct Gospels, but four "forms" or "ideas" (*AH* III, 11.9; II, 50) of the one Gospel. Thus Mark, for example, "presents us a winged image of the Gospel in full flight as it were," an "icon of the Gospel" (*ibid.*). Such a conception is perfectly faithful to the New Testament as well as to the earliest Christian tradition. For Paul too the Gospel is but one, as the term always refers to the oral preaching in his letters, and never to a written text.[26]

---

[24]Cf. Pius XII, *Mystici Corporis Christi*, (1943), *DS* 3808; Vatican II, *Lumen Gentium*, 7.

[25]A. Benoît, *Saint Irénée, Introduction à l'étude de sa théologie*, (Paris, 1960), pp. 111-112: "There is but one God, one Christ, one Spirit, one Church, and hence there can be but one Gospel."

[26]Cf. L. Vaganay, *Catholicisme*, IV, (1956), col. 767-769, article "Evangile."

C) As Christ Recapitulates Adam, Mary Recapitulates Eve

The struggle against the false gnosis also occasioned Irenæus' application of the idea of recapitulation to the Virgin Mary. It is no doubt difficult for us today to know exactly what a "gnostic mariology" would have been. Was such a thing even possible? Clearly not, for how could the gnostic disregard for matter and the body be reconciled with an esteem for Mary and her role in the economy of salvation?[27]

In exalting the mystery of the Incarnation of the Word, Irenæus inevitably finds Mary, intimately associated like a new Eve with the salvific work of the new Adam:

> Like the Lord, we also find Mary the Virgin obeying when she says: "Behold, I am the handmaid of the Lord; let it be done to me according to your word" [Lk 1:38]. Eve, in contrast, had been disobedient, even when she was still a virgin. For just as Eve, having Adam for her spouse, and nevertheless still a virgin—for they were both naked in Paradise and were not ashamed [Gen. 2:25] because, having just been created, they had no notion of procreation: they first had to grow up, and only then could they multiply—just as Eve, in disobeying, became the cause of death for herself and for the entire human race, so also Mary, having for her spouse one Who had been destined for her in advance, and nevertheless a virgin, became, by her obedience, the cause of salvation for herself[28] and for the whole human race.

---

[27] A collection and an analysis of the texts of the false Gnostics on Mary will be found in J. A. de Aldama, *Maria en la patristica de los siglos I y II*, BAC, (Madrid, 1970), pp. 40-62. For them, and most notably for Ptolemy, "Christ passed through Mary as water passes through a tube," but was not truly born of her (cf. *AH* I, 7.2); this explains the emphasis in our present text of the Apostles' Creed: "*natus ex* Maria Virgine."

[28] We do not share the opinion of J. A. de Aldama (*Eph. Mariologicæ* 16, 1966, 319-321: *sibi causa facta est salutis*); he believes that the *sibi* does not refer to Mary but to Eve; he supports his interpretation by the argument that it would be impossible to attribute to Irenæus the idea that Mary was the cause of her own redemption (p. 320); but it is by no means necessary to attribute such an idea to Irenæus in order to justify his expression (Mary cause of her own salvation) if we recall that Paul wrote to Timothy, "Pay close attention to yourself and to your teaching; continue in these things, for in doing this *you will save* both *yourself* and your hearers (1 Tm 4:16: the verb *sozein* is employed by the author, just as Irenæus, in the text in question, employs the related term *soteria*).

There is more. In the context of the *AH* III, 22.4, where Irenæus writes of Mary: "sibi causa facta est salutis," it is quite possible that he explicitly intended to allude to another passage of the same letter of Paul to Timothy, namely to 1 Tm 2:14-15: "Adam was not deceived, but the woman was deceived and became a transgressor. Yet *she will be saved through childbearing*, provided they continue in faith and love and holiness, with modesty." Is it not possible that, in the statement discussed by Fr. de Aldama, Irenæus meant that Mary was saved, having become for herself a cause of salvation, by accepting to become

This is why the Law applies to a woman who is betrothed to a man, even though still a virgin, the term spouse with respect to the one who has taken her for his troth [Dt 22:23-24], signifying thus the return [recycling: *recirculatio*[29]] which was effected from Mary to Eve. For what has been tied cannot be untied except by redoing in reverse the loops of the knot, such that the original series of loops is undone thanks to the second, and conversely, the second liberates the first.... The knot of Eve's disobedience was untied by Mary's obedience, for what the virgin Eve had tied through her unbelief, the Virgin Mary untied by her faith (*AH* III, 22.4). (This text was cited explicitly by Vatican II in *Lumen Gentium*, 56.)

This whole passage can be regarded as an exegesis of Luke 1:39 in the light of the second chapter of Genesis (with an additional marginal reference to Dt 22:23-24). Now one cannot but note that contemporary exegesis has returned to an analogous understanding of Luke's intention.[30]

---

the mother of not just any human being, but of the New Adam, the divine Savior? Indeed, the statement of Irenæus suggests that the general and universal law of salvation for woman, namly maternity, was fulfilled in a unique and transcendent way in Mary, to the extent that in saving herself she was actually saving the whole human race: she was accepting, for herself as well as for others, him who would be both her and their Savior. This comparison had been suggested by Fr. Spicq. Its particular merit lies in the fact that it shows how much more deeply rooted in Pauline thinking than had previously been suspected is the theology of Irenæus regarding Mary as the new Eve.

The interpretation of Fr. de Aldama seems to overlook the whole parallel drawn by Irenæus: Mary saves herself, just as Eve had lost herself. The point is not that Mary redeemed herself: the suggestion is merely made, as later theology will put it, that she cooperated (like each of us, but in a more sublime way) in her own *subjective* redemption, by applying to herself the merits of the one Redeemer who was the sole author of her *objective* redemption.

On *AH* III, 22.4 in connection with 1 Tm 2:14-15, see Bertrand de Margerie, *Introduction à l'histoire de l'exégèse des Pères latins*, chapter 3, notes 28-30.

[29]We note here the Greek term *anakyklesin*, which the Latin translator rendered *recirculatio* and which suggests literally a *recycling*. Etymologically, as Fr. Doutreleau (*SC* 210, *AH* III, vol. I, p. 376) points out, the Greek word signifies "the action of making an object come back by causing it to make a circular movement on itself. [...] The word corresponds, the present context, to the word *anakephalaiosis* (recapitulation): just as the second term expresses the work of salvation accomplished by the new Adam, the first (*anakyklesis*) suggests the participation of the new Eve in this salvific work." It is easy to see why Irenæus chose a different term to signify the action of Mary, because he underscores (in the same section) the faith of Mary who repaired Eve's lack of faith. He does not claim that Christ recapitulated Adam through faith. The transcendence implicit in the notion of recapitulation with respect to that of "recycling" manifests the transcendence of Jesus with respect to Mary, the believer.

[30]Cf. André Feuillet, "Marie et la nouvelle création," *Vie spirituelle* 81, (1949), p. 467-478; René Laurentin, *Court traité sur la Vierge Marie*, (Paris, 1967), (5), p. 40, note 32: "It is not unlikely that in presenting the dialogue of Mary with the angel Gabriel, Luke had in mind

Irenæus is faithful to Luke's profound intention in presenting us Mary's obedience as a salvific and divinely solicited response to Eve's disobedience. While, on the other hand, his presentation of the Virgin Mary as advocate of the *virgin* Eve (*AH* V, 19.1), by stressing Eve's virginity before sin, could be an interpretation—even perhaps a legitimate one—of the inspired text that goes beyond the explicit intentions of the author of Genesis, but not, to be sure, of the *sensus plenior* intended by the divine Author. If one prefers, it could be regarded as a doctrinal development, homogeneous to the biblical text, suggested by Luke himself in his inspired rereading of Genesis 2.

In summary, for Irenæus, Eve is the type, the prefiguration of Mary, as Adam is of Christ (cf. Rom 5:14). At the moment of their dialogues with angels, Eve and Mary are both betrothed spouses and virgins. By their free acts, both intervene in the historical drama of humanity.[31]

Recently, within the context of the theology of the Fathers of the second century as a whole, A. Orbe has shown how the Eve-Mary antithesis is, for Irenæus, deeper and more "existential" than has hitherto been thought. Satan was proposing to the first Eve, under the image of the forbidden fruit, a sexual activity that would anticipate the hour preordained by God and, consequently, a death-bearing motherhood. This explains Irenæus' insistence, in the passage cited, on the fact that Eve was still a virgin and that she had (as yet) no knowledge of procreation. In contrast, the archangel Gabriel proposes in God's Name, the Virgin Mary, without harm to her virginity, a life-bearing motherhood.[32] The interpretation of Orbe seems quite acceptable and certainly makes this text of Irenæus both more intelligible and more meaningful.

In any case, clearly Irenæus in the text commented on here ascribes a privileged role in the economy of salvation to the Virgin Mary herself and to her obedience to the word of God. Indeed, he goes so far as to proclaim her "cause of salvation for herself and for the whole human race," in dependence on Christ, of course. The Catholic Church would later invoke this reading of Luke's Gospel (1:38) and this insistence on the free consent of Mary to the divine maternity as implying an awareness on the part of Irenæus of the existence (in Luke and Paul) of a principle of privileged and unique association of Mary with Jesus Christ in

---

that of Eve with the serpent." Laurentin adds, however, "But if theologians have the right to develop these objectively valid hints in line with the Fathers of the Church, the exegete should remain more cautious."

[31]Cf. A. Orbe, *Antropologia de S. Ireneo, BAC*, (Madrid, 1969), pp. 247-251.

[32]*Ibid.*, p. 249; Aldama, note 27, pp. 285-286.

the redemptive work (*principium consortii*), an association that represents an implicit New Testament grounding of the doctrines of the Immaculate Conception and the Assumption of Mary, the second and new Eve.[33] For if Paul could view Christ as the second and new Adam, was he not also implicitly viewing Mary (cf. Gal 4:4-6) as the new and second Eve,[34] as Irenæus understood her to be?

We must even say that, perhaps without intending it, Irenæus objectively suggested the Assumption of Mary in his *Demonstration of the Apostolic Preaching*: "Adam had to be recapitulated in Christ so that what is mortal might be absorbed and swallowed up by immortality and Eve [had to be recapitulated] in Mary—in order that a virgin, becoming the advocate of a virgin, might destroy and abolish the disobedience of a virgin through the obedience of a virgin" (33).

This text, in its obscure richness and in its double parallelism (Adam-Eve on the one hand, Jesus-Mary on the other), clearly alludes to Paul's teachings on universal death in Adam and resurrection in Christ and with Him, to Adam's death and to Christ's resurrection (1 Cor 15:22: all die in Adam, all receive life in Christ; 1 Cor 15:54: when this mortal being puts on immortality). If the mortal Adam has been absorbed by the immortality of the risen Christ, and thus recapitulated, and if Eve is in an analogous situation with respect to Mary, does it not follow that Mary, cause of salvation for Eve (*AH* III, 22.4), was so precisely by swallowing up and absorbing Eve's death in her immortality as a risen one? If the recapitulation of Adam by Christ implies the latter's glorious resurrection, must we not conclude an analogous implication, in Irenæus' view, of Eve's recapitulation by Mary—Mary's privileged and anticipated resurrection?[35]

While insisting, in his denunciation of the anti-Marian reduction of false gnosis, on the mystery of the recapitulating new Eve, Irenæus was simultaneously fighting against another reduction touching specifically

---

[33]Pius XII, *Munificentissimus Deus*, 1950, (the bull that defined the Assumption of Mary), *DS* 3901-3902; in the context of the patristic theology of the New Eve, which had emerged with great clarity as early as the second century, the pope read Gn 3:15 in the light of Rom 5—6 and 1 Cor 15:21-26 and 54-57.

[34]Cf. J. M. Bover, *Teologia de S. Pablo*, (Madrid, 1952), pp. 440ff.

[35]Such an analysis should, however, be put forward with reserve. Cf. the cautious observations of Lucien Deiss: "By the use and exploitation (if we dare put it this way) of these texts, we should, however, take care not to exaggerate their sense. The passages cited earlier of the *Epideixis* (or *Demonstration of the Apostolic Preaching*) are found in the Armenian translation. Since we no longer possess the original, it is imprudent to read too much into terms that appear essential and that are perhaps already interpretations" (*Marie, Fille de Sion*, [Bruges, 1952], pp. 251-252).

on Mary's virginity, namely, that of the Ebionites and the Judeo-Christians who were attempting to minimize the sign announced in Isaiah 7:14:

God has then become man and the Lord Himself has saved us by himself giving us the sign of the virgin. In view of this fact, we fail to see how we could agree with those authors who now dare to translate the Scripture thus: "Behold, a young woman shall conceive and bear a son" [Isaiah 7:14]. It is so translated by Theodotion of Ephesus and Aquila of Pontus, both Jewish proselytes. They are followed by the Ebionites, who say Jesus was born of Joseph, destroying in this way, insofar as it is in their power to do so, the great economy of God and reducing to nothing the testimony of the prophets that was the work of God. This is a prophecy that was made before the deportation of the people to Babylon, i.e., before the hegemony of the Medes and the Persians. This prophecy was later translated into Greek by the Jews themselves long before the coming of Our Lord, so that no one can suspect them of having translated it as they did with the possible thought of pleasing us. For if they had known that we would exist one day and that we would use the testimonies drawn from Scripture, they would certainly not have hesitated to burn their own Scriptures with their own hands—those Scriptures which openly declare that all the other nations will have a share in life (*AH* III, 21.1).

After having shown at great length the "consonance" between the Septuagint version, anterior to Christianity, and the tradition of the Apostles, emphasizing especially the unity of the Spirit's action—the same Spirit who prophesied through Isaiah, interpreted[36] through the Septuagint and preached through the Apostles—Irenæus underscores the meaning of the prophecy. In Isaiah 7:10-16,

the Holy Spirit has revealed two things: the generation of him who comes from the Virgin, and his being, which consists in the fact that he is God —which the name Emmanuel signifies—and man, which is indicated by the expression "he shall eat curds and honey," by the appellation "child," and by the words "before he knows good and evil," for these are all traits that characterize a human being and a child. As for the expression "he will refuse the evil and choose the good" it expresses something proper to God. This is said lest the words "he will eat butter and honey" cause us to see in him simply a man

---

[36]Cf. J. A. de Aldama, *Maria en la patristica*, (cited in note 27), p. 115, note 46. The author correctly emphasizes that Irenæus offered the Septuagint as an interpretation (*interpretatus est*) without claiming, Sagnard notwithstanding, that the version was inspired (*SC*, vol. 34, pp. 257 and 432).

and lest, by excess in the opposite direction the name Emmanuel causes us to imagine a God not clothed with flesh (AH III, 21.4).

Irenæus is even more emphatic:

The phrase: "The Lord God himself will give you a sign" underscores the unusual character of His generation: this generation would never have taken place if the Lord, the God of all things, had not Himself given this sign in the house of David. For what would have been so remarkable, or what sign would have been constituted by the fact that a "young woman" conceived by a man and gave birth, since this is the normal way for a woman to give birth. But because the salvation that was to come to men through the divine assistance was extraordinary, extraordinary also was the childbirth that would have a virgin for its author: it is God Who would give this sign and man would count for nothing here (AH III, 21.6).

In short, Irenæus rejected the translations of Theodotion and Aquila that rendered the famous *almah* of Isaiah 7:14 not *parthenos*, virgin, but *neanis*, young girl, adolescent. Without claiming that the Septuagint version was inspired, Irenæus defended it and believed that it was a faithful guarantor of the originally inspired thought of Isaiah. For him, the prophecy was literally (and not typically) messianic. The debate has continued throughout the centuries and is still going on today. Indeed, few biblical subjects have caused so much ink to flow.[37]

We shall content ourselves here with two observations that corroborate Irenæus' exegesis of Isaiah 7:14. On the one hand, as the Protestant

---

[37]It might be noted that many modern exegetes still interpret Is 7:14 as a Messianic prophecy in the literal sense. We cite among others, C. Larcher, *L'actualité chrétienne de l'A. T.*, (Paris, 1962), pp. 69-73; André Feuillet, *De Mariologia et Œcumenismo*, (Rome, 1962), pp. 39-48. Some recent studies, in the view of A. Gelin, have contributed to a better understanding of Is 7:14 by situating the discussion "firmly on the terrain of royal Messianism" (*DTC, Tables*, I, [Paris, 1951], 1158). To some extent along this line, see also Cruveilhier, *DBS*, vol. II, (1934), 1041-1049 and A. Gelin, *DBS* 5, (1957), 1180-1182. We note especially this observation of J. Steinmann in the *Jerusalem Bible*, ([New York: Doubleday, 1985], p. 1201, note g): "Gk reads 'the virgin,' being more explicit than the Hebr. which uses *almah*, meaning either a young girl or a young, recently married woman. This LXX reading is, however, an important witness to an early Jewish interpretation, later adopted by the evangelist: Mt 1:23 understands the text to be a prophecy of the virginal conception of Jesus." This was already the position of Irenæus. The same author (*ibid*, note f) seems to favor a typological Messianic sense for Is 7:14: the prophecy would have first of all referred to a son of Ahaz, and beyond him, to Christ. But such an interpretation reduces the term *almah* to a banal sense and thus falls under the aim of Irenæus' criticisms and those of the Fathers, who are unanimous in their treatment of this text. The patristic interpretation was sustained in 1956 by P. H. Cazelles, (*Catholicisme*, vol. IV, col. 55-56, "Emmanuel") not, however, without some hesitation. See also notes 39-40 below.

exegete, O. Procksch[38] notes, if "Isaiah did not choose the term *betulah*, virgin, it is because this term would exclude every idea of childbirth." It was then natural that he should prefer the expression almah, which designates "a young marriageable girl not yet married: this word does not affirm virginity, but normally supposes it," writes A. Robert.[39] On the other hand, "the Emmanuel" is not just any son. When we read Isaiah 7:14 ("Behold the *almah*, the Virgin is with child and will give birth to a son, and call his name Emmanuel") in the context of the chapters that follow, the passage supposes a personage of exceptional dignity, situated in the sphere of the divine (9:5) and invested from birth with the Holy Spirit together with all his gifts (11.2). Although the prophecy has to do with a descendent of the line of David, it makes no mention (an unusual omission) of any monarch who was to be his father, and to whom, according to the custom of the times, ought to have been reserved the exclusive right of giving him a name. "The Emmanuel" announces then, by the very manner of his birth, that God means to take into his hands the interests of his people, without the cooperation of the declining dynasty. The prophecy is then, concludes A. Robert,[40] God's decisive response to the incredulity of Ahaz.

In summary, Irenæus is, together with Justin, one of the first patristic witnesses of the literally messianic interpretation of Isaiah 7:14. Now it is surprising to find that in this rather exceptional case, all the Fathers without exception, including those of the Antioch school, and including the Syrians such as St. Ephrem, would follow Irenæus and Justin in

---

[38]O. Procksch, *Jesaia*, I, (Leipzig, 1930), p. 121.

[39]A. Robert, La Sainte Vierge dans l'A.T.," *Maria*, vol. I, (Paris, 1949), p. 38, cf. p. 37: "It is impossible to prove from the biblical texts that the *almah* is married"; the author adds on p. 38 that Gn 24 (concerning Rebecca) "clearly establishes the equivalence of *almah* and *betulah* [virgin] as the comparison of verses 16 and 43 shows."

[40]*Ibid.* Therefore, it is for this author a Messianic and Marian prophecy of the first order; he agrees with E. J. Kissane (*Isaiah*, [Dublin, 1941] vol. I, p. 89) that "the prophet chose an elastic word to signify a virgin without excluding the idea of childbearing." Furthermore, we find a valuable bibliography on the present state of research on Isaiah 7:14 and a thoughtful treatment of the subject in J. Coppens, *Le messianisme royal*, (Paris, 1968), pp. 69ff. The author says especially, "We recall, supported by the hypothesis that sees in Emmanuel the Savior-king of the future, that no other explanation is entirely satisfactory and that to date no other has come to prevail." (p. 74). On the same subject we point out N. Füglister, *Mysterium Salutis, Les préparations de l'événement Jésus Christ*, (Paris, 1973), vol. IX, pp. 174-180; A. Feuillet, *Etudes d'exégèse et de théologie biblique, Ancien Testament*, (Paris, 1975), pp. 40-44; 210-214; 227-232.

interpreting this text of Isaiah as the antecedent and explicit annuncia-tion of the virginal birth of the Messiah.[41]

We have here one of the rare cases of unanimous agreement among the Fathers on the exegesis of a Scriptural text. It follows that members of the Catholic Church are required to hold the messianic exegesis of Isaiah 7:14, as Pope Pius VI stressed in 1779.[42] The Church, however, would not insist on a literally messianic reading but would admit, as D. Calmet points out, the possibility of a typically messianic sense.

In the light of the criteria proposed by Vatican I[43] and by Leo XIII,[44] and sharpened by Pius XII[45]—criteria accepted in substance by Vatican

---

[41]Cf. J. A. de Aldama, *Sacræ Theologiæ Summa*, (Madrid, 1951), vol. III, pp. 343-344; F. Cavallera, Saint Augustin et la prophétie de la Vierge Mère," *Rech. Sc. Rel.*, 1, (1910), pp. 380-384. In particular, concerning Irenæus, see also the parallel development in the *Démon-stration de la Prédication apostolique*, 53. Saverianus of Gabala, in a commentary on Gal 4:23-24, perhaps best qualified the prophecy of Is 7:14. Here is how this contemporary and adversary of John Chrysostom, two centuries after Irenæus, expressed himself:

> Certain prophecies are *only* verbal, such as, "Behold a virgin shall conceive in her womb [Is 7:14]; others are *only relative to certain facts*, such as, "Moses raised up a serpent in the desert [Nm 21:8 and Jn 3:14]; others are *both verbal and real at the same time*, such as what was said to Jeremiah in Jer 13:4-6; etc. [Quoted by C. Staab, *Pauluskommentare...aus Katenenhandschriften gesammelt*, p. 302; and by F. Ogara, *Gregorianum* 24, (1943), pp. 76-77].

In other words, for Severianus of Gabala, Isaiah's prophecy announced in words, a long time in advance, though not through a prefiguring fact, that a virgin would conceive the Messiah. Therefore it does not lend itself to the interpretation of Antiochian *theoria* (cf. Chapter VII) according to which certain prophecies have an initial fulfillment in the Old Covenant before reaching their fulfillment in the New Covenant.

We can easily understand why. The extraordinary miracle of a virginal conception couldn't take place in the case of an ordinary man, i.e., one who is not the Son of God.

[42]Pius VI, Brief *Divina* (September 20, 1779), *Enchiridion Biblicum*, (Rome, 1961[4]), # 74, condemning the thesis of J.-L. Isenbiehl (cf. Vigouroux, *Dictionaire de la Bible*, "Isenbiehl"), whose work, published in German in 1778, held that the reference to Isaiah 7:14 in Matthew 1:23 did not signify the fulfillment of a prophecy, but a simple allusion.

[43]Vatican I, *DS* 3007: "It belongs to the Church to judge concerning the true sense and interpretation of the Holy Scriptures and therefore no one is permitted to interpret them *against the unanimous agreement of the Fathers*." This does not mean that we can only inter-pret them *according* to such *unanimous* agreement. Cf. note 45.

[44]Leo XIII, *Providentissimus* (1893), *DS* 3824. After quoting the Vatican I text (given above in note 43), the pope specifies the reason for the Council's affirmation: their unani-mous agreement clearly manifests an apostolic tradition. This shows, in the case concern-ing us here, that the unanimous agreement of the Fathers on Isaiah 7:14, together with its use in the New Testament, takes us back to the interpretation and exegesis that the Apos-tles themselves left us concerning that prophecy.

[45]Pius XII, *Divino Afflante Spiritu*, (1943), *DS* 3831: "There are few biblical texts whose sense has been declared by the authority of the Church, or on which there is the

II[46]—one could doubtless go further and maintain that if the Church wished, she could actually define the literal messianic sense of Isaiah 7:14, or perhaps more easily, at least its typical messianic sense.

In a spirit of full fidelity to this unanimous agreement of the Fathers, the Church of Vatican II took up again, in a dogmatic constitution, the ancient text of Isaiah's prophecy by way of underscoring its importance:

> The sacred Scriptures of both the Old and the New Testament, as well as ancient tradition, show the role of the mother of the Savior in the economy of salvation in an ever clearer light and propose it as something to be probed into. The books of the Old Testament recount the period of salvation history during which the coming of Christ into the world was slowly prepared for. These earliest documents, as they are read in the Church and are understood in the light of a further and full revelation, bring the figure of the woman, mother of the Redeemer, into a gradually sharper focus.

> Likewise she is the virgin who is to conceive and bear a son, whose name will be called Emmanuel [cf. Is 7:14; Mic 5:2-3, Mt 1:22-23]. [47]

It is surely Irenæus' glory to have been a decisive landmark in this "venerable Tradition"[48] (which receives and transmits the Scriptures, not without interpreting them) and in the ecclesial understanding of the Isaian text. One could moreover regard his exegesis of Isaiah 7:14 as a particular instance of his more global vision of the *recirculation* of Mary

---

unanimous agreement of the Fathers," reinforcing the authority of the unanimous interpretation of the Fathers concerning Isaiah 7:14.

[46]See *Dei Verbum*, the Dogmatic Constitution on Revelation, 11 ("the books of the Old and New Testaments...have been handed on as such to the Church herself") and 12 ("...all that has been said about the manner of interpreting Scripture is ultimately subject to the judgment of the Church, which exercises the divinely conferred commission and ministry of watching over and interpreting the Word of God.") The fact that the church's judgment includes that of the recognized Fathers of the Church, is confirmed by the decree of the same council concerning the missions, *Ad Gentes*, 22, for all practical purposes placing the Fathers and the Magisterium on the same footing: "...the facts and the words revealed by God...explained by the Fathers and the Magisterium of the Church" (*facta et verba a Deo revelata...ab Ecclesia Patribus et Magisterio explicata*).

[47]Vatican II, *Lumen Gentium* 55. The Council text in no way claims that the pre-Christian reader of Gen 3:15 and Isaiah 7:14 would have learned nothing about the mother of the Messiah, but emphasizes the light shed on the texts of the Old Testament by the New Testament. Cf. O. Semmelroth's commentary, LTK, *Das Zweite Vatikanische Konzil*, (Freiburg, 1966), vol. I, p. 331. If these texts can tell us absolutely nothing about the mother of the Messiah without the clarification of the New Testament, how can we see them as prophecies?

[48]*Lumen Gentium* 55: "*veneranda Traditio.*"

with respect to Eve,[49] where the former recapitulates the latter, in subordination to Christ's recapitulation of Adam. It is this latter recapitulation that we meet again in Irenæus' exegesis of the parable of the Good Samaritan.

D) An Illustration of Irenæus' Recapitulation: The Good Samaritan

Irenæus devotes only a few lines to this parable, but they are extremely rich. They are as follows:

> The Lord entrusted to the Holy Spirit his own property, man, who had fallen into the hands of robbers, that man to whom he has shown compassion and whose wounds he himself had dressed, giving him two royal denarii in order that, after having received through the Spirit the image and inscription of the Father and the Son, we might make the denarius entrusted to us bear fruit and restore it to the Lord thus multiplied [AH III, 17.3].

Irenæus gives us this adaptation of the parable of the Good Samaritan in the context of a presentation of the gift of the Spirit to the Church in strife against the demon. Is this adaptation or exegesis? We would call it—and this will become clearer below—an exegetical adaptation and an adapted exegesis...not without a great wealth of biblical allusions.[50]

For Irenæus, the robbers are the demons that not only wounded man, but even left him half dead. The innkeeper to whom the Good Samaritan entrusts this man stands as a symbol of the Holy Spirit seen as the principle by which talents are rendered fruitful and multiply. Many details of the parable are left out. Irenæus takes up only what is of interest to him, while combining his selection with data drawn from other parables: dry wood (Lk 23:31), talents (Mt 25:15), tribute rendered to Caesar (Mt 22:20ff.).

As Irenæus sees it, indeed as all the Fathers see it[51] the Samaritan is a figure of Christ the Savior. He shows us (and this is less traditional) the

---

[49]Cf. note 29.

[50]At least to Mt 22:20; 25:14-30; Lk 19:12-27.

[51]Cf. W. Monselewski, Der Barmherizige Samaritaner, (Tübingen, 1967); A. Orbe, Parabolas evangélicas de S. Ireneo, BAC, (Madrid, 1972), vol. I, pp. 105-153 (we have taken our inspiration in the following pages largely from this remarkable work); J. Daniélou, "Le Bon Samaritain," Mélanges Bibliques A. Robert, (Paris, 1956), pp. 457-465, another work from which we have drawn inspiration; D. Sanchis, "Samaritanus ille," Rech. Sc. Rel., 49, (1961), pp. 414ff. (a thorough study of the treatment of the parable in Saint Augustine). We find in these authors an abundance of information on the patristic treatment of this parable. We can speak of the unanimous agreement of the Fathers concerning the double symbolism of the wounded man and the Good Samaritan (figures of mankind and its Savior,

Lord entrusting his humanity (an anti-gnostic allusion) to the Holy Spirit, which will not prevent him from saying a little further on (*AH* III, 19.3) that the same Savior offers and entrusts the same humanity to the Father. Is Irenæus contradicting himself? No. These two ideas can be synthesized. As Orbe suggests, the Spirit receives humanity in trust, from the hands of Christ, between the Ascension and the second coming or Parousia of Jesus, while the Father will receive this humanity at the end of history, in line with 1 Corinthians 15:24-28. It belongs to the Father to seal by means of the final resurrection the work accomplished in human flesh by his two hands, the Word and the Spirit.[52] At the second Parousia, the Spirit gives man back to Christ, who offers him to the Father. Such is the teaching that Irenæus received from the presbyters, disciples of the Apostles (*AH* V, 36.2). There is then no incompatibility between Christ's two acts of entrusting humanity, the first to the Spirit-Paraclete in the age of the Church, and the second to the Father on the last day.

At first sight, Irenæus would seem to be indulging in an exegetical sleight of hand to make the data of the parable agree with his pneumatological interpretation. To him the parable presents a Good Samaritan offering the innkeeper in advance the money necessary to pay for the hospitality given to the wounded man (Luke 10:35). This creates a problem for Irenæus. He does not want to say that the Lord Jesus pays the Holy Spirit for his services! He avoids the difficulty of proceeding as if the Lord had given the two denarii to the wounded man himself, just as in the parable the Good Samaritan had dressed his wounds by pouring oil and wine on them. By such a transposition, Irenæus means to imply that the two denarii are received by the wounded man, i.e., by ailing humanity, so that with the aid of the Holy Spirit, he might make his denarii—his talents—bear fruit.

But, by way of a new transposition, Irenæus shifts from the two denarii to the single denarius found in the parable of the eleventh hour workers (Mt 20:9ff.). We receive a denarius which is at once single and double, containing the image and the inscription of the Father and the Son, but we receive it through the mediation of the Holy Spirit, so that it

---

respectively) with all the doctrinal consequences that result in this case as in that of Isaiah 7:14: if the Church wished, she could define this sense as binding. Cf. Daniélou, p. 457.

[52]Cf. *AH* V, 6.1; V, 28.3, where the Son and the Spirit are called the hands of the Father or of God.

might be made to fructify and thus be able to be restored, multiplied,[53] to the Lord at the time of his second coming.

In other words, Irenæus is telling us that the wounded man, i.e., all of us—receives in the Holy Spirit a principle of salvific knowledge so as to recognize the Son, visible icon[54] of the invisible Father and, at the same time, the Father, invisible principle of the visible Son. The Spirit stamps anyone who is open to his action with the simultaneous knowledge of the Father and the Son, of the Father in the Son and of the Son in the Father (cf. Mt 11:27). The two denarii come thus to represent symbolically the Father and the Son, while the single denarius refers to our single eternal life with its double object, to the grace that orients us toward the single vision of the Father and the Son.

The wounded man—wounded mankind—must receive and accept, through the Holy Spirit, the coin that is the price of eternal life and of the vision of the Father and the Son. To receive that coin means to recognize and to confess the Son as one's King, and the Father of his King as Father of an only Son (cf. *AH* IV, 36.7: IV, 6.6). Hence the mention of the two royal denarii. It is only by the Spirit that man can recognize the Father and the Son in a saving way. The demons recognize Jesus as the Son, but only through their faculty of reason and not in a saving way (cf. Mt 8:29; Mk 1:24, 34: Jas 2:19 in the general context of 2:14-26).

What are we to think of this whole exegesis? At first sight, it seems to combine Irenæus' own theology concerning the role of the Spirit in man's knowledge of the Father and the Son with an already common interpretation going back to the Judeo-Christian presbyters,[55] according to which the Good Samaritan represents the Savior and the wounded man, mankind fallen into the hands of demons.

This seems to be a correct appraisal of the interpretation of Irenæus insofar as he sees in the innkeeper the image of the Spirit. Here he seems to be innovating. For Origen's presbyter, the innkeeper symbolized "the one who presides over the Church," which as Jean Daniélou notes, seems to be "the original sense," the sense that Jesus had in mind. Some will agree then with Daniélou that Irenæus' pneumatological interpretation of the innkeeper amounts to an allegorical exegesis which goes

---

[53]Obviously, this multiplication of the denarius of eternal life does not signify, in Irenæus' eyes, the multiplication of eternal life as an object, but the multiplication of the degree of subjective possession, by the creature, of the Creator as transcendent and unique object. Cf. *AH* V, 36.2.

[54]Cf. Col 1:15.

[55]Cf. J. Daniélou, pp. 458-459. However, Orbe, pp. 137ff., contests the identification of "presbyter" with "Judeo-Christianity."

beyond the intention of Jesus, an allegorism of inferior quality, undertaking "the extension of allegory to the least details" and thus anticipating a faulty type of exegesis later characteristic of the Alexandrian school. Daniélou adds that "as in many other cases, it would seem that the gnostics were in large measure responsible for this deformation, even though we do not have for this parable any exegesis of theirs comparable to what we have for the lost sheep and for the prodigal son" (for which we have very complete gnostic transpositions and interpretation). "In the process of correcting the gnostics," concludes Daniélou, "the Fathers were in fact being influenced by them, beginning with Irenæus."[56] In other words, in his exegesis, Irenæus would himself at times have fallen into the very shortcomings he was criticizing in the gnostics, though only in secondary details.

However, even this aspect of Irenæus' exegesis could perhaps be saved by noting that there is no contradiction between the presbyter's interpretation of the innkeeper ("the one who presides over the Church") and that of Irenæus. Is not the visible Church, in the theology of Irenæus, the manifestation of the Spirit? Is not the Good Samaritan, in entrusting mankind to the Church, in reality entrusting it to the Spirit? Moreover, nowhere does Irenæus deny that wounded humanity, entrusted to the Spirit, is at the same time being entrusted to the Church. We would even say that this is understood, in the context of his pneumato-ecclesiology.[57]

In any case, the allusion to the two royal denarii, symbols of the Father and the Son could correspond to the deepest intention of Jesus if

---

[56]Daniélou, p. 464. Thus for Daniélou, the Irenæan exegesis that sees the innkeeper as an image of the Holy Spirit "no doubt constitutes a replica of a gnostic exegesis" (*ibid.*, p. 463). But we must note with Orbe a point that seems to have escaped Daniélou: the false gnostics had also done a partial commentary of this parable. For them, if the Samaritan and the wounded man symbolized the Savior and sinful mankind respectively, then the wine and the oil represented love and the gnosis; the anointing with oil gave the health and the perfume of God. The only specific point of the false gnosis, in these commentaries on the *Gospel According to Philip* (of the Valentinians), 111, would be, according to Orbe (vol. I, pp. 108-109), the suggestion that only the spiritual man is ready for perfect health while the others, the "psychic men," can only participate in it to the extent that they live in union with the spiritual man.

[57]Cf. *AH* IV, 36.7; Eph 4:4: "There is one body and one Spirit..."; we know how the historical studies of recent years have shown the deep links in the earliest tradition, between the third article of the Apostles' Creed, relative to the Holy Spirit, and the ecclesiastical affirmations that flow from it. Cf. P. Nautin, *Je crois à l'Esprit Saint dans la Sainte Eglise pour la résurrection de la chair*, (Paris, 1947), especially p. 45, quoting in the sense that concerns us here *AH* III, 24.1 and III, 11.8. Besides this connection in Irenæus between Church and Spirit, we find a bond between the bishop (1 Tm 1:6) and the Spirit.

(as we think) Daniélou is right in following the view of Hoskyns that this parable of the Good Samaritan was situated historically in immediate sequence to the great hymn of exultation in Luke 10:21ff.[58] It too is a revelation of the secret of the Kingdom of which the wise are ignorant and the humble are aware. The parable then far transcends the range of a mere moral apologue (a fact which modern exegesis, in the vast majority of cases, fails to recognize, as Hermaniuk has shown), though a moral sense is not excluded.

Now specifically, on the one hand, the hymn of exultation reports these words of Jesus: "No one knows who the Son is except the Father, or who the Father is except the Son and any one to whom the Son chooses to reveal him" (Lk 10:22). On the other hand, according to Origen, the presbyter had already seen the two denarii, the "dispensing" of which is entrusted to the innkeeper, as the Father and the Son.[59]

The inevitable conclusion is that the discovery of the parable's true *Sitz im Leben* and its true nature—i.e., as not merely a moral apologue, but also a kind of divulging of the secrets of the Kingdom, with reference

---

[58]Daniélou, pp. 459-461. According to Daniélou, Luke modifies, for editorial reasons, the order of the pericopes in his chapter 10. The parable of the Samaritan is placed, as he indicates, in the course of Christ's itinerary from Galilee to Jerusalem by way of Jericho, but not in the course of the discussion on the greatest commandment and the definition of "neighbor." This discussion is later, in the Temple of Jerusalem. By contrast, the parable follows the hymn of exultation (Lk 10:21) and correspondes strikingly with the Johannine allegory of the Good Shepherd. Cf. E. Hoskyns, *The Fourth Gospel*, (London, 1947), p. 377: "The whole context of the parable of the Good Shepherd resembles that of the Good Samaritan, where God's love for the man, a victim of robbers (designated in both parables by the same word, *lèstai*) is manifested not by the leaders of Judaism (the priest and the Levite), but by the Good Samaritan."

[59]Origen, *GCS*, vol. IX, pp. 191 and 194. It is fitting to compare this last extract, which exists only in Latin ("the two denarii seem to me to be the knowledge of the mystery of the Father and the Son, how the Father is in the Son and the Son is in the Father") of the celebrated text and, more or less contemporary with Athenagoras, *Apology*, XII: "We who are driven by the single desire of knowing the only true God and his Word, [to know] what is the unity of the child with the Father, what the Father has in common with the Son, what the Spirit is, what is the union and the distinction of these united terms between them: the Spirit, the Child, the Father." To this question Athenagoras himself has an implicit response: "The Son is in the Father and the Father is in the Son through the oneness and the power of the Spirit" (*ibid.*, X). As Augustinian theology was to say later, it is the Spirit himself who constitutes the communion between Father and Son, who *is* their communion. It is therefore normal that the Spirit should receive man from the Son, the man whom that Spirit had created in the image of the Father and the Son (cf. *AH* III, 17.3 commented on here), to lead him to the knowledge of the *how* of the mutual inhabitation of the Father and the Son, i.e., of the Spirit himself in so far as he is their communion. We think this was the common perspective of the Christian writers of the second half of the second century.

to the Trinitarian mystery as well as to the double commandment of charity—such as emerges from the works of Hoskyns and Daniélou, makes it easier for us to justify Irenæus' exegesis of the Good Samaritan parable—one surely more faithful to Christ's intention, even in its details, than it might originally have seemed, including as it does the parable's trinitarian point, in accordance with the intention of Christ.

Conclusions: The lasting influence of Irenæus and of his "scriptural exposition" on the Church and especially on Vatican II

The enduring value of the exegetical method of Irenæus, in spite of all its limitations,[60] lies mainly, in our view, in the historical situation he had to confront—analogous to our own in many important respects—and also in his keen awareness of the mission of the hierarchical Church in the interpretation of the Scriptures entrusted to her. It is not surprising then that the Second Vatican Council resumed this method in some of its major aspects.

Irenæus constantly rejected and refuted "the gnostic theory of adapting both Old and New Testament Scripture to the way of thinking, to the environment, and to the prejudices of each individual as if through circumspection (and therefore out of human sympathy) the Prophets, the Lord, or the Apostles had not uttered the whole truth, but had spoken to the sick in terms suited to their condition. This theory, popular right up to our day (continues Hans Urs von Balthasar,[61] whom we are still quoting) is easily refuted by Irenæus. Indeed, he shows that the Lord and the Apostles were as fearless as the Prophets had been in provoking, by the undisguised clarity of their word, the most severe shock and scandal and in paying the price of the undesirable character of their preaching by undergoing all kinds of torments and even by death itself.[62] "If we were

---

[60]A. Benoît (*Saint Irénée, Introduction à l'étude de sa théologie*, [Paris, 1960]) has underscored some of these limits: "In general, the bishop of Lyon does not make direct use of the Old Testament; what he knows, he seems to owe in part to the *Testimonia*. And that disturbs us a little in a man who claims and wishes to be nourished on the Scriptures.... His knowledge hardly exceeded the level of current catechesis. (...) Irenæus knows the Old Testament very little and very badly" (pp. 89, 102). However the author concludes "[His] biblical culture [is] sufficient for demonstrating that the Old Testament foretold Christ."

[61]Hans Urs von Balthasar, *The Glory of the Lord*, vol. II, (San Francisco: Ignatius Press, 1980), p. 49, quoting *AH* III, 5.1.

[62]Irenæus, *AH* III, 5.2: "What physician, to heal a sick person, would conform himself to the wishes of his patient?"; III, 12.14: "Those who have given over their lives even to the

to ascribe to them the principle of adaptation and of the soothing word, every fixed norm of truth would be superfluous, and everything would remain in the old state of things," insisted Irenæus.[63]

In other words, exegesis was not a purely academic exercise for Irenæus. It was part of Christian preparation of martyrdom. To be a good interpreter of the Scriptures, one must be disposed to lay down one's life to be united to the witness of their authors (many of whom were martyrs), to render a testimony in blood to their testimony in writing. It is in this way that one will be able to go through and beyond the apologetic demonstration of the truth from the Scriptures[64] to the theological "self-demonstration" of the Trinitarian God himself.[65]

We could thus summarize the exegesis of Irenæus as follows: inseparable both from a continuous struggle against the gnostics and from the profession of faith of the sacred writers who sealed with their blood the writing of the New Testament (Matthew, Peter and Paul, John, James, and Jude), this exegesis was born, by way of the testimony of presbyters and successors of the Apostles, such as Polycarp, of the uncontrived truth of the flesh and blood of Christ that it confesses and with which Irenæus was nourished in the Eucharist. And this birth from that source was to lead him to martyrdom and to the vision of the glory of God. In his ecclesial exegesis, it is this very reality of the Incarnation that is developing and unfolding; it is the Church that is being built up in love, growing towards fullness in her Head, Christ (cf. Eph 4:15-16).

It is no wonder then that Vatican II recognized a kindred spirit in this exegesis. To appreciate this fact, it will suffice to assemble the texts in which the last council saw fit to make Irenæus' words its own:

> Existing with God, the Word, through whom everything has been made and who was always present in the human race, reveals the Father to all those to whom he wills and as the Father wills.[66] So that the Gospel might always be preserved intact and living in the Church, the Apostles left as successors the

---

point of dying for the Gospel of Christ, how could they speak in the sense of the ideas already received among men?"

[63]*Ibid., AH* III, 6.12.

[64]*Ibid.*, III, Preface.

[65]Hans Urs von Balthasar, p. 48. The author adds, "In an almost tedious way, Irenæus employs the terms *ostensio, manifestatio*: to show, to expose, to bring to light, to manifest. (...) The lexica of Dom Reynders, for the *AH* alone, [indicate] more than four hundred passages. (...) Irenæus thinks he can almost be content with this bringing to light, because the contrary doctrine refutes itself" (cf. note 71).

[66]Vatican II, *Ad Gentes*, 3, quoting *AH* III, 18.1; IV, 6.7; IV, 20.7.

bishops, to whom they gave over their own teaching function.[67] They are the depositories of the apostolic teaching.[68] The apostolic Tradition is manifested and preserved in the whole world by those whom the Apostles made bishops and by their successors down to our time.[69] What the Apostles, on Christ's command, preached, they themselves and certain men in their company transmitted to us, under the divine inspiration of the Spirit, in certain writings which are the foundation of the faith, namely, the four-sided Gospel according to Matthew, Mark, Luke, and John.[70] The Gospel message continues in entirety the books of the Old Testament.[71] Through the strength of the Gospel, the Spirit rejuvenates the Church and renews her unceasingly, keeping her on the path to perfect union with her Spouse.[72]

Still more concisely, one could recapitulate the entire exegesis of Irenæus with Hans Urs von Balthasar, in this way: "The one Church, in virtue of her unity, i.e., of her demonstrable tradition, guards the unity of Scripture in which is to be found the unity of the Revelation of the one and true living God."[73]

---

[67]Vatican II, *Dei Verbum*, 7, quoting *AH* III, 1.

[68]*Ibid.*, 25, quoting *AH* IV, 32.1.

[69]Vatican II, *Lumen Gentium*, 20, quoting *AH* III, 3.1; III, 2.1; IV, 26.2.

[70]*Dei Verbum*, 18, quoting *AH* III, 11.8.

[71]*Dei Verbum* 16, quoting *AH* III, 21.2.

[72]*Lumen Gentium*, 4, quoting *AH* III, 24.1.

[73]Hans Urs von Balthasar, vol. II, p. 42. On the exegesis of Irenæus see P. Bacq, *L'ancienne et la nouvelle Alliance selon saint Irénée*, (Paris:Lethielleux, 1978).

Chapter III
Clement of Alexandria
Integrates the Cosmic and Moral Symbolism of
Greek Paganism with Biblical Symbolism

Clement lived in the second half of the second century. A priest of the Church at Alexandria, there is little doubt that he died between 211 and 215. His exegesis is in basic harmony with that of Irenæus and Justin, which we have examined in the preceding chapters. Like them, he makes extensive use of typology, also within an anti-gnostic context, and he shares their convictions regarding the unity of the economy of salvation in and between the two Testaments. In contrast to Irenæus and Justin, however, he brings Philo and Greek symbolism into the service of Christian exegesis, drawing likewise on Judeo-Christian apocalyptic literature. What is more remarkable is that he succeeded in organizing all these diverse elements into a coherent synthesis, illumined by his personal vision.

It is a fact, however, that there is a perceptible gnostic contamination[1] in some of Clement's writings. This accounts for the shock experienced by Photius[2] in reading them, and for the reservations expressed by Pope Benedict XIV.[3]

---

[1]Cf. J. Lebreton, "Clément d'Alexandrie," *DSAM* 2 (1953), col. 957-961.

[2]Cf. J. Quasten, *Initiation aux Pères de l'Eglise*, (Paris, 1957), vol. II, p. 26. Photius, who still possessed the *Hypotyposes*, a work of Clement that is no longer extant, formulated on the basis of that work a severe judgment: "Clement lets himself be carried away by strange and impious ideas: he affirms the eternity of matter. ...He reduces the Son to the level of a

Without delaying over these aspects, to which we shall return at the
end of this chapter, we shall first present Clement's general conception
of Scripture and of its role in the economy of salvation, and then look
more closely at his way of understanding biblical symbolism, of which
we shall give some examples before offering a critical evaluation of
Clement's exegetical achievement.

We draw especially here on the works of Fathers Mondésert, Moingt,
and Daniélou.

A) The Mystery of Scripture in the Mystery of Salvation

Not only does Clement have a distinctly scriptural style in virtue of
close contact with and assimilation of the Scriptures (he quotes the Old
Testament thirteen hundred times, and the New twenty-four hundred
times), but also and above all he developed and set forth, within a Trinitarian context, a personal conception of their role in the economy of salvation.

For Clement, the two Testaments "are two as to name and date of
composition, having been dispensed according to a wise ordering that
followed growth and progress of humanity, but they are nevertheless
virtually one, deriving as they do from the same God through the mediation of the Son" (*Strom.*, II, 6, 29, 2). In his view, "the God of the two Testaments is one only, for the same promises have been made to us that
were made to the Patriarchs" (*Strom.*, II, 6). The Word speaks in the Old
Testament exactly as he speaks in the New Testament (the Word promised and announced in the Old Testament reveals himself in the New).
This is why the light of the Word is necessary for reaching an understanding of the sacred scriptures (*Pedag.*, I, 5, and I, 7).

"Concealed" beneath parables and figures, it is the Holy Spirit who
gives Scriptures the sacramental character of the mystery of God (*Strom.*
I, 9.49; 15, 115.5; 126.1). However, Clement does not appear to distinguish between the role of the Word and that of the Spirit, their respective missions, in the origin and the gift of the Scripture.

This Scripture presents various senses according to the level of interpretation one wishes to take. For example, if one were to summarize
Clement's train of exegetical thinking on Mt 18:20 ("For where two or
three are gathered in my name, I am there among them."), one would

---

simple creature. ...He imagines that the angels had relations with women and impreg-
nated them with children...."

[3]See note 24, below.

end up with the following picture: in the doctrinal and moral sense, the saying refers to the family (father, mother, and child); in the mystical sense, to God who is as much with parents who have given birth in accordance with their duty as he is with a person who remains chaste for the right reasons (against gnostic dualism); in the philosophical and psychological sense, the three represent the passions, desire, and reason, or again the flesh, the soul and the spirit (the meaning here would be more mystical). Again in the mystical sense, the three would represent the called, the elect, and the people chosen for the highest honor, i.e., gnosis; and finally, in the prophetic and religious sense, the three would be the Jews and the Gentiles who together make up the third people, the Church, which is one man, one race (cf. *Strom.* III, 10, 68, 1 to 70, 4).[4]

For Clement, the word of Christ, a human word addressed to men, is a sign that conveys the divine mystery in a concealed way to anyone who hears it in its materiality. God has to accommodate himself to our weakness to disclose himself to us. We must free ourselves of carnal affections to cease interpreting the Scriptures in a carnal way and come to know God as he is and no longer to our image. For the believer who has fallen back into the shadows of sin and who inattentively closes his eyes to the light of the teaching received, the word of Christ discloses only a faint fraction of his truth and his life. The fullness of the saving truths is, of course, given to the believer whole and entire in the word of Christ, but always through the mediation of the verbal sign and the precept to be carried out. To extract the meaning and the life hidden beneath that word, the believer must assimilate those truths, he must purify himself by the practice of the commandments to participate in the holiness of God. One must know and therefore study the precept to practice it, but the awareness from within, the ability to savor God's will is acquired only through practice.[5]

Such is the work of the true gnosis in its unique, double-faceted method:

the knowledge and clear elucidation of the witness borne by the Scriptures on the one hand, and training according to the Logos under the guidance of faith

[4]Cf. C. Mondésert, *Clément d'Alexandrie, Introduction à l'étude de sa pensée religieuse à partir de l'Ecriture*, (Paris, 1944), pp. 159-160. Henceforth, we shall refer to this important work as Mondésert, followed by the page number.

[5]Cf. J. Moingt, "La gnose de Clément d'Alexandrie dans ses rapports avec la foi et la philosophie," *Rech. de Sc. Rel.* 37 (1050), pp. 230-231. Fr. Moingt's study is pursued in many successive issues of *Recherches* of 1950 and 1951. We shall refer to his work as *Moingt*, followed by the year and page number.

and of the fear of the Lord on the other. Both of these grow together toward perfect charity. For I believe the true gnostic has two goals, at least on earth: on the one hand, contemplation in conformity with knowledge; on the other, action, praxis (*Strom.* VII, 15, 102, 1-2).

The true gnostic receives the precept "in its true sense, as it is uttered for the person who has knowledge in a more universal and more elevated sense" (*Strom.* VII, 11 at the beginning). "Taking the precept all the way according to the Gospel," the true gnostic extends the precept of fasting, for example, to include abstinence from all concupiscence, that of the keeping of the Lord's day to the interior re-living of the death and resurrection of the Lord (*Strom.*, VII, 12, 74, 6 to 76). He not only knows sin in its particular determinations, but also in itself (*ibid.*, VI, 12, 97, 3-4). Thus the true gnostic imitates the attitude of Jesus in the sermon on the Mount toward the Law: he sets up new commandments that contrast with it ("You have heard that it was said.... But I say to you" [Mt 5:21-27; 27-28; 31-32]) and nevertheless he claims not to leave out a single iota of the Law, but rather to bring it to its perfection (Mt 5:17); maintaining the letter of the Law, he extracts its full range of spiritual significance, which was restrained by an interpretation temporarily suited to a still carnal and infantile way of life (cf. *Strom.*, IV, 18, 113). From the negative precepts of the Old Law: "You shall not commit adultery; you shall not kill," Christ draws the positive precepts of purity of heart and of charity, whose signification was surely contained under the primitive letter, but concealed. Faced with the letter of the Gospel, the true gnostic imitates him, thus following Christ's invitation that summons us to seek the hidden meanings of his words.

As J. Moingt brings out,[6] Clement's gnostic method is not a critical method seeking to determine the literal sense of the texts; rather, it is an attempt discover in the Gospel a rule of life that will lead to the divine life. To perceive the truth hidden in the figure, the intention beneath the letter, to give to each word its total salutary value through which it extends to the totality of life: this method presupposes rather that one has discovered what we would call in our day the fundamental intuition of Christ, the essence of Christianity. This is the synthetic view that is characteristic of contemplation and as much so of an integral faith (cf. *Strom.*, VI, 15, 115, 1ff.).

In chapters 11 and 12 of *Stromateis* VII, Clement describes the true gnosis both as the spiritual sense of Scripture and as the sense of

---

[6]*Ibid.*, 1950, pp. 398-400.

supernatural values. To anyone who takes an overall view of *Stromateis* VII, without allowing himself to be hung up on certain equivocal expressions, evidently Clement is presenting the true gnosis as linked inseparably with a Christian and evangelical way of life. When he contrasts gnosis with simple faith, it is by way of reproaching the latter for retaining some carry-overs from paganism in its still carnal way of life, and not, therefore, for being inferior to gnosis precisely as faith. For Clement, true gnosis neither leaves aside the letter of the Gospel, nor does it use this letter as a springboard for uncontrolled, whimsical exegesis. Rather, it consists in interpreting the word of God in the Spirit of the Savior. Thus it amounts to a bringing to perfection of that faith that is common and available to everyone in its basic elements, but which is reserved in its full flowering to those who allow themselves to be guided by "a piety enlightened by knowledge" (*Strom.* VII, 12, 29, 6).

Thus, for example, Clement inquires whether the truest sense of the word "adultery" is given to us through the precept of the Law that prohibits adultery. Is it not found rather in the use that God himself makes of the word to designate the infidelities of the Jewish people or of the heretics in their relationship with him (cf. *Strom.* III, 12, 80, 1-2; VI, 16, 146, 3 to 147, 1)?

In spite of what has been said by some, Clement's biblical theology does not show a contempt for history. On the contrary, it insists on the importance of salvation history. Even where he tells us that "the Lord spoke only in parables" (in line with Mt 13:34), that "the style of the Scriptures is parabolic," he strives to show that this "parable" is inscribed within a historical context that gives it a certain and unalterable truth, and that Scripture is not to be treated according to whim, because it is a "deposit that must be returned to God." There is a rule of truth, the tradition of the Apostles, which establishes the way of understanding and of handing on Christ's teaching, and there is "the rule of the Church" that is the agreement between the Testaments (*Strom.*, VI, 15, 122, 1: 123, 3: 124 to 126). Scripture opens itself only to one who knows how to read it not only "letter by letter," but "by syllable." The sign Scripture contains manifests a triple event. Only he who has the knowledge of the origin and of the end of history—Christ in the glory of the Father—is capable of placing each event in its true place and of assigning its true significance, for "he possesses the most exact truth of the world from its beginning to its end, having learned it from Truth itself" (*Strom.*, 16, 131-132; VI, 9, 78, 2-79, 2).[7]

B) Biblical Symbolism in Clement of Alexandria

The fifth book of the *Stromata* (or *Tapestries*) is a treatise on the knowledge (gnosis) of the symbols used by the ancient Jewish and pagan wise men. For Clement, symbolism becomes a secret language whose aim is to withhold sacred things from profane eyes (*Strom.* IV, 4, 19, 3-20, 1). Prophets, poets and philosophers have used a symbolic approach. How does Clement justify this? He gives two reasons for it. First, symbol is used to conceal from the profane what they are not capable of understanding; second it serves to stimulate inquiry by concealing the truth behind a veil. Clement says:

> The meaning of the Scriptures is hidden for many reasons. First, in order that we might search and be always watchful in seeking out the words of salvation; then, because it was not fitting that everyone should know this meaning, lest they suffer harm as a result of understanding incorrectly what was said by the Spirit for the good (VI, 15, 126, 1).

Clearly Clement is extending to the whole of the Scriptures what Jesus said regarding the parables (Mk 4, 11-13).

In summary, while he never reduces the typology of the Scriptures to Hellenistic symbolism, Clement inserts the Bible's symbolism into the more general framework of a cosmic symbolism and of a symbolic universe.

First, for Clement, the figures of the Old Testament are unveiled in Jesus Christ, who is their content (*ennoia*). This unveiling was in a special way the role of John the Baptist:

> He who through his witness pointed to him who had been prophesied, having announced the event henceforth definitively present and manifest after a long preparation,[8] was really releasing the last words of the prophetic economy by unveiling the idea [*ennoia*] contained in the symbols (*Strom.* V, 8, 55, 2-3).

---

[7]*Ibid.*, pp. 406-408.

[8]Clement had just written: "The Lord's feet, whose thongs John loosens, are the last operation of the Savior toward us, that which is immediate, that of his coming, hidden until now by the symbol of Prophecy." The loosened thongs are therefore, for Clement, the symbol of the "last words of the economy." The humble gesture of the Baptist becomes an unveiling of the prophecies.

The symbolic genre is here biblical typology. It constitutes the hidden sense of the Old Testament, revealed by Christ and henceforth manifest.

Does a symbolism still subsist after Christ has manifested the hidden content of this Old Covenant? Clement thinks it does. He turns toward Paul, assembles those passages from the Captivity Letters that treat of revelation (*apokalypsis*) and of mystery (*mysterion*). Thus even after Christ, there is a hidden sense of Scripture. This sense is no longer typological, for the types stopped with John the Baptist. This hidden sense is the apocalypse, that is, the gnosis of the mystery, the knowledge of heavenly things. It is this Judeo-Christian gnosis, this apocalyptic exegesis that Clement sees, after the typology, as unveiling the meaning of Scripture.

Clement clearly distinguishes these two exegetical procedures and even relates them to the two levels of Christian teaching. Knowledge of the meaning of the figures belongs to the order of the common catechesis, whereas apocalyptic exegesis is to be identified specifically with gnosis. Clement confirms this by citing Hebrews 5:12—6:1, which contrasts "solid food" of adults with the "milk" of babies (cf. 1 Cor 3:2). Clement makes an extended reference in this sense to the *Letter of Pseudo-Barnabas*, reminding us that the latter is a gnosis (*Strom.*, V, 10, 60-64).

Clement makes no great cleavage between Greek allegorism and this biblical symbolism, though he stops short of reducing the latter to the former. He integrates Greek, Jewish, and Christian symbolism into a single unified and structured whole within the context of his central vision of the sequence of the Covenants:

- Greek allegory is the cosmic symbolism by which the pagans had some knowledge of God through the medium of his manifestation in the world, and the moral symbolism by which they were aware of God through his self-revelation within their consciences (cf. Rom 2:14-15);

- biblical typology corresponds to God's historical revelation to the People of Israel, where the actions of Yahweh in the Old Testament prefigure certain actions of Christ in the New Testament;

- finally apocalyptic exegesis corresponds to the manifestation of the future world and of its secrets that are being fulfilled in the Church.

All this enables Clement to incorporate Greek allegory organically in his vision of salvation history. We understand better, in this light, why his *Protreptic*, which is addressed to the pagans, is based on the Greek myths, his *Pædagogos* on the biblical figures, and his *Stromata* on Pauline apocalyptic. Clement's three books correspond to the three stages of salvation history as well as to the stages of the conversion of souls: "There is a first salutary change from paganism to the faith, and a second from faith to gnosis" (*Strom.*, VII, 10, 57, 4).

If one were to compare Clement's exegesis with the exegetical systems of Irenæus and Justin, one could say that it shares with them the catechetical and fundamental exegesis that is that of typology. Indeed, for Clement, typology is the axis of exegesis.

He extends this typology in two directions.

On the one hand he carries it further by way of a gnostic exegesis, which corresponds to the *didascalia*, to a knowledge more elevated than simple *kerygma*. He inherits this gnosis from Judeo-Christianity and in part from Philonian exegesis, which is also of Jewish origin.

On the other hand, he extends the typology by way of a cosmic, moral, and kerygmatic exegesis that corresponds to the cosmic covenant of Noah and which roots salvation history in cosmic religion. Here too he is largely dependent upon Philo.

By introducing typological exegesis into Philonian exegesis, he presents it in a historical perspective. The cosmic and moral exegesis is taken up within the context of a Christian vision of salvation history.[9]

In summary, the method of Clement regarding symbolism is based on a principle of Greek philosophy, a principle that is itself incorporated[10] into the Old and New Testaments (cf. Wis 7:27; 8:17; 9:17; 2 Pt 1:4; Heb 2:14). This principle affirms an intelligible bond that brings all beings together in an ordered hierarchy, giving them a unity beneath their apparent multiplicity and safeguarding their very multiplicity through their close cohesion and their unity. Thus, all beings have a kinship with one another and with God. There is a scale of beings, all beings enjoying a *participation* in Being.

In the domain of exegesis, Clement is applying the principle essential to Christianity—of the unity of creation and of the orientation of all beings, from the most material to the most spiritual, toward Being *par excellence* on whom all depend as on their final cause, but all of which

---

[9]Cf. Jean Daniélou, *Message évangélique et culture hellénistique*, (Paris, 1961), pp. 231-233, by which I have been deeply inspired here (pages taken from a whole chapter on Clement of Alexandria the exegete, *ibid.*, pp. 217-233) and Mondésert, p. 90.

[10]Certainly not habitually, purely and simply; the same principle is given in other categories. However, the Letter to the Hebrews presupposes it in many places, as does intertestamental Judaism. Cf. *Dictionnaire encyclopédique de la Bible*, (Paris: Brepols, 1960), "Participation."

reflect, each in its way, something of the divine perfection. All beings consequently reveal themselves, one to another, from one level to the next, all the way up to those with the greatest richness of being, those nearest to the divinity, although as finite beings and creatures these still remain far from the infinite divinity, author of all things.[11]

In other words, a moderately symbolic exegesis of the revealed and revealing Scripture is a necessity if one recalls that the Scriptures are situated within a symbolic universe, the work of a God who reveals himself therein in symbol, a universe in which beings are interdependent, existing each in relationship to the others. A symbolic exegesis is also necessary because the literal sense of Scripture is conditioned and completed by the meaning of the universe of which the Scriptures are a part. If the literal sense of the Scriptures is situated within the total context of the universe, the extension of this sense on the spiritual plane, when this was intended by God, becomes more intelligible.

C) *Examples of the Symbolic Exegesis of Clement of Alexandria*

We shall single out three examples of Clement's symbolic exegesis: Isaac, the rich young man, and the Good Samaritan.

The first case shows us an imperfect integration of Philonian elements into the Christian perspective. With clear reference to the Judaic and Targumic tradition, which attributes qualities of a redeemer to Isaac, and which Jews of the Christian era used against Christ,[12] Clement writes in his *Pædagogos*:

> Isaac is a type of the infant Lord as son (and in fact Isaac was the son of Abraham as Christ is of God), victim as was the Lord. But he was not cut down like the Lord; no, he only carried the wood of the sacrifice, he, Isaac, as the Lord did His cross. He laughed mystically by way of prophesying that the Lord fills us with joy, we who have been redeemed by his blood. He did not suffer, but left to the Logos, as is fitting, the first fruits of suffering. What is more, because he was not immolated, he signifies also the divinity of the Lord. For after His

---

[11]Mondésert, pp. 151-152.

[12]Cf. Jean Gribomont, "Isaac le Patriarche," *DSAM* 7 (1971), col. 1987-2005; Le Déaut, *La nuit paschale*, (Rome, 1963), pp. 198-207; R. L. Wilken, "Melito and the Sacrifice of Isaac," *Theological Studies* 37, (1976), pp. 53-69; Jean Daniélou, *Sacramentum Futuri*, (Paris, 1950), 1, III; Bertrand de Margerie, "Sens individuel ou collectif des Chants du Serviteur," *Esprit et Vie* 86, (1976), pp. 107ff. Cf. below, pp. 145-147.

burial, Jesus was raised up, thus leaving suffering behind, just as Isaac had escaped the sacrifice.[13]

Clement here is combining an allusion to Hebrews 11:19 and to an Isaac typology pointing to Jesus with a very forceful polemic against contemporary Judaism: Christ is superior to Isaac, for he really suffered and did not only carry the cross. There is even a possible allusion here to the mysterious harmony, in Christ crucified, between the impassibility (*apatheia*) of the divine nature and the passion (*pathos*) of the human nature.[14] Clement allots a privileged character to the personage of Isaac with the exceptional place he occupies (not surprisingly) with the Jew Philo.[15] But he integrates Philo's moral allegory (which identified Isaac with joy, in line with the etymology of his name) into a Christian perspective.

Previously, in the same book of the *Pædagogos*, Clement had offered us, still in connection with Isaac, a somewhat artificial Christian transposition of Philo:

> There is another way of interpreting the prophetic symbolism of the joy and the laughter that salvation procures for us as it did for Isaac. He too laughed over being delivered from death, playing and rejoicing with the spouse who is his companion [cf. Gn 26:8] in our salvation, the Church. The latter carries the strong name of patience [*hypomene*] both because she is alone in continuing [*menein*] to rejoice constantly throughout the centuries, and because her supporting structure is the patience [*hypomene*] of the believers, i.e., of all the members of Christ. And the testimony [*martyria*] of those who persevere to the end and the thanksgiving [*eucharistia*] for them—these constitute the mystic sport and the salvation that succors with holy joy. As for Christ, the king, he observes our laughter from on high and, looking through the window, as Scripture says [Gn 26:8], he contemplates the thanksgiving and the benediction, the exultation, and felicity, he beholds the patience that supports us in times of trial and the assembled totality of all these things, which is the Church, his Church. He shows only his face which the Church without him had lacked—the Church now complete, thanks to the head of the King. And

---

[13]Clement of Alexandria, *Pædagogos*, I, 5, 23, 1-2.

[14]It should be known that, shortly after Clement of Alexandria, Gregory of Neocæsarea, the Thaumaturge, published a treatise on *the impassibility and the passibility of God*, which is extant in Syriac (trans. by Pitra, *Analecta sacra*, IV, pp. 103-120 and 363-376) and which has been the subject of a study by Henri Crouzel, *L'homme devant Dieu*, (Mélanges de Lubac), (Paris, 1963), vol. II, pp. 263-279.

[15]Cf. Daniélou, *Message*, pp. 220-221 and Mondésert, ch. IX, pp. 163-186.

what then was that window through which the Lord showed himself? It was the flesh through which he revealed himself.

There is a paradox in this text[16] in that it presents both the pagan king Abimelech and the patriarch Isaac as types of Christ. We seem here to have gone far beyond the limits of a sound typology. Here we also meet the excessive allegorizing tendency of the Alexandrian school, where the simplest affirmations of Scripture must contain a hidden sense. Even a pagan king looking through a window....

We move on now to the rich young man. Clement has left us a homily on Mark 10:17-31.[17] The exegesis leaves the reader both stupefied and perplexed, but in the end he feels partially convinced.

Clement's general idea is that Christ is not commanding the rich young man to renounce his riches. It is not necessary to strip oneself of everything to be saved. If every Christian were to renounce his goods, it would soon become impossible to assist the poor. The words of the Lord are rather an invitation to avoid avarice.

"Go, sell what you own." These words, writes Clement, "do not mean what they seem to say on first sight, namely, strip yourself of your riches." He adds:

> The sacrifice of our riches is not one that would be new or unknown to men. Many had already made this sacrifice before the coming of the Savior. Some did so to dedicate themselves free of distractions to the study of letters and of a dead science; others, to acquire the vain renown of a shallow glory, as for example Anaxagoras, Democritus, and Crates. Is the mere fact of depriving oneself of riches, without thereby acquiring life, truly to be considered a heroic sacrifice worthy of imitation? One is reminded here of St. Paul: "If I give away all I have, and if I deliver my body to be burned, but have not love, I gain nothing" [1 Cor. 13:3].

However, Clement does not deny that a certain material renunciation might be implied in Jesus' counsel to the rich young man:

> Renounce troublesome possessions, keep those whose pious and moderate use can be profitable to you. Enjoy the goods the Lord gives you and whose use he himself points out to you:[18] reject your vices and your passions which corrupt

---

[16]Clement of Alexandria, *Pædagogos*, I, 5.

[17]Clement of Alexandria, *PG* 9, *Quis dives salvetur*, 609-652. The presentation given by A. Colunga, "Clemente de Alejandría escriturario," *Helmantica* I, (1950), p. 468, is questionable. This author cites our treatise as an example of Clement's recourse to the literal sense of the sacred author. We use here Quasten's summary, note 2, p. 26.

[18]In favor of the poor: cf. Mk 10:21.

those goods and which lead you to make criminal use of them; thus you will be obeying the Lord.

What are we to think of such an exegesis? We are surely dealing with a difficult text of which various interpretations have been proposed, even in our day.[19] Clement was right in perceiving that Jesus was inviting the rich young man to interior detachment. He does not appear to have seen that the Master was calling him to that inner detachment precisely by way of exterior and de facto poverty.[20]

It is in this very same homily that we meet the beautiful spiritual exegesis of the parable of the Good Samaritan, which is our third example. We quote the text:[21]

Who was our neighbor [cf. Lk 10:29, 36] more than the Savior himself? Who ever practiced greater mercies toward us? When we were very nearly perishing from the countless wounds inflicted on us by the spirits of darkness, when these were filling our souls with false fears, impure desires, blinding anger, deceiving and disquieting pleasures, he healed all our wounds, he rooted out and destroyed our vices, not like the Law whose effects are weak and impotent because still within the realm of the malignity connected with the origins of our vice themselves, but rather by himself applying the ax blade to the foot of the tree of evil and by pulling up all its roots with his own hands. He poured on the wounds of our souls a precious wine which is the blood of the vine of David. He drew forth from his own heart the oil of the Spirit with which he soothed our wounds. He bound our souls and brought them together with the indissoluble bandages of charity, faith and hope. He commissioned the angels and principalities and powers of heaven to serve us, and he pays them their wages for this service by freeing them from the vanity of the world through the revelation of the glory of the sons of God.

In summary, Clement sees Jesus as a physician who poured out the wine of his own blood for our sins. Having received the oil of his mercy

---

[19]See on this subject, S. Legasse, *L'appel du riche*, (Paris, 1966), pp. 84ff; R. Schnackenburg, *L'evangile selon Marc*, (Paris, 1973), vol. II, pp. 96-101. One should read pp. 227-260 of Legasse's book to measure the complexity of the history of the interpretations of the Gospel text, and J. Galot's critique of Legasse, *Gregorianum* 56 (1975), 441-467. Cf. also our chapter VI on St. Ephraem.

[20]Cf. S. Giet, "La doctrine de l'appropriation des biens, chez quelques-uns des Pères," *Rech. de. Sc. Rel.* 35 (1948), p. 61.

[21]Clement of Alexandria, *Who Is the Rich Man that Shall Be Saved?*, 29, PG 9, 634. We note here the very beautiful expression, "[Christ] drew forth from his own heart the oil of the Spirit," recalling both Jn 7:37-39 and 19:34. We also used in interpreting Clement's commentary on the Good Samaritan, A. Orbe's study on the patristic interpretation of the Gospel parables, *Parabolas evangelicas en S. Ireneo*, (Madrid: BAC, 1970), vol. I.

from the heart of his Father, he pours it out on us abundantly. In contrast to the law of Moses, he is a physician who really heals, for he removes sins and passions from the soul. That Law only treated the outward symptoms of the evil afflicting wounded man, that is, humanity, assailed by the demonic bandits before he found refuge, thanks to the Savior, with the angelic innkeepers.

We note here the order in which Clement presents the salvific wound-dressings: charity is named before faith and hope. Without charity, faith and hope of themselves cannot save.

What, according to Clement, is the recompense promised to the angels for their service to men (cf. Heb 1:14)? They will be freed from the necessity of serving a corruptible world, epitomized in the corruptible body of sinful man. Once men have been saved, the angels will no longer be bound to the service of men.

Surely such an exegesis is reminiscent of that of Irenæus, which we have already seen, but it is not entirely identical with it. In both cases, the parable is understood in a Christocentric manner. There is a good reason to think that the fundamental traits of this kind of exegesis derive from the Apostles themselves, through the presbyters.[22] Of course this in no way guarantees the apostolic origin of every allegorical detail found in Clement's interpretation or in that of the other Fathers regarding the parable of the Good Samaritan.

D) *Critical Evaluation*

We shall present first the most obvious criticisms that can be made, the same that were leveled against the exegesis of Clement of Alexandria. In almost every case, we shall offer some response; then we shall attempt to bring out some of the advantages his method can offer, even today, to exegesis.

First, Petau[23] accused Clement of Alexandria of favoring Arianism. Benedict XIV alludes to the hypothesis according to which, in contrast to Hilary of Arles and Vincent of Lerins (whose semi-Pelagian tendencies or errors predated the Church's condemnation of semi-Pelagianism), Clement would have sinned against already defined dogmas of the

---

[22]Cf. Orbe, *op. cit.*, note 21, vol. I, pp. 116-117 and 137.

[23]Petau, *Theol. Dogmata*, vol. II, *De Trinitate*, I, 4, (Paris, 1864), p. 359. Petau notes Clement's expressions, in the *Stromata*, which suggest a difference of natures between Father and Son, but he underscores the correction of Clement's language on the same subject in the *Protreptica*.

Church.[24] However, beyond the fact that the Pope refrains from making that hypothesis his own, it should be noted that the hypothesis appears to be without foundation, for, before the Council of Nicea, which was much posterior to the works of Clement, the universal and post-Apostolic Church seems never to have pronounced definitively on any subject. Some of Clement's views or exegetical interpretations might have contributed to setting the stage for the eventual emergence of Arianism, though it does not follow that for this reason he was himself a pre-Arian.

Clement has also been accused of esotericism and of favoring the idea of "secret traditions" in the interpretation of the New Testament. This accusation seems to have some validity (cf. *Strom.*, VI, 7, 61, and VI, 98; Lebreton, *DSAM*, vol. 2, col. 959-960). Still it must be observed that in Clement's view, the fact that not all Christians could attain to the "authentic gnosis" of the biblical text is not due to any intention on the part of Christ or the Apostles to hide the text's deeper meaning, but is due rather to a lack of generosity on the part of some in the keeping of the precepts: "he who does what is true comes to the light, every one who does evil hates the light" (Jn 3:21, 20) and cannot comprehend the profound sense of the divine word.

It seems to us, moreover, that later Catholic tradition has in no way rejected the idea of a relation between the generous exercise of freedom in the perfect obedience to the commandments of the Gospel on the one hand, and the knowledge of the divine mysteries on the other. In the eyes of Saint Thomas Aquinas, for example, only those who are in the state of grace can possess and exercise the Holy Spirit's gifts of knowledge, understanding and wisdom, and without these intellectual gifts, the divine will is not fully knowable.[25]

Some writers have also underscored the dangers of the allegorical interpretation of the Old Testament proposed by Clement.[26] Noting those criticisms, Mondésert admits that "if reduced to this method, exegesis risks foundering in fantasy, in the caprice of unbridled imagination,

---

[24]Benedict XIV, *De Servorum Dei beatificatione et beatorum canonizatione*, (Prato, 1841), pp. 119-125, XXVI-XXXVI, especially XXXI, all taken from an apostolic letter dated July 1, 1748 to Queen Joan of Portugal on the new edition of the Roman martyrology. It explained why the Church did not inscribe Clement of Alexandria in the martyrology and why his feast is not celebrated in the Roman liturgy.

[25]Cf. Thomas Aquinas, *Summa Theologiæ*, II, II. 8.3.3.

[26]Mondésert, p. 147ff.

and Clement is not always exempt from this reproach."²⁷ We have seen even here an example of this in connection with Isaac.

While acknowledging that sometimes, perhaps even often, Clement shows little concern for the sense that the biblical authors had in mind, it is also right to observe, again with Mondésert, that Clement was himself aware of the danger of neglecting the historical sense of the Bible. Evidence for this may be seen in the reproaches he aims at the heretics for forcing the texts of Scripture and in his constant appeals to biblical history, to the history of salvation.²⁸

Specifically, what Clement of Alexandria helps his reader better to perceive is the harmony between the two Testaments. He responds to both the Jews and the Gnostics by showing and by seeking "the accord between the two Testaments." He would remind the first, who reject the Gospel, that the latter authentically interprets and fulfills the Old Testament (*Strom.*, II, 6, 29) and he would warn the Gnostics, who scorned the Law, of its necessity for justification and of its enduring validity in the New Covenant (*Strom.*, II, 7 and 8; III, 11 and 12, 81, 6 to 83, 2). We even find in Clement certain formulæ that prepare for Cyril of Alexandria:²⁹ "true gnosis is a noetic understanding of prophecy," i.e., of the Old Testament (*Strom.*, II, 54, 1); "faith in Christ and the gnosis of the Gospel are exegesis and fulfillment of the Law" (*Strom.*, IV, 134, 3).

These views of Clement of Alexandria have lost nothing of their timeliness, even in our day. On the contrary, contemporary theology delights in recalling that "Christ himself unifies in himself all Christian history and grounds the unity-duality, or, if one prefers, the continuity and the discontinuity between the Old and New Testament, as fundamental historical expression of the Christian faith"; thanks to the foundation of the incarnate Word, it is possible to distinguish "the historicity of the Christian faith from a historicity in which man would be the creator of his own meaning."³⁰

---

²⁷Mondésert, p. 148. We underscore here the basic error of Clement and of the Alexandrian school, an error to which we shall return in connection with Origen: i.e., every sentence of the Bible has a hidden sense.

We note here with P. T. Camelot, O.P. (*Revue biblique* 53, [1946], pp. 246-247) that Clement's theology of inspiration commands his theology of the senses of Scripture and is inadequate. For Clement (*Protr.* IX, 87, 1; *Strom.* I, 65), all Scripture is inspired, even its letters and syllables. Therefore the slightest words are regarded as charged with divine meaning that must be discovered at any cost. See, however, pp. 223, note 38 and p. 236.

²⁸Mondésert, p. 148.

²⁹Cyril of Alexandria on 1 Cor 14:2, *PG* 74, 890-891.

³⁰M. J. Le Guillou, O.P., explaining certain theses of the International Theology Commission, *Doc. Cath.* 70 (1973), p. 461.

It is fitting here to underscore one of Clement's great merits, namely, that he orients his reader toward the consideration of the promises of God, of a God who promises, a God who is the future of man. Long before Augustine, Clement perceived that the faith does not call for blind adherence to invisible things still to come, for the present brings with it the realization of what was announced in the past and thus guarantees that what ought to be will be, thus "the present action serves as a confirmation of both time extremities" (*Strom.* II, 12, 52).[31]

This should give us some idea of the extent to which Clement could enlighten and excite the modern reader, much as he intoxicated Newman just over a century ago. Let us listen to the author of the *Apologia pro vita sua*:

> The broad philosophy of Clement and Origen carried me away; ...Some portions of their teaching, magnificent in themselves, came like music to my inward ear, as if the response to ideas, which, with little external to encourage them, I had cherished so long. These were based on the mystical or sacramental principle, and spoke of the various Economies or Dispensations of the Eternal. I understood them to mean that the exterior world, physical and historical, was but the outward manifestation of realities greater than itself. Nature was a parable: Scripture was an allegory: pagan literature, philosophy, and mythology, properly understood, were but a preparation for the Gospel... Holy Church in her sacraments and her hierarchical appointments, will remain even to the end of the world, only a symbol of those heavenly facts which fill eternity.[32]

---

[31]Moingt, 1951, pp. 83-84; cf. 1950, p. 417.

[32]John Henry Newman, *Apologia pro vita sua*. Modern Library Edition (1950), p. 55. Light was shed on the text by J. Seynaeve, "Newman," *DBS* 6, (1960), pp. 450ff.

N.B. We also draw the reader's attention to the works by two Protestant authors on the exegesis of Clement of Alexandra: E. Molland, *The Conception of the Gospel in the Alexandrian School*, (Oslo, 1938), pp. 5-84. The author treats in detail the relation between Law and Gospel in Clement's thought. O. Prunet, *La morale de Clément d'Alexandrie et le Nouveau Testament*, (Paris: PUF, 1966), p. 257 and especially pp. 175-248, where the author develops the thesis (pp. 234ff) of a non-recognition of the eschatological motivation in the Pauline moral understanding in Clement's thought.

We also note the recent and useful discussions of the presence in Clement of Alexandria of a doctrine of the triple sense of Scripture: Henri de Lubac, *Exégèse médiévale*, Part I, vol. I, (Paris, 1959), pp. 171-177; A. Méhat, "Clément d'Alexandrie et les sens de l'Ecriture," Ier Stromate, 176, 1 et 179, 3," *Epektasis*, Mélanges Daniélou, (Paris, 1972), pp. 355-366.

Chapter IV
Origen
His Greatness—Typology
His Weakness—Allegorizing

The name of Origen (c. 185-253) evokes in the majority of his readers a succession of very different reactions that are reflected in the different evaluations of his exegesis.

Sometimes we admire the methodical and monumental commentary of this "first scientific exegete of the Catholic Church." We would follow Quasten further with the observation that he "wrote on all the books of the Old and New Testaments in three different literary forms: the scholia, which are brief explanations of difficult passages, the homilies and the commentaries."[1] His concern for orthodoxy may be noted with Henri de Lubac: "not content with evoking the rule of the Scriptures, he appeals constantly to the rule of the Church, to the faith of the Church, to the preaching of the Church, to the traditions of the Church, to the doctrine of the Church";[2] for him, the bones of the Paschal Lamb symbolize the "holy dogmas of the Church,"[3] none of which should be broken.

At other times, Origen will be charged with major responsibility for all the "exaggerations of medieval allegorism." We will note, again with

---

[1]Johannes Quasten, *Patrology*, vol. II, (Westminster, Maryland: The Newman Press, 1953), p. 45.

[2]Henri de Lubac, *Histoire et Esprit*, (Paris, 1950), p. 62, where the author gives specific references to quoted works of Origen.

[3]*Ibid.*, p. 63.

Quasten, that "some of his symbolistic techniques become fantastic."[4] We will recall with insistence the philosophical and doctrinal errors with which, after his death, a number of popes and councils charged him, even to the point of anathematizing him:[5] the preexistence of souls, subordinationism,[6] *apocatastasis*.

All, however, agree in paying tribute to his genius, the sincerity of his faith, his knowledge of the Scriptures, his courage in the face of persecution—even to the point of martyrdom. Indeed, the great defender of Nicea, Athanasius, spoke of the "wise and hardworking Origen,"[7] cautioning us "among the opinions expressed in Origen's writings, not to confuse those he cites to refute them with the opinions that are his own."[8]

We shall not take time to consider here the enormous work of critical exegesis that Origen undertook in its entirety. We shall begin with an exposition of his exegetical principles and method, illustrating with examples as we go. Next, we shall retrace the influence of Philo and that of Gnosticism that color these principles and procedure, and finally we shall point out the positive and negative effects of his hermeneutics in the history of interpretation of the Holy Scriptures and in the Church. The subject is, of course, enormous. Our treatment will be brief, with frequent references to the works of specialists. We may confidently refer the reader to such works, especially in view of the significant progress that has been made in the last few decades in the study of Origen and in the knowledge of his works.[9]

A. *The Exegetical Principles and Method of Origen*

Origen explained for us the norms of his exegesis in his celebrated treatise, *Peri Archon*, or *On First Principles*, which he wrote in the years

---

[4]Quasten, p. 93.

[5]Especially Popes Anastasius I (*DS* 209) and Leo the Great (*DS* 298), and Canon 11 of the Second Council of Constantinople (*DS* 433); also the Lateran Council of 649, Canon 18 (*DS* 519).

[6]The doctrine that taught that Christ was inferior to the Father in everything.

[7]Athanasius, *Fourth Letter to Serapion*, PG 26, 649.

[8]*De decretis Nicænæ Synodi*, ch. 27, PG 25, 465.

[9]Especially works by Henri Crouzel, Henri de Lubac, Jean Daniélou, R. P. C. Hanson and Mrs. Harl, to mention only a few. The reader will find in the notes that follow their specific contributions. In H. Crouzel, *Origène et la connaissance mystique*, (Bruges-Paris, 1961), pp. 558-562, there is a valuable bibliography on Origen's biblical exegesis and theology up to 1960. It should be complemented by using the alphabetical index of the immense *Bibliographie critique d'Origène*, also by Father Crouzel (The Hague, 1971).

220-231, before his departure from Alexandria. We shall attempt to draw from this work the essential principle of his method that he never went back on and which was always present in the background of his thought, namely, his theory of the three senses, but we shall see that in fact, in his exegesis and in his homilies and commentaries, it is rather a typological theory of three levels (shadow, image, truth) that he applies with success and that constitutes the permanent value of his work.[10] Moreover, Origen himself does not seem to have attempted a synthesis of these two theories, even though the problem of effecting such a synthesis did not entirely escape him.[11]

Origen reveals a keen awareness of the need for an exegetical method that would take into account the divinely inspired character of the Scriptures. Accordingly, he makes it his explicit concern to set forth a correct way of understanding, governed by the rule and the teaching which Jesus Christ transmitted to the Apostles and which they transmitted by succession to their posterity, the teachers of the celestial Church.[12] His idea is then to develop a Christian, apostolic, and ecclesial exegesis of the Holy Scriptures of the Old and New Testaments. Better still: it is in Scripture itself that Origen seeks to discover an exegetical method. "We believe that the correct way to understand the Scriptures and to investigate the ideas they contain is that which Scripture itself teaches us to employ."[13] This then is the methodological result which Origen believes his biblical inquiry yields:

> In the Proverbs of Solomon, we find a commandment of this kind with reference to the careful investigation of the divine Scripture: "And you, write them down three times with reflection and knowledge, so that you may respond with words of truth to those who have questioned you" [Prv 22:20-21]. Everyone should then write the meaning of the Holy Scriptures three times in his soul. Then the simplest reader will be edified by what is, so to speak, the body of Scripture (as we call the ordinary interpretation which follows the narrative), but those who have already begun to advance a little, and whose perspective may be broader, will be edified by the soul of the Scripture; finally the perfect—those who have become like those of whom the Apostle said: "There

---

[10]Cf. Jean Daniélou, *A History of Early Christian Doctrine*, vol. 2, *Gospel Message and Hellenistic Culture*, (London: Darton, Longman & Todd Ltd, 1973), pp. 273-288, on Origen's exegetical method.

[11]This seems possible considering the references to Heb 10:1 in *De Princ.* IV, 2, 2 and 4 (11 and 13).

[12]*Ibid.*, IV, 2, 2.

[13]*Ibid.*, IV, 2, 4.

is, to be sure, a wisdom that we make known among those who are fully grounded; but it is not the wisdom of this world, or of this world's rulers, whose power is to be abrogated. What we make known is the wisdom of God, his secret, kept hidden till now; so, before the ages, God has decreed, reserving glory for us" [1 Cor 2:6-7]—will be edified by the spiritual law [Rom 7:14], which contains "the shadow of the good things to come" [Heb 10:1].[14]

There are then three distinct senses in Scripture, three meanings perceived respectively by the simple (or beginners), the advanced, and the perfect. The simple will be able to grasp only the first, the advanced only the first two; only the perfect will be able to grasp all three. Origen goes further in defining the anthropological paradigm of the three senses. "Man is composed of body, soul, and spirit (cf. 1 Thes 5:23); so too is the Sacred Scripture, given by God's generosity for man's salvation."[15]

Let us examine this construct of Origen's in greater detail.

The first of the three senses is sometimes referred to by Origen as *corporal sense*, and at other times, as the *literal sense*. For the Alexandrian master, this first sense must be investigated before any other. This is the "historical sense." While often regarded as an allegorist, and thus disdainful of history, Origen nevertheless writes: "There are many more things that have really taken place in the historical sense than there are things added to be understood simply in the spiritual sense."[16] Whenever he can, Origen regards the literal sense of Scripture as the essential one, and he generally begins by explaining it with great care. But he thinks that this sense is not the only one. Indeed, he even thinks that a literal sense is occasionally lacking altogether: "A diligent reader will sometimes hesitate and only after extensive research discover whether a particular fact is literally historical or not."[17] How is it possible, in Origen's view, to arrive at this conclusion that one or another fact reported by Sacred Scripture is not literally historical? Because—and Origen is following Philo here—since the Scripture is divine, the sense it offers must always be worthy of God and beneficial for man. Being God's word whose aim can only be to instruct man, it cannot contain anything foreign to that purpose. "We strive," says Origen explicitly, "to find in the Scriptures, which we believe to be inspired by God, a meaning worthy of God."[18] Now, "often...the literal sense designates not only illogical things, but

---

[14]*Ibid.*

[15]*Ibid.*

[16]*Ibid.*, IV, 3, 4 (20).

[17]*Ibid.*, IV, 3, 5 (21).

[18]This position reappears in various ways in the *De Principiis*, especially IV, 3, 4 (20).

even impossible things."[19] We need not be shocked. We should seek to understand what Origen is trying to say here. Let us grant with Daniélou[20] that this principle of Origen is "susceptible of a perfectly legitimate understanding." How? In his work *Origène, theologien et exegete*, Prat makes two important observations. First, we are dealing here with an absolutely indisputable principle of exegesis; "the fundamental principle that one must abandon the corporal sense, i.e., the proper sense, wherever something impossible, absurd or false results from it is indisputable and there is no Catholic exegete who would not subscribe to it."[21] His second observation is that what Origen calls the literal sense is not what we understand by that term (namely, the sense intended by the human author in the inspired text). This is, rather, the proper sense. In Scripture, the literal sense is often a figurative sense. Hence his principle obviously applies in all cases where the literal sense is figurative. If we remember that certain passages are not to be taken in the proper sense, we can agree with Origen that not all the texts of Scripture have a literal sense. The Song of Songs is allegorical in the very intention of its author.[22]

The *psychic sense* that is superimposed on the corporal sense is more difficult to define. Origen only rarely attempted to define it. It seems to be equivalent to what was later called the tropological sense.[23] The Alexandrian is often content with contrasting the letter and the spirit. Having noted the literal sense of a text, he passes rapidly to the spiritual or allegorical sense that is the aspect that holds his entire attention.

Unlike the literal sense, the *spiritual sense* is always present in a text. To show its importance, Origen appeals not to Philo but to St. Paul, with explicit references to Heb 8:5; 10:1; 1 Cor 10:11, 4; Gal 4:21-24; Col

---

[19]*Ibid.*, IV, 2, 9 (16) ff.

[20]Jean Daniélou, *Origen*. Translated by Walter Mitchell, (New York: Sheed and Ward, Inc., 1955), p. 179. Part II is concerned with Origen and the Bible.

[21]Prat, *Origène, le théologien et l'exégète*, (Paris, 1907), p. xix.

[22]Daniélou, p. 181. Father Camelot made a similar observation in 1946 concerning Clement of Alexandria: "He did not see, nor did many after him, that the figured sense is a 'primary' sense. When he hears the sacred author speak of the arm or the eye of God, these anthropomorphisms are for him a literal and primary sense, and he seeks a spiritual or allegorical sense to isolate the figurative sense hidden beneath those metaphors which is in truth the literal sense intended by the author. Cf. Thomas Aquinas, *Summa Theologiæ*, I.1.10.3, (*Revue Biblique* 53 [1946], p. 247: "Clément d'Alexandrie et l'Ecriture").

[23]In the *De Principiis* (IV, 2, 6), Origen gives the Pauline interpretation in 1 Cor 9:9-10, of Dt 25:4, as example of the sense which is as the the soul of Scripture. With Bardy (*DTC*, XI, 2, [1932], col. 1508, "Origène"), we could also mention *Sermon* XVII, 1 on Genesis (*PG* 12, 253).

2:16-17. In Origen's view,[24] these texts show the existence of a spiritual sense both in the Pentateuch and in the historical writings of the Old Testament.

We quote here an excerpt from the *De Principiis* that best reveals the thought of Origen:

> The Holy Spirit wished to enclose and to conceal secret mysteries in ordinary words behind the screen of a story and an account of visible things....Through the narrative of war and the description first of conquerors and then of the conquered, some of the ineffable mysteries are revealed to those men who are able to penetrate to the depth of texts of this kind.... All these texts have been woven with divine artistry so as to form a sort of covering and veil for spiritual meanings, and this is what we have referred to as the body of Holy Scripture; and the purpose was that, through what we have called the covering of the letter woven by the art of divine wisdom, as many persons as possible might receive instruction and be able to progress, which would otherwise have been impossible.[25]

There is no body without a soul, no letter without a spirit. The marvel of Scripture in Origen's eyes—but this is also what makes us uneasy reading him—is that every line has a hidden sense that we will have to discover. Such a view has no foundation in the Pauline texts cited by Origen. These texts show the existence of a spiritual sense beyond the literal sense in a certain number of cases, but not as a rule.

How do we explain this theory in Origen's writings of the universal spiritual sense that is present throughout Scripture and which must be discovered? As Daniélou saw clearly, what Origen calls the spiritual sense contains in reality three different elements.[26]

First, this spiritual sense embodies a Platonist view of the universe. All visible nature is but the symbol of the invisible world and each individual has its correspondent, its type, its model in the ideal world. It follows that all things, including Scripture along with everything else, have two distinct aspects. The first is the corporal, sensible aspect, accessible to the mass of the simple. The other is the spiritual and the mystical aspect that only the perfect perceive. The corporal sense is not false, but it is incomplete. It is the spiritual sense that reveals the full truth to those who are capable of grasping it. Whether it be a question of narratives,

---

[24]*De Principiis*, IV, 2, 6 (13).

[25]*Ibid.*, IV, 2, 8 (15).

[26]Jean Daniélou, *Studia Patristica*, vol. I, (Berlin, 1957), "Origène comme exégète de la Bible," pp. 284-287. We use Daniélou's thought, modifying his presentation and organization.

prescriptions, names, or numbers, there is nothing that is not expressed in figure. It is the privilege of the masters to interpret these images and symbols correctly.

More precisely, in this Platonist view of the universe, the contrast is more between the *aistheta* and the *noeta* (the former being the figure of the latter) rather than between the *historika* and the *pneumatica*. Following Philo, Origen often interprets the scriptural data as allegories of moral realities. Accordingly, the trees of Paradise are the virtues, the Ark of the flood is the soul, Hagar represents profane culture, Sarah, wisdom. Philosophical symbolism replaces biblical typology. Ambrose will inherit this aspect of the spiritual sense in Origen.

On the other hand, what the Alexandrian calls spiritual exegesis contains at another level elements that belong to literal exegesis. Origen understood that the meaning of many passages of the Old and New Testaments is not the proper sense. Rejecting a certain "fundamentalism," his intention is to undertake a sound "demythologization" of Scripture, notably in the interpretation of the first chapter of Genesis. For him, the seven days of creation are not to be taken in the proper sense; rather, they express an order (*taxis*).[27]

Finally, the spiritual sense in Origen embraces a third element: the entire typology or analogy between the way God acts in the events, institutions, and personages of the Old Testament and the New. Here, Origen, as bearer of the heritage of Justin and Irenæus, is aware that he is carrying on the common tradition of the Church. The departure from Egypt prefigures the baptismal liberation; Joshua entering into the promised Land announces Jesus opening Paradise to all human beings; the temple of Jerusalem prefigures his Body.

With its triple structure that we shall define a little more precisely, this typology must be received in faith. Only faith gives the true understanding, gnosis of Scripture and of its mysteries. Gnosis is a further development of faith, an understanding, through the action of the Spirit, of what is Spirit beyond the letter. Exegesis becomes here contemplation, through reflection on God's words, of his only Word, the Logos, hidden under the appearance of the Letter. This is the aspect retained by Henri de Lubac in his work *Histoire et Esprit*: under the action of the Spirit, the Christian receives today, through the medium of Scripture, the Word sent by the Father.

---

[27]*Ibid.*, p. 284; cf. Origen, *PG* 12, 97B.

In fact, this third, the typological element of the spiritual sense in Origen is that which he takes from the Letter to the Hebrews and from the tripartite structure it proposes: shadow, image, truth. The shadow of the Old Testament is succeeded by the image of Christ and his Church, which will be consummated in the truth of the Kingdom. *Skia, eikon, aletheia.*[28]

Thus, in the *Sermons on Joshua*, Origen shows that the fall of Jericho can be seen as variously prefiguring the collapse of paganism by the preaching of the Gospel, the fall of the interior Jericho found within each person through his conversion to the word of God, and finally the destruction of the Kingdom of Satan at the Parousia.[29] The historical entrance of Joshua into Jericho symbolizes Christ's entrance into our sinful world, his Paschal victory over idolatry, and the conquest of our souls, rescued from vice by his virtues, to be conducted thus to the truth of his final triumph on the last day.

In other words while the shadow is single, the image and the truth reveal three aspects: the nature of the Christian mystery (Christ-Church), the virtuous life and activity that that nature entails, the consummation of that nature and that activity in the eschatological Kingdom. Later tradition will express these three aspects in terms of the allegorical sense, the tropological sense, and the anagogical sense understood as subdivisions of the spiritual sense.

The shadow refers to the literal or corporal sense, the image covers both the allegorical and tropological senses, while the truth means the anagogical sense. Through the reading of Scripture, the Christian passes from the shadows through the images to the truth. As Newman put it, he moves *"ex umbris et imaginibus in veritatem."*[30]

Origen has given us a magnificent resume of the shadow-image-truth typological dialectic in a homily on Psalm 38:2:

> Paul distinguishes three levels in the law: the shadow, the image, and the truth.... The law contains the shadow of future good things, but not the very

---

[28]Cf. Henri de Lubac, *Histoire et Esprit*, p. 200, note 149. We note (cf. the text of Origen referred to in note 24) with Daniélou the historical relationship between the Temple of Jerusalem and the eschatological Temple in Heb 8:5 and 10:1. It is this, Daniélou thinks (*Gospel Message and Hellenistic Culture*), that Hanson showed against Spicq: *Allegory and Event, A Study of the Sources and Significance of Origen's Interpretation of Scripture*, (London, 1959), pp. 83-93.

[29]Daniélou, *Studia Patristica* I, p. 286; above all, by the same author, *From Shadows to Reality*, (Westminster, MD: Newman Press, 1960), pp. 276-286.

[30]We know that Newman summed up his intellectual and spiritual odyssey in such terms: *Meditations and Devotions*, p. 439.

image of the realities and this clearly shows that the image of the realities is different from what is designated as the shadow of the law. If anyone can describe the ceremonies of the Jewish worship, let him view the temple as not having had the image of realities, but only their shadow. Let him see the altar as a mere shadow, and the rams and the calves brought to sacrifice also as a shadow, according to the Scripture: "our days on earth are like a shadow"[1 Chr 29:15].

If someone wishes to go beyond this shadow, let him come to the image of the realities and let him behold the coming of Christ made flesh: let him contemplate him in his role as High Priest offering victims to the Father henceforth and in the future; let him understand that all this is an image of spiritual realities and that heavenly functions are denoted by corporal functions. We employ the term image to refer to that which is intelligible at present and which human nature can observe.

If you can penetrate the heavens with your understanding and your mind and follow Jesus who has penetrated the heavens and who stands as our intercessor before the face of God, you will find there those good things whose shadow the law contained and whose image Christ revealed through his Incarnation, those good things that have been prepared for the blessed, which neither eye has seen nor ear heard, and which man has never even imagined or thought of.[31]

As Henri Crouzel brought out with great precision, this passage may indeed be viewed as a synthesis of the various, even conflicting interpretations which Origen offers us in various parts of his work on the relationship between shadow, image, and truth.

Sometimes, struck by the symbolic and imperfect character of all Scripture, he applies to both Testaments without distinction the notions of shadow and image, e.g., the soul of Jesus is the shadow of the Word.[32] At other times, however, he sees that in his Incarnation, Christ has gone beyond the symbols to usher in the authentic reality and he refuses to attribute these terms to the Gospel.[33] His way of thinking is antithetical. But in view of Hebrews 10:1 he makes a first attempt at synthesis—the Old Testament as shadow, and the New Testament as image are distinguished in their figurative function—but he does not go far in investigating the nature of this distinction in this text.[34]

---

[31]Origen, *Hom. in Ps.* 38, II, 2; *PG* 12, 402A.

[32]*Comm. in Joann.* I, 6 (4); *GCS*, IV, p. 60, 1, 17.

[33]See the file of Origen's texts set up by Henri Crouzel on this point, in his volume, *Origène et la connaissance mystique*, (Bruges, 1961), p. 219, note 1.

[34]*Ibid.*, p. 219. In contrast, see M. Harl, *Origène et la fonction révélatrice du Verbe incarné*, (Paris, 1958), p. 105.

We should note with Crouzel that this was Origen's *first* attempt at a synthesis. We do find others, such as his three Testaments, his three Paschs, and his three successive peoples, namely, Israel, the Church, the Assembly of the Kingdom in which, after the first Pasch has been replaced by the second, we shall celebrate the eternal, the only definitive, the only perfect Pasch,[35] "among myriads of Angels, in a blessed exodus."

Above all—and Henri de Lubac stressed this at length, pointing out why it is that Origen cannot be considered a precursor of Joachim of Fiore[36]—the Alexandrian distinguishes the temporal and corporal Gospel, which is proclaimed by the Church here below, from the eternal Gospel that is to be promulgated at the Parousia.

Taking up the expression of the author of the Book of Revelation (14:6), Origen deduces from the text, by distinction and apposition, the existence of a Gospel that is temporal. As the first Mosaic law was followed by Deuteronomy, which is essentially still the same law, but which is "clearer and more manifest," so also the Gospel of time promulgated by our Savior in the humility of the form of a slave will be succeeded by the Gospel of eternity that he will promulgate at the time of his second and glorious Parousia. Then all those who have lived spiritually on earth according to the laws of the first Gospel, shall live in the Kingdom of Heaven according to the laws of this eternal Gospel.[37]

However, this striking distinction should not lead us to believe that there is a real duality of Gospels in Origen's view. On the contrary, for him there is only one Gospel, delivered on earth partially, as through a mirror, darkly (cf. 1 Cor 13:12), under the veil of the letter, but contemplated in heaven in its fullness. Its character as image results from our weakness. The more the soul conforms, through the reception of grace and the practice of the virtues, to the resurrection of Christ, the more it surrenders itself to the Logos growing within it, allowing the Word to transform it into his likeness, the more the divinity begins to show through the glorified humanity of Christ and the letter of the Scripture and the mysteries begin to be perceived beneath their clothing as image.[38]

Such are the fundamental principles of Origen's exegesis: the search for a threefold sense in Scripture, of which the third, the spiritual sense,

---

[35]Cf. Lk 22:16.

[36]de Lubac, *Histoire et Esprit*, pp. 220-221. Contrary to Joachim, Origen's eschatological vision has no admixture of millenarism.

[37]*De Principiis*, IV, 3, 13. Cf. H. de Lubac, *Histoire et Esprit*, p. 227.

[38]Crouzel, p. 368.

on which the emphasis is placed, itself includes three distinct aspects: the allegorical, the tropological, and the anagogical. From the shadow of the old Law, through the image of the new Law, the exegete works his way toward the face-to-face vision of the truth.

These principles, we must remember, are not coordinated in a rigorous system. On the contrary, the meaning given to the different expressions to which we have just referred vary according to the context. Origen is not afraid to contradict himself, which explains how it has been possible to interpret him in contradictory ways by stressing one affirmation or one commentary to the detriment of another. In view of this, we readily admit that our presentation amounts to a systematization and simplification of Origen's thought.

In concluding this brief presentation, it remains for us to clarify two areas in which Origen lays the groundwork for the later synthesis of Athanasius and John Chrysostom; both relate to the content and to the fundamental purpose of Scripture.

For the Alexandrian,

> the principal doctrine revealed through these men filled with the Divine Spirit[39] is that concerning God, i.e., the Father, the Son and the Holy Spirit; then come the mysteries relative to the Son of God—how the Word became flesh and why he went so far as to take on himself the form of a slave [Jn 1:14; Phil 2:7]. It was also necessary, by logical necessity, that they give this mortal race a teaching in the divine word—concerning creatures endowed with reason, those of heaven as well as those on earth, the blessed as well as those here below.... Then it was necessary that we should learn through the divine words what this world is and why it was made, why it is that the evil on earth is so enormous and so serious and whether evil exists only on earth or also in other places.[40]

The Trinity, the redemptive Incarnation, the spiritual and the physical universe, the raison d'être of evil: these are the things, according to Origen, that the authors of the Scriptures—human, but divinely inspired—intended to teach us.

We should note that, in his exposition of biblical themes, Origen does not differentiate between the Old and New Testaments. However, he cites excerpts only from the New Testament to document his position. Nevertheless, since he reads the Old Testament in the light of the New, the problem does not arise for him in exactly the same way as it does

---

[39]Origen refers here to the inspired authors of the Old and New Testaments.
[40]*De Principiis*, IV, 2, 7 (14).

today in the minds of some exegetes. In writing that the Old Testament was speaking of the Father and of the Son and of the Spirit, the Fathers believed that Moses and the prophets had already had the revelation, however imperfect, of the Trinitarian mystery.[41] They went on then to a Trinitarian reading of the Old Testament texts on the Word and on the breath of God. We generally continue to do this today, but not so much by way of attributing infused knowledge of the Trinity to the patriarchs and prophets as in the context of "biblical themes," as a reflection on the action of the Spirit, who inspires and directs the course of biblical history, on the concepts of word and of breath-spirit.

It is in this context that we may understand the thinking of Origen. Considered as a whole, the Scriptures speak to us of the two forms or conditions of the Incarnate Word, at the same time as they speak to us of the Trinity on the one hand and of the world of angels, of men and of matter on the other. As we shall see in the next chapter, Athanasius will isolate the Christological theme as the fundamental purpose (*skopos*) of the Scriptures.

Likewise for Origen, it is the Scriptures taken as a whole that manifests the *sugkatabasis* or "condescension" of the transcendent and immaterial God for the sake of mankind sunk in matter, a condescension of which the Incarnation of the Son, with his divine form, in the form of a slave, is the culminating point.[42] It is specifically this divine condescension, Origen thinks, that enables us to understand Moses' toleration of divorce[43] and the toleration of the bloody sacrifice of animals, which God was able to use as an antidote against polytheism. Indeed, it was impossible that Israel should worship the animals it was immolating.[44]

Thus the Alexandrian was preparing the way for the biblical theology of Chrysostom, in which the idea of the divine condescension is the principal axis, as we shall see in Chapter VIII.

Again we should note, with Henri de Lubac, that Origen's doctrine of the divine condescension, while emphasizing the design of a divine

---

[41]For Origen, Moses and the prophets had an imperfect and partial knowledge of the Trinity and of Christ: *Comm. on John*, XIII, 48; *Sermons on Joshua*, III, 2. Cf. Daniélou, *Origen*, pp. 124ff.

[42]Origen, *Contra Celsum*, IV, 15, *PG* 11, 1045; cf. K. Duchatelez, "La condescendance divine dans l'histoire du salut," *Nouv. Rev. Theol.* 95 (1973), p. 598.

[43]Cf. Dt 24:1ff; H. Pinard de la Boullaye, "Les infiltrations païennes dans l'ancienne loi d'après les Pères de l'Eglise: la thèse de la condescendance," *Rech. de Sc. Rel.* 9 (1919), p. 205.

[44]Origen, *Serm. XVII, 1 on Numbers*, *PG* 12, 703; *SC* 29, pp. 337-340; and a text of Origen quoted by Pinard (see note 43), pp. 205-206.

economy already preparing in the Old Testament for the revelation of the New, was in no way viewed by Origen as conflicting with his emphasis on allegory: "How could the preparation of a reality to come not be symbolic of that reality?"[45] This had already been recognized by Newman, in contrast to the later view of Harnack.[46] And it is the contemplation of this divine condescension in the economy of salvation that enables Origen to temper and to limit the neglect of history to which his inclination for allegory might have led him, had he cultivated it onesidedly.[47]

B. Negative and Positive Evaluation

We have just mentioned the temptation, inherent in Origen's love for allegory, to empty history of its meaning and to obscure the progressive character of biblical revelation. These remarks serve as an introduction to a summary presentation of the critical observations that can be made of Origen's exegesis. We shall first describe the major objections that can be made to this exegesis, and then we shall briefly describe its merits and the extent of its influence on subsequent exegesis.

Non-Christian philosophies and thought-systems weighed heavily on Origen's exegesis: specifically, Gnosticism and the Platonic systems of thought. How and why was this so?

1. While reacting against Gnosticism, Origen was under its influence.

As Irenæus had already observed,[48] it is characteristic of Gnostic exegesis to employ biblical expressions, but to invest them with a meaning derived from a system that is foreign to their authentic sense. Gnostic exegesis is a case of alienation into the imaginary.

In his *De Principiis*, Origen proposes as a "deeper" hermeneutics the idea that "the *Archons* and the souls from neighboring countries (Egypt, Babylon, Tyre, Sidon) came down, from the places they were living in, according to the way they had behaved there while dispersed in captivity."[49]

---

[45]de Lubac, p. 250.

[46]Newman, *Apologia pro vita sua*, ch. 1: "Certain parts of Clement's and Origen's teachings were based on the mystical or sacramental principle and dealt with different economies or dispensations of the Eternal." However, we shall come back to the criticisms Newman addressed to Origen later. Cf. H. de Lubac, *Histoire et Esprit*, pp. 250-252.

[47]*Ibid*. See also de Lubac, "A propos de l'allégorie chrétienne," *Rech. de. Sc. Rel.* 47, (1959), pp. 5-43.

[48]See chapter II.

[49]*De Principiis*, IV, 3, 9 (25).

A transformation has here taken place. While the events of Jewish history are the prefiguration of the future Jerusalem, they have also become, by a kind of reversal, the image of a prior history, the reflection and the result of a heavenly history. This is evidenced by the following excerpt:

> The prophecies pronounced concerning various peoples should be taken as referring rather to souls and to their various heavenly dwellings. Likewise the relating of events that were said to have happened to the race of Israel or to Jerusalem, under the attacks of this or that nation, ought to be thoroughly examined and investigated because it would appear that most of the time those things did not take place corporally, but rather they represent more properly those races of souls who once dwelt and should still be believed to dwell in that heaven that is said to pass.[50]

We see here the influence of an idea that can in no way be assimilated by Christian thought: the preexistence and the fall of souls.[51]

Let us state with greater precision the exact meaning of a Gnostic exegesis of the New Testament.[52] We are not dealing, as in the case of Philo, with a transposition of the events to the states of the soul, but with a symbolic system in which the acts and the framework of the life of Jesus are viewed as symbolic of a heavenly history, that of the eons of the pleroma, of which the earthly life of Jesus is an inferior reproduction. This is Platonic exemplarism, to be sure but with an important difference. We no longer have here the immobile archetypes, the eternal ideas that are reflected in the sensible world, but rather a heavenly drama of which the earthly drama is but a shadow.

A characteristic element is common to the disciples of Valentinus, Ptolemy, and Heracleon, and to Origen: the application of a symbolic system of numbers and of places—not only to the Old Testament, but also to the New—to symbolize the places and times of the heavenly world. The whole Gospel thus becomes a kind of esoteric teaching where

---

[50]*Ibid.*, IV, 3, 10 (26).

[51]We must at the same time note with Céline Blanc: "Though Origen generally regards preexistence as probable, he clearly rejects metempsychosis and reincarnation" (Origen, *Comm. on John*, vol. I, SC 120, [Paris, 1966], p. 30).

[52]Cf. J. Daniélou, *Origen*, pp. 191ff.; C. Barth, *Die Interpretation des Neuen Testaments in der valentianischen Gnosis*, (Leipzig, 1911). It is not certain that the numerous recent works on Gnosticism have cleared up the basic data of the exegesis of the heterodox gnosis as much as other points. Except those of Daniélou: cf. the following note, or the work of R. M. Grant and H. Schlier, "Gnose," *Encyclopédie de la Foi*, (Paris, 1965), vol. II, pp. 179-183.

the secrets of the gnosis, i.e., of the heavenly world, are hidden and revealed.

Let us take John 2:12, for example, where it is said that Christ went down to Capharnaum. For Heracleon, Capharnaum represents "the lower parts of the world, matter," and "since that place was not propitious for him, Christ is said to have done and said nothing in that place."

Origen takes a strong stand against such an exegesis, pointing out that in other Gospel passages, Jesus is said to have performed miracles in Capharnaum. But a little earlier, he himself had written:

> We must seek to discover why it is that he is not said to have entered, nor to have gone up, but rather to have gone down to that place. Let us see if in this passage we should not understand the brothers of Jesus to mean the powers that went down with Him, powers that were not invited to the wedding...but which are helped in lower things and in another way.[53]

Origen does not limit himself here to the exercise of his usual method of interpretation. For him, places represent spiritual states. To go up and to go down correspond to spiritual movements. In the text we are concerned with here, still more may be perceived. The brothers of Jesus represent angelic powers. The descent represents the Incarnation where the Word is accompanied by his angelic brothers who came down with him, according to a doctrine known to Origen. He allows of an incarnation of angels, as well as an incarnation of the Word. We are very close here to the method of Heracleon that we criticized above, although a transposition has taken place from the doctrine of the *pleroma* to that of the Incarnation. Angelic history is a kind of double of human history.

In the view of someone like Daniélou, Origen's gnosis is an end product of Jewish and Judeo-Christian apocalyptic, of which it represents a continuation within the great Church. In its philosophical tendency, it contains questionable elements.[54]

---

[53]Origen, *Comm. on John* X, 37-40; *SC* vol. II, (Paris, 1970), pp. 408-409. The translator Céline Blanc, expresses in the first note (p. 408) her disagreement with Daniélou's interpretation who sees here an example of gnostic exegesis.

[54]Daniélou, *Gospel Message and Hellenistic Culture*, (London/Philadelphia, 1973), pp. 494-500. However, we can admit, with J. Pépin, (*Philon*, [Paris, 1967], p. 161), that for Philo, "certain texts only come out from literal interpretation." On the exegesis proposed by Daniélou concerning Origen's allegorism, we refer to Crouzel's criticism that denies in the Alexandrian a clear distinction between typology and allegory (*Bull. de Litt. eccles* 65, [1964], 173). However, Crouzel concedes in Origen insufficient consideration of the inspired author and of history in themselves; they have their own consistency at the same time as they prepare for the coming of Christ (*ibid.*, 70 [1969], 262).

2. *Origen was too much under the influence of the allegorism of Philo.*

It was from Philo that Origen presumably learned that the literal sense is not always proper, but at times symbolic; carrying this insight a little too far, Origen goes on to propose the idea that all passages of Scripture have a symbolic as well as a proper sense. Although Christ is indeed prefigured in the Old Testament, the methodological distortion here exposed results in many errors of detail.

At the beginning of the fifth century, Saint Isidore of Pelusium will give perfect expression to the criticism that one could make of Origen's system, though without mentioning his name:

> Those who wish to apply the Old Testament in its entirety to Christ are far from correct. In doing so, they provide arguments to the pagans and heretics who reject this principle. They do violence to the texts in attempting to extract from them a Christological sense they do not have, and in so doing they end up throwing into discredit the texts that speak quite clearly of Christ. There is a truth that seems evident to me: if the Old Testament does not always speak of Christ, it does at least sometimes, refer to him.[55]

We could not put it better, as long as we still agree to acknowledge that all Scripture is indeed ordered to the manifestation of the mystery of Christ even when it is not speaking of him explicitly: everything is for Christ because "all things have been created through him and for him" (Col. 1:16). But while we cannot deny their ultimate Christological orientation, many realities mentioned in the Scriptures nevertheless have their own consistency, meaning, proximate or immediate finality. An Alexandrian mind could find it difficult at times to acknowledge this fact.

From Philo, Origen borrowed the best (as mentioned above) and the worst, namely, the conviction that not only a few individual episodes, but even the details of Scripture have a typical sense. Almost every line is assumed to be filled with mysteries and the role of the exegete to consist in detecting the reality of the Savior beneath the clothing of the letter. Origen's exegesis is essentially the detection of figures and of symbolic correspondence.

The principle according to which every passage of Scripture has a symbolic sense is foreign to the primitive Christian conception. It is the principle of universal allegory. Origen is so penetrated with this principle that he does not hesitate to write: "Everything in Scripture is mystery."[56] Two negative consequences follow from this. On the one hand, the

---

[55]St. Isidore of Pelusium, *Epist.* 195, *PG* 78, 642.
[56]Origen, *Tenth Sermon on Genesis*, IX, 1.

typological interpretation of Scripture is frequently reduced in Origen to hardly convincing subtleties (especially in the case of Leviticus); on the other hand, his perception of a historical development in the Old Testament is sometimes imperiled. The general tendency of allegorism is toward the negation of history.

To reread Scripture in the light of Jesus is not to transpose every one of its pages into as many Gospel scenes. In reliving the entire history of his people, in taking up again the appeals of the prophets and the prayers of the Psalms, Jesus, while transforming those experiences, left intact the personal details of their historical character and of their concrete situation. If the meaning of the Old Testament changes with the Incarnation, it is not by way of becoming Gospel, but rather by revealing the chasm—which Jesus alone could bridge—that separated him from that Israel according to the flesh that he comes to recapitulate. Origen himself was of course fully aware of this chasm.[57]

This did not however prevent the Alexandrian from replacing the Pauline typology with a literary allegorism of three levels. First, it is no longer the historical realities that are important, but rather the Book that employs the historical realities as symbols. Secondly, past events and institutions are no longer figures of other events and other institutions to come; rather, visible realities, bodies, are symbols of invisible realities— past, present or even future. Historical typology is shifted into a vertical symbolic system characteristic of Hellenized gnosis. Finally, there is no progress in the knowledge of realities, for they have always been known by the "spiritual" and they always remain hidden to the "psychic." A hierarchy of degrees of perfection replaces a succession of stages of revelation.[58]

While it is true that Origen shows no disdain for history, it is also correct to say with Henri de Lubac that "the Alexandrian Platonism that Origen inherited created a dangerous climate. Like the world of natures, the world of history lacked, so to speak, real solidity. Hence the tendency to attach no greater importance to literal exegesis than an exegete would attach to the natural sciences."[59]

Thus, without justifying it we can excuse Origen's excessive allegorism by which he spiritualized everything that appeared to him

---

[57]Cf. J. Guillet, "Les exégèse d'Alexandrie et d'Antioche," *Rech. de Sc. Rel.*, 35 (1947), p. 195.

[58]Daniélou, *Gospel Message and Hellenistic Culture*, pp. 286-288. Cf. R. P. C. Hanson, *Cambridge History of the Bible*, (Cambridge, 1970), vol. I, p. 436.

[59]*Histoire et Esprit*, p. 377.

incompatible with the holiness of the Old Testament saints—e.g. the polygamy of the Patriarchs, the drunkenness of Noah.

We can also attempt, with Cardinal Newman, to give a psychological explanation for Origen's allegorism. A mind occupied and preoccupied with some immense object is prepared to detect in every new datum some aspect of his prior vision. Thus the biblical writers illuminate particular providential interventions of God by means of allusions to the relationships that bind them to the new Covenant. Origen carries their methodical principle further, and for him "history becomes the outer garment of prophecy."[60]

3. Brief notes on Origen's merit and influence.

For Origen, the allegorical exegesis that he abuses is in theory limited and controlled by the rule of faith of the Church. He goes on in his own way, with an independent mind, to the treatment of disputed questions. In his time, the Church had not yet fixed or crystallized her dogma in any ecumenical council. The abuses of his allegorical exegesis were not heresies at the time he was writing, any more than were his serious doctrinal errors. It was his firm and constant intention to be a man of the Church, a loyal and submissive son of the Church.[61]

Origen was always—and one might even say he was almost exclusively—a man of Scripture. From his earliest years, his father trained him in the Scriptures and made him learn them by heart. Even as a child, according to Eusebius, Origen was already seeking their deepest meanings.

Eusebius tells us that as a catechist, he spent the greater part of his nights in the study of the scriptures.[62] As a master of the *Didascalia*, he was the founder of biblical science and brought spiritual exegesis of Scripture to its highest brilliance. As a preacher in Cæsarea, he preached on Scripture every day for many years.

So, continues Cardinal Daniélou, nothing would be more false than to judge the exegesis of Origen on the basis of some of his questionable allegorical interpretations. He is the first great master of exegesis. All who came after him, even those who reacted against him, such as Saint

---

[60]John Henry Newman, *The Arians of the Fourth Century*, (London, 1901), p. 58. Pages 46-64 contain an extremely penetrating judgment of Newman on the exegesis of Alexandria and therefore that of Origen.

[61]Cf. G. Bardy, *DTC* XI[2] (1932), 1507-1511 on the exegesis of Origen.

[62]Eusebius, *Ecclesiastical History*, III, 8.

Jerome, owe nearly everything to him in every domain.[63] In a word, one could rightly ask where would exegesis today be were it not for Origen.

In short, what is Origen's attitude toward the Bible? What one must admire in him is that he is a complete exegete. The Bible is for him first of all a literary text that must be studied scientifically like any literary text;[64] it is in the second place a word of God directly addressed to the Church and, in her, to individuals—a word pregnant with the power (*dynamis*) of the Spirit; finally, it is the point of departure for a theological speculation that opens up a total vision of the universe and of history. When Origen contrasts the letter of Scripture and its hidden sense, he means that Scripture contains this global interpretation of the world which human intelligence has the duty to extract.

This is an admirable task, which Origen accomplished only in part. The culture of his time—that of the grammarians as well as that of the philosophers—did not supply him with the instruments needed for its proper execution. But the partial failure of his attempt cannot conceal the capital role he played in the history of exegesis. He opened to exegesis all the directions it has followed since his time, and even those who have rejected his errors have always been obliged to acknowledge themselves as his disciples.[65]

In the West, the exegesis of the four great Doctors of the Latin Church (Jerome, Ambrose, Augustine, Leo)—to which St. Hilary and a number of others should be added as well—depends directly on that of Origen.[66] In the East, the authors of the *Philokalia* (St. Basil and St. Gregory Nazianzen) reproduced almost in its entirety the fourth book of Origen's *De Principiis*. As Henri de Lubac again observes, Origen's first great adversary, Methodius of Olympus, is for all practical purposes his complete disciple in exegesis as well as in mysticism.[67] The complex attitude of the Magisterium of the Church toward Origen and his thinking reveals the back and forth movement of such negative and positive criticism. After the condemnation of a certain number of propositions

---

[63]Daniélou, "Origène," *DBS*, vol. VII, (1960), col. 885.

[64]We have not even touched on this point here, which was dealt with at length by Daniélou, *DBS* VI, col. 886ff.

[65]Daniélou, *TU* 63, p. 290.

[66]*Histoire et Esprit*, p. 36; cf. Bardy, *La question des langues dans l'Eglise ancienne*, vol. I, pp. 247-272. We in no way imply that the Fathers mentioned followed Origen in everything. Augustine criticized him vigorously. However, those Fathers do not seem to have criticized Origen's exegesis as such.

[67]*Ibid.*

excerpted from *De Principiis* in 543[68]—and it is not absolutely certain if this condemnation was confirmed by Pope Virgilius[69]—comes the anathema cast on Origen (qualifying him as a heretic) by Constantinople II in 553.[70] However, this does not mean that in the view of that Council Origen himself had persevered in defense of any heresy that had already been formally condemned; rather it meant that he was regarded in 553 as the protagonist of propositions judged then to be heretical. The Roman Council of 648—not ecumenical—presided over by St. Martin I, went one step further and anathematized those who refused to cast the anathema on Origen and some others, all considered heretics.[71]

Although those condemnations have never been lifted by the Church, they should all be interpreted in the context of the silence observed at Florence regarding Origen when that Council of Reunion reconfirmed the anathema placed on a good number of heretics of the first centuries,[72] and above all in the context of the praises lavished on Origen by Leo XIII in his encyclical on biblical studies:

> From those schools of catechesis and theology came the majority of the Fathers and writers whose profound studies and notable works followed one another during three centuries in such great abundance that this period has been called the golden age of biblical exegesis. Among those of the East, the first place belongs to Origen, admirable for his diligence of mind and for the constancy of his labors; it is from his numerous works and from his immense *Hexapla* that almost all his successors have drawn.[73]

With no real contradiction, for the two evaluations are not dealing with the same aspects of his thought, the anathematized author of heretical propositions has become an "admirable" man. We should note too that Leo XIII's judgment concerns Origen's exegesis, in contrast to earlier condemnations that were aimed at certain doctrinal propositions (not, however, without exegetical implications).

There is more: the same encyclical of Leo XIII in a manner quite characteristic of Origen, though citing Augustine, sets forth the Pope's own way of understanding the literal sense: "in no way to deviate from the literal and as it were obvious sense unless some reason prevents one

---

[68]*DS* 403-411.

[69]The confirmation is suggested by Cassiodorus, *De instit. divin. Litterarum*, c. 2, PL 70, 1111D.

[70]*DS* 433.

[71]*DS* 519.

[72]*DS* 1339-1346 (the Bull of union with the Copts).

[73]Leo XIII, *Providentissimus* (1893).

from holding to it or forces one to abandon it."[74] Leo XIII was sounding the appeal "not to neglect the allegorical sense especially when that meaning flows naturally from the literal sense and rests on numerous authorities."[75]

The teaching given during the pontificate of Pius XII was to show itself much more reserved toward what constitutes the substance of Origen's method. In 1941, Pius XII approved a document of the biblical commission declaring that it was a serious excess of the Alexandrian school to attempt "to discover a symbolic sense everywhere, even to the detriment of the literal and historical sense."[76] Without further allusion to the Alexandrian school, in his 1943 encyclical *Divino Afflante Spiritu*, Pius XII set forth in a profound way (as we saw in our introduction) the relation between the literal sense and the spiritual sense and the necessity for the exegete, as distinguished from the preacher,[77] "not to put forth metaphorical significations of things as the authentic sense of Scripture."[78] The exegete, Pius XII insists, "may expound the spiritual sense, provided it is clearly intended by God," for "God alone could have known this meaning and revealed it to us."[79] Clearly this limiting affirmation, followed by precise criteria, cannot be reconciled with either the theory or the practice of Origen.

It follows that, even apart from questions of orthodoxy on particular points, while retaining an admiration for Origen, the Church shows marked reserve regarding his theory and his practice of exegesis. This does not prevent her from employing a whole series of selections from the Alexandrian's biblical commentaries in the new *Liturgy of the Hours* published after Vatican II as the official book of prayers in the Latin rite. To be sure, this does not mean that the Church considers Origen a Father of the Church (since the Church has never revoked the anathe-

---

[74]*Ibid.*, quoting St. Augustine, *De Genesi ad litt.*, 1, VIII, c. 7, 13. It will be noted that Leo XIII is not defining here any more than St. Augustine the exact nature of this literal sense; still the words that follow his mention of it (almost obvious) suggest that, like St. Augustine, Leo XIII does not distinguish between metaphoric sense and literal sense intended by the author (cf. note 22 above).

[75]*Ibid.*

[76]DS 3792.

[77]Pius XII, *Divino Afflante Spiritu.*

[78]*Ibid.* The Latin text is "alias *translatas* rerum significationes," DS 3828. There is no question of metaphors in the Latin text.

[79]DS 3828

mas placed on his errors), but as a presbyter and an ecclesiastic writer,[80] and hence as a partial witness of the Tradition.

---

[80]*Liturgia Horarum, ed. typica,* (Vatican City, 1971), vol. I, p. 67: *Instituto generalis de Liturgia Horarum,* ch. VII, 160. Origen's name is not mentioned here, but there is an allusion to the general category of ecclesiastical writers of whom the Office includes certain extracts, together with those of the Fathers.

Chapter V
Polemical, Doctrinal and Spiritual Exegesis of Saint Athanasius

Athanasius of Alexandria (295?-373) is famous above all as the heroic defender and apostle of the divinity of Jesus, Son of God, who was defined at Nicea in 325 during the first ecumenical council as "consubstantial" (*homoousios*) with his Father. But Athanasius is less known as an exegete. His commentators however have all underscored his exceptional knowledge of the divine Scriptures to which most of his works bear witness, from the beginning to the end of his long career as an episcopal writer.

This exegesis has attracted the attention of numerous specialists in recent years.[1] In this study, which does not claim to be more than an introduction, we shall limit ourselves to the examination of the exegesis of Athanasius in the three-fold context of Arianism, Judaism, and monasticism, which we see as the three *loci* in whose context the Alexandrian doctor worked out and applied his exegetical principles.[2] This will explain why the exegesis of Athanasius has at once both doctrinal and

---

[1]Especially H. J. Sieben, "Studien zur Psalterbenutzung des Athanasius von Alexandrien in Rahmen seiner Schriftauffassung und Schiftauslegung," (unpublished doctoral thesis, Institut catholique de Paris, 1968); "Athanasius über den Psalter, Analyse seines Briefes an Marcellinus," *Theologie und Philosophie*, 48 (1973), pp. 152-173; "Herméneutique de l'exégèse dogmatique d'Athanase," *Politique et Théologie chez Athanase d'Alexandrie*, (C. Kannengiesser: Paris, 1974), pp. 195-214, referred to henceforth as *Herméneutique*, followed by the page number.

[2]T. E. Pollard, "Exegesis of the Scripture and the Arian Controversy," *The Bulletin of the John Rylands Library*, 41 (1959), pp. 414-429.

ascetico-mystical characteristics. The anti-Arian polemic made Athanasius look at the literal sense of the New Testament, while the anti-Judaistic polemic encouraged him to examine the spiritual sense of the Old Testament; and his monastic exegesis was situated at the confluence of his doctrinal and ascetical preoccupations. We shall enlarge our presentation of this last aspect of his exegesis by adding an appendix devoted to the biblical formation of the desert monks, one that reveals a comprehensive notion of the role of Scripture in the search for perfect union with God.

A. Against the Arians, Athanasius Displays a Literal Exegesis of the New Testament

We must keep in mind the important fact that from the beginning to the end of his career, Athanasius had to fight against the Arian exegesis. What were the essential characteristics of the latter?

Without a comprehensive study of Arian exegesis, which does not yet exist, we will content ourselves with a review of its major characteristics, considering recent works.[3]

Arius (256?-336), a priest of Alexandria, was charged by his bishop, after his ordination, we are told by Theodoret,[4] "with expounding the divine Scriptures." Arius interpreted biblical assertions regarding God's oneness, his eternal immutability, his indivisibility and his incomprehensibility as attributes reserved to the supreme Monad in contrast to the properties of the Son. He wanted to explain the Scriptures—and above all the mystery of the relationships between the Father, Son, and Spirit—from without, and even against, the tradition of the Church, so as to demonstrate that the Son could not be the only true God. According to Arius, Catholic exegesis, by maintaining the consubtantiality of the Son, was introducing into the one God a division into parts, a composition, a change. To counter this view, in its attempt to prove that the Son was created by the Father and is inferior to him, Arian exegesis used three groups of biblical verses:

• Proverbs 8:22: "The LORD gave me being at the beginning of his way," wrongly translated: "The Lord created me at the beginning of

---

[3]The best presentation of Arian exegesis is probably E. Boularand's *L'hérésie d'Arius et la foi de Nicée*, (Paris, 1972), Part I, pp. 85-93. We take our inspiration here from this work. There are complementary indications in Sieben, *Herméneutique*, p. 198, n. 10; and A. Grillmeier, *Christ in Christian Tradition*, (Oxford 1975), pp. 220ff.

[4]Theodoret, *Hist. Eccles.* I, 1, PG 82, 885A; GCS 19, 6.

His ways";[5] this verse was seen as taken up and developed in Hebrews 1:4 and 3:1;

- in the light of 1 Corinthians 1:24, the Arians interpreted Joel 2:26 and Psalm 103:21 as signifying that Christ is one of the created powers;

- finally, and above all, they saw in John 14:28 ("...the Father is greater than I") the decisive proof of the inferiority of the Son in relation to his Father.

Failing to distinguish between the two natures of Christ, Arian exegesis attributed directly to the Word such things that are proper to human nature. Athanasius, on the contrary, reads the Scriptures in the light of the doctrine of the two conditions or natures, human and divine, of Christ the Savior, such as he receives it from the the Scriptures themselves[6] (cf. Phil 2:6-8) through the Church and the tradition of the Fathers.

In close connection with his deep conviction on this matter, Athanasius enunciates a general principle that he sees as applicable to all of Scripture:

> The purpose and the character or distinctive mark of Holy Scripture [*skopos kai charakter tes hagias graphes*], as we have often said, is its twofold declaration concerning the Savior, namely, that he is God from all eternity and Son, as Logos and Resplendence and Wisdom of the Father and that it is also he who later took on flesh for our sake from Mary, Virgin and Mother of God, and became man: cf. John 5:39: "You search the Scriptures, and it is they that bear witness to me."[7]

How should we understand the sense of this Athanasian rule regarding the purpose and character of the Scriptures?

Athanasius depends here on Origen,[8] but with certain modifications. For Athanasius, the purpose or *skopos* of Holy Scripture no longer supposes, as it did for Origen, the communication of a "compendium of

---

[5]The Hebrew says only, "Yahweh has given me being as the first fruits of his ways," which Wisdom in its turn presents "under the figure of a first-born, the most exquisite product of the life of God" (A. Robert, "Les attaches littéraires de Prov. 1-9," *RB* [1934], p. 193).

[6]Read in their totality in the Church.

[7]Athanasius, *Third Discourse Against the Arians*, 29, PG 26, 385A; cf. the saint's second letter to Serapion, 8, PG 26, 620C. This character of the Christian faith comes from the Apostles through the Fathers, cf. M. B. Handspicker, "Athanasius on Tradition and Scripture," *Andover Newton Quarterly*, (1962), pp. 13-29.

[8]Origen, *De Principiis*, IV, 2, 5-6; cf. Sieben, *Herméneutique*, p. 206ff.

human destinies in the form of hidden mysteries"; rather it constantly returns to the communication of a single truth, that of the mystery of the only-begotten one whom Origen, for his part, had also mentioned as holding first rank. This reduction of the sense and of the content of Scripture to the mystery of Christ marks a fundamental difference between Athanasius and Origen. Scripture is no longer for Athanasius the letter that veils every conceivable truth and wisdom that may in principle be thought up; rather, it carries the message of its own proper truth.[9]

In saying that "the purpose—*skopos*—and the distinctive mark of Holy Scripture consist in the two-fold teaching about the Savior, namely, that he is God from all eternity and Son and that for our sake he later took flesh from Mary and became man," Athanasius is not referring only to the distinction of the two conditions, states and natures of Christ, but also to that of the two time periods in the existence of the Logos.[10]

His principle does not so much mean that a particular passage of Scripture should be interpreted considering the whole Bible. It points rather to the final content of Scripture, read as a whole in the light of the New Testament. Of course, the Athanasian principle is only enunciating a permanent datum of the Christian faith, and one might even say that it was substantially reiterated and so to speak canonized by Vatican II when it declares: "The raison d'être of the Old Testament economy was to set the stage for the coming of Christ the Savior...to announce that coming in prophecy and to represent it by means of various figures.... The books of the Old Testament attain and reveal their full signification in the New Testament."[11]

For Athanasius, as for John and Paul, this Christ-centered content is not something projected from without and as it were imported into Scripture. On the contrary, this "two-fold message" constitutes for him the internal and the central affirmation of the Bible. In other words, Scripture as a whole would have no sense except in the communication of such a key message. In this connection, Pollard[12] is right in saying that since the different parts of Scripture should be interpreted considering such a basic principle whose aim is to reach its total content, this principle requires that Scripture be interpreted by Scripture itself.

---

[9]*Ibid.*

[10]*Ibid.*, p. 202ff.; cf. p. 214; Athanasius, referred to in n. 7 (*Third Discourse Against the Arians*).

[11]*Dei Verbum*, 14-15.

[12]Cf. Sieben, *Herméneutique*, p. 211, n. 68.

How did Athanasius come to see the two-fold mode of existence of the Son as the central affirmation of Scripture and hence to designate that affirmation as normative for the interpretation of Scripture as a whole? It must be said that there is no doubt some relationship between that twofold mode and the New Testament's declaration of the fulfillment, in itself, of the Old Testament and of its promises. Could this explain why the bishop of Alexandria, in the same passage of his *Third Discourse against the Arians*, goes on to say: "For one who studies Holy Scripture, the Old Testament will serve as a starting point for the understanding of the texts; let the Gospels bring him to the contemplative vision of the Lord made man."[13] The formulation is, however, a little obscure.

We quote some examples to show how Athanasius applies his principle.

In his *Fourth Letter to Serapion*, Athanasius explains the sense of Mt 12:31 concerning the unforgivable sin against the Spirit as distinguished from the forgivable sin against the Son of Man. He writes: "The sin that can obtain forgiveness is said by Jesus to relate to the Son of Man, a term used to designate his corporal being; but as for the unforgivable blasphemy, he showed that it amounts to an offense against the Spirit. In using the term Spirit to describe a contrast with his corporal being, he thus pointed to his own divinity."[14]

In commenting on John 10:30 ("the Father and I are one"), Athanasius stresses only the divine condition of Christ: the harmony and the unity of the Father and the Son in thought and in will, in teaching and in activity, can be understood only as the external manifestation of their internal unity of essence.[15]

---

[13] Athanasius, *Fourth Discourse Against the Arians*, III, 30, PG 26, 388A.

[14] Athanasius, *Fourth Letter to Serapion*, 19, PG 26, 665. In 8ff. of the same letter, Athanasius criticizes at length the interpretation Origen had given of the same text concerning the sin against the Holy Spirit, to propose his own as having discovered its deeper sense, relative to Christ's divinity and human nature. It is interesting to note that a modern exegete of Lagrange's stature comes to Athanasius' position without referring to him: "We can be excused up to a certain degree for not recognizing the dignity of him who hides himself beneath the humble appearance of a man, but not for finding fault with the obviously salutary works that reveal the action of the Holy Spirit" (*Evangile selon saint Marc*, [Paris, 1920], p. 69).

[15] Athanasius, *Third Discourse Against the Arians*, 55, 10-16, PG 26, 437; 26, 341-357. We will note the constant presupposition of Athanasius: the "I" of the Johannine Christ is that of the eternal person of the Word; there is no distinct "I" of Christ's humanity as such. A good presentation of the Athanasian argument on Jn 10:30 is in T. E. Pollard, "The Exegesis of John 10:30 in the Early Trinitarian Controversies," *New Testament Studies*, 3 (1957), pp.

Still another example: the exegesis of Mark 13:32: "But about that day or hour no one knows, neither the angels in heaven, nor the Son, but only the Father." According to the Arians, Jesus was here confessing his ignorance of the day and the hour (an interpretation widely revived today![16]); he was proclaiming then, in the Arian view, that he does not have fullness of divinity.

Athanasius answered them: "What madness! You accuse of ignorance the all-knowing Word, Creator of heaven and earth, the Son Who knows the Father" (cf. Mt 11:27); now the context of Jesus' words shows that he who knows the antecedents of the day certainly knows the day.[17] The Son is not ignorant as Son, but as Son of man, according to the flesh.[18]

Thus Athanasius reads each passage of Scripture, not in isolation, but considering other passages and under the illumination supplied by his fundamental principle on the purpose of the Scriptures that is to manifest the divinity and the humanity of the Savior.

In his well-known *Letter to Marcellinus* on the reading of the Psalms, Athanasius complements this principle or rather, explains its implications with the observation: "all divine Scripture is the mistress of virtue and of true faith."[19]

Indeed, the Word became man to deify us[20] through the practice of the virtues that refashion our souls as images of the unique Image. Christ has given us the incomparable example of these virtues and the Scriptures relate that example to us. The ascetic finality of the Scriptures may

---

334-349, especially, on Athanasius, pp. 341ff. If the Arian interpretation of John 10:30 was correct, we would also have to say that the angels and the very stars are one with the Father, since they are in harmony with God (*PG* 26, 341).

[16]Thus A. Vögtlé wrote that "the Son does not know as Son," which Arius would gladly have said. See our study on the pre-Paschal *Human Knowledge of Jesus*, (Boston: St. Paul Books and Media, 1980), 29.

[17]Athanasius, *Third Discourse Against the Arians*, 42-50, PG 26, 411-429. Many present-day exegetes who write on Mark 13:32 without knowing the patristic treatment of the subject would be interested in Athanasius.

[18]*Ibid.*, 43, PG 26, 414. We refer the reader to the commentaries of John Henry Newman, *Select Treatises of Saint Athanasius*, The Library of the Fathers, (Oxford 1877), pp. 461 and 464 especially, nn. b and f. We also note that the later doctrine of the Church on Christ's triple human knowledge (acquired or experiential, prophetic-infused, and beatific) can be reconciled with what Athanasius wrote: it is in fact not sense experience or the use of reason that teaches Christ the day and hour of judgment, at that level he knows nothing of these things, but he knows them, even humanly, as prophet and as one who sees the Father. See also my study on this subject referred to in n. 16.

[19]*Letter to Marcellinus*, 14, *PG* 27, 25; cf. Sieben thesis, p. 340.

[20]Athanasius, *passim*, especially *On the Incarnation of the Word*, 9, 1.

be viewed then, in the overall theological perspective of Athanasius, as a logical consequence of its Christocentric content.

Athanasius' commentary on Mark 13:32 constitutes a validation of this ascetic and salvific finality of the Scriptures. The reason for Jesus' response ("the Son knows neither the day nor the hour") is that it is good for us, as human beings, not to know the last day so that we will not be negligent, just as it is not good for us to know the day of our death: the Word has hidden from each individual the end of all things and his own end, for the end of all things and the end of each individual are mutually immanent, and the Word knows the beginning and the end—of each individual as of all things.[21]

One cannot but be impressed with the rarely equaled human and existential depth of this exegesis. Its intuitive insights anticipate, and even already surpass, some of the better commentaries of our time.[22] Especially noteworthy is the sharpness of mind which Athanasius brings to the task of understanding and of expounding the intentions underlying the sayings of Christ and the Apostles, i.e., what we today call the "literal sense." We shall see in a moment how his typological exegesis builds on and develops this literal exegesis.

B. Against Judaism, Athanasius Interprets the Old Testament Typologically

Here again, the Alexandrian bishop takes his inspiration from the same fundamental principles concerning the purpose and character of the Scriptures. It is especially in his *Festal Letters*, where his intention is to bring out the elements that distinguish and specify the Christian Pasch as compared with the Jewish Pasch, that Athanasius offers reflections of a typological character. We will quote from two of the *Festal Letters*, the sixth letter of 334, and the fourteenth letter, written in 342.

In these *Festal Letters*, Athanasius is frequently concerned with warning his faithful against celebrating the Pasch in the company of heretics, of schismatics, and above all of Jews. The temptation was not imaginary. The bishop has to continually re-affirm that the figures have fulfilled their role, reached their term: the true Lamb has been immolated once

---

[21] Athanasius, *Third Discourse Against the Arians*, 49, PG 26, 28B.

[22] Concerning Jesus' eschatological discourse, of which Mark 13:32 is a part, many contemporary exegetes say that he was speaking both of the destruction of Jerusalem and the end of the world simultaneously, and of the former as symbol of the latter. Does not Athanasius, in the text referred to in the preceding note, suggest that the end of each person is symbolized by the ruin of Jerusalem?

and for all. Athanasius gives special emphasis to the fact that "it was not the death of Isaac that was to deliver the world, but the death of our Savior" Jesus, and his alone.[23]

Quoting John 8:56 and Hebrews 11:17 (two texts relative both to Isaac and to Jesus), Athanasius recalls that it was through the expectation and the vision of Christ, not through legal observances, that Abraham experienced the festive joy. Then Athanasius adds: "When Abraham offered his son [Isaac], he was worshipping the Son of God; when he was prevented from immolating Isaac, it was Christ that he saw in that ram offered as a substitute in immolation to God."

What is the sense of this worship of the Son of God? Is it to the Word, inquires Jean Gribomont, that Isaac is offered? He answers: "To judge from parallel passages where this theme is treated [Mellitus, Clement, and numerous Fathers], the distinction between the unbloody offering of Isaac and the immolation of the animal should suggest, more or less clearly, the distinction in Jesus between his immortal divinity and his crucified flesh."[24] This answer appears entirely correct and it brings us back indirectly to the fundamental principle of Athanasius referred to above: "The distinctive mark and the purpose of Holy Scripture is its twofold declaration concerning the Savior: being God from all eternity, he took flesh from Mary and became man." It is worthy of note that Athanasius, in contrast to so many other interpreters of Gn 22:2-18, sees in Isaac not only the type of Christ the immolated Lamb, but also the type of the Son of God. Clearly, it is his exegetical method that leads him to this conclusion.

---

[23]We know that there was, for a number of centuries, a polemic between Jews and Christians over the role of Isaac in salvation history: cf. R. L. Wilken, "Melito and the Sacrifice of Isaac," *Theological Studies*, 37 (1976), pp. 53-69; "Isaac (Patriarche)," *DSAM*, referred to in more detail later; I. Speyart, "The Iconography of the Sacrifice of Isaac," *Vig. Christ.*, 15 (1961), pp. 214-255; Le Déaut, *La Nuit Paschale*, An. Biblica 22, (Rome, 1963), pp. 198-207; F. M. Braun, *Le Mystère de Jésus-Christ*, vol. III, 1, *Jean le Théologien*, (Paris, 1966), pp. 157ff., especially p. 160 (John 3:16 wished to make allowance for the existing rabbinical tradition concerning the voluntary sacrifice of Isaac); B. de Margerie, "Sens individuel et collectif des Chants du Serviteur," *Esprit et Vie*, 86 (1976), pp. 107-109; L. Deiss, *La Cène du Seigneur*, (Paris, 1975), pp. 64-66.

We also note the works of H. J. Shoeps, "The Sacrifice of Isaac in Paul's Theology," *JBL* 65 (1946), pp. 385-392; R. J. Daly, "Soteriological Significance of the Sacrifice of Isaac," *Catholic Biblical Quarterly*, 39 (1977), pp. 45-75; P. R. Davies and B. D. Chilton, "The Akedah: A Revised Tradition History," *Catholic Biblical Quarterly*, 40 (1978), pp. 514-546 (a detailed response to the preceding study).

[24]Jean Gribomont, "Isaac le Patriarche," *DSAM* VII, 2 (1971), col. 1997.

We return, after this explanatory digression, to his *Sixth Festal Letter*. The lines that follow are directed explicitly against a Jewish theology, that of the Targums, according to which Isaac, through his voluntary self-offering, merited the redemption:

> Abraham was really put to the test. However, the one who was sacrificed was not Isaac, but he who was foretold in Isaiah 53.

> Abraham was commanded not to lay his hand on the child, lest the Jews, on the pretext of the immolation of Isaac, distort the messianic prophecies, particularly those of Psalm 39:7 ("You wanted neither sacrifice nor oblation, you prepared for me a body..."), by denying them their application to our Lord. In fact, so far as Abraham's son is concerned, the sacrifice did not consist in an offering of Isaac, but was that of Abraham himself who was put to the test here; and it is not the death of Isaac that will deliver the world but the death of our Savior alone.

This response as a whole[25] lacks neither depth nor grandeur. For Athanasius, Abraham offers the Lamb that is to come, in place of Isaac, to the eternal Word. This does not yet take us as far as the Augustinian vision (which is really Paul's), according to which both the sacrifice of Abraham and that of Isaac were integrated, according to the eternal divine plan, in the unique and total sacrifice of Christ and of his Church.... In the framework of such an all-encompassing perspective, no Christian could really deny a co-redemptive value to the sacrifice of Isaac as integrally related to the sacrifice of the one redeemer, Jesus of Nazareth. It was perhaps the polemical climate of the time that did not yet favor the presentation of such a synthetic view. Would not such a synthesis, however, be perfectly compatible with all of Athanasius' principles? In any case, the answer given by Athanasius, within the context of a commentary on Psalm 39:7, brings out the spontaneous character of Jesus' sacrifice, of which Isaac is a representative type. In spite of Athanasius' strong insistence on the divinity of the Savior and in spite of his weak theological understanding of the human soul of Christ,[26] his reflection on the sacrifice of the cross leads him to stress the human self-offering of Jesus. At least to this extent then he remains faithful to the second part of his fundamental principle: "The distinctive mark of

---

[25]*Ibid.* The original Greek text is lost; there is a Latin translation of Athanasius' text in *PG* 26, 1387. The personal commentary, following Athanasius' extract in the current text, develops a deeper view in our work, *Christ for the World*, (Chicago: Franciscan Herald Press, 1975), ch. XI.

[26]Cf. A. Grillmeier, *Christ in Christian Tradition*, (Oxford, 1975), pp. 308-328.

Holy Scripture and its purpose consist in the teaching on the Savior who is God and Son become man."

Already in Paul (cf. Rom 5 concerning the two Adams), typological exegesis has the character of an antithesis, through which the superiority of the antitype, Christ, is exalted over the Old Testament type.[27] Athanasius is pursuing the same goal when he emphasizes the transcendence of Jesus, the new Isaac, the true Lamb of God, both in relation to Isaac and to the ram that replaces him.

It is again this type of exegesis, typology by antithesis, that comes to the fore in the *Festal Letters* XIV and XLIV.

In the first, written in 342, Athanasius sees in the summons of Christ: "Let anyone who is thirsty come to me, and let the one who believes in me drink" (Jn 7:37), words pronounced "on the last day of the festival," an allusion by Jesus to the fact that he is fulfilling, at the end of time, the Mosaic law concerning the eating of the paschal lamb (cf. Ex 12:2-3): "The prophet Moses said: 'The LORD your God will raise up for you a prophet like me from among your own people; you shall heed such a prophet' [Dt 18:15]." In those times, Athanasius observes,

the prophet and the lawmakers read the Scriptures but avoided drawing attention to themselves, taking care rather to refer what they read to others.... The Lord, however, did not refer what he said to another, but applied it to himself: "If anyone is thirsty, let him come to me": not to another, but to me, he said: "let him drink of me, not of others": meaning: not of Moses! For the Well-spring of life took on our thirst to invite us to the feast which he himself is: "If anyone is thirsty, let him come to me and let him drink." And if after having crossed the Red Sea, we are oppressed by heat, if we come upon some bitter water, it is here that the Lord makes his presence felt, fills us with his sweetness, from his life-giving spring, and says to us: "If anyone is thirsty, let him come to me and drink."[28]

Festal Letter XLIV states the idea with even greater clarity; from reflection on the one from whom we are to drink (not Moses, but Jesus) the letter moves on to describe the one who constitutes the drink itself, the spirit given by Jesus. The beautiful text of Athanasius reads as follows:

[27]We are using the word "antitype" in the sense in which it is used in 1 Pt 3:21, where the word signifies the reality prefigured by the type.

[28]Athanasius, *Festal Letter* XIV, 3-5, *PG* 26, 1420-1422. We have modified the order of the saint's thoughts. Sieben, thesis, p. 300, justifiably calls attention to the importance of this text.

When the servants of the high-priests and the scribes heard Jesus saying: "Let him who is thirsty come to me and drink," they recognized quite clearly that He was not a mere man like themselves, but rather the one who was to provide the saints with water, the one whom the prophet Isaiah had foretold [cf. Is 12:3].[29] He is truly, as it were, the radiance of primeval light and the word of God, the river that flowed from the springs and watered paradise [cf. Gn 2:10] way back then; now, he is for ever the one who imparts the Spirit to every individual and he says: "If anyone is thirsty, let him come to me and drink. He who believes in me, as the Scripture says, rivers of living waters will flow from his heart." These words, concludes Athanasius, cannot be said of a man, but of the living God, who alone truly imparts life and who gives the Holy Spirit.[30]

In the view of Athanasius, ordinary men[31] cannot give the Holy Spirit. In promising the Holy Spirit, Christ reveals that he is God the Savior.

While seeking to discover the spiritual sense of the Johannine text, Athanasius has succeeded remarkably in drawing out the literal sense and its point. A modern exegete is really doing little more than this when he observes:

In this messianic self-revelation shines forth Jesus' sovereign claim, namely, that he is not only the new messianic Moses, not only God's instrument in bringing about eschatological salvation—like the Messiah of the Jewish expectation—but something much more—something which Judaism reserved exclusively to God: he claims, as the new Temple, to be the very well-spring of the eschatological water, with the capacity of fully quenching the thirst for messianic salvation in all who would believe in him: he claims to be the source of the gift of the Spirit, the gift that reveals.[32]

We again note that such an exegesis of John's Gospel, at once literal and spiritual, reveals perfect continuity on the part of the Alexandrian bishop with what Jesus and the beloved disciple had in mind in their way of understanding and expressing the relationship between the new Moses and the Old Covenant, in the context of a polemic with Pharisaic

---

[29]The comparison made here between Is 12:3 and Jn 7:37-39 is taken from Pius XII, *Haurietis Aquas*, (AAS 48, [1956], 309-410), an encyclical whose title alludes to Is 12:3.

[30]*Festal Letter* XLIV, PG 26, 1441-1442. There are other beautiful texts of Athanasius that could support a biblical-patristic renewal of the worship of the heart of Jesus in Sieben's thesis, pp. 321-322.

[31]If it is not, Aquinas would add, in virtue of Christ's instruments. Cf. *Summa Theologiæ*, III.8.1.1; Bertrand de Margerie, *Christ for the World*, p. 458, where this whole problem is discussed in the context of certain statements of contemporary theologians.

[32]S. Sabugal, *Christos*, (Barcelona: Herder, 1973), p. 290.

Judaism. The exegesis of Athanasius is compatible with the text he is expounding even in the matter of polemical style.

We shall now see how this doctrinal exegesis, at once anti-Judaic and anti-Arian, serves as the basis for the last form of exegesis found in Athanasius, namely, monastic exegesis.

C. In Conflict Both With the Arians and With Judaism, Athanasius Develops a Spiritual and Monastic Exegesis

This monastic exegesis is revealed most strikingly in two of Athanasius' writings: the *Life of Anthony the Great* and the *Letter to Marcellinus* on the Psalter.

It is common knowledge that the life of Anthony (*VA*), written by Athanasius around the year 357, shortly after the death of its hero, is really a "monastic rule in the form of a narrative" (Gregory Nazianzen[33]), following as it does the Athenian canons of panegyric and the techniques developed by the rhetoricians, a manifesto in support of a culture, not a profane, but a biblical-ecclesial one.[34]

Before examining it in greater detail, we must emphasize that such an undertaking by Athanasius would be perfectly compatible with his constant striving, against Arian and Jewish opposition, to develop an exegesis that would bring out the twofold aspect—divine and human—of the promised and granted savior. The monastic exegesis retains the emphasis on dogma and typology. As evidence of this, we cite the great apology of Anthony in confrontation with the two Greek philosophers:

> Why, in recalling the cross, do you remain silent concerning the signs and prodigies that show Christ to be not only man, but God? You seem to me to be cheating yourselves. You seem not to have read our Scriptures with sincerity. Read them through and you will observe that the works of Christ give witness to the fact that he is God come for the salvation of men.[35]

Athanasius' purpose in writing the life of Anthony is to reach and ultimately to convert the pagan reader by convincing him that Christ is the Son of God (*VA*, 93). It is this that inspires him to recall the dying admonitions of Anthony: "Have no communion with the Arians, whose impiety is evident to all.... Their presence will cease, it is mortal and will

---

[33]Gregory Nazianzen, *Orat.* 21, 5, on the *Life of Anthony*, see the following note.
[34]Cf. Sieben, thesis, p. 45; Quasten, *Patrology*, vol. III, pp. 39-45, presents a good general introduction to the *Life of Anthony* (henceforth referred to as *VA*, followed by the paragraph number).
[35]*VA* 75.

not last long.... Preserve the tradition of your fathers and above all the pious faith in our Savior Jesus Christ, which you have learned from the Scriptures" (*VA* 89).

We see here that the virtue St. Athanasius wished to inculcate through the fostering of a biblical culture, the virtue whose cultivation is, in his view, the very raison d'être of the Bible, as we pointed out above,[36] is not a flat moralism, but rather an ethical attitude founded on the theological virtue of faith and specifically on faith in the divinity of Christ. Primarily, the Scriptures inculcate a "pious faith," a faith full of piety, full of *eusebeia*.[37] Only after this comes the concern for solitude and contemplation toward which this faith leads. The reading of the Scriptures with sincerity—and this remark, placed on Anthony's lips, is actually an autobiographical insight into the life of Athanasius himself—helps to establish the testimony that Christ refers to his divinity through his works.

It is only against this background of a biblical faith in the divinity of Christ that we can understand the biblical existence attributed by Athanasius to Anthony and proposed by him as a pattern to be followed by monks—a type of existence which will later so powerfully attract the young Augustine of Tagaste during his stay in Milan, contributing decisively to his conversion to Christianity and to the divinity of Jesus.[38] What else could have inspired Anthony to leave all things and to follow Jesus in his poverty? How else could he have recognized the voice of Christ in that of the village priest who but echoed the call of the Palestinian Christ, addressed alike to the rich young man and to Anthony himself: "If you would be perfect, go, sell what you possess and give it to the poor, and you will have treasure in heaven; and come, follow me." (Mt 19:21)? "As though inspired by God with a vivid memory of the saints[39] and as though the Gospel reading had been directed to him," we are told by Athanasius, "Anthony immediately left the church...took the goods he had received from his parents and gave them away to the people of the village, sold his entire personal estate and distributed the proceeds among the poor, except for a small amount that he set aside for his sister" (*VA*, 2).

---

[36]Cf. n. 19 and the commentary given in the present text.

[37]Cf. Javier Ibañez, "Naturaleza de la *Eusebeia* en S. Atanasio," *Scripta Theologica*, 3 (1971), pp. 31-73.

[38]Augustine, *Confessions*, VIII, 6, 14. On Augustine's christology before his conversion, see *Confessions* VII, 19, 25.

[39]It is a question of the Apostles and the first Christians, according to the New Testament use of the word "saints."

The text of Athanasius just quoted is of interest in two respects: not only does it bring out the immediacy[40] of the divine call, but it also points to the way in which the Church mediates this call, a mediation that conditions the call in some way without destroying its immediacy. But how does it do so?

During his earthly life in Palestine and now, in Egypt, at the heart of his Church, it is the same Christ who calls his disciple to perfect poverty. In the second case, however, Christ wills that his call be conditioned by mediation—not only by that of human language, but also by the double mediation of Scripture and of the liturgy. None of these forms of mediation (human language, Scripture, liturgy) will disappear until we arrive at the direct vision of God in heaven. Scripture crystalizes the mediation of the human and multi-faceted language used by the one Divine Word. But Scripture itself is in turn mediated by the liturgy of the Church and it is through this liturgical mediation that the immediate call of the Redeemer reaches the center of awareness of one baptized and brought up in the faith. Anthony recognized the biblical-liturgical call of Christ ("if you wish to be perfect") only because he had been "raised as a Christian by Christian parents...and listening attentively to the reading, he lay up its fruit in his heart" (VA, 1) to the point where "on his way to church according to his custom, he would become absorbed in thought, reflecting as he went on how the apostles left everything to follow Christ and on how, in the Acts of the Apostles, the faithful sold their possessions placing the proceeds at the feet of the apostles to be distributed to those in need (VA, 2).

It is clear then that the biblical culture which Athanasius extols in his life of Anthony is not independent of the Church, rather, it is above all an ecclesial and liturgical reading that is fostered. He is urging those living the solitary life to read the Bible with the Church. Without the Church and without the event par excellence of its most intense existence, namely, the celebration of the Eucharist, Scripture would not in fact have reached[41] Anthony, and he would never have heard the call of the Redeemer. This can hardly cause surprise when we remember that the New Testament is itself posterior to the Church.

---

[40]A point stressed by Sieben, thesis, p. 55.

[41]Cf. two texts of Vatican II: Liturgy, § 7, "Christ is speaking when the holy scriptures are read in the Church"; Ecumenism, § 21, "It is in the scriptures that they [our separated brethren] seek God as he speaks to them in Christ." The Latin text says it in a more nuanced manner: "Deum...quasi sibi loquentem in Christo." This tends to underscore the mediation of the Church founded by Christ in the hearing and interpretation of the word of God, as is shown in the course of the text.

If then the ecclesial reading of Scripture is the origin of the call to the monastic life, it will come as no surprise that such a reading continues to serve as a beacon and a guide to the monk as he journeys toward the Kingdom.

Scripture purifies the monk. As his Lord once did in the desert, he struggles against the temptations of the demon with the help of scriptural quotations and he thus sees Satan fall from the heavens like a lightning bolt (cf. Lk 10:18), that is he sees the temptations cease (*VA*, 40). The self-exorcism by which the ascetic biblically repels the demonic temptations is, in the view of Athanasius, even more important than therapeutic exorcism.[42]

After Elijah and Paul, but before Augustine and Monica,[43] Anthony and Athanasius do not look to the past in the tension of their continual movement toward the kingdom; rather, they strive each day to advance along the way, ever remembering the words of St. Paul: "Forgetting what lies behind and straining forward to what lies ahead, I press on toward the goal for the prize of the heavenly call of God in Christ Jesus (Phil 3:14; *VA*, 7). Thus Scripture causes the monk to progress, especially by helping him to become convinced of the necessity of mastery over his flesh (cf. 1 Cor 9:27; 2 Cor 12:10, both texts quoted in *VA*, 7). The process by which virtues are acquired included, as an essential gesture, the verbal usage of the Scriptures.[44]

Finally, in the fourth stage[45] of his life of Anthony, Athanasius sets forth with biblical coloring the perfection to which his hero arrives. Like the prophets of the Old Testament, like John the Baptist, Moses, and like Jesus himself, Anthony lives alone in the desert, but alone with God. He reproduces in his life the graces characteristic of Adam in his innocence, of the patriarchs and the prophets as well as of the apostles and martyrs of the New Testament. Wiser and more powerful than the great men of the world, he wins their reverence, and in this way he plays the role of the prophets who often lived in deserts but who, on occasion, were clothed by God with wisdom and strength for directing the powerful of this world (*VA*, 50-52, 66-75, 81-85).

---

[42]Sieben, thesis, p. 57, n. 69. On this point, see below, nn. 81, 82.

[43]Cf. Augustine, *Confessions*, IX, 10, 23. It is possible that the life of Anthony drew Augustine's attention to the spiritual value of this Pauline verse.

[44]Sieben, thesis, p. 69.

[45]*VA* 49-88; cf. Dom E. Bettencourt, "L'idéal religieux de saint Antoine et son actualité," *Studia Anselmiana*, 38 (1956), p. 56; Sieben thesis, pp. 62-63. For Steidle, the image of Moses, though not named, is underlined.

Athanasius shows then, in his *Life of Anthony*, how Scripture purifies and fortifies the monk until he has reached perfection. Although it is no longer necessary to him when he has arrived at this point, it continues to describe and to illuminate the state in which he finds himself. Athanasius would certainly never have contradicted what his disciple Augustine was to write on this matter and what he himself had been able to observe in his friends, the monks of the desert:

> For one who stands firmly on faith, hope, and charity and guards them with steadfast fervor, Scripture is needed only for instructing others. This is why many, thanks to these three virtues, live without holy books, even in solitude.... Possessing a perfect good, they do not seek a partial good. Perfect, of course, insofar as one may possess such a good in this life. For, compared to the future life, even the life of a just and holy man cannot be perfect.[46]

In summary, Scripture seems to be viewed as that which nourishes the faith of the solitaries by leading them to perfect charity toward God and toward men. Even when it is no longer useful for the exercise of charity toward God, Scripture never loses its usefulness for the exercising of charity toward men. This is undoubtedly what Athanasius wishes to express symbolically when he shows us his hero leaving the desert on two occasions to return to Alexandria, first of all, to seek martyrdom there (in vain) and then to refute the Arians, which is another way of carrying on his struggle against the demons, their teachers.[47] We see here the two limits of the solitary life—which reminds us to what extent, for Athanasius, the practice of the moral virtues and of ascesis is subordinated to that of the theological virtues and, consequently, how completely the moralizing function of the Scripture is controlled by the idea of our conformity to Christ, God and man, whom it is their purpose (*skopos*) to reveal. It was in him, through him and for him that Scripture so haunted the memory of ascetics and monks that it could be said to have become their memory.[48]

---

[46]Augustine, *De Doctrina Christiana*, I, 34, 43—Scripture is a partial good relative to the total good of charity. Cf. 1 Cor 13:2, 9-12.

[47]Cf. Bettencourt, p. 45. Cf. *VA*, 82, 89. We would like to underscore the absence of all historical testimony to the existence of religious life in the Arian churches. Everything indicates that the faith in Christ's divinity conditions, in different ways, the possibility of following the evangelical counsels and especially of following them in a collective and organized way. The silence of M. Meslin (*Les Ariens d'Occident*, pp. 335-430, [Paris, 1967]) on this point is doubtless significant: he has nothing to say concerning any monastic life in the Arian churches, while he speaks at length of their liturgical life.

[48]Cf. *VA*, 2; Sieben thesis, p. 63.

To sum up, Athanasius seems[49] to make his own the words he places on Anthony's lips, the very first words that the latter pronounces before the crowd that gathered to greet him, at the end of a twenty years' solitude: "The Scriptures suffice for our instruction" (*VA*, 16).

In his *Letter to Marcellinus*,[50] the bishop of Alexandria seems again to reduce "what suffices for our instruction" to the reading of the Psalter.

Athanasius is here summing up for ascetics and for virgins, indeed for all Christians, the principles that should guide them in their study of Scripture. For Athanasius, the Psalter represents the ideal synthesis, both objective and subjective, of spiritual and Christian prayer and life.

Athanasius begins by describing his "conversation with an old man who was a student of the Psalms." It is to this old man, who remains anonymous, that he attributes the essence of the instruction delivered to Marcellinus.

On the one hand, the Psalms recall and recapitulate the teaching contained in the Pentateuch concerning the origin of the world, the exodus from Egypt, the gift of the Law, and in the historical books on the Kings, the deliverance from captivity and the return of the people, the reconstruction of the temple and of the city, as also the teaching of the prophets regarding the coming of the Savior, whose passion, resurrection, and ascension they describe.[51]

On the other hand, "the book of Psalms has a certain grace of its own and demands special attention. Beyond what it has in common with the others, it is peculiarly endowed with the merit of embracing all the movements of the soul." Athanasius defines the therapeutic function of the Psalms as follows:

> In the other books, we only hear the law as it is laid down about what we should or should not do; we listen to the prophecies only to learn of the fact of the Savior's coming; and the stories we are told merely inform us regarding the lives of the King and of holy men.

---

[49]Perhaps he means that the Scriptures suffice for our instruction in the faith, without denying the usefulness of human instruction. Everything makes us believe that Athanasius had received a careful Greek formation. He presents Anthony, his hero, as unlettered (*VA*, 73), which at least means he did not know Greek (as Bardy writes, *Catholicisme*, vol. I, [1948], 665).

[50]Of this letter, we have only an incomplete French translation: F. Cavallera, *Saint Athanase*, Textes et Etudes, (Paris, 1908), pp. 298-317. We use the letter here and refer to it with indication of the paragraph.

[51]Athanasius, *Letter to Marcellinus*, 2, 7 and 8; *PG* 27, 11 and 15-18.

But in the book of Psalms, besides learning these things, the hearer may recognize and learn the movement of his own soul; hence this book may supply him with a model of expression for the things he experiences or the sufferings that weigh him down. Thus the reader learns not only how to escape what hurts by listening but how to heal it by appropriate words and actions.[52]

While the other books, Athanasius continues, give certain precepts (do penance, bear tribulations, live in gratitude, accept persecutions for the sake of justice), the Psalms teach us how to carry out these precepts and "what we should say, how we are to converse with God, what words render an acceptable homage."[53]

In other words, the Psalms teach us simultaneously how to pray to obtain the grace necessary for fulfilling the divine law and, thus, to observe it.[54]

Athanasius insists on this and demonstrates at length how the Psalms help us to appropriate, through and in prayer, the values inculcated in the historical and prophetical books:

In the case of the other books, the reader refers what the saints say or what they write about to the subject of the book. The hearer perceives himself as distinct from those involved in the narrative, so that the actions recorded arouse only admiration or the zealous desire to imitate....To one who reads these books, evidently the words they contain are to be read not as his own, but as belonging to the saints or as referring to the objects of which they speak. With the reading of the Psalms, however, a wonderful thing happens: except for what refers to the Savior and the prophecies concerning the nations, they become personal expression of the reader. Each individual sings them as if they were written for himself. One does not keep a respectful distance here as in the case of words uttered by the patriarchs or Moses or the other prophets. No. One singing the Psalms dares to use the words as though they were his own, as though they were written to describe his situation.[55]

One could summarize by saying that, in Athanasius' view, it is as if God intentionally gave us the Psalter so that the spiritual man, the disciple of Christ, might be able—under the New Covenant, and in the light of the suffering and risen Christ—to relive not only all the typically human situations, but also, through a process of appropriation, the entire

---

[52]*Ibid.*, 10; *PG* 27, 20-22; cf. Sieben, thesis, pp. 82-86.

[53]*Ibid.*, 10; *PG* 27, 21; Cavallera, p. 306.

[54]Which stands out particularly in Ps 118. This is the theme that Athanasius develops so magnificently in *De Spiritu et Littera*.

[55]Athanasius, *Letter to Marcellinus*, 11; *PG* 27, 22.

history of the saints of the Old Covenant in their varied responses to the divine offer. The point may be demonstrated by the following citations from the letter to Marcellinus:

> The Psalms as I view them are like a mirror in which the reader can see himself and the movements of his soul; he can recite these prayers as though this were actually so. Even the hearer receives the song of praise as if it concerned himself. Either he will come to repent, having been convicted by conscience and filled with confusion, or, by hearing words of hope in God and of the assistance accorded to those who believe, he will rejoice as though this grace were now being granted to him and he will begin to thank God.... The Psalms apply whether one has kept or transgressed the commandments.[56]

We could follow Sieben in observing that Athanasius is here describing a kind of "Psalmotherapy"; and he would readily admit that this psalmotherapy is at once essentially spiritual or pneumatic, psychological by accident, and indirectly, even somatic. The "Psalmotherapy" practiced by monks is in effect "pneumatopsychosomatic."[57]

There is more. For Athanasius, the Psalms are a gift and grace of Christ. He intended to give us a portrayal of his life in advance and to prepare us for meeting him:

> Those among the Greeks who make the laws can promulgate them verbally. The Lord, however, as true Lord of the universe who cares for his handiwork, not only lays down the law, but also gives himself as a model so that those who are willing may know the power of doing. This is why even before his coming into our midst, he was instructing us of these things in the Psalms that were sung so that just as he revealed himself as the earthly and the heavenly man of the types, in the like manner anyone who wished might be able to learn from the Psalms the movements and affections of the soul, finding therein the cure for each movement as well as its proper ordering.[58]

Clearly, for the bishop of Alexandria, the reading of the Psalms makes the Christian conform to Christ. Psalmotherapy is Christocentric to the point of being an integral part of the salvific design of Christ the Redeemer. It is that in the Old Testament that goes beyond the Law by recapitulating it to touch, to reach, to obtain, in prayer, the grace of the New Testament. In this therapy and through it, Christ, who is sung and who sings in the Psalms, heals and saves.

---

[56]*Ibid.*, 12; PG 27, 22.
[57]Sieben, thesis, part II, ch. 6 and 7, pp. 78ff.
[58]Athanasius, *Letter to Marcellinus*, 13; PG 27, 25.

Psalmus, vox Christi—Athanasius anticipates Augustine. In view of this, it is all the more striking[59] when we consider that while the letter to Marcellinus takes verses 16-19 of Psalm 21 as words of Christ crucified, its focus is limited to the physical sufferings of Christ prefigured here, passing over in silence the initial cry of dereliction ("My God, my God, why have you abandoned me?"). In spite of his principle *Psalmus vox Christi*, it is as if Athanasius did not dare to put into Christ's mouth words of the psalms that express interior suffering, even in spite of the example provided by the authors of the New Testament (cf. Ps 41 and Mk 14:34; Ps 68 and Jn 15:25).[60] We have here undoubtedly a product of the great bishop's inadequacy in Christology, his tendency to accord no more than physical existence, deprived of theological significance, to the human soul of Jesus,[61] an unconscious deficiency in that fullness of *eusebeia* and of piety in the faith which he longed for and preached.[62]

Conclusions: Limitations and merits of Athanasius' exegesis, where doctrine and piety (asceticism, mysticism) are inseparable

The limitations to which we have just alluded are not the only ones. Even the ascetic and therapeutic aspect of Athanasius' exegesis—so true, so beautiful, and so impressive—does not yet reach, it seems to us, the depth that Augustine will later reveal when he will see the practice of the two-fold charity as the purpose[63] or *skopos* of all Scripture (just as, conversely, Augustine will not try to link up this double charity with the

---

[59]M. J. Rondeau, "L'Epître à Marcellinus sur les Psaumes," *Vigilae Christianae* 22 (1968), p. 186.

[60]B. Fischer, "Psalmus vox Christi," *Politique et Théologie*, pp. 305ff., especially p. 307.

[61]Cf. n. 26.

[62]We can wonder, in the light of the mystery of the human soul of Jesus, and in light of its theological importance in the mystery of salvation, if Athanasius was right in thinking that nothing was lacking in the faith of Nicea (*Letter to the Antiochenes*, 5; *PG* 26, 800C.); the Councils and professions of faith that have followed do not seem to prove that judgment; the fullness of piety, suggested as desirable by Athanasius (*ibid.*) seemed to them to require an explicit profession of belief in the soul of Jesus. Thus, for example, Constantinople III in 681 (*DS* 554).

[63]Augustine, *De Doctrina Christiana*, I, 35, 39: "The end of all the divine Scriptures is the love for the Being in which we should rejoice and love for the being that can rejoice with us in that love " (Rom 13:10; 1 Tim 1:5). It is noteworthy that Augustine does not seem to have passed from that double love toward God and man to a christological (two natures) concentration whereas John Chrysostom caught sight of this movement in his commentary on Mt 22:37ff.: Jesus wanted to suggested to the Pharisees that they should love him, and love him as the nearest neighbor and, as God, more than any neighbor. Cf. *PG* 58, 663.

two natures of the Savior, nor will he define the purpose of Scripture by reference to the two states of Christ).

Likewise, Athanasius has not yet penetrated as profoundly as Chrysostom will into the mystery of the Incarnation as a mystery of precise condescension (with a precision at once human and divine, as we shall see) although he has brought out magnificently the condescension of the Word both in creation and in his Incarnation.[64]

What is more—and this limitation is by no means distinctive of the bishop of Alexandria since it is common to all the Fathers except, implicitly at least, Augustine[65]—Athanasius practiced a *typology of contrast* through which he brought out, in complete fidelity to the New Testament, the transcendence of Christ with respect to his Old Testament types, without, however, developing this into a *typology of integration* that would show how the sacrifice of the total Christ includes in some way all those of his types in the Old Testament. Nevertheless, we must acknowledge with Sieben the merits of Athanasius' typology. Perceiving in the typology a relation between a *fact* of the New Testament and the *institution* of the Old, the author of the *Festal Letters* notes well that Christ is the cause of the type of the Old Testament—not the reverse—and that a typology so conceived establishes the possibility of explaining the Old Testament from the perspective of New Testament.[66]

Having admitted the limitations of Athanasius' exegesis—in large measure those proper to his times—we may be more at ease as we go on to exalt its merit and its enduring value.

Athanasius recognized that the authors of Scriptures, and above all God by means of them, intended to give us a doctrine, epitomized in the Messiah, the Incarnate Word, and at the same time to rouse us to the practice of those virtues which the possession of the truth in faith conditions and causes to bloom, effecting a kind of extension by imitation of that same Incarnate Word.

By constantly re-focusing our attention on the two states and the two natures of Christ as Savior, the Christological concentration in Athanasian exegesis, far from relegating the ethical goal of the Scriptures to a secondary level, succeeds rather in making that goal more intelligible. As man, our Savior shows us, through the Scriptures, the virtues that lead to

---

[64]Athanasius, *Treatise Against the Pagans*, 47, PG 25, 93C; *On the Incarnation*, 15; PG 25, 121C; cf. Duchatelez, "La condescendence divine et l'histoire du salut," *Nouv. Rev. Theol.*, 95 (1973), pp. 600-601.

[65]Cf. Augustine, *De Civitate Dei*, book X.

[66]Sieben, thesis, pp. 294-298.

salvation. As God made man, he brings about in us its difficult yet easy realization.[67] Because the Scriptures essentially treat of a Christ who is divinely and humanly our Savior, their purpose is to help us to save ourselves through the imitation of his human virtues and of his divine perfections—of which the former are a reflection—and especially of his piety (cf. Is 11:2).

Being both literal and spiritual, the exegesis of Athanasius is that of a Christian, of a bishop who is not only believing, but devout. For the bishop of Alexandria, the exegetical act is an act of piety (going well beyond our modern notion of piety as an adherence—not entirely free of constraint—to the duties and practices of religion), an act which, in the manner of the aged Paul of the pastoral letters, integrates the moral aspect of Roman piety within a larger synthesis where the soteriological and eschatological nuance dominates.[68] Athanasius makes exegesis an act of *eusebeia*, a means of pursuing the acquisition of that *piety* whose exercise constitutes the noble combat of faith and enables one to take hold of eternal life (cf. 1 Tim 6:11-12; 2 Pt 1:6-7).

We are in no way suggesting here that Athanasius worked out in a conscious or complete way the views we have just set forth regarding the exegetical act as an exercise of *eusebeia*, of piety. Indeed, Athanasius seems never to have commented explicitly on the texts of the pastoral epistles concerning piety or *eusebeia*.[69]

All this is true; nevertheless, it does not preclude the extreme importance of this *eusebeia* in the ensemble of Athanasian thought. Indeed, so central was this notion in his writings that it could not but affect his exegetical act, even in an essential or constitutive way.

To justify the validity of this formative influence of *eusebeia* on the work of Athanasius, suffice it to recall[70] the content of this notion as we so frequently meet it in his writings.

---

[67]Difficult for nature because of vices and temptations, but easy with the aid of Christ's grace.

[68]Cf. C. Spicq, *Les Epîtres pastorales*, (Paris, 1969), vol. I, Excursus IV, pp. 482-492: "Piety" in the pastoral letters. See especially pp. 487-488, n. 3.

[69]Cf. the almost complete absence of biblical references to the word *eusebeia* in the *Lexicon Athanasianum* of G. Müller, S.J., (Berlin, 1952). However, it must be noted that in his celebrated *Festal Letter* 39 on the Scriptures, Athanasius writes: "Only in the canonical books [of the Scriptures] is the teaching of piety preached." This text (*PG* 26, 1437 C) therefore implies that all the Scriptures present the doctrine of piety and that they do it to the exclusion of the apocryphal writings.

[70]Ibañez, p. 53.

For Athanasius, piety or *eusebeia* signifies an attitude of respectful religiousness, constant fidelity to the deposit of Revelation, the awareness of progressive penetration of the revealed mystery, the capacity to expound and to formulate that mystery in ever new ways, while at the same time being able to criticize the novelties that arise during history trying to pass themselves off as profound or developed statements of the Gospel kerygma. The proper function of *eusebeia* is to reveal whether a vital continuity exists between these new interpretations of the faith and the apostolic heritage. According to Athanasius, *eusebeia* effects such a discernment by means of a Christian sense (*phronema*); it is a gift of God; it is grace; it is charism.[71]

For Athanasius, piety or *eusebeia* perfects faith and goes beyond it.[72] Scripture itself is its principle.[73] Piety is a participation in that Christian sense which, under the action of the Spirit, lives permanently in the Church.

In short, for Athanasius, Scripture is a gift of the Spirit to Christian communities and to their members, given them so that they might better know and imitate Christ, God and man, for their salvation.

Appendix: The biblical formation and the biblical life of the monks of Egypt

Athanasius was "the most zealous and the most persuasive apostle" of the sacred reading of Scripture in the monastic circles of Egypt.[74] In what sense and in what ways was the monks' life in the desert biblical?

We could answer this question in the following manner: sensitive to the dangers that in fact accompany the use of the divine Scriptures, the monks made of them an instrument in the struggles against the demons, an instrument of correction and of fraternal conversation, of meditation and of prayer.

For the monk, Scripture was a means, not an end. Certain old and experienced monks used to say that possession of a codex of the Bible is harmful if it constitutes an obstacle to the Gospel ideal of self depriva-

---

[71]*Ibid.*, p. 71.

[72]*Ibid.*, p. 47; cf. Athanasius, *De Synodis*, 3; PG 26, 684D.

[73]Cf. n. 69. Athanasius' emphasis on *eusebeia* is more impressive since the term is unknown in Justin and the Apostolic Fathers (Spicq, *op. cit.*, p. 486).

[74]P. Rech, *La doctrine ascétique des premières maitres ègyptiens du IVᵉ siècle*, (Paris, 1931), p. 164. We have used the author's general presentation of the theme of reading and study of Scripture (*ibid.*, pp. 157-167) for the composition of part of this Appendix.

tion; that one should not take more trouble to recopy the Bible than to put it into practice.

The monks deplored the tendency to boast of knowing the meaning of a difficult term. An old monk, Ammon of Rhaiton, avowed to Sisoes: "When I read holy Scripture, my mind is eager to search for something to inquire about." Whence the reaction of Abba Pambo: "If one asked me to explain a word of Scripture, I would say that I did not know; if one were to insist, I would not respond."

We should note that such precautions were never aimed at the Bible as such, but at certain abusive ways of employing Scripture that are ultimately at odds with its message.[75] Respect and fidelity require of the monk that he not profane the Word of God by treating it as an object for discussion or by supposing that intellectual reflection will suffice to bring out its deepest meaning.[76]

What we have just said concerns the semi-anachoritic monks, whose 948 apophthegms contain less than 150 scriptural references.

The situation appears different in the case of the cenobitic communities of Saint Pachomius, whose letters seem to consist entirely of paraphrases of Scripture or of "chains" of citations taken from the sacred texts.

His rule prescribes the study of Scripture for all the monks, including the illiterate. All must learn by heart at least the New Testament and the Psalter; one must be able when necessary to recite Scripture, and the latter is in fact the only subject of conversation allowed by the Rule.

Scripture is even employed as a means of fraternal correction. To monks who implored Saint Theodore to point out to them their faults the saint would respond by indicating what passage of Scripture addressed their particular state.[77]

For Evagrius of Pontus (who lived as a monk in the deserts of Egypt from 382 to 399), the Bible even became a weapon for fighting against the demon. His originality consists in his having collected "the words that we would wish to use in driving back our foes, the cruel demons, but which we do not find on the field at the hour of combat, since they

---

[75]Cf. 2 Pt 3:16: "There are some things in them [the letters of Paul] hard to understand, which the ignorant and unstable twist to their own destruction, as they do the other scriptures."

[76]Cf. J.-C. Guy, "Ecriture sainte et vie spirituelle," *DSAM* IV, 1 (1960), col. 163-166. We took our inspiration here from this work.

[77]Rech, pp. 165-166, especially several passages of the Rule of Saint Pachomius.

are scattered throughout the Scriptures and accessible only with difficulty."[78]

These words of Evagrius quite well express the goal he was aiming at when he wrote his *Antirrheticos* whose eight sections, corresponding to the eight capital vices that must be combated, are as many webs of scriptural citations adapted to the thousand subtle forms that temptation can take. The work as a whole amounts to a ritual of exorcisms, an arsenal from which every individual can draw at will.[79] We see here the implementation of a principle referred to by Athanasius in his *Letter to Marcellinus*: "In the words of Scripture we find the Lord whose presence the demons cannot abide."[80] The Bible is a sacramental.

However, Evagrius recognized the dangers of this antirrhesis or "contradiction of the demon": "the Evil One will not be short-changed…when we enter into conversation with the enemy, we are defrauded of our conversation with God."[81] In this connection, Barsanuphius (born in Egypt at the end of the fifth century) adds: "There is no other way to overcome demons than to invoke the name of God. For God said: 'Invoke me in the day of your affliction, and I will deliver you.' The battle with demons is not for everyone to wage, but only for those who are strong according to God; for such the demons obey."[82]

To sum up we would say that under the influence of Anthony, Pachomius, and Athanasius, the monks of the Egyptian deserts perfected the various elements that enter into the use of the Bible in the struggle against the vices-the acquiring of virtues, union with Christ, God and man, in faith, hope and charity.[83] To all succeeding generations, to all the schools of spirituality, to us also if we are willing, the monks of Egypt bequeath the treasure of a biblical return to paradise lost. Under their influence, at least indirectly, the saints will learn the Scriptures by heart.

---

[78]J. Kirchmeyer, "Ecriture sainte et vie spirituelle," *DSAM* IV, 1 (1960), col. 165-166, referring to Evagrius, *Antirhétique*, ed. Frankenberg, (Berlin, 1912), pp. 472-473.

[79]Kirchmeyer, col. 165.

[80]Athanasius, *Letter to Marcellinus*, 33; *PG* 27, 45A.

[81]Cf. J. Muyldermans, "A travers la tradition manuscrite d'Evagre le Pontique," (unpublished thesis, Louvain, 1943), p. 89, n. 32; however, it is not certain that the text quoted is really of Evagrius.

[82]Barsanuphius, referred to by Kirchmeyer, col. 166.

[83]See also Le Leloir, "La Bible et les Pères du désert," *La Bible et les Pères*, (Paris, 1971), pp. 113-134.

Chapter VI
The Biblical Poetry of Saint Ephraem, Syrian Exegete (300-373)

There has been a great revival of interest in the work and in the biblical commentaries of St. Ephraem in recent years, as is evidenced by a whole series of studies.[1] A number of reasons account for this renewal: the poetic charism of the Syrian doctor pervades a large part of his biblical commentaries; Ephraem represents a non-Greek exegesis, close to the Semitic soil of the Old Testament, much more like a Judeo-Christian and oriental approach to the Scriptures than is that of many of the other Fathers; further, it is quite possible that he stands, at least in part, at the very origin of the school of Antioch and of its *theoria* as of its unique way of reading the Old Testament.

Drawing upon the recent works we just mentioned we will first take a brief look at several examples of his exegesis of the Old and the New Testaments, emphasizing the importance Ephraem gave to the relationship between Moses and Jesus. Then we will attempt to define the principles that guide the exegesis of the Syrian doctor, the Bonaventure of the East.

Let us further point out that the study of Ephraem's exegesis is no easy undertaking, for many of his writings have yet to be published in

---

[1]Especially L. Leloir, *Doctrines et méthodes de saint Ephrem*, CSCO 220, subs. 18, (1960); C. Bravo, *Notas introductorias a la noematica de S. Efrem*, (Rome, 1956); S. Hidal, *Interpretatio Syriaca*, (Lund, 1974); R. Murray, *Symbols of Church and Kingdom*, (Cambridge, 1975).

critical editions. This situation has, however, been improving in recent years.[2]

A. Some Examples of Saint Ephraem's Exegesis

The poetic flights of Saint Ephraem are more impressive because his was primarily and consistently a literal exegesis. His procedure was to explain the sacred text verse by verse, objectively, taking existing controversies into account, noting the opinions of other exegetes, anticipating objections, and frequently confronting them with his own opinion.[3]

Although he wrote commentaries on many books of Scripture, Ephraem concentrated much of his attention on the first chapters of Genesis, examining them both in themselves and in the light of the New Testament.

For example, here is how Ephraem understands Gn 2:21-23 and the account of Eve's creation from a rib of Adam:

> Man, wide awake, surrounded by splendor and until then not knowing sleep, fell naked to the earth and slept. And during that sleep, Adam probably received in a dream a vision of what was happening within him. His rib was removed in the wink of an eye and it was replaced immediately by flesh. The removed rib was arranged in all form and beauty, and God conducted it to Adam and presented it to him. Two had been fashioned out of one, man and woman.... Adam said: this at last is *bone of my bones and flesh of my flesh*. She will be called woman because she was taken out of man. "At last" means that she who came after the animals was not made like unto them. They come from the earth, while "this at last is bone of my bones and flesh of my flesh." Certainly either this was said prophetically, or else Adam saw and knew it by a vision in his sleep, as we said above. Since all the animals were given generic names on that same day, Adam did not call Eve by a personal name, but called her woman, a name given to the whole genus.[4]

There are a number of original insights in this interpretation. Before sin, man is, like the angels, a wide awake being who does not sleep;

---

[2]Cf. the fine-tuning of D. Hemmerdinger-Iliadou and J. Kirchmeyer on Ephraem's works in the *DSAM*, IV, 1, (1960), col. 800-822.

[3]Cf. R. Leconte, "Saint Jean Chrysostome, exégète syrien," (unpublished thesis, Institute Catholique de Paris, 1942), pp. 70-72. See pp. 290-301 for a more detailed excursus.

[4]*Sancti Ephrem Syri in Genesim et in Exodum Commentarii*, Latin trans. by R. M. Tonneau, O.C.S.O., vol. 153, Scriptores Syri, vol. 72, (Louvain, 1955), p. 24. It is generally known that the Syrians referred to the angels as "watchers."

Adam's sleep does not prevent him from experiencing a vision of God's creation of Eve from his side.[5]

A little earlier, Ephraem had seen in Gn 2:19 an indication of the wisdom given (by God) to Adam.[6]

Ephraem then sees Adam as a being *wide awake*, a contemplative, a prophet, a visionary, master of the creation. Such is the meaning of these verses of Genesis, according to Ephraem. Would it be their literal sense? We would scrupulously avoid this expression, because the literal sense implies a distinction between the sense that the human author of Genesis had in mind and that which God wished to communicate to his reader, and we cannot be sure, at least here, that the Syrian doctor had this distinction in mind.[7] Clearly for Ephraem, read today, the sense of the text is already singularly spiritual. We could put it this way: this literal exegesis, which follows each verse, makes us take flight and transports us already into the omniscience of an eternal divinity who makes the first man a sharer in his perfections.

Let us take a look at Ephraem's poetic transposition of the literal exegesis we have just brought out. We find it in his *Twelfth Hymn on Paradise*, in the following two stanzas:

> Two trees He placed
> In Paradise,
> The Tree of Life
> And the Tree of Knowledge,
> This pair of fountains
> Blessed with every good.
> By this
> Glorious pair,
> Can man become
> A likeness of God:
>
> In immortal life
> In infallible Knowledge
> The knowledge of the visible
> which He had given to him

---

[5] The reader will note the lack of force in this reasoning: the name of the woman does not designate, as the names of the animals do, a distinct species.

[6] *Sancti Ephrem Syri in Genesim et in Exodum Commentarii*, p. 23.

[7] Cf. X. Ducros, "Le dogme de l'inspiration chez saint Ephrem d'après ses commentaires de l'Ancien Testament," *Mélanges Cavallera*, (Toulouse, 1948), pp. 163-179, especially pp. 165-167.

> And which alone allows him
> To name Eve and
> [all] the beasts,
> God did not use this
> When he revealed to him the mysteries.
> And the Tree of Knowledge,
> This pair of fountains.[8]

If we compare the concluding verse here with the explanation offered above by Ephraem, we will note that the Syrian exegete is hinting at the limitations of the first Adam's infallible knowledge. Though God had given such knowledge of the animal species and even of his own role in the creation of Eve to this wide awake being, nevertheless, Ephraem suggests, the latter remained ignorant of the mysteries, i.e., of Christ and his Church, even though he and Eve prefigured them. His is a knowledge of the visible rather than the invisible.

Ephraem is not content with this poetic transposition. He goes on from here to make a mystical transposition of the account of the first Eve's creation. For him, as for the other Fathers, Eve prefigures both Mary and the Church, but in different ways.[9]

First, "Eve born of Adam without carnal encounter" suggests "Joseph and Mary, his virgin spouse." To be noted here is the originality of Ephraem's typological application, with Adam prefiguring Joseph. Ephraem goes on: "The conception of the virgin teaches us that He Who, without carnal link, gave birth to Adam by bringing him out of the virgin earth, has also formed the second Adam in the womb of the virgin without any carnal link. The first Adam returned into his mother's womb; through this second Adam, who did not return there, he who had been buried in his mother's womb (i.e., buried in Adam) was taken out again."[10]

This first typological approach is situated essentially in the line of the Incarnation. A second approach accentuates above all the Redemption:

> Thanks to the side pierced through by a lance, I have entered into the paradise guarded by the lance. We enter by the pierced side, for it is because of the rib that was taken from man that we have been stripped of the promises. A fire of concupiscence burned in Adam because of his rib. This is why the side of the

---

[8]Ephraem, *Hymns on Paradise*, SC 137, (Paris, 1968), XII, 15-16, pp. 161-162.

[9]Cf. R. Murray (n. 1), p. 144; by the same author, "Mary, the Second Eve, in the Early Syriac Fathers," *Eastern Churches Review*, 3 (1971), pp. 372-384.

[10]Ephraem, *Diatessaron*, SC 121, (Paris, 1966), p. 66: II, 2 (Syr. Arm.).

second Adam was pierced, and out of it flowed a stream that was destined to extinguish the fire burning in the first Adam.[11]

In other words, the second Adam gave to Ephraem the knowledge he had refused to the first, namely, the knowledge of the invisible mysteries visibly prefigured in the first chapters of Genesis, which this Doctor of the Syrians reads eschatologically, in the light of the New Testament.[12]

This typological polyvalence is somewhat ambiguous. The same Eve who prefigures Mary and the Church in a first typological approach, prefigures the seduction of sin in another. If there is no strict contradiction here, there is also no great typological rigor.

Ephraem's exegetical universe is very precise and consistent in some instances, but rather lyrical, vague and imprecise in others. It does not seem to have been his principal concern to read and explain what the human author or even what the divine author meant or did not mean, but rather what the inspired text suggests to the believing reader whose concern is to read it within the analogy of the Church's faith. To be sure, Ephraem is not the only one of the Fathers to leave us with this impression. But it is more accentuated in his case, and we cannot deny that the interpretations he offers and especially the comparisons he makes generally give us some insight into the sense that the divine author wished to communicate to us.

We move now to an example[13] of Ephraem's exegesis of the New Testament—his commentary on the rich young man (Mt 19; Mk 10), who, moreover, in the Syrian doctor's view, is not a young man, but just a man. His interpretation revolves essentially around two themes: the old law and the new law, and the meaning of the expression "God alone is good." Let us review them briefly. Saint Ephraem combines the two themes harmoniously.

For Ephraem, the rich man "had enriched himself according to the blessings of the law, and he had full confidence in his earthly opulence that the law had promised him. He came to Our Lord, fully expecting to receive approval for his riches and for his works."

When the rich man came and said: "What do I still lack?" [Mt 19:20], expecting our Lord to speak to him of some details of that law in which, like Paul, he was perfect [Phil 3:6], our Lord told him not what he was hoping to hear him say, but what he did not want to hear.... He restated the truth of the law, but he

---

[11]*Ibid.*, pp. 379-380 (XXI, 10: Syr. Arm.).

[12]Cf. F. Graffin, Introduction, *Hymnes sur le Paradis, SC* 137, (Paris, 1968), p. 17.

[13]Ephraem, *Diatessaron*, ch. XV (Syr. Arm.), pp. 263-271.

added the seal of a solid food: "Go, deposit these earthly riches in heaven and then entrust yourself to them, because they have been reserved for you...." Seeing right away that the man's heart was totally submersed in this earth's goods, the Lord took him by surprise and lifted him up from the dust of this earth to make him run toward heaven: No one is good, except One alone in heaven [Mk 10:18]. Instead of earth, he shows the man heaven. Instead of his fathers, he shows him a single Father. One alone is good, and he is in heaven. Elevate your love from the earth toward the Good that you love.

Saint Ephraem thinks then that the rich man incarnates and symbolizes the justice of the law that is neither willing to open itself to the justice of the Kingdom, nor ready to replace "the milk and the honey of children with the nails and the cross of the perfect." Those who trust in their riches find it difficult to raise themselves toward God in heaven. "They believe that the earth is gain." "If the law blesses you and says: possess the goods of the earth and be rich (Dt 28:1-16), and if you strip us of what we have, and say: you fall short in one thing only, namely, that your fullness falls short of the law."

Having arrived at this point, Ephraem gives us a thoroughly Pauline analysis of the dialogue between the rich man and Christ:

As a man who believed himself to be perfect, the rich man had come for the purpose of praising himself. When he saw that something was lacking to him, he was troubled [Lk 18:23], for he saw his vainglory crumbling. He had attended to his justice so as to take glory from the law and he had received possessions because of his observance of the law.

Because his justice was according to the law...he had placed his hope in his riches, as if they were the recompense for his justice...those who think that their riches are the just retribution of their justice cannot abandon those riches.

This analysis is appealing, but is it accurate?

There is one serious difficulty. At first glance, the rich man had an ardent desire for eternal life, as his question to Jesus at the start of their dialogue seems to indicate: "Master, what good must I do to win eternal life?" (Mt 19:16), with the rebound following, "what do I still lack" (Mt 19:20). He does not appear then to be really satisfied with the "justice of the law." Indeed, the grace of the new Law seems to be pushing him further. The least that one could say is that one entire aspect of the rich young man hardly corresponds to Ephraem's analysis.

Nevertheless, the final attitude of the rich young man, his refusal to renounce his possessions on behalf of the poor, thereby acquiring a treasure in heaven, confirms that Ephraem's analysis corresponds to another, much more decisive dimension of the personality described. More exactly, it helps us better to perceive the inner conflict that was tearing the rich young man from Christ in His poverty. It offers the notable advantage of underlining that the rich man's avarice had deep roots; not only vainglory, which led to his quest for justice according to the Law, but also an attachment to earthly life even at the expense of a real pursuit of eternal life.

In summary, Ephraem unmasks the rich man's unconscious hypocrisy[14] that was already secretly present in his initial questions to Jesus regarding the conditions of attaining eternal life and the things that transcend the old law and condition access to that life.

Ephraem insists too on bringing out the opposition, in the dialogue, between earth (the domain of men) and heaven (the domain of God). At times like this he goes beyond the letter of the Gospel expressions (where we will seek in vain a fusion of the themes of God and heaven), but he remains perfectly faithful to the Spirit of the text, to its deeper meaning, which he extracts in a remarkable way.

It is hardly necessary to dwell on the fact that Ephraem's exegesis keeps the text in its immediate and remote Old Testament context more than the exegesis of the same passage by Clement of Alexandria two centuries earlier (cf. Chap. III, C.).

Another, still subtler, aspect of Ephraem's exegesis in our passage deserves our attention. The Syrian doctor thinks that the rich man regards Jesus as simply a man and an earthly being, like the masters of Israel. The sense of Jesus' response: "There is only one who is good" is to be understood as meaning: "The Son knows only one Good so good that he learned from no one to do good. This epithet by which the flattering rich man honored the Son, the latter employs to honor the Father, not to please him with flattery but rather to witness to him." Ephraem adds later: "If you were aware that I came from above and that I am the son of the Good One, you would be right in calling me Good; but if I am of the earth, as you think, it is wrong." While these thoughts obviously go beyond what Jesus wished to have his interlocutor understand at the time, they are nevertheless in perfect harmony with the mind of Jesus

---

[14]Others prefer to speak of successive and differing sincerities in a freedom whose options follow one another incoherently, but without hypocrisy—it is strange to observe that some modern exegetes such as S. Legasse, *L'appel du riche*, (Paris, 1966), who often refers to Clement of Alexandria and his exegesis of the passage in question here, does not mention Saint Ephraem's general interpretation, no doubt because the *Source Chretiennes* edition was issued at the same time as his book.

himself and with what the Evangelist intended in presenting to the Christian community the dialogue that transpired between the rich man and the poor Christ, the good Christ who is even now the only Son in heaven, the true treasure of his Church.[15]

We move now to another example, no less original, of Ephraem's New Testament exegesis: the interpretation of Matthew 27:46 in the context of verses 50-53 that follow shortly afterwards. We cite from Ephraem:

"My God, my God, why hast thou forsaken me? Eli, Eli lema sabachthani?": But the scoffers said in untruth: "Let us see whether Elias will come to deliver him"! They had ridiculed his first cry, saying: "How is it that Elias has not delivered him?" So he cried out a second time [vv. 49-50] and it was the dead who heard and who answered him [vv. 51-53]. He showed thus that if dead people, without hearing, had heard him, how much more should the living be listening to him! But why was it the dead who answered when it was to his Father that he was crying? The Father wished to show through the dead that he had heard him, in order to instruct the living and in order to persuade them, through the obedience of the dead, to listen to him. They [the scoffers present] strayed far from the truth at the time of his first cry, but his second cry brought them back with force. His first cry had provoked laughter on their lips and scoffing in their words, but the second put "Woe is me!" on their lips and caused them to beat their breasts [Lk 23:48]. His first cry was turned into derision, the second was aimed at saving his enemies from divine vengeance.... Dead men are killing one who is alive, and the victim is engaged in bringing the dead to life!.... The corpse of Elisha raised a dead man to life [2 Kgs 13:21-22], a figure of Him Who, by his death, opened the tombs and emptied them of their dead who would condemn his murderers.... In order to reduce his adversaries to silence, He commanded the very stones and they were cleft asunder; He commanded death and it did not prevent the just from leaving Sheol at the sound of his voice.[16]

We have here a rather startling interpretation. Ephraem sees this resurrection of the just, described in Mt 27:53, both as an act of the Father, responding to the prayer of his Son in a manner perceptible even to his enemies, and as an act of the Son, raising the dead to life through his very death. It is the triumphant response of the Father who does not abandon his Son and of the Son who suffers insult but is nevertheless

---

[15]Cf. the distinction among the three stages of the transmission of the Gospel in the Instruction of the Pontifical Biblical Commission of April 21, 1964, on the historical truth of the Gospels, *DC* 61 (1964), pp. 713-714.

[16]Ephraem, *Diatesseron*, XX, 30 and 24 (Arm.).

victorious. Ephraem pursues his theme further, introducing a pneumatological note very appropriate in an age of discussions on the divine nature of the Holy Spirit:

> The tombs split open [Mt 27:52] to show that the Lord could, if he wished, split them open and crush the wood of his cross. But he did not split the wood and did not crush it because he was to make use of it to dissolve the kingdom of Israel and to crush sin among the gentiles. Now the Spirit split the veil instead of the wood of the cross; and to prove that he had left the temple, he convoked as witnesses of his exit the just who were leaving their tombs. These two exits from the tomb, that of Christ and that of the just, mutually herald one another.[17]

Here Ephraem's commentary views the text in its more remote and more global biblical context. A number of themes are interwoven: that of Christ's victory over his enemies and that of the Spirit's going over to the pagans. This exegesis points more to the spiritual sense, but not without firm footing in the literal sense.

It is characteristic not only of the various examples we have quoted thus far but of Ephraem's work as a whole that he is constantly referring to the Old Testament to explain the New.

To be more specific, one could, for example, study especially Ephraem's theological exegesis of the relationship between Moses and Jesus. The texts are numerous and rich in significance. We cite here only a few, all of which bring out the thought of the inspired authors of the New Testament.

Commenting on Jesus' discourse on the bread of life, Ephraem writes:

> Sated in the desert as were the Israelites of old at the prayer of Moses, the people shouted: "This is indeed the prophet of whom it is said that he is to come into the world" [Jn 6:14]. They were alluding to Moses' words: "The Lord will raise up for you a prophet" [Dt 18:15], not just any prophet, but a prophet like me, who will satisfy you with bread in the desert. "Like me" means he has walked on the sea [cf. Mt 14:25-31], he has appeared in the cloud [cf. Mt 17:5], he has liberated his Church from circumcision, he has replaced Joshua, the son of Nun, with John who was a virgin and he entrusted him with Mary, with his Church [cf. Jn 19:25-27] just as Moses entrusted his flock to Joshua [cf. Dt

---

[17]*Ibid.*, XII, 6 (Arm.); cf. Ez 8—11 and 47. For the prophet, the glory was going to leave the temple of Jerusalem. It is interesting that, a little after Ephraem, Gregory of Nyssa will see the glory (Jn 17) as an allusion to the Holy Spirit: *Hom. 15 in Cant*, PG 44, 1116-1117.

31:7-8]. All of this happened so that the expression "like me" might be fulfilled.[18]

Could one show in a more condensed and convincing way, concerning a single episode of the Gospel, but also alluding to others, that Jesus is the new Moses, who supersedes the first while bringing what he prefigured to fulfillment?

Ephraem likewise shows that there are more reasons for us today to believe in Jesus than the Jews and Pharaoh had for "believing in Moses," "For then," he insists, "no revelation had been made on this subject by a prophet and no voice had been heard in heaven." It is characteristic of Ephraem to insist on the importance of signs and miracles for evoking faith, whether in Moses or in Jesus.[19]

Ephraem's enormous interest in the figure of Moses is doubtless explained not only by his importance in the history of God's people, but also by the influence, even though contested, of ambient Judaism. For Ephraem—and this is decisive—Moses is not only the lawgiver, the one who transmitted the Old Law to Israel; he is also the prophet who, with his actions and words, announces Jesus, the new Israel and even his Church, "the Jerusalem from on high, our mother, which was shown to Moses on the mountain" (cf. Ex 24:10).[20] As he examines the person and the destiny of Moses in the light of Jesus, Ephraem is close to the Jewish world and to that of Jesus, though he does not fail to perceive the transcendence of the latter. One trait particularly manifests the superiority of Jesus over Moses: the account of the Transfiguration, read considering Mt 27:53, teaches us that Jesus brought back to life this Moses whose burial no one had seen (cf. Dt 34:6).[21]

Henceforth, in the Church which Moses had contemplated on the mountain, Jesus has exalted his disciples and envoys, making them

similar to Moses: indeed, just as Moses carried with him the bones of the just, the Apostles were likewise to carry with them the body which justifies all bodies.[22] And if Moses, by evoking three names of Abraham's house, reconciled God with His children who had transgressed the law [cf. Ex 32:13], how much

---

[18]Ephraem, *Diatesseron*, XII, 5. It should be noted that, for Ephraem as for Ambrose, Mary standing at the foot of the cross, contains the Church.

[19]*Ibid.*, XIII, 12 (Syr. Arm.).

[20]*Ibid.*, III, 5 (Arm.).

[21]*Ibid.*, XIV, 9 (Syr. Arm.).

[22]An allusion to Ex 13:19: "And Moses took with him the bones of Joseph who had required a solemn oath of the Israelites, saying 'God will surely take notice of you, and then you must carry my bones with you from here.'"

more do the Apostles, by evoking the three names of the divinity, purify all the nations which constitute the family of Adam?[23]

Clearly reading Ephraem would help us to renew our understanding of the New Testament in the context of the Old, to grasp better the originality of Jesus, the new Moses, the new Adam, and of his Church, the new Israel.

How did Ephraem come to such a reading? What principles guided him?

B. Ephraem's Exegetical Principles

We can trace these principles back to several laws: a rejection of fundamentalism; a cosmic-biblical symbolism that involves the exercise of liberty; antithetical parallelism; synthetic and integrating association of ideas in the context of the mystery of the Incarnation.

While the last word on the subject is far from being said and could not even be pronounced at present (given the lack of critical editions of many of Ephraem's writings), we think that the following remarks could serve to summarize accurately the results of recent works.

FIRST LAW: THE REJECTION OF BIBLICAL FUNDAMENTALISM

We understand this expression, not in the technical and modern sense,[24] but as referring to an exegesis that would be content with the mere facts, without admitting that these may themselves ever be symbolic of other facts, or that there may be a place for a careful study of the literary forms of the biblical texts.

To be sure, Ephraem did not perceive many of the problems that command the attention of present-day exegetes, neither does he drift, in the opposite direction, into the allegorism of an Origen. Nevertheless, he clearly rejects anti-symbolic literalism as a method. If he had to choose, he would probably even prefer Origen: "...do not stop at the outer splendor of the words that, by their outward shell, conceal the true

---

[23]Ephraem, *Diatesseron*, VIII, 2 (Arm.). For Ephraem, who was aware of two distinct fulfillments of a triple structure, Abraham, Isaac and Jacob become a foreshadowing of the Trinity.

[24]Fundamentalism excludes all critical study of texts and even any consideration of literary genre, claiming to be faithful to the confessional doctrinal foundations, which include some form of millenarism (cf. Yves Congar, *Catholicisme IV*, [1956], col. 1413).

meaning of the account. Apply yourself rather to investigating their deeper meaning and to ascertaining what they are truly saying."[25]

SECOND LAW: HUMAN LIBERTY IS THE INTERPRETER OF A UNIVERSAL COSMIC-BIBLICAL SYMBOLISM

Ephraem does not separate biblical symbolism from cosmic symbolism For him the biblical types are not cut off from the cosmos.

The Bible is at once a part of, and the special interpreter of, the entire world and of its history. Scripture contains symbols of Christ because the entire universe contains these symbols. If types of the cross can be seen in the many trees of the Old Testament, it is because, for the eyes of faith, every tree is pregnant with the mystery of the cross. Likewise, the rebirth of nature in the Spring is, each year, a cosmic image of the resurrection of the dead.[26] Thus God created the universe of material reality in the image of the paschal mystery of his Son.

If, in his exegetical works, the Syrian doctor comments with sobriety on the typological sense of certain episodes of the Old Testament, anticipating the reserve characteristic of the Antiochian school, in his hymns he will frequently synthesize cosmic and biblical symbolisms, offering a justification for this synthesis that is itself biblical.

> Wherever you look, His symbol is there;
> Whatever you read, you find there His types;
> For in Him were all creatures created
> And He sealed all His possessions with His symbols when He created the world.[27]

It is in the context of this universal analogy that Ephraem reacts against Arian univocity and determinism by exalting, as inseparable, the transcendence of God the creator and the freedom of man created in his image. As a poet, he recognizes and affirms the primacy of symbol in

---

[25]Ephraem, *Diatesseron*, XXII, 3 (Syr. Arm.). Cf. R. Murray, "Symbolism in S. Ephraem's Theology, " *Mélanges Graffin, Parole de l'Orient*, (Kaslik, Lebanon, 1975-1976), p. 6.

[26]Cf. *ibid.*, VIII, 3 (Arm.): "...in spite of the prefiguration of the mystery of the resurrection of bodies, a mystery which inanimate things express, when the light comes and the dawn appears to chase away the night."

[27]Ephraem, *Hymn on Virginity*, 20, 12; *CSCO* 223, Syr. 94, p. 70. We note the allusion to Col 1:16: "...in him all things in heaven and on earth were created...," the biblical justification for Ephraem's universal Christocentrism. Whence also Ephraem's moving cry: "This Jesus has multiplied the symbols for us; I have fallen into an ocean of symbols," (*Carmina Nisib.*, 38, 17).

human discourse and the access to the reality of God revealed in Christ that our earthly names, terms and symbols supply. But why, in Ephraem's judgment, do symbols facilitate access to the realities of faith? Because the symbol functions heuristically and not in an apodictic way. Open to a plurality of significations, the symbol invites us to discovery. The heuristic technique of the symbol respects and requires liberty, presupposing as it does even the freedom to refuse the divine invitation.[28]

To be sure, Saint Ephraem does not employ the terms we have just used to express his vision of the cosmic-biblical symbol as a challenge to the freedom of man, a being both material and spiritual. But this is the only way in which we can understand this vision today. For it stands as a challenge both to our present-day rationalism, and to all the contemporary forms of Arianism. We take the liberty of citing in this connection some admirable selections from Ephraem's hymn on faith:

> Man is too small to understand all languages;
> If he could understand the language of the Watchers,[29]
> Then perhaps he could be raised to an understanding of the silence
> That is spoken between the Father and the Son.
> Our language is foreign to the voice of the animals,
> The language of the Watchers is foreign to all language.[30]
> The silence in which the Father speaks to His Son
> Is foreign even to the Watchers.
> Oh! What goodness! Just as He assumes all forms
>   so that we might be able to see,
> So does He assume all voices in order to instruct us.
> His nature is one, it can be seen;
> His silence is one, it can be heard.[31]

We note the breadth of vision here: it extends from the cosmic forms and from the voices of animals (Ephraem carefully avoids speaking of their non-existent languages) to the angelic Watchers who never sleep and who speak continuously, and even to the silence between the unique Word and his Father, a silence that transcends all human and angelic understanding. Likewise we note that Ephraem is at the same

---

[28]Cf. R. Murray, p. 17; and T. Jansma's study on a connected theme, "Ephrem on Ex 2:5: Reflections on the Interplay of Human Freewill and Divine Providence," *Or. Christ. Period.*, 39 (1973), pp. 5-28.

[29]An allusion to the angels.

[30]Cf. 1 Cor 13:1.

[31]Ephraem, *Hymns on Faith*, 11, 7-9, CSCO 154 (Syr. 73). This poem, with its first and third stages in tension, reminds us of St. John of the Cross.

time affirming that our understanding, by nature incapable of hearing and of seeing the diction of the only Word, can nevertheless see his nature, which is shared by both that Word and his Father. Rather than see, we should say glimpse that Nature.

The Son leads man to see not only this Nature but also the distinction present in it between Father and Son, and it is to this end that he assumes all the cosmic voices. And this illumination comes to us particularly through Scripture.

If one were to object that this law of cosmic-biblical symbolism concerns not so much Ephraem's exegesis as his theology, we would reply that it conditions, affects, and qualifies his exegesis taken as a whole. To overlook this law would be to misunderstand the hermeneutics of the Syrian doctor. In short, it signifies that the creator has placed the entire universe at the service of the understanding of his Word.

THIRD LAW: RECOURSE TO THE DISCORDANT CONCORDANCE OF ANTITHETICAL PARALLELISM

Dom L. Leloir has laid particular stress on St. Ephraem's constant use of this law in his hermeneutics.[32] One could say that it pervades his *Commentary* on the concordant Gospel. The passage cited above regarding Moses could be quoted to illustrate this point. Indeed, the reader will sometimes experience a feeling of fatigue before the artificiality of this or that parallelism, though more often he will be moved to wonder at the perspectives they open up. Who could fail, e.g., to appreciate the following extract?[33]

They offered him wine to drink, mingled with gall [Mt 27:34]; he had cheered them with a delicious wine and they offer him vinegar: in exchange for the gall, he sweetens the bitterness of the nations through the power of his mercy. His tunic was without a seam [Jn 19:23], because it represented his divinity—not divided because not composed. And his garment was divided into four parts, symbolizing his Gospel, which was to acquire the four parts of the world [cf. Jn 19:23].

Out of love for him, then, share in the body of him who, out of love for you, shared his garments among those who crucified him. Take it everyone, absorb it entirely, just as he took to himself alone and absorbed into his own the death

---

[32]Leloir, chapter III.
[33]Ephraem, *Diatessaron*, XX, 27 (Arm.).

that belongs to you all. Open the doors of your heart to him who opened to you the gates of his kingdom.

Mary saw Our Lord in him who had rested on his breast [Jn 13:23-25; 21:20] and John saw our Lord in her whose womb gave him to the world; this is why he entrusted her to this disciple, in preference to all the others.

Each one of these statements shows at once concordance and discordance—sometimes in itself, and sometimes in relationship to what precedes or to what follows, in the context of a complex symbolism: wine and vinegar, tunic without seams and divided garments, the body to be shared yet taken entirely.

Recourse of this kind to the discordant concordance of antithetical parallelism frequently (though not always) goes beyond what the human and inspired author of the Scriptures consciously and explicitly had in mind. But can we say that it goes beyond the intention of the infinite Wisdom of the one supreme Author of all the Scriptures, of this one Author whose will it was that the Scriptures form a single book? We think not. On the contrary, what we have here is an implementation of the analogy of faith, an anticipated application of the ideal proposed to the Christian exegete by the Second Vatican Council: "Since Holy Scripture must be read and interpreted according to the same Spirit by whom it was written, no less serious attention must be given to the content and unity of the whole of Scripture, if the meaning of the sacred texts is to be correctly brought to light. The living Tradition of the whole Church must be taken into account along with the harmony that exists between elements of the faith."[34]

FOURTH LAW: SYNTHESIZING AND INTEGRATING ASSOCIATION IN THE CONTEXT OF THE MYSTERY OF THE INCARNATION

In our view, the preceding laws and their application by the Syrian doctor are polarized by the law stated here. For Ephraem, Christ is the symbol par excellence; and it is above all in him that we see the radiance of the concordance of antithetical parallelism between his divine nature and his human nature, without any discordance whatsoever. It is because of this concordance that Christ expiated the discordances of sin. Ultimately, the oppositions brought out by Ephraem are intended only to manifest the supreme unity of Christ and of the entire universe in him.

---

[34]*Dei Verbum*, 12.

How may these assertions be justified? We could first invite the reader to reread, from the perspective of this fourth law, the passage we cited to illustrate the third, a passage that deals with the Passion of Jesus. But it is in the hymns more than anywhere else, as we might have expected, that we find the most splendid examples of this kind of reading that integrates the contrasting elements that Scripture sets before us in the unity of the mystery of Christ:

> His whole body was hanging on the Cross
> But His power was wholly free with all things.[35]
> In fact, when he was on the cross, He was raising the dead to life
> Just as, when in his mother's womb,
> He was fashioning all children in their mothers' wombs.[36]

These examples illustrate perfectly how Ephraem loves to pair off the action of Jesus' divinity with the passibility or the passion of his humanity. This tendency is quite prevalent in his writings. In speaking of the man Jesus, Ephraem never forgets that he is the eternal Son of God, enjoying all the perfection of divinity. This memory continuously transforms his reading of the Gospel. Conversely, he reads the Old Testament in the light of the Paschal Mystery and then goes on to contemplate the God of the Old Covenant from the perspective of the humanity of Jesus.

St. Ephraem sees the Incarnation as the Word clothing Himself with our humanity.[37] He applies the same image of a clothing of the divinity to Scripture, suggesting thereby the idea of the Bible as the preparation for and the extension of the mystery of the Incarnation, an idea that helps us to understand that the integrating association of the human and the divine constitutes the exegete's horizon, the key that opens for him the profound understanding of the divine and human Scriptures.

We cannot but cite here three beautiful stanzas from the Hymn XI on Paradise:

> One who speaks cannot
> Dispense with words
> By means of which visible things
> Are designated here

---

[35]Ephraem, *Hymn on the Nativity*, 4, 168; *CSCO* 186/187; 82/83. Referred to by Pierre Youssif, "La croix de Jésus et le paradis d'Eden," *Mélanges Graffin*, p. 36.

[36]*Ibid.*, p. 37; referring to Ephraem's hymn on the Nativity, 4, 170.

[37]Murray, *Symbols of Church and Kingdom*, pp. 310-311. The author thinks that this image is not of the New Testament. However, Paul shows us Christ stripping himself (Phil 2) and John (1:14) shows us the Word becoming flesh and not putting on flesh as mere clothing.

To represent for his hearers
    The image of invisible things.
If then the Creator
    Of the garden [of Eden]
Has clothed his Majesty
    With the words of our earth
One could all the more speak of his garden
    In terms of our comparisons,
If one should, through error,
    Retain only the names
Which the Divine Majesty has himself borrowed
    He turns these figures
Which He took on in coming to his aid
    Into slander and blasphemy,
And toward the Goodness, who came down from the heights
    Even to his infantile level, he shows himself ungrateful,
Since he had nothing in common with this Divine Majesty,
    Now His Majesty is concealed
In man's own images
    So as to bring him himself to his likeness.[38]

In these magnificent stanzas, Ephraem's method of integrating association leads him to examine more closely the idea of the divine condescension, which will later become the major theme of the biblical theology of Saint John Chrysostom (cf. our Ch. VIII): "The Divine Majesty clothed itself with these figures to bring us help, Goodness came down from the heights to meet our infancy." Although the Incarnation is not explicitly mentioned here, Ephraem is scarcely unaware that the truth of his affirmations is most brilliantly reflected in this mystery. This is clear from the fact—as we have mentioned—that he applies to it also the image of clothing.

That the double nature of the one person of Jesus, the Son of God, constitutes the integrating horizon of Ephraem's entire exegesis is clear also from his typology in three levels, which the deacon of Edessa summarized as follows:

The type was in Egypt, the reality in the Church:
the seal of the recompense [will be] in the Kingdom.[39]

---

[38]Ephraem, *Hymns on Paradise, SC* 137, p. 147.
[39]Ephraem, *Hymn on the Azyme*, 5, 23, *CSCO* 169, Syr. 76; referred to by Murray, *Mélanges Graffin*, p. 8.

It is thanks to the Incarnation that the Church is fulfillment or realization in comparison with the Old Testament, while being itself a type of the eschatological kingdom. For Ephraem, the whole of human life is a voyage from Eden to Zion, from Zion to the Church, from the Church to the Kingdom.[40] We have here a vision of salvation history that harmonizes perfectly with that found consistently in the Letter to the Hebrews[41] when it presents us with the dialectic: shadow, image, truth (Heb 8:5; 9:24; 10:1). He who is the First-born and the Image of the invisible God, after having announced himself in shadows, becomes, by fulfilling them, the visible Image of the invisible God to conduct men to the full truth of his vision.

The objection will undoubtedly and rightly be raised, that Saint Ephraem is not always speaking of Christ in his exegetical commentaries. This is why we carefully avoided giving this impression when we were stating this supreme law of his exegesis. On the other hand, we think that the constant tendency he shows toward the integrating association of elements often antithetical (contrary without being contradictory) is discretely conditioned by his faith in the mystery of the Incarnation, the horizon that illuminates his particular interpretations even when he does not direct our attention to it. In other words, we could pose the following question: without Ephraem's faith in the two natures of the one Word, would he have developed the contrasts in such a systematic way? Everything suggests that it was his faith in the contrasts of the Paschal Mystery of the Man-God that impelled him to seek out, in the Christocentric universe,[42] the various contrasts with which it abounds.

---

[40]Ephraem, *Hymn Against the Heresies*, 25, 4; *CSCO* 169, Syr. 76; referred to by Murray, *Mélanges Graffin*, p. 8.

[41]We also find in Ephraem, in the context of certain Old Testament texts, another triple movement. According to R. Leconte, p. 72; cf. pp 295ff.:

It comes to him to have the type enter into a prophetic whole in three terms, constructed according to the following schema:

a. an utterance of the Old Testament directly predicts an event which must happen in the history of the Hebrew people;

b. that event, that generally belongs to the Assyrian, Persian, or Maccabean periods, plays the role of type with respect to a person or a fact of the New Covenant;

c. the third term is represented by the evangelic reality itself.

Leconte then gives a series of specific examples, involving especially the books of Isaiah and Zechariah, Here too, Ephraem is clearing the way for Antioch.

[42]Ephraem even worked out a rule that Athanasius had already presented: "All the texts of Scripture that speak of the abjection of the Savior refer to his humanity; his

Conclusions

Ephraem's exegesis culminates in a Christocentric love of the Scriptures and a biblical love of neighbor. The interpretation of the Scriptures left us by the Syrian doctor is not, any more than it is in Augustine,[43] cut off from practical love of God and of neighbor, found together in Christ: "All the Lord's teaching is sustained as by two wings in the two precepts: charity toward God and charity toward men."[44]

Since he loves Christ, Ephraem cannot but love his least words, in the Gospels, for they contain immense treasures.[45] Let us listen rather to this hymn in which the poet-doctor sings his love both for the Scriptures and for him who inspired them:

> Who is capable of understanding the richness of even one of your words, oh God? What we understand of them is much less than what we leave behind, like thirsty people drinking from a fountain. The perspectives of Your word are countless, numerous as the perspectives of those who study it. The Lord has colored His word with multiple beauties, so that everyone who examines it can contemplate what he pleases.
>
> (...) His word is like the rock opened up in the desert, which became for every man, everywhere, a spiritual drink: They all ate the same prophetic food, and all drank the same prophetic drink [1 Cor 10:4].[46]

For Ephraem, to nourish oneself with Christ's word is in a way to feed on Christ himself, in love and gratitude. But this will occur only if we avoid isolating certain words from others, as the heretics do in the manner of the demon: they take some words found in Scripture and omit others.[47]

In its turn, prayer nourished by the word of God will bear the fruit of love of neighbor, a love that will go even to the point of sacrificing one's life for him:

---

divinity is above all those weaknesses" (*Opera Syr. Lat.*, III, 98-99; referred to by Lamy, "L'exégèse en Orient au IV siècle ou les commentaires de saint Ephrem," *RB* 2 [1893], 11). However, the information given by Lamy, often based on texts of doubtful authenticity, is not dependable, as was emphasized by articles on his work that appeared in the *DBS* and *Catholicisme*. In any case, Ephraem's criterion is more nuanced, distinguishing three orders in our Lord: divinity alone (Jn 1:1); divinity and humanity united (Jn 3:13); humanity (Jn 7:19): *Diatessaron* XIV, 28, (Syr. Arm.).

[43]Augustine, *De Doctrina christiana.*
[44]Ephraem, *Diatessaron*, XVI, 23 (Syr. Arm.).
[45]*Ibid.*, XVI, 31 (Syr. Arm.); cf. Leloir, p. 62.
[46]*Ibid.*, I, 8 (Syr. Arm.).
[47]*Ibid.*, IV, 8 (Arm.).

Thou shalt not kill: he who loves does not kill. Thou shalt not steal: he who loves does more: he gives his own substance. Thou shalt not bear false witness: he who loves tells the truth and will not tell a lie [Mt 19:18].

Your love for one another is to be like the love I have borne you. This is the greatest love a man can show, that he should lay down his life for his friends [Jn 13:34; 15:13]. If we give our lives for You, will our charity be equal to Yours? Even if we do not die for You, we are still only mortal beings. But You have undergone the suffering of our death, yet You are (essentially and eternally) living. How then should we explain His words: like the love I have borne you? Let us die for one another, He is saying.

But we do not even want to live for one another. If I, Who am your Lord and your God, die for you, how much more should you die for one another?[48]

In other words, Scripture, which contains the word of Christ, leads us to martyrdom and to the sacrifice of our lives for the love of neighbor and of Christ the Savior.

Still today, through the writings he has left us, Ephraem continues to intercede for us and to exercise for us the charity that Christ, whom he now sees face to face, has always enjoined on him. By his writings, he enters into our hearts with the greeting "that the Lord Himself might enter there and dwell there." The mystery of the salutation which Ephraem addresses to us with his writings always opens up the mystery of our salvation in and by Jesus. This mystery of missionary salutation Ephraem has described in unforgettable terms:

This greeting is the mystery of His faith[49] that shines forth in the world. Through it, enmity is stamped out, war is stopped, and people mutually acknowledge one another....This greeting is more than sufficient for all men....It entered into all who heard it; it singled out and set apart as His sons those who acknowledged it. It remained in them, but it would denounce those who were strangers to it, for though once sewn in them, it has now left them.

This greeting was not corrupted in those who welcomed it, showing thereby that the gifts of the giver were stable and secure. It was present in those who gave it and in those who received it, but suffered neither diminishment nor division. It announced of the Father that He is near to everyone and in everyone. It announced of the Son's mission, that He is in the fullest manner with all and that His end is at His Father's side. This greeting is an Image of the Father, and it does not cease to preach, does not flag in its proclamation until the

---

[48]*Ibid.*, XIX, 13 (Arm.).
[49]That is, of the faith announced by Christ and asked for by him.

coming of the certitude which fulfills the typical figures, until the truth has put an end to images, until the shadows are replaced by the body itself and the symbols dissolved by true representations.

So we proceed to sow the word of the Lord into its hearers and familiars as a coagulant which will separate and unite: separate, by removing them from all impurity and unite them to the Lord who is gathering the community together.[50]

The mystery of the peace-bringing greeting whose basis is found in Jesus' missionary discourse (Mt 10) is, in Ephraem's view, the mysterious proclamation of the word whose aim is to convoke and assemble the Church. What the silent voice of the deacon of Edessa can no longer do, his pen continues to effect,[51] when we read his writings. His loving exegesis is entirely directed to the building up of the Church, to make us move on from the types toward the Kingdom.

---

[50]Ephraem, *Diatessaron*, VIII, 3-5 (Arm.), commenting on Mt 10—12.

[51]We are not claiming to equate the written word with the spoken word in the work of evangelization. Cf. my article on "The Spread of the Bible and the Economy of Salvation," *American Ecclesiastical Review*, 168 (1974), 96-121.

Chapter VII
History, "Theoria" and Tradition in the Antiochian School

Like that of the School of Alexandria, the historical influence of the School of Antioch was immense, particularly in the patristic era and in the Middle Ages.

This influence, it must be acknowledged, was not always positive, nor has it been evaluated as such. Many would be tempted quite simply to equate the school of Antioch with a Nestorian, rationalist exegesis whose effect would be to divide Christ and his mystery.

Is it fair to reduce the school of Antioch to its great masters, Theodore of Mopsuestia and Diodorus of Tarsus? Is not their fellow student and disciple, John Chrysostom, whose authenticity the universal Church recognizes to the point of proclaiming him a Doctor, the chief figure of this school?

Moreover, the two schools of Antioch and Alexandria have often been set in neat, systematic opposition to one another. The former supposedly lays heavy emphasis on the literal sense, the latter on the spiritual sense of the Scriptures. The former, it is imagined, holds closely to all the historical roots of the biblical realities, the latter takes leave of history to soar into an ethereal and somewhat mythical sphere.

Contemporary works are generally unimpressed with such excessive over-simplifications, while acknowledging the element of truth they contain. Drawing on these works, we will try to bring out the fundamental values which Antioch seems to have grasped, in its understanding of prophetic activity as at once history and contemplation (*theoria*), and its formulation of criteria that allow one to recognize when the sacred writer is resorting to *theoria*. We will also note a number of particular points at which the fundamental intuition of Antioch was applied in a way that is still suggestive today.

We will then raise the question, given this possible future for the Antiochian views, of what was to be their destiny in the Church, how the Tradition was to evaluate them. We will conclude by examining the possible ways in which the Antiochian *theoria* could tie in with the *sensus plenior* that has been the object of so much reflection in our century.

A. History and Theoria with the Antiochians

1. MEANING OF THE TERM *THEORIA*

Generally, as is well known, the term *theoria* signifies contemplation, vision.

In a biblical context, at Antioch, the word acquires a technical signification with the prophetic vision of the sacred author.[1]

Neither the Antiochian authors nor their modern interpreters agree on the meaning of this idea.

Drawing on the works of Fathers Vaccari and Mariès, we will first present the views of Julian of Eclana and of Diodorus of Tarsus; next, those of Saint John Chrysostom, which are, we believe, significantly different in character.

In the case of *theoria*, as the first two writers see it, the sacred author is primarily concerned with an event of Israel's history and this event is a figure of a messianic reality. But these two series of objects that relate to one another as type to antitype both belong to the literal sense that the human author had in mind and which he "intentioned." The contemplation or *theoria* of the human and inspired author would conceal a true typology within the literal sense, or, if you prefer, a typical-literal sense. This is the technical meaning of Antiochian *theoria* in the view of many modern authors.

We could go on with Vaccari to specify four characteristics of *theoria*:

---

[1]On the Antiochian *theoria*, see A. Vaccari, *Biblica* 1 (1920), pp. 1-36; P. Ternant, *Biblica* 34 (1953), pp. 145-158, 354-383, 456-486 (henceforth referred to as Ternant); J. Guillet, "Les exégèses d'Alexandrie et d'Antioche, Conflit ou malentendu?" *Rech Sc. Rel.*, 34 (1947), pp. 257-302; R. Devreesse, "La méthod exégétique de Théodore de Mopsueste," RB 53 (1946), pp. 236ff. We should remember that Diodorus died in about 392, Chrysostom in 407, Theodore in about 428.

a) hagiography, in his understanding of *theoria*, presupposes the historical reality of the primary matters described;

b) beyond this first reality, another, ontologically posterior, is herewith encompassed;

c) of these two objects, the first relates to the second not only as the small to the great, but also as the image to the person himself or as the sketch to the completed portrait;

d) these two objects are both direct terms of the cognitive activity of the human and inspired author, as he understands *theoria*, but in different ways: the minor object is the means through which or by way of which this activity reaches the loftier and the more noble object.[2]

Considering Bishop Diodorus of Tarsus (bishop of the fourth century, teacher of Theodore of Mopsuestia and of John Chrysostom) and of his commentary on the Psalms, let us give a few examples of *theoria* that illustrate the three last points that we have just presented.

For the second point, the bishop of Tarsus shows how beyond Israel (Ps 15), David (Ps 21), the Maccabees and Israel (Ps 68), and Solomon (Ps 71) who are presented historically (*historikos*) by the texts, another object, Christ, is present to the mind's eye (*theorematikos*) of the human and inspired author.

But—and here we illustrate the third point—the first object is related to the second (*pros huperbolen to kata to alethes*) either as the small to the great (as with the relationship Solomon-Jesus in Ps 71) or as first draft to subsequent realization (as with the relationship David-Jesus in Ps 17c).

Finally, as for the fourth point, Diodorus writes apropos of Ps 68 (Maccabees):

The words of the Psalms are at the same time both history and prophecy. Words are uttered, from the historical point of view, with "hyperbole" (that is to say that they go beyond the historical situation that occasions them), but the same words, from the prophetic point of view, are realized in truth.[3]

For Antioch, then, the prophet is a contemplative historian: a historian of the present—in which, however, he contemplates the glorious

---

[2] Cf. Ternant, p. 144. The author comments on a text of Julian of Eclane that repeats the Antiochian position. Cf. Vaccari, *Biblica* 15 (1934), pp. 94-101.

[3] Cf. L. Mariès, *Etudes prèliminaires à l'éd. de Diodore de Tarse sur les Ps.*, (Paris, 1933), p. 136; Ternant, pp. 144-145. We note with Ternant (p. 137, n. 2) that the attribution of this commentary to Diodorus is contested by Devreesse (*DBS*, vol. I, col. 1128-1130), who nevertheless acknowledges that it expresses the best of Antiochian thought.

Messianic future in all its intricate detail. The prophet, according to the Antiochian exegetes, is fully aware of the figurative value of the primary object his words intend to convey. We could even say that there is *theoria* in the strict sense when the prophet contemplates and beholds, within a future event of the Old Testament, a future event of the New. Such is, at least, the interpretation given by a number of modern authors.

We could say too that the *theoria* or contemplation of the Antiochians is properly speaking a literal sense, not a sense added to the literal sense, as would be true in the case of allegory, anagogy or even the ordinary typology of other ages. In the theory of Antioch, the Messianic sense stands in contrast not to the literal but to the historical sense. This in no way introduces a duality of literal senses. The adequate literal sense is no more than one, but, if the expression may be pardoned, it is virtually double. "There is a single prediction only, which is twice fulfilled: a first time partially, a second time fully."[4] We would prefer to speak of a proximate historical sense and of a more remote historico-messianic sense. This would avoid giving the impression that the Messianic sense is not historical, which would certainly not correspond to the thinking of the Antiochian writers. On the contrary, for this school, the two aspects of the literal sense were historical.

Does the Antiochian *theoria* disclose a typical sense? Are type and prophecy the same thing? Here the Antiochians seem to be divided.

On the one hand, Theodore of Mopsuestia denies it. His disciple, the African bishop Junilius, expressed the thought of his master remarkably well in his *Instituta regularia*. For him, prophecy foretells a future event by means of words, taken either in their proper sense or in a figurative sense, while in the case of the type, the event is announced by deeds or by persons to which the biblical words point.[5] Theodore of Mopsuestia goes so far as to identify type and allegory[6] (indeed, on the occasion of his commentary on the prophet Jonah, he leaves us a veritable treatise on types and on the typical sense in the Old Testament[7]).

---

[4]Ternant, p. 150.

[5]Junilius, an African layman, lived in Constantinople in the sixth century (cf. L. Pirot, "Junilius," DTC, VIII, 2 [1925], col. 1971-1976) and wrote *Instituta regularia divinæ legis*. The expression referred to here is taken from Book II, ch. 16 (critical edition of Kihn, p. 510). Cf. L Pirot, *L'œuvre exégètique de Théodore de Mopsueste*, (Rome, 1913), p. 195: 'Prophetia est typus in verbis, secundum id quod verba sunt et contra typus prophetia est in rebus, in quantum res esse noscuntur." This is still the text of Junilius.

[6]Pirot, p. 192.

[7]*Ibid.*, p. 193. Cf. the evaluation by Pesch, *De inspiratione S. Scripturæ*, p. 567: this treatise is "perfectly Catholic."

On the other hand, St. John Chrysostom seems to put things better when he distinguishes verbal prophecy from typical prophecy: "Prophecy in type is that which takes place in deeds or in historical realities; the other prophecy is one in words. For God has persuaded some by highly insightful words, while he has bolstered the certitude of others, the less sophisticated, through the vision of events."[8]

The obvious inference is that in the view of Chrysostom the prophet is not always explicitly aware of what he is announcing. The type does not know, at least does not necessarily know, what he represents.

This example shows that there is no rigorous uniformity within the Antiochian school. A more thorough investigation would possibly reveal similar differences within the thinking of each of the masters of the school. There is nothing surprising about this. The period that spans the development of a system is not yet that of the perfect reciprocal ordering of every one of its elements, with the precise and logical recognition of the presuppositions and consequences of its basic positions.[9]

We recall still another distinction of Saint John Chrysostom that fairly well sums up the exegetical tendencies of the Antiochian School:

All the statements of Scripture fall into three categories:

- some reveal, beyond their letter, a more profound sense, the object of *theoria*;

- others can be understood only according to their literal affirmation (ex. Gen. 1,1);

- still others can be understood only according to a sense different from that suggested by the sound of the words.[10]

This last category implies that among the Antiochians it was admitted by some that the literal sense of Scripture—that intended by their human and inspired authors—can be expressed by means of words taken not in

---

[8]John Chrysostom, *Sixth Sermon on Penance*, n. 4, *PG* 49, 320; cf. F. Ogara, "De typica apud Chrysostomum Prophetia," *Gregorianum*, 24 (1943), 62-77, especially 66-67. The parallel will be noted between this view of Chrysostom and that of Junilius (n. 5). For Chrysostom, the allegory of which Paul speaks to the Galatians (4:23-24) is in reality a type (cf. *PG* 61, 662.)

[9]This is what the Canadian theologian Bernard Lonergan emphasizes: cf. Bertrand de Margerie, *The Christian Trinity in History*, (Petersham, Massachusetts: St. Bede's Publications, 1983), pp. 93-96. Ternant's extraordinary study seems not to have noted these fluctuations in the Antiochian ideas, especially the incoherence respecting the understanding of the *theoria* itself.

[10]John Chrysostom, *In Ps. 9*, *PG* 55, 126-127; cf. *In Ps. 46*, 1: *PG* 55, 183-184.

their proper sense, but in a figurative or metaphorical sense.[11] This meaning, which we would call the literal-metaphorical sense, and which Alexandria referred to as a spiritual sense, was viewed at Antioch as a true literal sense.

But John Chrysostom is careful to note, commenting on Is 5, that we have no right to interpret according to our fancy the passages of Scripture that appear to be metaphorical:

> Nowhere does Scripture depart from this rule. It always supplies the key for the allegories it employs, wishing in this way to prevent minds that are keen on such figures from straying off at random and without purpose, from letting their imaginations go wild.[12]

Does *theoria* come in already with the literal-metaphorical sense? It would seem that it does, to judge from the expressions of the Antiochian authors.[13]

The complexity of the material available shows that we still undoubtedly await the definitive work that will give us an exact understanding of the meaning of Antiochian *theoria*, or, better still, of the different meaning of the term found in the authors of the School and even within the same author.

2. CRITERIA FOR THE APPLICATION OF THEORIA ACCORDING TO ANTIOCH

A number of exegetes of our century[14] have questioned whether the fundamental principle of Antioch, that is, to express it in other categories (employed notably in England[15]), the "compenetration" of type and antitype in the mind of an individual ahead of the crowd, is tenable. Why this a priori deduction of a revelation?[16]

Without taking time to point out that a negative response would entail the denial of all possibility of prophecy, we shall take the

---

[11]Pirot, p. 178, n. 3; cf. pp. 181, 201. Cf. P. Benoît, commenting on Thomas Aquinas on *Prophecy*, (*Summa Theol.*, II-II, 171-178, [Paris, 1947], pp. 355-356): "This literal sense is encountered in every case, for an author does not speak in order to say nothing, but it could be proper or improper, inasmuch as he takes the words in their direct or figurative meaning.... The figurative sense is also a literal sense." This was unknown in Alexandria.

[12]John Chrysostom, *PG* 56, 60.

[13]See a list of these expressions in Pirot, p. 178, n. 3.

[14]Especially R. E. Murphy, *A Study of Psalm 72 (71)*, (Washington, 1948), p. 103; cf. Ternant, pp. 330ff; Dubarle, *RSPT*, 31 (1947), p. 45.

[15]For example, E. f. Sutcliffe, *The Old Testament and the Future Life*, (Oxford, 1946), interpreting in this way Dn 12:1-2.

[16]Ternant, p. 361.

opportunity presented by these difficulties to set forth with great insistence the criteria for the application of *theoria* employed by the Antiochian writers, according to their modern interpreters.

Theoria is the rule to follow "when an apostle of the New Testament, by citing an oracle as having been verified in Jesus of Nazareth, guarantees at least implicitly that the prophet was aware of the messianic signification of his words, even if the context makes it clear that these same words do refer to another, more proximate, historical object (compare, for example, Ps 16 with Acts 2:30; Zec 9 with Mt 21:4 and Jn 12:16); and when, even in the absence of such an apostolic witness, one finds in the same prophetic context hyperbolic traits which could only apply to the Messiah together with other features that better describe a historical personage who prefigures the Messiah.[17]

Vaccari, whom we have just cited, acknowledges the validity of each of these two criteria, even when considered independently of the other.

Pirot is not, however, of this opinion. In his view, Theodore of Mopsuestia takes the position that we should apply to Christ and to his Messianic kingdom those passages of Scripture that apply also to persons or events of the Old Testament only when there is a New Testament citation that invites us to do so. But Theodore is only negatively faithful to this principle. While he never interprets in a typical sense a passage for which he does not find clear and precise pointers in the New Testament, still, he is careful not to explain in a typical sense all the texts of the Old Testament that are so interpreted by the New Testament.[18]

There is, however, general agreement among scholars in recognizing the importance of hyperbole for the exegetes of Antioch. These would be expressions that, while not suppressing the historical personage or the event of Jewish history immediately or primarily intended by the prophet,[19] are nevertheless disproportionate to this personage or to this event, even allowing for the imaginative style of Orientals and for the

---

[17]Vaccari, *Biblica*, 31 (1950), 258; cf. Ternant, p. 369.

[18]Pirot, p. 210-212. Pirot adds: "...and this is why he was unable to avoid in his exegesis a certain rationalism from which the School of Antioch would have preserved him, had he remained faithful to its principles"; however, "the works of Theodore provide excellent arguments for refuting the moderns who deny prophecy, miracles, and the supernatural." He is not rationalist in the sense of our contemporary meaning of the term.

[19]What we are saying is therefore valid for both cases of *theoria*. In the case of *theoria* in the strict sense, with prophecy that has a double object, the one more proximate, the other more remote in time; and also in the case of *theoria* in the broad sense, when the prophet sees the messianic event in the context of an historical event that is already known and present, or past.

exuberant temperament of the prophet. The hyperboles of "court style" are not sufficient to allow us to suppose that the inspired author consciously intends to portray the Messiah or the Messianic blessings through the immediate realities he is describing.

The only hypotheses that would allow us to conclude to such an intention are those which Vaccari effectively defines when he lays down the following rule: when the facts predicted or the benefits promised exceed the capacities of a single people or the limits of the human species during history.[20]

Let us give some examples of hyperboles that must be considered insufficient to warrant the application of *theoria*. The prayer for "length of days for ever and ever" does not mean that the author of Psalm 21 was pointing beyond a king of Judah to the Messianic King. Such hyperbole is fully "within the style of the good-wishes addressed to the ruling monarch (cf. Neh 2:3; 1 Kgs 1:31, where the formula contains a touch of irony in view of the circumstances)," as E. Podechard observes.[21]

The criterion of hyperbole, then, requires delicate handling. Only rarely would it allow us to discern a case where the idea of *theoria* should be applied. However, if it receives the support of New Testament attestation, we can no longer hesitate to make this application.[22]

3. SOME EXAMPLES TAKEN FROM THE GOSPELS, THE ACTS OF THE APOSTLES AND THE PAULINE EPISTLES

We begin with two examples that are more apparent than real. This will help us to perceive more clearly, by means of contrast, the specific point being made by the writers of Antioch.

Mt 2:14-15 refers us to Hos 11:1: "Then Joseph got up, took the child and his mother by night, and went to Egypt and remained there until the death of Herod. This was to fulfill what the Lord had spoken by the Lord through the prophet, 'Out of Egypt have I called my son'." For Saint John Chrysostom, these last words were said "not so much of those who worshipped the golden calf and offered their children in sacrifice to demons, as of him who was son by nature and who honored his Father;

---

[20]Cf. Ternant, pp. 355ff.

[21]*Ibid.*, p. 371; E. Podechard, *Le Psautier*, (Lyons, 1949), vol. I, p. 101.

[22]Ternant, p. 373; cf. L. Cerfaux, "Simples réflexions à propos de l'exégèse apostolique," *Eph. Th. Lov.*, (1949), p. 573.

if he had not come, the prophecy would not have had its worthy fulfillment."[23]

The same preacher-exegete supplies another example, considering Hebrews 7:3: "[Melchizedek is] without father, without mother, without genealogy, having neither beginning of days nor end of life, but resembling the Son of God, he remains a priest forever." "In what way," asks John Chrysostom,

> is Melchizedek without father and without mother, without beginning or end? How is this so? In the sense that Scripture does not supply this information. What does this mean? Just as Melchizedek is without father because his gene-alogy is not reported, so Christ is such in a very real sense. Just as we do not know either how Melchizedek's life began or how it came to an end, because these things are not written, so we do not know the beginning and the end of Jesus, not because they are not written, but because they are lacking in fact [i.e., Jesus—as God—has no beginning or end].[24]

The objection might here be made, and not without reason, that the two examples chosen, while giving a suggestive idea of the exegetical methods employed by Antioch, do not however amount to examples of *theoria*. If the latter is taken in a rather strict sense, implying on the part of the prophet at least[25] a twofold prophetic insight (one relative to the proximate future absent here, the other to a more remote, Messianic future), the objection would hold. We must however acknowledge—and

---

[23]John Chrysostom, *Hom. 8 in Mt.*, n. 2; *PG* 57, 85-86; cf. Pirot, p. 266: "In the literal sense there is absolutely no doubt that Hosea's prophecy is alluding to the departure from Egypt; but in the typical sense, we must understand it as referring to Jesus Christ, of whom Israel was a figure." Cf. Ogara, n. 8.

[24]John Chrysostom, *In Ep. ad Hebr.* 7; *PG* 63, 97-98; Ogara, pp. 70 ff.

[25]For Theodoret of Cyr, the prophecy of Is 60:1 is also a prophecy in three stages: "It announces the building of Jerusalem in the time of Cyrus and Darius: this is the shadow; then comes the image, i.e., the church; finally there is the archetype, i.e. the future life and the heavenly citizenry" (Theodoret, *Commentary on Isaiah*; cf. Ternant, p. 148. We recognize here the classical distinction from the Letter to the Hebrews: shadow, image, archetypal realities). Here, Antioch already includes what medieval tradition was to call the allegorical and anagogical senses of Scripture, by adding to it a prophecy that was located in the inte-rior of the Old Testament: "All these things foretold therefore apply in a certain way, to the ancient Jerusalem, which received the first illumination that went beyond hope." This is what L. Mariès also emphasizes: "Antiochian exegesis sees the great majority of the prophecies as fulfilled within the very history of the Jewish people, before Jesus Christ" (*Rech. Sc. Rel.*, 22 [1932], 387). We can regard this idea as the specific point of Antioch and as the result of the Jewish influence on the Antiochean authors (cf. Ternant, p. 142, n. 2). But we could not say that the universal church has retained this idea of a prior fulfillment, within the Old Testament, of the messianic prophecies.

this is surely one of the difficulties of a clear presentation of the Antiochian "system," which is hardly a system at all—that the immediate
vision of the prophet can also be focused, as Diodorus would contend,
on events contemporary to the prophet himself.

> In predicting events of the future, the prophets adapted their discourse both to
> the ages to which their utterances were made and to subsequent ages; their
> words were hyperbolic as expressing the realities of the contemporary era, but
> they were in perfect harmony and proportion with respect to the events which
> were to fulfill the prophecies.[26]

There is more. In the eyes of John Chrysostom, the author of Genesis
is himself a prophet even when he is describing the past.[27] It is perfectly
legitimate then to admit in theory the possibility of a case of *theoria*
where one of the two terms of the inspired prophetic "vision" would be
an event of the past (the return of the Jewish people to Palestine, recalled
by God in Hosea, on the one hand, and on the other, the presentation of
Melchizedek in Genesis, in the two cases we have just considered)
through which this prophet would "see" in his *theoria* the future Messiah
thus typified.

There is more: one would have to have been able to say that the
inspired writer—in this case, Hosea or the author of Genesis, in the passage considered—had the Messiah in view, even if only indistinctly
when he was speaking of the Jewish people or of Melchizedek. Now it
must be stated quite clearly that it is not possible to affirm anything of
the kind,[28] even on the basis of the New Testament (which is far from
suggesting such an idea).

We cannot say, then, that Hosea 11:1 or Genesis 14:17-20 are true
cases of *theoria*, in strictly Antiochian terms. We give now some examples
that are more convincing, at least at first sight.

Zechariah 9:9 cited by Matthew 21:5, supplies us with a first example:

Rejoice greatly, O daughter Zion!
Shout aloud, O daughter Jerusalem!
Lo, your king comes to you;
triumphant and victorious is he,

---

[26]Text attributed to Diodorus of Tarsus by L. Mariès, *Rech. Sc. Rel.*, 9 (1919), 97; cf. Ternant, pp. 145-146.

[27]John Chrysostom, *Homily 2 on Genesis*, PG 53, 27. This idea is biblical: cf. Nm 11, 24-29;
12:6; Dt 18:18; 34:10.

[28]Above all else, Abraham's case appears to be different in John's (12:41) judgment;
however, we shall see that John Chrysostom does not seem to be of the same mind.

humble and riding on a donkey,
on a colt the foal of a donkey.

Theodore of Mopsuestia cannot support the idea of dissecting this prophecy in such a way as to apply a part of it to Zerubbabel and a part to Christ. Such a procedure, in his view, would be the height of madness. He goes on therefore to apply the entire oracle to Zerubbabel from the historical and literal point of view, but at the same time he shows how this royal personality is a figure of Christ. He then reminds us in this connection that the Law was not more than the shadow of realities to come, that an innumerable posterity was promised to Abraham, that an everlasting kingdom and preservation from the tomb were announced to David only because these men were both types of Christ. The same is true in Zechariah. Zerubbabel was the shadow, Christ is the reality. True and lasting joy is to be had only in Christ. He alone is truly the just judge of the universe; he alone, the true Savior. The Gospels are right then in applying this prophetic text to him.[29]

To put it another way, in the view of Theodore, the Prophet Zechariah's exhortation to joy, while applying first to Zerubbabel, is expressed in such hyperbolic language that the prophecy could not have its complete fulfillment in him. Its ultimate fulfillment can take place only in Christ.[30] The reasoning here is convincing if we situate the text of Zechariah in the context of what follows immediately on the passage cited (v. 10):

He will cut off the chariot from Ephraim
and the war horse from Jerusalem;
and the battle bow shall be cut off,
and he shall command peace to the nations;
his dominion shall be from sea to sea,
and from the River to the ends of the earth.

It is noteworthy in this regard that a contemporary exegete, Fr. Lamarche, interprets the Messianism of Zechariah 9 in a very Antiochian

---

[29]Cf. Pirot, 566-567. It is noteworthy that another Antiochian, Theodoret of Cyr, presents us a diametrically opposed exegesis: he rails against the stupidity of the Jews who try to apply this prophecy to Zerubbabel(*PG* 81, 1921; cf. Pirot, p. 264). Vaccari also thinks that the prophecy of Zec 9 is exclusively messianic (*Biblica*, [1920], p. 19).

[30]Cf. Ternant (referring to H. N. Bate), p. 147.

way, without however referring to the idea of *theoria* or to the authors of the School of Antioch.[31] There is nothing new under the sun!

We select as a final example an expression of hope found in Ps 16 and quoted in Acts 2:27-31; 13:35ff. The two chiefs of the Apostles both cite Ps 16:10 ("For you will not abandon my soul to Hades, or let your Holy One experience corruption") and both interpret it as a prophecy of the resurrection of Jesus: "...our ancestor David...both died and was buried, and his tomb is with us to this day. ...Foreseeing this, David spoke of the resurrection of the Messiah...," said Peter (Acts 2:29-31). Paul, for his part, goes on to say: "For David...died, was laid beside his ancestors, and experienced corruption; but he whom God raised up experienced no corruption" (Acts 13:35-37).

Commenting on this Psalm, Theodore of Mopsuestia points out that verse 10 of Ps 16 found its complete fulfillment in Christ.[32] But—and this seems at first sight difficult to reconcile with the apostolic interpretation that appears to exclude any fulfillment of verse 10 at the level of Davidic reference—he sees also a certain fulfillment of Ps 16:10 in David as type and even in the entire Jewish people.

Such a view is not satisfactory either if we recall with John Chrysostom that the typical sense is that which is expressed not by words but by things.[33] The relationship between type and antitype can and normally does remain outside the ken of the sacred writer. Now if we were dealing here with a simple case of the typical sense, how could Peter say that the Prophet David foresaw and spoke of the resurrection of Christ?

It is easy to see then why the Second Council of Constantinople frowned[34] on the interpretation of Ps 16:10 given by Theodore of

---

[31]P. Lamarche, "Zacharie IX-XIV," *Structure littéraire et Messianisme*, (Paris, 1961), pp. 45, 120-121, 156: "We have adopted this nuanced solution which according to literal exegesis sees in the King-Shepherd of Zec 9-14 both a person who is a contemporary of the prophet and the Messiah."

[32]Cf. n. 34; Theodore of Mopsuestia, *PG* 66, 657-660. Pirot does not seem to have noticed a different and short commentary of the same passage of Ps 16 within the commentary that Theodore of Mopsuestia left us of Zec 9; cf. *PG* 66, 557-558. Theodore states there that verse 10 was pronounced hyperbolically by David concerning the whole Jewish people, but that it was only fulfilled in truth in Christ. This is the text of Theodore that Pope Vigilius had in mind (*Mansi*, IX, 77). See n. 34.

[33]Cf. John Chrysostom, *PG* 4, 320; 6, 396; Thomas Aquinas, *Summa Theol.*, I.1.10 and ad 1m.

[34]Cf. Pirot, p. 247, n. 5. We can only note with astonishment the lack of any mention in the *Enchiridion Biblicum* as well as in *DS* of the condemnations issued by Pope Vigilius in his *Constitution* of May 14, 553 and by the Second Council of Constantinople concerning certain exegetic views of Theodore of Mopsuestia. It is even more strange to observe that the

Mopsuestia. Preferable to this explanation is another which was given in the eighteenth century by Dom Calmet[35] and which is actually more faithful to certain Antiochian norms: the entire psalm is to be interpreted as referring both to David and to Christ, but verse 10 is realized in David in its metaphorical sense—death and sepulcher with its corruption signifying calamity and depression, resurrection being a symbol of liberty[36]

---

authors of the decree of the biblical commission of 1933 on Ps 16:10 (*DS* 3750) seem to have been unaware of the condemnation issued by Pope Vigilius (*Mansi* IX, 77), which concerns specifically the interpretation that Theodore has given us of that Psalm, and which was repeated by Constantinople II (*Mansi* IX, 211-212). R. Devreesse (*Essai sur Théodore de Mopsueste*, [Vatican City, 1948], p. 248) writes that the text of the pope's and the Council's constitution "gives an unfaithful and tendentious reference to a passage that is conserved in its entirety," in the *Commentaire de Théodore sur les Psaumes*, published by himself ([Vatican City, 1939], pp. 99-100). However, this great specialist in Theodore did not notice that the propositions condemned by the Pope and the Council, concerning Ps 16:10, are mainly taken from another commentary of Theodore concerning the minor prophets (*PG* 66, 557-558; cf. n. 32). This oversight is all the more paradoxical because Devreesse, in the same book (p. 88; cf. p. 72), even quotes the Greek text of his commentary *per transennam* of Ps 16:10 in the framework of a commentary on Zechariah. By comparing these works of Theodore with the propositions condemned by the Pope and the Council, we will see that their quote does not appear to be substantially tendentious, although both of them fell short of understanding exactly the true thought of Theodore. See in the same sense Sullivan *op. cit*, n. 52, pp. 135-138. It must be acknowledged also that the Latin text of the dossier supplied by Leontius of Byzantium (and to whom Vigilius referred) was an imperfect translation, especially in the case that concerns us here, of the thought of Theodore of Mopsuestia; moreover, the Pope's condemnation was directed not at his person and not even at his writings as such, but at certain doctrines "presented under the name of Theodore of Mopsuestia," and the Pope took care to emphasize that the condemnation applies to a certain interpretation of the text (*videtur dici*): every interpretation of Ps 16:10 according to which this verse constitutes a prediction concerning *not* the Christ, *but* the Jewish people, is anathematized; the Pope says nothing against the exegesis of the text or against seeing a prophecy in two stages. The Latin translation shows no understanding of the "hyperbolic sense" of Antioch. On the other hand we no longer have the Greek text of either Pope Vigilius or of Constantinople II. The reader should consult on this extremely complex subject F. X. Murphy and P. Sherwood, *Constantinople II and III*, (Paris, 1974), pp. 99 and 288ff; bibliographical orientations, pp. 335-340; E. Amann, *DTC* XV.2 (1950), 1923: Vigilius' judgment, in his *Constitution* of May 14, 553, is extremely subtle and it expresses at its best the thought of the Church on this difficult question. It is this document that contains the condemned exegesis and particularly that of Ps. 16:10; the texts of Theodore of Mopsuestia which were condemned at Constantinople II have been published with notes by R. Devreesse, *Essai sur Théodore de Mopsueste, Studi e Testi*, (Vatican City, 1948); and *RB* 53 (1943), 207-241; the text of the *Constitution* of May 14, 553 will also be found in *PL* 69, 67-114 and (better) in *CSEL*, 35a, 230-320, besides *Mansi*, already referred to.

[35]Referred to by Vaccari in his remarkable article: "Antica e uova interpretazione del Salmo 16" (Volg. 15), *Biblica* 14 (1933), pp. 408-434. D. Calmet's views are on p. 432.

[36]Cf. Ez 37:1-14.

and of return to the fatherland—while the same verse is fulfilled in Jesus Christ in its proper sense.

Still another explanation might, however, be more in conformity with the full range of norms established by the Antiochian School. The reference is to Christ and to the author of the Psalm (David or some other) throughout, though it is less rigorously so in one case than in the other. There is no question that Peter seems to exclude that the Psalmist is speaking of anyone other than Christ. In biblical language, the formula "not A but B" very frequently means, according to Hebrew usage, "not so much A as B." Examples of this abound (1 Sm 8:7; Mk 9:37; Jn 6:32; 12:44; Acts 5:4).[37] "You will not let your holy one see corruption" (Ps 16:10). The deliverance that the inspired poet is soliciting for himself is not, as in the case of Christ, exemption from the immediate consequences of death on the human body. Rather it is deliverance from perpetual corruption.[38] He writes with an awareness of the messianic signification of his words that bear, therefore, a double signification.[39]

This interpretation would cover the implications of a truly Antiochian understanding of Ps 16:10. Clearly the Antiochian authors had very profound methodological intuitions that they did not always manage to exploit correctly. Contemporary and future exegetes will perhaps come to a renewed understanding and application of the Antiochian *theoria* by retaining and perfecting their criteria.

Both John (12:41) and Peter (Acts 2:34-36) seem to have maintained that at least in certain cases the prophets had Christ in view when they delivered their oracles. The point is of capital importance since the exegesis of the apostles is inspired. One could affirm then that, according to the interpretation sanctioned by the Holy Spirit, the prophets intended to speak of Christ or of Christian realities in a sense that we today call literal. It is possible to demonstrate that, in the oracles that the New Testament certifies as literally messianic, the prophets had in mind also and primarily a historical personage as figure of the Messiah or certain historical realities as types of the realities of the messianic era. In such cases

---

[37]Vaccari, *Biblica*, 14 (1933), 431.

[38]Ternant, p. 377; cf. Vaccari, 433. The author refers there to Robert Bellarmine, in his commentary on Ps 16:10: "We can all apply this verse to ourselves, not in the strict sense, in which it is said of Christ alone, but because we are all members of Christ and because God has raised us in him (Eph 2:5ff), because our souls will not be abandoned in Purgatory and because our flesh will not see eternal corruption."

[39]Cf. Ternant, pp. 367 and 377ff.

we would be obliged to acknowledge, according to Antiochian terminology, that the prophet in question was exercising *theoria*.[40]

Have we not perhaps "attributed" too much either to John or Peter or to the prophets to whom they referred? If what we have just written corresponds fully either to the views of the apostles or to the view of the prophets, would we not necessarily be affirming that Abraham saw in advance the day of Christ's resurrection, not in figure but in its proper reality, and that we are assured of this by both Jesus and John (8:56): "Your father Abraham rejoiced that he was to see my day; he saw it and was glad"?

The great Antiochian writer, John Chrysostom, does not seem to have interpreted the inspired text in this way—long before the last edition of the *Jerusalem Bible*.[41] He writes:

How did he see, so many years in advance: By way of a figure, by way of a shadow [*dia tou tupou, dia tes skias*]. Indeed a spiritual lamb has been offered for the world just as a ram was offered for Isaac. The fact is that the truth had to be presignified in the shadow. Everything was prefigured by way of shadow. Here as well as there you have an only and well-beloved son. Here as well as there you have a father who gives over....[42]

It will be noted that there is no question in this commentary[43] on Abraham's foreknowledge of the reality prefigured but only of an awareness of the type, without even an admission that the type was recognized as such.

It would appear then that it is not so easy to find an example of *theoria* proposed by an Antiochian author that fulfills all the conditions supposedly laid down by the school. Can we overlook in particular that Theodore of Mopsuestia does not say that Zechariah had a clear vision into the future of Zerubbabel and Jesus and that he saw Jesus in Zerubbabel? He is content to point out the hyperbolic character of what was

---

[40]*Ibid.*, p. 373; Cerfaux, "Simples réflexions à propos de l'exégèse apostolique," *Ephmerides Theologicae Lovanienses*, 25 (1949), 565-576, especially 573.

[41]"Abraham saw Jesus' Day (as Isaiah saw his glory: 12:17), but 'from a distance,' cf. Nb 24:17; Heb 11:13, because he saw in it the birth of the promised Isaac (at which Abraham 'laughed,' Gn 17:17f) which was an event prophetic of Jesus' birth. Jesus claims to be the ultimate fulfillment of this promise made to Abraham; he is Isaac according to the spirit." (*The New Jerusalem Bible*, [New York: Doubleday, 1985], p. 1765, n. s.).

[42]John Chrysostom, *Hom. 47 on Genesis*, PG 54, 432. The whole passage deserves reading.

[43]Nor in the Commentary that the saint has left us on the Johannine Gospel, concerning Jn 8:56.

asserted regarding Zerubbabel,[44] a prophetic utterance that found its complete fulfillment only in Christ. Ancient authors generally did not have the same concerns as ours. What interested them was not so much the subjective awareness of the biblical writers as the objective fulfillment of what they announced.

As for the text of Acts where Peter cites Ps 16:10, asserting its fulfillment in the Resurrection of Christ, only the full genius of a modern exegete like Vaccari could find here the affirmation of a final non-corruption of David alongside that of a total non-corruption of Christ. Peter had on the contrary pointed out in his speech that the prophecy of David did not refer to himself (2:29), but to Christ (2:30-31).

Without wishing to state our case absolutely, we are not clearly aware of a single case of genuine *theoria* attributed by the Antiochian authors to Old Testament prophets with a foundation in the New Testament and in the sense of a conscious two-stage prophecy.

With the research we have done, it seems likely that the *theoria* of Antioch was intended rather to allude to a two-fold objective realization of a prophecy than to a subjective awareness of a two-stage prophecy. This would be true at least in a great number of cases.[45]

The discussion of *theoria* as an explanation of the prophetic phenomenon would remain, however, an interesting one, fully deserving of further and more intensive study.

Such a study would have to avoid introducing our modern categories into the analysis of Antiochian thought. This is no easy matter.

The urgency and need for such study is all the greater when we see the number of exegetes who are attempting today to resolve various biblical problems in a line that could be characterized as Antiochian in a broad sense. J. Cambier, for example, suggests applying to the Emmanuel oracles what J. Coppens[46] allows for the case of Psalms 2 and 110, namely, that the psalmists had in mind simultaneously the historical kings of the Davidic dynasty and the Messiah. For Roland de Vaux,[47] the oracle of Gn 49:10-12 can no doubt be taken as referring to David, but to

---

[44]Theodore of Mopsuestia, *Commentary on Zechariah*, PG 66, 557-558.

[45]Especially concerning Zec 9: cf. the preceding note. But it must be recognized that in many cases, especially concerning the Psalms, Theodore of Mopsuestia does not admit a "two-termed prophecy," "the events marked by prophecy have already received their first and total fulfillment" (Devreesse, *Revue Biblique*, 53 [1946], 222) while he more easily admits a two-termed prophecy in connection with the Minor Prophets (*ibid.*, 235-237). Theodore has more than one exegesis.

[46]Ternant, p. 478; cf. *Eph. Theol. Lov.*, 28 [1952], 289.

[47]R. de Vaux, "La Genèse," *Bible de Jerusalem*, (Paris, 1951), p. 212. Cf. Ternant, p. 476.

David as type of the Messiah. Other exegetes resort in their interpretation of the royal psalms (2, 45, 72, 110) to the hypothesis of a messianic rereading, by an inspired author, of a psalm that was originally not messianic in reference. Likewise, in the view of Feuillet, Benoît and Spadafora, our Lord, the Prince of Prophets, saw beyond the destruction of Jerusalem, which appears to be the primary object referred to in the entire eschatological discourse, the final cosmic catastrophe of the end of the world—a view we find already expressed in Theodoret of Antioch.[48]

In a number of these cases, the "law of the blurring of vistas" would be at play,[49] a law in virtue of which the prophets, contemplating different horizons to come, would be seeing them all on the same plane.

Such a formulation is deficient, besides being not quite faithful to the Antiochian idea according to which the antitype was glimpsed through the type, but without any real confusion. It would be better to speak of compenetration between type and antitype.

Confronted with this possible future (in the Church) for the ideas of the Antiochian School, we could raise the question of how these ideas have fared in the tradition.

B. Antioch and the Tradition of the Church

One may say that the Church has broadly speaking made its own several of the fundamental principles and attitudes of the School of Antioch, while severely condemning the "Nestorian" tendencies already present in a number of interpretations of Theodore of Mopsuestia, whose disciple Nestorius was.

In contrast to Alexandria, Antioch held that every passage of Scripture had a literal sense, whether proper or figurative. By comparing parables and metaphors with similar passages of other sacred authors and by grammatical and historical explanation the School extracted from them their literal sense.

Moreover, Antioch allowed a typical sense as well by way of or along side of this proper or metaphorical literal sense. This sense was always based on the literal sense and frequently aimed at expressing the relationships that existed between the two Testaments.[50]

---

[48]*Ibid.*, p. 484.

[49]J. Bonsirven, *Théologie du Nouveau Testament*, (Paris, 1951), p. 169.

[50]Pirot, p. 40. Devreesse, pp. 238-241, examines in detail the destiny Theodore reserved to typology, specifying the rules he followed.

On these fundamental points, one could say with some nuances that the Church has made its own the principles and attitudes of Antioch. On other points, however, the Church has kept her distance regarding the School of Antioch and especially regarding Theodore of Mopsuestia.

In the fourth century, a number of exegetical interpretations of Theodore of Mopsuestia were condemned by Pope Vigilius and the Second Council of Constantinople.

In his dogmatic constitution of May 14, 553, while carefully avoiding any condemnation of the person of Theodore, Vigilius anathematized fifty-four propositions taken from his writings, a good number of which are made up of scriptural interpretations affected by "Nestorianizing" tendencies. The Pope explained with great precision in what sense each of these propositions had been condemned.[51]

By way of example, we cite two interpretations of John's Gospel given by Theodore. In his view, Christ did not give the Holy Spirit to the apostles by breathing on them on the day of his Resurrection (Jn 20:22) and the word of Thomas ("My Lord and my God," Jn 20:28) did not refer to Christ, but was rather an exclamation of praise addressed to God who had raised Christ from the dead.[52] Theodore does not accept the idea that the apostles could ever have recognized Christ's divinity during his mortal life or even in the period after Easter and before Pentecost.[53]

The Fifth Ecumenical Council establishes as a principle that every commentary on Scripture, if it is to remain within the realm of orthodoxy, must take into account the analogy of faith. God does not

---

[51]Cf. n. 34.

[52]Cf. Theodore of Mopsuestia, *CSCO*, vol. 116, *commentarium in Evangelium Johannis Apostoli*, (Louvain, 1940), pp. 254-256. For Theodore, in Jn 20:22, Jesus uses a present in the future sense; he does not give, but promises the Spirit. Pirot, p. 319; *Mansi*, IX, 73 (Theodori capit. XV et XVI); Devreesse, *Essai...*, p. 247; J.-M. Vosté, "L'œuvres exégétique de Théodore de Mopsueste au IIe Concile de Constantinople," *RB* 38 (1929), pp. 382ff., especially (for the texts referred to here), pp. 387-389. Vosté notes, in connection with Theodore's opinion on Jn 20:22: "a singular opinion which contradicts the obvious sense of Our Lord's words, at the very moment He was conferring the power of absolving sins"; in connection with Theodore's interpretation of Jn 20:28, Vosté remarks: "According to the Syriac version, Theodore immediately makes an objection against the possibility of such a confession of Jesus" divinity by the apostle Thomas: 'How is it that Thomas, who did not even believe that the Savior was raised from the dead, could now call him "Lord and God"? This is difficult to believe.'"

We also note that F. A. Sullivan, after a long analysis (*The Christology of Theodore of Mopsuestia*, [Rome, 1956], pp. 130-132), also comes to the conclusion that the text of these two propositions and exegeses, in the form in which they are presented by Vigilius and the Council, correspond to Theodore's thought.

[53]Cf. Vosté, p. 384.

contradict himself in his Revelation. Many of Theodore's explanations were rejected because they ignored this rule. These explanations were wrong either in positing two distinct subjects of attribution in Christ (the Word, to whom the miracles were referred and the man Jesus to whom suffering and death were attributed[54]), or in distinguishing two sonships in Christ, a human, natural sonship—that of Jesus—and another, participated sonship—that of the Word that was understood as something very much like an adoptive sonship.[55]

Recent attempts to effect a complete, or nearly complete, rehabilitation of Theodore[56] have cleared up a subject that remains complex, but they have not convinced all historians.[57] In spite of the disappearance of the original Greek text of a large portion of his work, modern study of the Syriac translations of Theodore have confirmed both his limitations[58] and his merits.

The rationalism with which he has not unfairly been charged is, however, very different from the exegetical rationalism of our times. For Theodore of Mopsuestia, prophetic vision or *theoria* is situated in the context of the theory of the "two catastases" that is fundamental to his entire theological system. The first "catastasis" or state is the world that passes, the present life together with its entire framework; the second, is the future condition, our state of conformity with Christ.[59] We quote here the beginning of Theodore's commentary on John, where he expresses this global view that is, to be sure, closely correlated with the idea of *theoria*:

The same God, who alone is Lord of both Testaments, master and author of all things, ordered the content of the two covenants to a single goal. He had decided already at the beginning to reveal the future state whose principle he

---

[54]Thus Vigilius and the council condemn some interpretations of Jn 1:49; 20:17; Mt 5:11; 8:9; Heb 1:9. Cf. Pirot, p. 320.

[55]*Ibid.*, p. 321, in relation to Mt 3:17; Lk 3:22.

[56]It is a question especially of Devreesse, E. Amann, P. Galtier, J.-L. MacKenzie; see the bibliographical orientations of Murphy-Sherwood, indicated in n. 34.

[57]Especially M. Jugie, W. de Vries, F. A. Sullivan. Cf. Murphy-Sherwood, p. 26, note. We must also refer to the unpublished thesis of I. Bolonek, "De œcumenitate Concilii Constantinopoli a 553 habiti deque decretorum ejus valore dogmatico," (unpublished thesis, Gregoriana, Rome, 1969).

[58]Cf. Vosté, *RB* 38 (1929), p. 553, to be nuanced considering the research of F. A. Sullivan, especially p. 157.

[59]Cf. the New Testament view on the "present age," "dominated by a usurped kingdom of created powers in revolt against their Creator," while the "age to come" will be entirely back in the hands of the Creator again. However, in Christ, the world to come has unexpectedly arrived in the world it is supposed to replace," as Louis Bouyer put it so well, *Dictionaire Théologique*, (Tournai, 1963), p. 439, art. "Monde."

displayed in the economy of Christ. He judged it necessary, however, to set us first in the present condition and only then to transfer us to the other through the resurrection of the dead. His purpose here was to help us to come, through the comparison of the one state with the other, to appreciate the grandeur of the good things that await us. But he had also to make clear how his plan was twofold so that we would not be lead to imagine that we might someday be the object of a new scheme or of a subsequent resolution. This is why we find him at work in the history of humanity leaving numerous hints regarding the coming of the Lord Christ. And it is why the Jews were awaiting him for so long before he came.[60]

In other words, types and prophecies, history and *theoria* are ordered to the second catastasis, to the future age that has already been inaugurated in this world. The outlook expressed here can hardly be more traditional and we are lead to ask ourselves what relationship might exist between the Antiochian *theoria* and the views of some exegetes and theologians of our times regarding the *sensus plenior* of the Scriptures.

C. The Antiochian Theoria and the Sensus Plenior of the Scriptures

The Antiochian *theoria* must be distinguished from what we call the *sensus plenior* to the extent that the writers of this School thought that the prophet sees, in a single vision, both the events of a proximate future, interior to the Old Testament, and, in these events, the more remote Messianic future. The prophet is, moreover, in their view, fully aware of the relationship of prefiguration existing between the Old Testament events and those of the Messianic era.

The *sensus plenior*, in contrast, is viewed as a true scriptural sense, conveyed by the words of Scripture, intended by God, but not necessarily understood by the human and inspired author, who, while writing under the impetus of the charism of inspiration, actually employed the words in question in a more modest and restrained sense. To put it

---

[60]Theodore of Mopsuestia, *PG* 66, 317C; cf. Devreesse, *RB* 53 (1946), 237; cf. in an analogous sense Theodore's prologue to his commentary on Amos (*PG* 66, 241 AB):

> If God separated the Hebrews from the pagans, if he gave them the circumcision, if he settled them in a region apart, if he imposed on them a special form of worship, it was so that Christ, coming into the world in line with the promises of the Prophets, might convince *all men* that God's designs for the salvation of mankind were not of recent date, but since he had, by the testimony of Saint Paul, fixed his decision in the most ancient and remote time, he chose for himself Abraham so as to make a people that he would care for, so that Christ our Lord, upon his arrival in the flesh for our salvation, might appear as coming to fulfill the ancient plan.

another way, the notion of the *sensus plenior* is close to that of the type or of the figures of the Old Testament, with respect to which the sacred writer was not necessarily aware that God had ordained that individuals and institutions about which he is writing, should in fact represent New Testament realities.[61]

If, on the other hand—and this we feel is the only correct interpretation—one understands the Antiochian teachers to be saying that Scripture, the psalm, ultimately the text, points to the immediate historical future in a hyperbolic manner, and beyond this in reality, to Christ (these teachers making no mention here of the prophet, the psalmist, the sacred writer) is one not equivalently saying that in a certain number of cases (though not in all) the sacred writers, in the view of the Antiochian teachers, have an implicit knowledge of the typological character of the proximate historical events they are describing? But can we really, without violence, identify this implicit knowledge with the *sensus plenior*?[62] The fact is that the *sensus plenior* as scientifically understood today focuses on the words rather than on the deeds or event described. It is difficult to imagine that the Antiochians, in their study of Old Testament types, would have gone on to focus their attention on themes and on the evolution of the meanings of notions as is done today in a useful and even necessary way by the proponents of the *sensus plenior*. In sum, it is hard to imagine that the Antiochians could have extended the notion of *theoria* to include a perspective inherent in words. A notable presupposition for such an investigation would be a good knowledge of Hebrew. Though it would not be impossible to undertake the investigation in a limited way on the basis of the Septuagint.

It must even be said that some of the Antiochian criteria regarding the investigation of authentic types place us on guard even today against the abuse of imaginative speculation in our supposed discovery of the *sensus plenior*.

While giving considerable importance to the typological sense, Theodore of Mopsuestia invites us to an attentive reading of the Old Testament: "We should be careful not to rely (in looking for types) on fortuitous or fleeting similarities between words of the ancient text and expressions of the new, but rather on serious study of an entire personality, event, or institution prominent in sacred history and of what

---

[61]Cf. E. F. Stucliffe, "The Plenary Sense as a Principle of Interpretation," *Biblica* 34 (1953), pp. 333-334, especially p. 334.
[62]Cf. Ternant, p. 355.

is believed to correspond to these in our salvation story. Above all, we must allow ourselves to be guided by the intuitions of the New Testament authors."[63]

In short, the Antiochian criteria of a sane typology provide us also (though the Antiochians were not aware of this) with criteria for the sane usage of the method that investigates biblical themes, an instrument employed in research on the *sensus plenior*. In the analysis of a "continuity of consciousness"[64] relative to words which is being pursued by contemporary exegesis, Antioch can make a contribution by its insistence that we never separate words from the institutions and events to which they refer, but rather study them precisely in context, in the light that these events and institutions supply.

In our judgment, then, the Antiochian notion of *theoria* is not identical to the *sensus plenior* we speak of today, but the Antiochian criteria relative to the types could help contemporary exegesis to better perform its task of following the biblical themes and of attempting to determine the *sensus plenior* of the words of Scripture.

Thanks to the School of Antioch and to its insistence on the prophetic aspect of Old Testament typology,[65] of a typology of events, we can better appreciate today that a number of Old Testament words and themes, while not saying anything explicit about Christ, announce him nonetheless because they are charged with connotations which point to a future fulfillment within the New Testament.

In spite of its numerous weaknesses and limitations, indeed in spite of its internal contradictions, the School of Antioch challenges us today to transpose the *theoria* of events to words, while not forgetting the link that binds the latter with the former.

Appendix: Bibliographical indications on the School of Antioch

We indicate here a few studies not mentioned in the text of our chapter with the intention of opening up avenues of research to readers who would like more precise information on certain points:

R. M. GRANT, *L'interpretation de la Bible des origines Chrétiennes jusqu'à nos jours*, ch. VI, pp. 76-86, American edition (original) 1948; excellent presentation of the whole question, at once broad and precise.

---

[63]Cf. E. Amann, art. "Type," *DTC* XV.2 (1950), 1943.
[64]Cf. J. Guillet, p. 300-301.
[65]*Ibid.*, pp. 274ff.

A. VACCARI, "Le teoria esegetica antiochena," *Biblica* 15 (1934), 94-101: the author examines in a critical way the hypothetical reconstruction, proposed by J. M. Bover (*Estudios ecclesiasticos* 12, [1933], 405-415), of the Greek text that stands behind the definition of the Antiochian *theoria* presented by Julian of Eclane.

M. WILES, *The Spiritual Gospel, The Interpretation of the Fourth Gospel in the Early Church*, (Cambridge, 1960), ch. VIII: The Christological exegesis of Theodore and Cyril; the author shows the presuppositions common to Cyril of Alexandria and Theodore of Mopsuestia in their respective exegeses of the Gospel of John, notably (in his view) the doctrine of the two natures (cf. pp. 131-133).

R. A. GREER, *Theodore, of Mopsuestia, Exegete and Theologian*, (Westminster, 1961), ch. V, VI and VII: the author, an American Episcopalian, also studies the Johannine exegesis of Theodore of Mopsuestia; it is his view that there was interaction between his theology and his exegesis, but that it was above all his exegesis that influenced his theology.

M. J. RONDEAU, "Le commentaire des Psaumes de Diodorus de Tarse et l'exégèse antique de Ps 109-110," *Rev. d'Hist. des Relig.*, volumes 176 and 177 (1968-1970). A study that forms part of a general study on the commentaries on the Psalms by the Greek Fathers.

M. J. RONDEAU, "Le Commentaire Patristque du Psautier, IIIe-Ve siècles," vol. II, *Exégèse Prosopologique et Théologie, Dz. Christ. Analecta,* 220, (Rome, 1985).

C. SCAUBLAN, "Untersuchungen zu Methode und Herkunft der Antiochenischen Exegese," *Theophania* 23, (Koln, 1974): the author examines the usage of hypothesis, a technique common in Greek rhetoric of the period, as employed by Theodore of Mopsuestia; he stresses his major contribution, namely, his grasp of the Hebraisms of the Septuagint; cf. C. Kannengieser, *Recherches des Sc. Rel.*, 66 (1978), pp. 403-406.

Chapter VIII
Saint John Chrysostom,
Doctor of Biblical "Condescension"

It is primarily through the work of Saint John Chrysostom that the school of Antioch, whose orientations and aspirations we have just examined, has influenced the Church and Christian exegesis.

There is a tendency today in sophisticated circles to regard the exegesis of the Syrian doctor[1] as no more than a moralizing and psychologizing exposition, devoid of any lofty doctrinal content.[2]

A reaction to this assessment is, however, taking shape. The doctrinal richness of Chrysostom is being rediscovered. Daniélou insists particularly on the liturgical context within which the Patriarch of Constantinople penetrated the splendors of Sacred Scripture,[3] and, in its light, of God's incomprehensibility.

---

[1]Cf. René Leconte's unpublished thesis, *Saint Jean Chrysostom, exégète syrien, d'après les homélies sur saint Matthieu,* presented in 1942 at the Institut Catholique de Paris, ch. III, conclusion: in his exegetic method, Chrysostom was more under the influence of the Syrian monks than of the Greeks.

[2]However, the recent articles do not seem to be subject to this prejudice: for example, see A. Wenger, *DSAM* 8 (1974), col. 4331-355, with a rich bibliography, especially in connection with Chrysostom's exegesis; D. Stiernon, *Catholicisme* 6 (1967), col. 498-511; *DTC*, Tables, II, 2452-2459 etc.

[3]Cf. Jean Daniélou's introduction to Chrysostom's treatise on the *Incomprehensibility of God,* SC 28ᵃ, (Paris, 1970), pp. 15-62; A. M. Ritter, *Charisma im Verständnis des Johannes Chrysost. und seiner Zeit,* (Göttingen, 1972); E. Nowak, *Le Chrétien devant la souffrance, Etude sur la pensée de Jean Chrysostome,* (Paris, 1972): even while underscoring the influence of Stoicism on the great Antiochian exegete, the author does not fail to add: "John preaches all the dogmas of Christianity, the Trinity, the Incarnation, the Redemption, retribution after

189

This helps to explain the enthusiasm generated during history by the biblical commentaries of this man whom the Church has proclaimed heavenly patron of all Christian preachers.[4] If, for Henry IV, Paris was worth a Mass, Saint Thomas Aquinas[5] was prepared to sacrifice the beauties of the capital for those of Chrysostom's commentary on the Gospel according to Saint Matthew; and Charles de Foucauld never tired of reading and re-reading the works of the Antiochian exegete and preacher which provided solid nourishment for his prayer.[6]

Is it not remarkable to think that great minds like those of the two cardinals Newman[7] and Daniélou, although much more Alexandrian than Antiochian, more drawn to the spiritual than to the literal sense of the Scriptures, found the charm of the Syrian doctor irresistible?

He continues to instruct his readers today, not only on the virtues and the vices (which, by the way, he treats in a very biblical manner), but on the economy of salvation as well.

We will be able to test this by viewing the Scriptures, in the light of the biblical homilies and commentaries[8] of the great Antiochian Doctor, as a manifestation of the very meticulous condescension of God our Savior who leads us exiles to the most lofty *theoria* and vision of his Face

---

death, eternal life, the universal resurrection, the divine judgment, the Church and her salvific mission that is extended to all men.... These truths obviously are hardly to be credited to Stoicism" (pp. 227-228).

[4]By a decision of Leo XII to which Saint Pius X referred on July 22, 1907, in his letter *Prope est*; Saint Pius X, *Actes*, (Paris: Bonne Presse), vol. III, pp. 81-84.

[5]Cf. C. Spicq, "Saint Thomas d'Aquin," *DTC* XVI.1 (1946), 701: "Our doctor possessed St. John Chrysostom's Homilies and Commentary on St. Matthew. At the time of his first teaching assignment in Paris (1256-1259), he is said to have expressed the wish, according to Bartholomew of Capua, to obtain a good translation of the Homilies, which he regarded as a more valuable treasure than the whole city of Paris."

[6]Cf. these remarks by B. Jacqueline in his Introduction to a retreat of Charles de Foucauld, *En vue de Dieu seul*, (Rome-Paris, 1973), pp. 23-24: "Charles de Foucauld read John Chrysostom..., a reading recommended to him on various occasions by Fr. Huvelin: 'Follow your St. John Chrysostom, who suits you so well'" (Sept. 16, 1897). He was still pursuing that reading in 1898: "St. John Chrysostom," writes Charles de Foucauld, "is far from finished." This reading corresponds to a principle of Charles: "to read the books of the Catholic doctors who comment on it (namely, the Scriptures), not just any books, but books of very sound doctrine, books of great spirits and great saints: Saint Augustine, Saint John Chrysostom, Saint Thomas Aquinas" (*ibid.*, p. 105).

[7]John Henry Newman, *Historical Sketches*, (London, 1873), vol. II, pp. 217-302, where the author emphasizes at length, pp. 288-289, the merits of Chrysostom's literal exegesis.

[8]We note here the hypothesis developed by M. L. Guillaumin during a study on "Bible and Liturgy in the Preaching of John Chrysostom," *Jean Chrysostome et Augustin*, (Paris, 1975), pp. 161-174: after having been solely a preacher for some years, our doctor ended up producing a biblical teaching separated from the liturgical year.

through the humility of his Letters and of his unique Book: *sugkatabasis, akribia, theoria.*

This will help us to see that Scripture is for Chrysostom an extension of the Incarnation. It set the stage for the Incarnation and it now unfolds this mystery, manifesting it fully in the Liturgy that is the place par excellence of the reception and the efficacy of the divine Word that it transmits.

It is clear then why the teachings of the "Golden Mouthed" Doctor have found such an echo in the texts of Vatican II as well as in the Christian confessions that are in real, albeit not yet perfect, communion with the Catholic Church.

A) *Scripture manifests the Condescension* (sugkatabasis) *of God the Savior*

Like Origen[9] and Saint Athanasius,[10] perhaps even under their influence (at least indirectly), Chrysostom makes use of the notion of "condescension" to express the way in which God behaves in his relations with humankind, particularly in his gift of Scripture. His use of the idea is undoubtedly more systematic than that of his predecessors—so much so that he has become known, in the apt expression of H. Pinard de La Boullaye, as "the doctor of divine condescension."[11]

What exactly is this condescension, this *sugkatabasis* of God in the mind of the Antiochian preacher? He himself gives us the following definition:

---

[9]Origen, *Contra Celsum,* VII, 60: the "divine nature condescended to the ignorance of the multitudes of hearers: thus, using terms which were familiar to them, that divine nature won the hearing of the multitude of simpletons: once they have been initiated, they can easily aspire to grasp even the most profound thoughts in the Scriptures." Cf. IV, 12: God adapts himself even to the intellectual weakness of man, just as it is the human custom of teachers to condescend to the level of children.

[10]Mainly in a christological context: cf. K. Duchatelez, "La condescendance divine et l'histoire du salut," *Nouv. Rev. Théologique,* 105 (1973), pp. 593-621; on Athanasius, see pp. 600-601.

[11]An expression of H. Pimard, "Les infiltrations païennes dans l'ancienne loi, d'après les Pères de l'Eglise, la thèse de la condescendance," *Rech. Sc. Relig.,* 9 (1919), pp. 197-221; the expression mentioned is on p. 209; on this theme in Chrysostom, see also F. Fabbi, *Biblica* 14 (1934), 330-347. The author wrongly believes that this theme is ignored and even combated by Origen; P. Moro, *Euntes docete* (1958), pp. 109-123; F. Asensio, *Estudios Biblicos* 32 (1973), pp. 223-255 and 329-356. We have made much use here of the works of Pinard and especially of the works of Fabbi and Duchatelez.

It is that God appears and shows himself, not as he is, but such as he can be seen by one who is capable of such a vision, adapting the character of his self-presentation to the weakness of those who contemplate him.

If condescension is at work even in the beatifying vision granted to the angels[12]—and ultimately to human beings—it is present too from the beginnings of the religious history of humanity.

The notion was already familiar to Greek paganism,[13] although it was strangely rebuffed by the neo-paganism of Julian the Apostate: "The excellence of their superior nature prevents the gods from descending to the level of earthly objects."[14]

The idea of condescension does on the contrary imply a descent to the level of the inferior, an adaptation to the capacity of another. In the view of Chrysostom, the concept serves magnificently to express the way in which the transcendent God fits his revelation and his work of salvation to the measure of man in his littleness and weakness, whether in the Old Testament, in the New Testament, or even through the pastoral activity of the Church. Like a master with his pupils, like parents who go so far as to imitate the babblings of their little children, God adapts himself to our measure.[15] The teachers of children who are just beginning school always give them the primary elements first and reserve the more elevated teachings for later. In like manner, Moses served as a pedagogue, inculcating the rudiments and leaving it for Paul and John to clarify and complete them.[16]

Chrysostom's homilies on Genesis bring out admiringly and emphatically the extreme condescension of God (*tês sugkatabaseôs tên huperbolên*) in his relations with human beings. In the beginning, God conversed with men familiarly. He spoke personally with Adam, Cain, Noah, Abraham. There was no need for writing. As humanity began to degenerate, the Creator did not totally turn away from it, but to those who were now living somewhat estranged from him he sent a letter, through the agency

---

[12]John Chrysostom, *On the Incomprehensibility of God*, Discourse III, SC 28ᵃ; PG 48, 722A; Discourse I, PG 48, 707B. You might as well say that infinite Being is never seen by a finite creature as much as he is visible, which is to say infinitely. Some even think that Chrysostom denies the face-to-face vision of the divine essence by the saints in heaven: Tixeront, *Histoire des dogmes*, vol. II, p. 201; this would be a good theme for further study.

[13]Æschylus, *The Choephores*, 727.

[14]Julian the Apostate, Discourse VIII, 11; cf. Duchatelez, p. 598.

[15]Cf. John Chrysostom, *Hom. III.2 on the Letter to Titus*, PG 62, 678.

[16]Chrysostom, *Hom. II on Genesis*, PG 53, 26ff.

of Moses, to recall them to his friendship. We are the recipients of that letter, living as it were in a great foreign country.[17]

It is in this context that Chrysostom often exalts not only the condescension of God, but also that of the divine Scripture: apropos of Gn 2:21—Eve taken from the side of Adam—he declares that God employed these words by way of condescending to our littleness and he asks us to carefully observe the *"sugkatabasin tes theias graphes."*[18]

What is the proximate foundation of this salvific condescension? It is rooted, as the Antiochian exegete sees it, in God's will to establish a relationship between his immaterial being and the materiality of the human person. Let us listen to the Saint himself as he comments on Ps. 6:

> When you hear God spoken of in terms of anger or wrath, be careful not to take these words in their usual human and material significance; what we have here is merely a language of condescension. When we speak with uneducated people we use their language to make ourselves understood by them. We babble with tiny children, and, no matter how sophisticated we are, we do not hesitate to descend to their level. There is nothing surprising in this language, since, to correct children, we often wring our hands, and find all kinds of ways of feigning anger. In like manner we see God adopting the language which David puts on his lips, to discipline people who are uncultured or uncouth. When God speaks to us, he considers less his dignity than the good of those to whom his words are addressed.[19]

> That he is immune from anger he himself declares by the mouth of the Prophet: "But am I the one they are provoking? ...Are they not rather harming themselves, to their own shame?" (Jer 7:19).

> How would you want God to have talked to the Jews? Could one really have said: God is never angry, never would hate the evildoer, because anger and hatred are passions of the soul?

> Then we would also have to say: God does not keep an eye on human affairs because seeing is an act of a bodily organ; he does not hear either, because hearing belongs to the body.

> But [a more spiritual language] would have obfuscated the dogma of the divine Providence.... How many minds would have remained in complete ignorance of God?

---

[17]Chrysostom, *PG* 54, 582.

[18]Chrysostom, *PG* 53, 121.

[19]Chrysostom, *Exposition on psalm VI, PG* 55, 71.

In sum, recourse to the consideration of God's condescension constitutes Chrysostom's great response to the problem that Ambrose and Augustine had not long ago examined[20] in more fully Alexandrian terms, namely, the expounding of the anthropomorphic and apparently shocking passages of the Old Testament. We were careful to say in more fully Alexandrian terms, because Origen had already resorted, for the same reason, as we brought out above, to an explanation of condescension; nevertheless, at times, with him as in the Alexandrian school in general, the idea of a metaphorical literal sense was lost sight of; in contrast, with Chrysostom, it was retained.

As his commentary on Ps 6 so beautifully shows, it is the concept of divine condescension that enabled Chrysostom to justify God's speaking of his totally spiritual Self in such a way as to be understood by human beings who were as yet material and primitive, imperfectly aware of their own spirituality, rather than simply remaining silent regarding himself under the pretext that whatever might be said could deceive them. Thanks to the idea of condescension, an eternally impassable God was able, without denying his impassibility, to adopt the language of human passions to make himself understood by men endowed with passions.

For Chrysostom, the prophets went beyond the language of Genesis and of David and spoke more clearly of the spiritual nature of God: "to one who believes that there is no Providence and God does not even exist, what good would it have done to speak of the impassibility of God?" On the other hand, after having convinced his contemporaries of the existence of God, the prophet can then "elevate them to the dogma and discourse of the divine impassibility" and can say to them: "God does not grow tired" (Is 40:28).[21]

Thanks to the concept of the divine condescension, Chrysostom was able to show that there is no complicity in the Old Testament with the pagan representations of gods moved by passions like those of sinful

---

[20]Johannes Quasten, (*Initiation aux Pères de l'Eglise*, [Paris, 1962], vol. III, p. 610), emphasizes that Chrysostom's commentaries on the Psalms date from the end of his Antiochian period; these discussions have come to us under the title of *Interpretations* (*Hermènéiai*) and not homilies; it is therefore not certain that Chrysostom had actually delivered these discourses with his own lips, but they are by far his best commentaries on the Old Testament. Now, at the end of the Antiochean period, about 397, it was a long time—more than ten years—since Ambrose and Augustine had broached, in a very different way, the same subject of the difficulties the fourth-century reader found in the Old Testament.

[21]Chrysostom, *Exposition on Psalm VI*, PG 55, 71.

men; he was likewise able to reject more easily the theses of the Egyptian anthropomorphists who maintained that it was necessary to hold to a strictly literal interpretation of all the biblical expressions on God's anger, God's hands, fingers, face etc., God being thus viewed as a bodily, not a spiritual being.[22] For Chrysostom, all such biblical expressions pointed to the condescension of a spiritual Being who merely wished to provide us with the means of attaining him, through metaphors suited to our materiality.

The Antiochian doctor often insists on this point: we find in the Bible metaphors,[23] parables, similes, enigmatic expressions,[24] symbols,[25] metonymies,[26] etc. This is God's way of lowering himself to a language that might appear unworthy of him, but which he employs because he has in mind not his dignity, but our good—as Chrysostom brings out in commenting on Ps 6[27]—and our salvation.

It is the same salvific will that explains both what is still obscure and what is already clear in the prophecies and in the Old Testament—a theme brilliantly developed in the two celebrated homilies "on the obscurity of the prophecies."[28] For Chrysostom, certain things are obscure in the Old Testament, but not all, "Otherwise they would have been told us in vain."[29] He brings this out strongly in his *Homily* 32 on Genesis: "God in his mercy did not intend that all the truths contained in the Scriptures should come to us clear and luminous at a simple reading. In this way he would shake us out of our sleep, that through our vigilance we might laboriously extract what is useful for us. For what we find through painful and diligent search usually becomes more deeply engraved in our minds than that which we rapidly understand and

---

[22]Audius, who died in 372, and who lived in Syria at the time of the Council of Nicea, thought that God has a human form because (Gn 1:27) he created man in his image and likeness. If God sees, hears, speaks, becomes angry or threatens, it is because he has, like man, senses and passions: cf. Bareille, *DTC*, I, 2 (1923), 1371. Chrysostom denounces anthropomorphic exegesis in the *Exposition on Psalm VII*, 11, PG 55, 97-98.

[23]Chrysostom, *In Ps. XLIV*, 10, PG 55, 225-226.

[24]Chrysostom, *In Ps. XLVIII*, 5, PG 55, 225-226.

[25]Chrysostom, *In Ps. XLIV*, 8, PG 55, 197.

[26]Chrysostom, *In Ps. XLIII*, 20, PG 55, 179; *In Ps. 147*, 1, PG 55, 478.

[27]Cf. note 19.

[28]Chrysostom, PG 56, 163-192.

[29]Chrysostom, PG 56, 173.

which we just as rapidly forget."[30] This theme was being developed by Saint Augustine in roughly the same period.[31]

The condescension of the Revealer is not manifested only in the Old Testament, but is continued, Chrysostom believes, even in the words of Christ. To the most sublime affirmations Christ joins "humble expressions; he thus lowers himself" to provide for our salvation! "It is not that I must have a man's witness; I say this only in order that you may be saved" (Jn 5:34).[32]

The Antiochian doctor goes even so far as to list four reasons for the condescension of Christ in his discourse: to make his words more easily credible for those who would be disturbed by their sublimity,[33] thus demonstrating the weakness of the flesh with which he was clothed; to take into account the intellectual weakness of his audience; to teach them by the example of a humility, not only in words, but even in deeds, the humility which he came to inculcate; and finally to keep us from falling into the error of believing that the Father and the Son are one and the same person because of the great and immense proximity of their hypostases or persons.[34]

We see then how profound is the level of Chrysostom's reflection on the condescension of Christ in his activity as revealer. He wishes to bring out the connections between the behavior of Christ, on the one hand, and his person and mission on the other, in the context of the mysteries of the Trinity and the Redemptive Incarnation. In order to distinguish himself clearly from the Father whose sublimity is unique, the Son was lead to speak a humble language reflecting the humility of his human nature with respect to the divine nature; moreover, how could he, if he used only sublime words corresponding to the sublimity of his divine nature, effectively teach the humility he had come, as the second Adam,

---

[30]Chrysostom, *Homily XXXII on Genesis*, PG 53, 292-293.

[31]Augustine, *Epist. 149 ad Paulinum 34*, (CSEL 44, 379); *Enarrat. in Ps. 146*, 12 (Cch 40, 2130ff.); texts referred to by Pius XII, *Divino Afflante Spiritu*, AAS 35 (1943), 318-319.

[32]Chrysostom, *Homily XXXIX on the Gospel of John*, PG, 59, 221.

[33]The saint notes, about Jn 8:28 and Jn 8:30, that many were drawn toward Jesus when he presented himself as one taught by the Father, and they believed in him (PG 48, 761).

[34]Chrysostom, *Discourse on the Son Consubstantial with the Father*, delivered at Constantinople in 397 (Quasten, p. 632), PG 48, 761-762: "He who taught us to be humble and who moved us to humility by his words and actions had many opportunities to speak humbly," the saint said before quoting Mt 11:29 and Mt 20:28.

to offer and demand of human beings to rescue them from the pride of the first?[35]

It might appear that these considerations of Chrysostom that we have here recalled have made us stray from our purpose that was to present his biblical exegesis; do they not concern the Person who is the unique Word of God rather than the multiplicity of his human words reported by Scripture? Can a proper understanding of the human language of Jesus really be separated from a correct perception, within the parameters of faith, of his theandric Person?

For Chrysostom, the enormous advantage offered by the notion of *sugkatabasis* was that it could serve simultaneously to exalt both the transcendence of a God who cannot *descend* among men except by remaining *above them* (*kata* meaning: from above to below) and correlatively his immanence: his superiority does not prevent Him from being *with* (*sun*) human beings.

God's *sugkatabasis* or condescension allowed Chrysostom to demonstrate, in his dialogue with the Anomean Arians, that Scripture did not separate the Creator's philanthropy from his superiority: "God resorts to condescension in virtue of his great philanthropy."[36] For the Antiochian exegete and theologian, the *sugkatabasis* is almost equivalent to the notion of *economy*: Chrysostom frequently employs the latter term in the sense of an accommodation, a condescension that again derives from a certain reserve in the revelation of the truth.[37] The two words seem to remain distinguished by a nuance: condescension implies the idea of an assistance granted in adaptation to a lack of capacity; economy, that of a reserve imposed by the intrinsic exigencies of God's salvific plan.[38]

Having seen the double context, the sublime and the humble, of the divine condescension in Chrysostom, we are in a better position to grasp the hermeneutical consequences of his doctrine.

If one accepts the premise that God has been educating humanity progressively, one will not be shocked at the rough edges of history, nor at the imperfections of the Old Testament. The exegete will accept the past in its objectivity. History will not be an embarrassment.

---

[35]It can be observed here that the God of the Old Testament, in his preparing mankind for the Incarnation of his Son, was already speaking in a language of humble condescension.

[36]Chrysostom, *Hom. IV.2 on the Letter to the Colossians*, PG 62, 328.

[37]Cf. Chrysostom, *Hom. III, 1 on Matthew*, PG 57, 32; *XXXIX, 1 on John*: PG 59, 221.

[38]Duchatelez, p. 60, n. 1.

Similarly, if we accept that God has been willing to employ the ordinary language of human beings, deficiencies in style or vocabulary will appear normal. At the same time, each word, since it is a divine medium of expression,[39] will be of enormous interest to us and we will have to subject the sacred text, without reserve, to a minute literal analysis. Grasping the human thought present in the text will enable us to discover at the same time the thought of God who condescends to express himself in human terms.

Thus the idea of divine condescension should normally lead the biblical scholar to an exegesis that is both historical and grammatical. This is why Saint John Chrysostom, in spite of the popular character of his homilies and the limits of his erudition, nevertheless imposes on himself the rule of not rising to spiritual considerations till after having attentively examined the obvious and natural meaning of the texts.

Even if, as we have already said, Origen had already perceived how much the consideration of the divine condescension could affect exegesis,[40] it does not seem that he saw clearly, as did Chrysostom, the services that this notion was to render in favor of a more objective interpretation of the Sacred Books.

When he comes across a passage of Scripture that denotes a somewhat primitive faith, morality or mode of expression, Origen refuses to take it seriously and he resorts to allegory. There is some internal contradiction in his work in the fact that he is here "judging moments of

---

[39]Cf. P. Benoît, "Inspiration," *Catholicisme*, V (1962), col. 1717-1718:

The divine influx goes even into the very text, which is its true term. We can therefore speak of verbal inspiration. This expression used to frighten us, in so far as inspiration was conceived in the fashion of a revelation. The sacred writer was supposed to be nothing more than a passive instrument writing under the "dictation" of God.... [But] he is actually the man who seeks and finds, with all his human resources and faculties, the most suitable words to express his thought; but he does this under God's impetus, in such a way that the text he works out will truly be that which God wished. ...This is of capital importance for establishing the *sensus plenior*. This is why God has made his interpreter adopt such and such a term which the interpreter was keeping for later, for another writing, a term which he has made part of a "biblical vocabulary" where the words have a history: their later uses give to their more ancient uses an unsuspected value that the first author did not perceive, but which God himself already knew and which he prepared in that earlier writer and which is therefore scriptural.

However, it is true that Chrysostom's relative ignorance of Hebrew (which he only knew, it seems, through Syriac: cf. R. Leconte, pp. 98-104) did not permit him to benefit fully from all the consequences of his doctrine on inspiration.

[40]Cf. below, note 9.

providential condescension to be unworthy of God,"[41] in the words of Fr. Prat.

All these advantages[42] were still further reinforced by Chrysostom's idea of *exactitude*, which serves to complement the criterion of condescension. For—and this should be obvious—the exclusive application of this latter principle could detract from the holiness of Scripture and from the dignity of the One who inspired it.

B. God's Condescension is Likewise Revealed in "Acribeia," the Precision, the Exactitude and the Inerrancy of the Inspired Text

If the Golden Mouth frequently speaks of condescension, of the *sugkatabasis* of the Scriptures, he no less frequently underlines their *akribeia*, their exactitude: "note well the precision of the teaching (*akribeian tes didaskalias*)";[43] "observe the exactitude of Scripture,"[44] etc.

Speaking of this exactitude, the Antiochian doctor affirms that the veracity of Scripture surpasses every other testimony,[45] including even that of a dead person restored to life[46] or of an angel come down from heaven.[47]

Thus, Scripture contains nothing superfluous[48] nor any contradiction;[49] its veracity extends even to the circumstances of place, time and person[50] and to historical circumstances in general,[51] for this Scripture is after all the word of the infallible God on whom any error it might be thought to contain would reflect.[52]

Of course, the Patriarch of Constantinople concedes that there are divergences, dissonances or "diaphonies" regarding time and place between the various Gospel narratives, but he does so only to insist that these do not imply any contradiction, in contrast to what we find among the orators and the philosophers; on the contrary, these diaphonies more

---

[41]F. Prat, *Origène, le théologien et l'exégète*, (Paris, 1907), p. xix, cf. p. 180; Cf. Origen, *In Principiis*, 1, IV, notes 11-16, PG 11, 341-414.

[42]Cf. R. Leconte, pp. 258-260

[43]Chrysostom, *PG* 53, 120.

[44]Chrysostom, *PG* 53, 121.

[45]Chrysostom, *PG* 55, 36.

[46]Chrysostom, *PG* 48, 1009-1010.

[47]*Ibid.*

[48]Chrysostom, *PG* 53, 256.

[49]Chrysostom, *PG* 53, 42, 286.

[50]Chrysostom, *PG* 53, 180, 187.

[51]Chrysostom, *PG* 60, 171.

[52]Chrysostom, *PG* 56, 156

strikingly bring out the truth of what is told because they show that the four evangelists did not get together and conspire before sitting down to write.[53]

We will confirm these general affirmations by some concrete examples.

One of the goals pursued by the Syrian exegete in his homilies on the Gospel according to Matthew is clearly stated by him at the beginning of his work in the following terms: "We will attempt to demonstrate throughout this work that the evangelists were not contradicting one another."[54] He was certainly thinking, as he wrote these words, of the many in Antioch who were listening to the objections of the heretics and using some supposed contradictions to argue against the absolute veracity of the holy Books.[55]

As he moves forward in expounding the text of Matthew's Gospel, Chrysostom manifests the desire to show that the sacred writers "had the truth alone in view and never concealed the facts";[56] their "love for the truth is evident in the fact that they tell with perfect exactitude (*akribeia*) even things that are regarded as shameful; they conceal nothing, they are embarrassed by nothing."[57]

Far from contradicting one another, the Evangelists represent a "symphony" (reminiscent of the "consonance" of Irenæus[58]) which itself reflects something deeper: the kinship of every affirmation of Scripture with all other affirmations:

> When we take a part from the flank [of an animal] we find in that part everything that goes to make up the living organism as a whole—nerves, veins, bones, arteries, blood—a miniature, if I may put this way, of the entire organism. So also concerning Scripture we can see that a kinship with the whole manifests itself in each part of the text.[59]

Each biblical affirmation is illuminated by many other statements in the Bible. This is Chrysostom's way of pointing out what we today call the analogy of faith.

The apparent disagreements regard only minor points (*mikra*), such as: "expressions or turns of phrase (*remata kai tropous lexeon*)" or again

---

[53]Cf. note 63.

[54]Chrysostom, *Hom. I in Matt.*, PG 57, 18.

[55]*Ibid.*, col. 45, 349; *Hom. IV*, 28 and 29.

[56]*Ibid.*, *Hom. LXXX*, col. 727.

[57]*Ibid.*, *Hom. LXXXV*, col. 757.

[58]Cf. our chapter II, note 16. Some influence by Irenæus is not impossible.

[59]Chrysostom, *Hom. I in Matt.*, PG 57, 18.

"time and place,"⁶⁰ for chronological or topographical specifications reflect the point of view of the inspired author.

On the other hand, there is perfect agreement among the inspired authors on the essential and fundamental truths of the faith (*kephalaia*), necessary and urgent questions, for example, which pertain to life and to the kerygma:

> ...the fact that God became man, that he worked miracles, that he was crucified and buried, that he rose again, that he went up [to heaven], that he will judge us, that he has given us special teachings to lead us to salvation, that he introduced a new Law that is not contrary to the old, that he is God's only true Son, that he is of the same nature as the Father, and things of this kind.⁶¹

Even the differences on secondary points (*mikra*) do not amount to contradiction.⁶² Moreover, without a surface "diaphony," the profound "symphony" would become suspect:

> If their story were identical down to the tiniest detail of circumstance—the place, the exact words, etc., none of their enemies would have believed that they wrote what they wrote without having come together and made some private agreement with one another. But it is precisely this difference we find in the details of the story that removes all suspicion from these writers and clearly testifies in their favor.⁶³

What rule then will the exegete apply, according to Chrysostom, to reconcile the texts, all inspired by the same Spirit, without ending up in some forced harmonization and without doing violence to the texts themselves? Chrysostom responds to this question when he attempts to reconcile Mt 11:2-3 and Lk 7:18-19: "This does not provoke the slightest difficulty but simply makes room for *theoria*."⁶⁴ What he must mean here by "theoria" is an overall view of history and of the economy of salvation

---

⁶⁰*Ibid.*, 57, 16. R. Leconte shows that this point was badly understood by Foerster (*Chrysostomus in seinem Verhältnis zur Antiochenischen Schule*, [Gotha, 1869]) and S. Haidacher (*Die Lehre des Heil. J. Chrysostomus über die Schriftinspiration*, [Salzburg, 1897]). The difference (which is in question in the course of our present text) between *kephalaia* and *mikra* "should not be interpreted from a purely quantitative and extensive point of view, for it is not meant to introduce a hierarchy in the texts of Scripture, but simply to underscore the difference that exists between a particular truth and the way it is expressed by each author" (Leconte, p. 190, and in general, pp. 169-190).

⁶¹Chrysostom, *Hom. I in Matt.*, PG 57, col. 16-17.

⁶²*Ibid.*, col. 18: "one thing is" *diaphoros eipein*, "another thing" *machomenous eipein*.

⁶³*Ibid.*, col. 16 (RJ 1170).

⁶⁴Chrysostom, *Hom. XXXVI*, col. 413. Cf. Leconte, pp. 189 and 250.

which, in the words of his teacher Diodorus of Tarsus[65] "neither under-mines history nor destroys our understanding of it" and which looks at a particular point of history in the light of the double objective pursued by the inspired author and by the One who inspired. We must remember that in Chrysostom's view there is matter for *theoria* even in the New Testament, as will become clearer below.[66]

The point of view here presented is very close to that which Augustine was expressing at approximately the same period in his *De Doctrina Christiana*: the objective of Scripture is that its reader advance in the love of God and of neighbor.[67] But Chrysostom does not take the liberties with the sacred text that Augustine sometimes takes.

The harmonization techniques of Chrysostom will perhaps appear somewhat artificial to us today, for example, when he is commenting on the conversion of the Good Thief.[68] The fact remains that he wanted to take into account every nuance, every insinuation or preference of each author to extract from their diverse accounts a harmonious and exact view of what they were describing—in each case the same event.

His search for the *symphony* among the human authors of the New Testament is inseparable from his concern for *akribeia* and for the exact and precise truth.

When we reflect on it more deeply, this *akribeia* appears to be not so much a necessary complement to condescension as one of its intrinsic aspects. When the God who is beyond every extrinsic determination, the God who is transcendent, takes the initiative to address finite, limited, circumscribed entities like human beings, in their language which is con-crete, and when he wishes to be understood by them and to enable them to know the particular historical events of his saving economy, he is low-ering himself to be *with* them (condescension) through a clearly deline-ated exactness of ideas and expressions.

---

[65]An extract from the *Commentaire de Diodore de Tarse sur les Psaumes*, preface, *Rech. Sc. Relig.*, (1919), p. 88, 1, 23; on the *theoria* and the economy of salvation, see Leconte, pp. 278-279.

[66]Cf. Chrysostom's text, referred to in n. 64.

[67]Augustine, *De Doctrina Christiana*, III, 10, 15-16.

[68]Chrysostom, *Hom. LXXXVII on Matt.* 27, 44, *PG* 57, 772. Cf. on the same subject the saint's homily on the paralytic let down through the roof, *PG* 51, 54. The great doctor of Antioch thought that the Good Thief was converted after having blasphemed Christ when both were being crucified; Augustine's interpretation is preferable, according to which usage permits Matthew to use the plural for the singular: *De Consensu Evangelistarum* III, 16, *PL* 34, 1191.

In opposition to Anomean Arianism and to the rationalist claims of Eunomius ("God does not know any more about his being than we do and everything he knows of himself we find it easily and without any difference in ourselves"),[69] Chrysostom tirelessly underscores the incomprehensibility of God: "You claim," he says to Eunomius, "to circumscribe his essence"![70] We do know the existence of God, but we do not know his essence. "What Chrysostom considers impious is the claim to a complete (*akribes*) knowledge of the divine essence: a term he continuously employs is *akribeia*," Daniélou remarks.[71] "If even the prophets (a term which in Chrysostom's terminology refers to the sacred writers) cannot describe the divine essence with exactitude, how great is the folly of those who believe they can subject his very essence to their own reasonings?"[72]

For the Antiochian Doctor, the "inexpressible, inconceivable, invisible and incomprehensible God surpasses the power of any human language, escapes the grasp of any mortal intelligence; only the Son and the Spirit know Him."[73] Except for them, "no one has ever seen God, that is to say, no one has ever known God in his essence with full exactitude," *meta akribeias apases*.[74]

For Chrysostom, we do not know perfectly, *meta akribeias*, the essence of the angels,[75] nor that of the soul;[76] the Anomean Arians "know neither the angels nor their own souls, yet they claim to know perfectly (*meta akribeias*) the Master and Creator of the universe!"[77]

Conversely, Christ said: "No one knows the Son except the Father and no one knows the Father except the Son (Lk 10:22); not that anyone has seen the Father except the one who is from God, he has seen the Father (Jn 6:46)." He thus indicates, Chrysostom comments, "both the perfection (*meta akribeias*) with which he knows the Father and the reason why he knows Him. And what is this reason? It is that he comes

---

[69]The text of Eunon referred to by Socrates, *Hist. Eccles.*, IV, 7, *PG* 67, 474B.

[70]Chrysostom, *On the Incomprehensibility of God*, SC 28a, (Paris, 1970), (henceforth referred to by the title followed by the indication of the homily and page), Homily I, 231-234, p. 120.

[71]Jean Daniélou, "Introduction to the Homilies of Saint John Chrysostom," *On the Incomprehensibility of God*, Homily I, 196, p. 116.

[72]Chrysostom, *On the Incomprehensibility of God*, Homily I, 196, p. 116.

[73]*Ibid.*, Homily III, 53-59; p. 191. Cf. Homily V, 285-319, p. 297.

[74]*Ibid.*, Homily IV, 222, p. 246. Cf. Homily V, 55-77, p. 276.

[75]*Ibid.*, Homily V, 257, p. 292.

[76]*Ibid.* Homily V, 265, p. 294.

[77]*Ibid.*

from Him. And conversely, the fact that he comes from Him is proved by the perfection of the knowledge he has of Him" (*meta akribeias eidenai*).[78]

If we, in contrast to the Son, do not know the Father "meta akribeias," do not enjoy the vision of His essence, this is precisely because we are not the Son in the unique sense of the term, but only created intelligences; "though we do not know what his essence is, we do know that he exists" and we are not "ignorant of the fact that God foresees, sustains and governs everything with precision, *meta akribeias.*"[79]

The many texts we have just cited on the divine "akribeia," the non-"akribeia" of human beings regarding God and the "akribeia" of the language of the Scriptures call for a number of observations.

On the one hand, it is clear that the Antiochian Doctor did not himself synthesize the opposite poles of his own thinking: man cannot know God and his inner life with *akribeia*, with exactitude, but even so he can recognize the expressions charged with *akribeia* which God, the author of Scripture, employs when he chooses to speak with man in a circumscribed situation of time and space—this man who is governed by God with an *akribeia* that the human being is also capable of recognizing.

It is quite probable that Chrysostom was not perfectly equipped, from the philosophical point of view, to effect such a synthesis; his one-sided insistence on negative theology did not lend itself to the exercise of the method of analogy thanks to which a Thomas Aquinas was to surmount these antinomies.[80]

On the other hand, the *akribeia* and the precision of man's situation is the condition which enables him, through the *akribeia* and exactitude of the written word which God addresses to him through human instruments, to come to the knowledge of God who surpasses all created *akribeia* while knowing himself with a perfect and infinite exactitude and *akribeia*, with no inner vagueness. In this respect, the divine condescension expresses itself through the *akribeia* of the saving word and more generally through the *akribeia* of the divine governance of the world.

One could say at least that the sphere of *akribeia* is what one would call, in modern terminology, the categorical domain—the domain of the finite. It stands in contrast to the supra-categorical infinitude of the divine being. The Being who is above all *akribeia* expresses himself with *akribeia* through condescension for the sake of those who inhabit its

---

[78]*Ibid.*, Homily V, 240-249, p. 292.

[79]*Ibid.*, Homily I, 291-301, p. 126.

[80]We go more deeply into this subject in a work published on "The Perfections of the God of Jesus Christ," (Paris, 1981), chapter I.

sphere. The *akribeia* of his biblical word is no more than an anticipation (the Old Testament) or an extension (the New Testament) of his condescending assumption of a human nature subject to the *akribeia* of the present.

Just as Christ's condescension in His language manifested not only the sublimity of His divine nature, but also the humility of His human nature with respect to His brother human beings, so the *akribeia* of His language, while recalling His double self-lowering, His divine and human, or theandric condescension, at the same time brings out the circumscribed character of His human nature and the perfect and uncircumscribed knowledge which He, as Word, has of His Father.

We see all of this as implicit in Chrysostom's thinking and in his use of the categories of condescension and *akribeia* to express the dialogue between the Word of God and human beings, which takes place through the human word. What Chrysostom is trying to tell us, what he is suggesting, without having said so explicitly, is that the Christological confession conditions exegesis itself. One cannot adequately grasp the condescension and the *akribeia* of the divine Scriptures without first having acknowledged in faith the One who is in person the divine condescension made human *akribeia*. One cannot comprehend in depth the words of Christ until one has recognized the One who pronounces them, the divine Word become human word.[81]

If acknowledgment of the situation of the divine Speaker and Writer conditions the perfect exegesis of his message, the nature of the latter as well as its role is better seen when we underline the exiled condition of those to whom the message is addressed.

C. Through the Condescension and Akribeia of his Word God is Leading Us to the Theoria of his Being.

The letters written by the Patriarch of Constantinople[82] during his exile are a moving auto-biographical description of a long agony, the ultimate preparation of the great preacher and exegete for the *theoria* of the beyond, but also the reverse symbol in act of an aspect of his biblical theology which we have not yet underlined and which was brought out

---

[81]It would be good to see researchers examine carefully and specify the different senses Chrysostom gave to the terms: *sugkataasis, akribeia, theoria*. This would be particularly facilitated if there were a critical edition of all the works of Chrysostom, which is still lacking. Cf. A. M. Malingrey, *Studia Patristica*, III, *TU* 78, (Berlin, 1961), pp. 81-84.

[82]Cf. Chrysostom, *Lettre d'exil à Olympias et à tous les fidèles*, (Paris, 1964), *SC* 103; *Lettres à Olympias*, (Paris, 1947), *SC* 13.

by J.-M. Leroux: Chrysostom could never have written his exile letters unless he had spent hours and hours—before his personal exile and with a consciousness of his participation in the collective exile of humanity from Paradise in Adam—reading and re-reading the correspondence which God addresses to this humanity to bring it back to Himself by revealing to it his merciful love.

Let us listen to the Antiochian orator:

> In the beginning, the Creator of men spoke to men, conversing with them in a manner proportionate to human nature. Thus it is that God approached Adam, accused Cain, conversed with Noah, became Abraham's guest.
>
> But when, in the course of the ages, the whole human race fell into the abyss of evil, God its Creator did not wish to withdraw from it completely; although human beings had shown themselves unworthy of this familiarity, he wished to renew his friendship with them. So he sent them a letter as to persons living far from home, in an effort to draw to Himself the whole human race.

The messenger who bore this letter, Chrysostom concludes,[83] was Moses.

The idea is profound: the word manifests the proximity regarding God of those who were the partners in dialogue of the Creator.[84] The letter form, on the contrary, manifests a certain distance, even though its objective was to bring together. It is likewise worthy of note that in Chrysostom's view the divine letter is addressed, not only to Israel according to the flesh or to the Israel of God that is the Church, but also to the entire human race, as a gesture of salvific friendship.

Chrysostom then views the whole collection of the biblical books as one immense correspondence addressed by God to humanity. By linking Scripture to the epistolary genre, Chrysostom rescues it from the

---

[83]Chrysostom, *Hom. II, 2 on Genesis*, PG 53, 28. Cf. J.-M. Leroux, "Relativité et transcendance biblique d'après saint Jean Chrysostome," in *La Bible et les Pères* (colloquy of Strassburg), (Paris, 1971), pp. 67-78. This writing seems to have been taken from a work in preparation. Without embracing all the author's views, certain interpretations that strike us as rather questionable, we have used this study very extensively here, nuancing it here and there. The basic thesis of Leroux seems to us to be well presented in these words: "The doctrinal system [of Chrysostom] is directed toward that spiritual union which prefigures the beatific vision" (p. 77). This does pose a problem (cf. n. 12). Does the great doctor of Antioch really believe in the beatific vision of the *divine* nature by the soul? Moreover, what exactly is Chrysostom's conception of *theoria*? Nothing in the pages published by Leroux (and mentioned above) leads us to suspect that he has perceived this two-fold problem. See, however, n. 88.

[84]We note that Chrysostom (see preceding note) uses here the Greek word *dialekthè*.

anonymous and impersonal character of literary works; into the heart of each of the books, even those which we call historical, he introduces the affective bond proper to correspondence.

For this reason, the Bible cannot be regarded as a dead writing to which are consigned the history of a chosen people and the commandments dictated by God; it is the living document wherein is expressed the exchange of thoughts between God and humanity, the letter which vibrates with a divine philanthropy, determined at any cost to maintain contact with a rebellious humanity, the means invented by God to keep in touch with humanity.

At the same time, the letter is the mirror image that adequately expresses the present imperfection of the dialogue between God and the human race. God continues to address man and to communicate his message to him, but unfortunate circumstances resulting from sin no longer allow the exchange of a direct conversation. God's message has become fixed within the framework of a writing and its form has been determined by the human condition. Scripture is bound to the vicissitudes of history that compromises its transmission. An effort of understanding is necessary therefore to rediscover the profound meaning of the divine message. Man weakened by sin cannot discover that meaning without asceticism.

Moreover, the epistolary character brings to light more than any other genre the dynamic nature of Scripture through which the divine pedagogy is expressed.[85] Indeed, if the entire complex of a correspondence expresses the thought of its author, each of the letters taken singly reflects a moment of this thought and corresponds in principle to the actual concerns of the two interlocutors.[86]

So it is with Scripture where each of the books corresponds to a stage of the Revelation willed by God. The Bible is in fact dominated by this educative concern of God who is progressively leading humanity from the abyss into which it had fallen to the salvation accomplished by the Incarnation, to dialogue between man and God, restored initially in the Liturgy and completely in the beatific vision of the human being raised from the dead. Here below, Scripture constitutes the prop of this renewed dialogue, such as it takes place in the liturgy. The human being distant from God, to whom the divine letter of Scripture is addressed, becomes, in the presence of the preacher, one who hears a God who has

---

[85]Leroux, pp. 75-76.
[86]*Ibid.*, p. 76.

come near, a God who now speaks to him and who even makes Himself his food in the Eucharist.

If God is closer to man through His Word than through His Writing, this Word and the dialogue which it entails constitute a less immediate relationship between man and God than the vision promised to those who hear Him: "Let us have a veritable passion for God, not out of fear of hell, but out of a desire for the Kingdom. What can compare in fact with the sight of Christ? Nothing.... The eye has not seen what God has prepared for those who love him."[87] "The virgin desires to die," insists Chrysostom, "and life weighs heavily on her, for she is hastening toward the face to face vision of her spouse."[88]

The fact remains, however, that the reading of Scripture greatly facilitates the flight toward that face to face vision in which Scripture itself will definitively disappear. Not only do the sacred books contain very precise rules for the healing of pride, concupiscence, love of riches, excess of sorrow,[89] but the remedies they provide us with are also like magic and divine chants that need only be applied to the evil in question to see it vanish.[90] We need only look at these books and we experience sorrow for our sins; we need only touch them and they impart a wonderful harmony to our thoughts.[91]

It is impossible, our Saint goes on, for one to thus converse with God and listen to his word without deriving some profit therefrom.[92] Chrysostom goes so far as to intone a hymn honoring the Scriptures as the path of salvation:

How sweet is the reading of Holy Scripture, sweeter than any meadow, more pleasing than paradise, above all when knowledge accompanies the reading. The meadows, the beauty of the flowers, the verdure of the trees...delight the eyes; but after a few days, all of this fades.

But the knowledge of the Scriptures strengthens the mind, purifies the conscience, uproots enslaving passions, sows virtue, elevates the mind, prevents us from being overwhelmed by the unexpected vicissitudes of events, raises us above the ploys of the devil, causes us to dwell close to heaven itself, frees the

---

[87]Chrysostom, *Hom. XV, 4 on the First Letter to Timothy,* PG 62, 584.

[88]Chrysostom, *De Virginitate,* 59; PG 48, 580.

[89]Chrysostom, *Hom. XXXVII on the Gospel of John,* PG 59, 207.

[90]Chrysostom, *Hom. XXXII, 3;* PG 59, 187-188.

[91]Chrysostom, *De Lazaro,* III, 1-2-3; PG 48, 992-996.

[92]Chrysostom, *Hom. LIII, 3 on the Gospel of John,* PG 59, 295-296.

soul from the bonds of the body, lightens our wings and brings everything good that has ever been described into the reader's soul.[93]

Clearly the memories and the personal experience of John Chrysostom have entered into this hymn. During his years as a hermit in the region of Antioch where he dwelt in a cave, John memorized the whole of the New Testament. Could he otherwise ever have become the eloquent preacher that he was, the preacher whose writings we continue to read today? Could he otherwise have been transformed into a dynamic apostle, urging all to the frequent and reflective reading of the Scriptures? We quote him again:

> Hear then, people of the world: get hold of these books that contain the remedies of the soul. If your ambitions are not too high, get hold of the New Testament at least, the Acts of the Apostles, the Gospels. You will find in them good lessons for every occasion... Have you just suffered a loss of money? Is death at your door? Are you about to lose a loved one? Let your eyes scan these divine formularies, enter into them, keep them always with you. Ignorance of the Scriptures is the source of all evils. Not to know them is to march unarmed into battle, is to be totally defenseless![94]

Thus, in this passage as in the preceding ones, the reading of Scripture becomes a singular instrument for the return to God through the practice of the virtues. Hence the insistence with which the saint demands of his readers that they prepare in advance for listening to his sermon by reading the biblical passage on which he was to comment.[95] If ignorance of Scripture is the source of all evils, does not its knowledge bring with it all good things? Hence once again the importance given to the least words of Scripture, in a statement which could seem more Alexandrian than Antiochian at first sight: "Let us not neglect the words of Scripture, even those we believe are without importance, for they too are the gift of the Spirit and the gift of the Spirit is never weak and without fruit; on the contrary, it is great, wonderful and worthy of the generosity of the One who bestows it."[96]

---

[93]Chrysostom, *Hom. V, De Studio præsentium*, 1, PG 63, 485. On the biblical pastoral of Chrysostom, see L. Meyer, *Saint Jean Chrysostom, maître de perfection chrétienne*, (Paris, 1933), pp. 298-316.

[94]Chrysostom, *Hom. IX on the Letter to the Colossians*, PG 62, 361-362. Cf. Bruno H. Vandeberghe, *Saint Jean Chrysostome et la parole de Dieu*, (Paris, 1961), pp. 66-70.

[95]Chrysostom, *Hom XI, 3 on the Gospel of John*, PG 59, 77-78.

[96]Chrysostom, *Hom. I on Statues*, PG 49, 17.

The biblical reading to which Chrysostom exhorts is not only individual, but also familial,[97] indeed social:[98] through the Bible, society as such should be returning to God and joining in a *theoria* that anticipates the beatific vision.

CONCLUSION

Ecumenical significance of Chrysostom

We have been able to give here only a very limited and inadequate idea of the exegesis of Saint John Chrysostom as well as of his biblical theology. The reader has at least been able to perceive the charm of his literal exposition of the Scriptures, the charm of this Chrysostom that rebounds—as Newman well observed[99]—on his method. Leaving mystical commentary to the Alexandrians (not always, however, as we had occasion to remark on the question of the divine incomprehensibility), more concerned to see in the Scriptures the nature and the attributes of God rather than his works, Chrysostom charms us by the ease with which he enters into the minds of others when he comments on Scripture. He lovingly scrutinizes the apostles, or better, he photographs them such as they reveal themselves in their writings. Who has ever spoken and written on the apostle Paul like John Chrysostom?[100]

As J. Quasten rightly observed,[101] no Father of the Church has left behind a literary heritage (and we would add, an exegetical heritage) as significant in volume as is that of Chrysostom. He is the only early Antiochian whose writings have survived almost in their entirety.

---

[97]Meyer (n. 93) put together a valuable dossier on this point; see his book, pp. 304ff. It is especially in the whole *Homily XXI on the Letter to the Ephesians* that the great doctor of Antioch treats the subject of education.

[98]Chrysostom foresees group reading of the Scriptures to which he invites families, especially in the setting of a review of instructions received in the Church; he foresees for the same purpose and in the same setting a gathering of friends for the reading of Scriptures at one of their homes: *Homily V, 1 on Matthew* (PG 57, 55); *Sermon VI, 2 on Genesis,* (PG 54, 607). It is in this sermon that we find a recommendation orchestrated by Vatican II: "Each of you, make your home a church," said Chrysostom. "In what might be regarded as a domestic Church, the parents, by word and example, are the first heralds of the faith with regard to their children" (*Lumen Gentium*, 1); *Hom. XIV, 5 on Genesis, PG 53, 117-118,* etc. We also note that, for Chrysostom, God's word and Scripture are not only a social tie, but they even provide teachings on what are called today social problems: cf. L. Daloz, *Le travail chez les Pères Antiochiens,* (Paris, 1959).

[99]John Henry Newman, *Historical Sketches,* pp. 288-289.

[100]Cf. B. Vandenbeghe, chapter IV: Chrysostom and Saint Paul.

[101]Quasten, p. 602.

This privilege is to be attributed to the author's personality as much as to the intrinsic value of the writings themselves. No Oriental writer (and again we add, no Greek patristic exegete) has earned the admiration and favor of posterity to the degree enjoyed by Chrysostom.

He placed the Attic and classical purity of his Greek language, already brought out by another Father, Isidore of Pelusium,[102] at the service of the Word and the Writing of the God of the Old and New Covenants, while insisting on their transcendence with respect to any purely human word or writing.[103]

At the same time, the work of Chrysostom manifests his condescension relative to his readers in the service of the precise condescension of the divine message.

It is for this reason that he will continue, through the private, pastoral and liturgical reading of his works[104] to influence those catechists and preachers who would conscientiously carry out their theological[105] or exegetical ministry, even when they are not professional theologians and exegetes, and to lead them to *theoria* and to a contemplative life based on the Bible.

All the more so now that we have entered into an ecumenical era. The influence of the biblical work of Saint John Chrysostom has been and remains enormous in the Orthodox Churches. Though obviously less pervasive, this influence is however not nonexistent in the Protestant world. Thanks to Chrysostom, and perhaps through the mediation of Luther, a number of Protestant patrologists of the Seventeenth and Eighteenth centuries developed the theme of the divine condescension.[106] H. Lauerer even argued in 1928 for a Lutheran spirituality of condescension.[107] Not only did Vatican II cite Chrysostom and his biblical

---

[102]Isidore of Pelusium, *Ep V, 2.* Referred to by Quasten, p. 603.

[103]Leroux, pp. 68-69.

[104]We note that the new *Liturgy of the Hours* or post-conciliar breviary, now translated into many languages, accords an important position to John Chrysostom's sermons in its Office of Readings, introducing its many readers to Chrysostom's exegesis. Similarly, Jean Daniélou has emphasized the importance of Chrysostom's moral and sacramental catechesis for catechists: *La catéchèse aux premières siècles,* (Paris, 1968), pp. 167-170 (he is speaking of post-baptismal catechesis). For the use of preachers, we should also note Chrysostom's influence on Bourdeloue and Bossuet, both of whom quoted him copiously. Through them, John Chrysostom has penetrated into French literature.

[105]Cf. Congregation for Catholic Education, *Doc. Cath* 73, 8, (1976), p. 458, on the theological formation of future priests.

[106]Cf. Duchatelez, p. 620.

[107]H. Lauerer, "Die Kondeszendenz Gottes," *Festschrift F. Ihmels,* (Leipzig, 1928), pp. 258-272.

commentaries more than any other Father, Greek or Latin, (with the sole exception of Augustine),[108] but it even incorporated his basic exegetical idea relative to the divine condescension into the dogmatic constitution *Dei Verbum* on the divine Revelation:

> In sacred Scripture, therefore, while the truth and holiness of God always remain intact, the marvelous "condescension" of eternal wisdom is clearly shown, "that we may learn the gentle kindness of God, which words cannot express, and how far He has gone in adapting His language with thoughtful concern for our weak human nature."[109] For the words of God, expressed in human language, have been made like human discourse, just as of old the Word of the eternal Father, when he took to Himself the weak flesh of humanity, became like other men.[110]

N.B. We would like to bring to the attention of the reader the study of R. Hill, "Saint John Chrysostom's Teaching on Inspiration, in the Six Homilies on Isaiah," *Vig. Christ.* 22 (1968), pp. 19-37.

---

[108]Chrysostom is referred to at least thirteen times in the sixteen documents of Vatican II, especially in the Constitution on the Church—more than Cyril of Alexandria, even more than the Cappadocians.

[109]Chrysostom, *Hom. XVII, 1 on Genesis 3, 8*, PG 53, 134. Note 11 of the Council text (cf. n. 110 below) stresses that the Latin term *attemperatio* is meant as a translation of the Greek term *sugkatabasis*.

[110]*Dei Verbum*, 13.

Chapter IX
Saint Gregory of Nyssa
Theoretician of Biblical Connections or Chains:
Skopos, Theoria, Akolouthia

Gregory of Nyssa (335-395), brother of Saint Basil, is generally regarded as the deepest of the three Cappadocians. His theological work won him high regard at the Second Council of Nicea (787) which bestowed on him the title *Father of the Fathers*.

He has left us commentaries[1] on Genesis, Exodus, the Psalms, Ecclesiastes and the Song of Songs; what has come down to us of his New Testament exegesis appears less impressive but includes a number of treatises on the Beatitudes and the Lord's Prayer,[2] in addition to the biblical commentaries which his liturgical homilies contain.

After having presented the dominant principles of Gregory's exegesis, drawing especially on the works of Cardinal Daniélou,[3] we will show

---

[1]See the detailed list of these works in Quasten, *Initiation aux Pères de l'Eglise*, (Paris, 1963), vol. III, pp. 376-384. On Nicea II and Gregory of Nyssa, see *Mansi*, vol. 13, col. 293.

[2]There is an English translation, the work of H. C. Graef, in the collection *Ancient Christian Writers*, vol. 18 (1954).

[3]See his introduction to the *Life of Moses* (SC 1a, [Paris, 1955²], pp. X-XVIII); Jean Daniélou, *L'être et le temps chez Grégoire de Nysse*, (Leiden, 1970), chapters I and II about *theoria* and in *Ecriture et Culture Philosophique dans la pensée de Grégoire de Nysse*, (Actes du Colloque de Chevetogne, Sept. 22-26, 1969, [Leidan: M. Harl, 1971], referred to henceforth as *EC*). Daniélou's study: "Orientations actuelles de la recherche," pp. 9-12. See also, *ibid.*, M. Alexandre, "La theorie de l'exégèse dans le *De Hominis opificio* et l'*In Hexæmeron*," pp. 87-110. Other studies on the exegesis of the great bishop of Nyssa will be referred to during this chapter.

their application in the interpretation of some data of the Old and New Testaments.

A. The Three-fold Key to the Reading of Scripture: the Determination of its Goal and of its Structures (skopos, theoria, akolouthia)

The goal (*skopos*) of Gregory, in his exegesis, may be stated thus: in view of the objections and above all of the apparent contradictions, in the biblical text itself, between the past grandeur and the present misery of mankind, "to form for ourselves a coherent and connected view of the creation of the world,"[4] "to resolve oppositions with the help of the scriptural account and by means of what our reasonings allow us to discover, and thus to invest this whole matter with a concatenation (*eirmos*) and with an order between things which appear to be opposed but which in fact tend toward the same goal, thanks to the divine power."[5]

Necessary connection, link, order, harmony, adaptation—all of this exists in the history of the world and of man willed by God, and all of this is obscurely present in the Scriptures; it is this *akolouthia* that the exegete attempts to restore. This gives Gregory a comprehensive way of responding to isolated contradictions.[6]

A similar exegetical principle is not foreign to the biblical text itself in its finality. In the view of the Bishop of Nyssa, it corresponds in part to the goal of the sacred author: "Moses' objective or goal (*skopos*) is to take men who are subject to the slavery of the senses, and lead them, through the mediation of the sensible, to that which transcends sensible perception."[7]

There is more: for Gregory, the goal of the human author coincides with that of the divine Author.[8] In this respect, he stands very much within the tradition of Origen.

In his exegetical works, the bishop of Nyssa affirms that Scripture teaches us God's design, gives us a certain number of "dogmas" (*dogmata*)[9] to learn; it takes us by the hand and introduces us to these things; it offers a doctrine on the world and on man in their relationships

---

[4]Gregory of Nyssa, *In Hexæmeron*, PG 44, 68D.
[5]*De hominis opificio*, PG 44, 128B.
[6]M. Alexandre, *EC*, p. 95.
[7]*In Hexæmeron*, PG 44, 69D.
[8]*De hom. opif.*, PG 44, 128 A B.
[9]Cf. the texts referred to by M. Alexandre, *EC*, p. 97, n. 1.

with God.[10] Thus Moses "is philosophizing about nature" and "about the soul."[11] In this insistence on the *skopos* of Scripture, we recognize the influence of Origen, for whom, as we have seen, the principal *skopos* of Scripture is to impart a teaching on God and the Trinity, on rational creatures—heavenly and earthly—on the world and on the origin of evil.[12]

The bishop of Nyssa is however indebted to Origen not only in his investigation of the *skopos* of Scripture but also in his search for *akolouthia*. For both, the object of allegorical exegesis is to discover this systematic order that stands behind the letter of the text;[13] but there is an important difference between the two in the way they go about this. For Origen, the knowledge of this *akolouthia* is a gnosis that stands in contrast to a simple knowledge of the facts presented by Scripture, while Gregory's concern is precisely with the knowledge of these facts that must be linked as in a chain.[14]

What is significant, however, is that one meets the term *akolouthia* constantly in the writings of Gregory. It represents a leit-motif of his thought. Sometimes—and this is its weakest sense—it designates the succession of the historical events as they are found in Scripture;[15] at other times it signifies the sequence, at the logical level, of necessarily linked propositions—and this sense shows a dependence on Plotinus[16] at least; finally—and here we arrive at the properly theological sense—the term *akolouthia* sometimes refers to the unfolding of God's plan in nature and in history, and recapitulates various formerly held philosophical beliefs within a theological perspective. In Gregory, *akolouthia* describes a growth process; it gives expression to a force that is at once immanent

---

[10]*In Hexæmeron*, PG, 44, 69D and 76D; *De hom. opif.*, PG 44, 181C and 256B.

[11]*In Hexæmeron*, PG 44, 61 A B, 72C; *De hom. opif.*, PG 44, 144D, 148B.

[12]Origen, *De Principiis*, IV, 2, 7; see also our chapter IV.

[13]Daniélou, *L'Être et le temps*, pp. 49-50. Clement of Alexandria had already previously written in his *Stromates* (I, 28): "We must approach Scripture armed with the dialectic sciences, as much as we can, to track down the sequence [*akolouthia*] of the divine teachings." By contrast, in Marrou's opinion, St. Augustine's exegesis is something else again: "He only discovers the concatenation, the sequence of ideas, *a posteriori*, in proportion as it manifests itself; he almost always comments on the text with assurance, without concern for what is going to follow, satisfied with adapting more or less laboriously the commentary of what comes to his interpretation of what preceded it" (Marrou, *Saint Augustin et la fin de la culture antique*, [Paris, 1958⁴], p. 429).

[14]Daniélou, *L'Être et le temps*, p. 49.

[15]*Ibid.*, pp. 37ff.

[16]*Ibid.*, p. 45, referring to *Enneads* I, 8, 2: "Our intellects reason and speculate on the concatenation of propositions [*hé tou akolouthou theôria*] to know the truths thanks to that concatenation [*akolouthia*]."

and transcendent; it underscores the organic solidarity of the revealed data, so that the latter appear, not as a complex of inner necessities, but as the action of a free divine causality; reduction to the highest principles is conducted in such a way as not to ignore the facts, which is precisely what Gregory accuses Eunomius of doing.[17]

In short, we could summarize the complex sense of Gregory's *akolouthia* with Jean Daniélou as follows: "The term designates at once the material sequence of the biblical text, the necessary interconnection between the realities of salvation history and the analogical correspondence which exists between these two planes."[18] It is clear that, in his study of *akolouthia*, Gregory is inseparably exegete and theologian; his undertaking shows us already at work in the fourth century a methodical effort aimed at discovering the connections between the mysteries and the meaning which the divine author of the Scriptures had and still has in mind, as the First Vatican Council,[19] and later Pope Pius XII (in *Divino Afflante Spiritu*) were to bring out.

One can and one must say that Gregory's method of exegesis which culminates in the search for the *akolouthia* of the divine plan of salvation coincides in advance with the wish expressed by Pius XII: "may professors establish the literal, and above all the *theological* sense of Scripture in such a solid fashion, may they explain it in such relevant terms, may they inculcate it with such warmth that their pupils will have happen to them what happened to the disciples of Jesus Christ on their way to Emmaus, when they exclaimed: were not our hearts burning within us as he opened to us the Scriptures (Lk 24:32). May their exegesis bring out above all the *theological contents* of Scripture."[20] This is precisely the major preoccupation of Gregory of Nyssa: to establish the *literal theological meaning* of the Scriptures.

If the goal of exegesis is, for Gregory, to arrive at the discovery of the articulations that constitute the *akolouthia* of the divine plan of salvation,

---

[17]Daniélou, *L'Être et le Temps*, p. 49.

[18]*Ibid.* We note that this chapter of *L'Être et le Temps* reproduces an article by the same author in *Rev. Sc. Rel.*, 27 (1953), pp. 219-249, with certain modification.

[19]*DS* 3016: "De mysteriorum nexu inter se et cum fine hominis ultimo": the mutually illuminating *connection* between the mysteries, which is present in the thought and work of Gregory as it is to the thought and work of the other Fathers, is on the horizon of the research on *akolouthia*, although it is distinct from the research itself.

[20]Pius XII, *Divino Afflante Spiritu*, AAS 35 (1943), 322: "sensum *litteralem* quem vocant ac præsertim *theologicum* ita solide proponant.... Exegetica ratio *ad rationem potissimum theologicam* spectet." This is precisely what Gregory was practicing when he expounded the sense of Jn 20:17 and Phil 2 as we shall see below.

what means must be employed to arrive at this end? Primarily *theoria*, with the special sense and the nuances that distinguish Gregory's use of the term. What then does *theoria* mean for Gregory?

As in the case of *akolouthia*, Gregory inherits earlier meanings and imposes his personal meaning on this term. For the Bishop of Nyssa, as for Origen, it designates the hidden meaning discovered behind the letter of Scripture which pertains to spiritual realities; but also, as with Eusebius, the Christian economy as already contained in the prophecies of the Old Testament, or, as with the Antiochians, the prophetic vision of the authors of this Old Testament. But Gregory applies the term also to texts—and here we arrive at the meaning proper to this author. For the Father of the Fathers, *theoria* designates the search for or the investigation of the meaning of a biblical text. This sense is extremely frequent in his writings.[21] The term can also designate the actual understanding of the sense of the text (or, if you will, the result of the research), particularly of the literal sense (*historike theoria*[22]). *Theoria* is the grasp of the meaning of events, beyond a mere observation of the facts. There is *theoria* from the moment that there is interpretation.

One cannot then equate Gregory's *theoria* purely and simply, in the exegetical domain, with the spiritual or typological sense. It integrates an exegesis that intends to be scientific into a general system according to which visible realities are symbols of spiritual realities, to discover—and this is the object of *theoria*—the *akolouthia* of these realities. Thus the Bishop of Nyssa will speak of "seeing (*theorein*) the connection between facts, their *akolouthia*" or again, in his *Life of Moses*, of the "connection (*akolouthia*) of things contemplated (*theoretenton*) analogically."[23] Most often—and especially in the *Life of Moses*—the object of *theoria* is to go beyond the historical events and to grasp the spiritual teaching.[24]

For Gregory, the books of the Bible are first historical books that report real events whose chronology is worked out by the historical science. But in these books the Holy Spirit is likewise providing a spiritual instruction, pertaining to the stages of the spiritual life. As we will see regarding the Book of Psalms, this teaching also involves an *akolouthia*, which may differ from chronology. This *akolouthia* is not arbitrary,

---

[21]*In inscriptione psalmorum*, II, 1; 69, 11 (GNO): this sigla will be explained later (n. 36).

[22]*Ibid.*, II, 2; 72, 10. Cf. Daniélou, *L'Être et le temps*, chapter I, "Theôria," pp. 9ff. On Eusebius see C. Sant, "Interpretatio Veteris Testamenti in Eusebio Cæsariensi," *VD* 45 (1967), 78-90.

[23]*In Hexæmeron*, PG 44, 117C; *Life of Moses*, II, 150; cf. Daniélou, *L'Être et le temps*, p. 11.

[24]*Ibid.*, pp. 11-12.

because it corresponds to the intention of the Holy Spirit who inspires Scripture. The *noete theoria* is the search for this *akolouthia*. The latter constitutes the object of Gregory's treatises on the *Psalms*, of the homilies on *Ecclesiastes*, on the *Song of Songs*, of the *Life of Moses*. The disposition of the text, its *taxis*, corresponds in certain cases with this spiritual *akolouthia*, thus manifesting the intention of the sacred writer. But the proper object of *theoria*, of the hermeneutical undertaking, remains that of showing the *akolouthia*, whether historical or spiritual or both. This is a method to which Gregory of Nyssa is constantly returning.

Gregory's originality has then to do neither with the existence of a spiritual sense, as object of *theoria*—Origen had recognized this—nor with the principle of *akolouthia*—already admitted by Clement of Alexandria, Origen and Eusebius of Cæsarea.[25] What Gregory does is to extend this principle to biblical books taken as whole: not only to each Psalm, but to the Book of Psalms as a whole. Moreover, Gregory makes the quest for this *akolouthia* the object of *theoria*, a connection found neither in Eusebius, nor in the Alexandrians or Antiochians who came before him.

In all of this, Gregory appears to have been influenced by the rhetoric of his time. In his most developed works (*De mortuis, De infantibus*), the presentation implies a clearly defined goal (*skopos*) toward which the thought continues through a logical sequence (*akolouthia*). He conceives the structure of the Sacred Books in the same way, inquiring into their intention or goal, and the manner in which they methodically pursue this goal. Now Iamblichus had already applied the theory of the unique goal (*heis skopos*) and of *akolouthia* to the dialogues of Plato and the Neo-Platonism of the school of Athens will continue to do so.

For the Bishop of Nyssa, in his capacity as exegete, *theoria* does not have primarily a contemplative sense, for "its ascensions do not give vision[26] and the immediate grasp of reality" to the soul," even if it does continuously progress in this "*theoria ton atheoreton*,"[27] in the vision of the invisible. Nor does it have a primarily philosophical sense, as discernment of the natures constitutive of created being. The exegetical *theoria* of Gregory introduces us rather to one of his fundamental intuitions: that of the historicity of created being and of the way in which

---

[25]Cf. n. 13 and *ibid.*, pp. 49-50.

[26]In Greek, *theôria*.

[27]*Cant. II*; 326, 1; the preceding quotation comes from *Cant. V*, 138, 9-10. Cf. Daniélou, *L'Être et le temps*, p. 16.

God causes this being to unfold into an ordered history, into an *akolouthia*. Unlike God, Scripture is not above and beyond *theoria*.[28]

It is perhaps this linking of exegetical *theoria* to the contingency of created being which enables us to understand, with Gregory even better than with Philo or with Origen, whose affirmations he borrows, why it is that he regards his own exegesis not in magisterial terms, but as no more than an "exercise based on conjectures."[29] Gregory often returns to this theme: "The poverty of our nature is incapable of seeing the principle of wisdom which reveals itself in each being; a certain connection, or sequence of facts (*akolouthia*) following an order established by the Creator can however be discerned—and it is this discernment, an interiorized contemplation (*entheoresai*), together with some conjectures, that is accessible to those who know how properly to observe the concatenation."[30] The interpretation of a contingent Scriptural passage, given in the midst of a universe and of a Church that are themselves contingent, is itself contingent and not necessary in many cases. This is the feeling and the opinion of many modern exegetes as well. Such a speculative character of exegesis is perfectly in harmony with the intention of Gregory to engage in a hermeneutics that would integrate literal sense and theological sense, history and contemplation.

But did his achievement match his intention? Did not Gregory in fact abuse Origenian allegory? The question is an obvious one, and it will be better to respond to it in the conclusion of this chapter, after having presented a few concrete examples of the exegesis of the Bishop of Nyssa. For the moment, we terminate this presentation of Gregory's exegetical principles with a citation from Cardinal Daniélou: "We find in Basil and Gregory a type of exegesis which is neither the allegorical exegesis of Alexandria nor the literal exegesis of Antioch, but rather an effort to reconcile theological data and scientific thought. Now this concordistic exegesis has an antecedent only in the writings of Acacius of Cesarea."[31]

---

[28]Daniélou, *L'Être et le temps*, p. 17.

[29]*In Hexæmeron, PG* 44, 68C. Cf. M. Alexandre, p. 99. Philo: "It is necessary that it be God alone who knows the absolutely true cause; but the cause that appears to be convincing and possible with a probable conjecture does not have to be hidden" (*Opif.* 72, commenting on Gn 1:26); on Origen, see Henri de Lubac, *Histoire et Esprit*, (Paris, 1950), pp. 322-335.

[30]*In Hexæmeron, PG* 44, 117C.

[31]Daniélou, *EC*, p. 11. Cf. also *L'Être et le temps*, p. 10: "Acacius of Cæsarea belonged with Melicius of Antioch to the group of *homoean* theologians, and it was to this environment that Basil and Gregory of Nyssa were originally connected.... This exegesis

B. *Gregory of Nyssa, Exegete of the Old and New Testaments*

Gregory's exegesis of the Old Testament includes widely differing forms: literal exegesis with respect to the creation of the world and of man (Genesis), haggadic exegesis (*Life of Moses*, viewed primarily as a model of virtue), moral allegorism inspired by Philo and Origen (in the second part of the same work and in the Commentary on the Song of Songs). But, in the *Sermons* and elsewhere, Gregory is a witness of the traditional typology, which is an integral part of the Church's catechesis.[32]

After having given here several examples of typological exegesis, we will look more closely at Gregory's original presentation of the *akolouthia* of the Psalter as such, and finally we will discuss the ethical and theological interpretation of a number of major New Testament texts in the thinking of Gregory.

If the *Life of Moses*, in a number of its procedures,[33] shows some similarity to the spiritual exegesis of Exodus inaugurated by Philo, this current of interpretation is joined by another which will invest it with a completely different signification: the Christocentric reading, begun within the New Testament, particularly in John and Paul, according to which the events and institutions of the Exodus are not primarily figures of purely spiritual realities, but rather of another reality, at once historical and spiritual, namely, the reality of Christ and the new order He instituted. Gregory gave us the very principle of his method and affirmed that it was but the development of the Pauline exegesis found in a very characteristic passage on the subject of the tabernacle:

> We affirm then, with the help of Paul who treated this mystery in part and in whose words we find a point of departure, that Moses taught in advance, in

---

attempted to reconcile the text of the Bible with the data of science." See below the opinion of E. Pfister, n. 97, which is quite different.

[32]Jean Daniélou, "La typologie biblique de Gregoire de Nysse," *Studi e Materiali di Storia delle Religioni* 38 (1967), p. 185.

[33]Cf. Daniélou, Introduction to the *Vie de Moïse*, SC 1a, (Paris, 1955²), pp. XIV-XV:

> The *theôria* constitutes the essence of the work.... The life of Moses becomes the symbol of the mystical itinerary of the soul. Here also Gregory is connected to Philo, but it is to the Philo of the *Questions on Exodus*: they share the same general conception of Moses' life as well as of the mystical migration; they have the same major episodes, particularly the burning bush and the climbing of Sinai; and the whole thing is all the more notable in that they are at the first stage of the typical New Testament exegesis; there is the same general structure of the spiritual life, entailing first the purification of the fleshly life, then the illumination, and finally the mystery of inaccessible Being.

figure, the mystery of the true tabernacle which contains all things, that is to say, Christ, the Power and the Wisdom of God.... And since Paul said that the veil of the earthly tabernacle was the body of Christ [Heb 10:20], it will be of good method to extend this partial explanation to the whole: the enigmas of the tabernacle are illuminated then by the very word of the Apostle.[34]

Thus, not only the brazen serpent or the rock—as in John (chap. 3) or Paul (1 Cor 10)—but also the burning bush, the prayer of Moses with outstretched arms, the restoration of the broken tablets of the Law, etc., all become so many Christological symbols. The transfiguration of Moses' countenance is likewise related to Christ, not however to the transfiguration which took place during his first coming, in the company of Moses on Mount Tabor; rather, it is seen as a figure of the manifestation of Christ in his final glory, at the time of the Parousia, when sinners will be unable to bear his radiance:

He who restored the broken tables of our nature, transforming them by the Divine Finger, is no longer visible to the eyes of the unworthy, but is inaccessible to them, by reason of the excess of his glory. Later, when He comes in glory, as Scripture says, with all his angels with Him, even the just will hardly be able to look at Him and contemplate Him.[35]

This type of exegesis takes its inspiration from an earlier tradition, and in particular from Origen. Gregory is more original when he is engaged in the search for the logical sequence, the *akolouthia* of the Psalter.

As M. J. Rondeau has remarked,[36] Gregory of Nyssa's treatise *On the Titles of the Psalms* stands out for its powerful originality among the many works devoted by Christian antiquity to the Psalter. This originality does not consist in the search for the spiritual signification of the Psalm titles or the attempt to find in them pointers for the spiritual life, following the example of Athanasius in his *Letter to Marcellinus* (cf. our chapter V). Rather it consists in the extremely synthetic, unifying, chaste character of his exegetical method and in the rigor with which he applies it.

[34]*Life of Moses*, PG 44, 381D; 384A.

[35]*Ibid.*, 397D.

[36]M. J. Rondeau, "Exégèse du Psautier et Anabase spirituelle chez Grégoire de Nysse," *Epektasis, Mélanges Daniélou*, (Paris, 1972), pp. 519-531. The following pages are largely inspired by this remarkable work. We refer to Gregory's treatise on the *Titres* or *Inscriptions des Psaumes* according to the McDonough-Jäger edition, *Gregorii Nysseni Opera*, vol. V, (Leiden, 1962), pp. 24-193, henceforth abbreviated as *GNO*.

To be sure, Eusebius[37] had already attempted to work out the *akolouthia* between successive Psalms, but he had not looked for a single *akolouthia*, based on a single *skopos* of the Book of Psalms as a whole. For Gregory, the Psalter as a whole is ordered to a single goal: access to beatitude, the term of the virtuous life. Eusebius practiced a prophetic reading of the Psalter, focusing his attention on the economy of salvation; Gregory prefers a sapiential reading.

Of course, Gregory admits that the Psalter does not follow the historical order of the life of David; he resolves the classical difficulty of this historical *"anacolouthon"* by saying that the Holy Spirit is not concerned with chronology but rather with spiritual progress.[38] The Psalms are ordered according to the *akolouthia* of meaning, of an intelligible progression from the less good to the better, as Eusebius had already observed.[39]

But Gregory's originality is most radical when he assigns a significative value to the division of the Psalter into five sections.[40] When the *skopos* and *akolouthia* principles combine with the observation of this division, Gregory is lead to attribute a structuring value to this framework. It becomes a *"technike diairesis,"* capable of grounding intelligibility, or, if you will, the way that leads to beatitude. The division of the Psalter into five parts makes it possible, Gregory believes, to distinguish the five great stages of the rigorously logical progression towards eternal beatitude that constitutes the basis of its teaching.

In order to define the contents of the five sections, each of which is viewed as a homogenous unit (though Gregory does not provide proof of such a postulate), the bishop of Nyssa resorts to an implicit presupposition, namely, that the beginning of a given section of a work has a decisive character: it contains in seed the entire subsequent development of the section; the initial Psalm of the section functions as a mother-cell capable of determining its character. Gregory is not always faithful however to the principle he has laid down. Thus, for example, he comments on Psalm 4 (first section) in terms that relate it to the third.

---

[37]Eusebius, *Commentary on the Psalms*, PG 23 and 24, 9-76. Cf. Quasten, vol. III, p. 477; Rondeau, *Epektasis*, p. 518.

[38]*GNO*, V, pp. 115-118.

[39]Eusebius, *In Ps. 51*, PG 23, 444C-448A; *In Ps. 58*, PG 23, 532D-533A.

[40]Cf. Rondeau, p. 519: "This division, determined by the recurrence of a formula of praise almost identical with the end of Psalms 40, 71, 88, 105 and 150, is very often found in ancient exegesis, for example, in Eusebius who refers to it often, but without seeing in it anything significant."

Is Gregory of Nyssa successful in demonstrating that the initial psalms of each of the five sections and the final psalm of the entire Psalter (Ps 150) outline the successive degrees of a spiritual ascension?

He sees Psalm 1 as an invitation to renounce evil and to adhere to the good; Psalm 41, as the expression of the ardent desire for participation in God. In Psalm 72, man, initially scandalized by the misfortune of the good and the prosperity of the wicked, is able to discern in a flash of visionary insight where the true good resides. Psalm 89 is a meditation on the changing nature of man and the immutable nature of God. Psalm 106 recapitulates the stages of the divine plan of the salvation of Israel; through the device of identically structured successive units it brings out the miseries of man, the mercies of God and the thanksgiving of saved humanity. Finally, in Psalm 150, we find the praise of God sung by all created beings.

We give here an example of these commentaries of Gregory on the Psalms. For the Bishop of Nyssa, Moses, the author of Psalm 89 according to its title, had a limit experience and basically played the role of a mediator between God and men (a view that is in perfect harmony with the biblical data). In trying to explain this experience and this role by way of Ps 89 and the psalm by way of the experience, Gregory can legitimately view Moses not only as pronouncing Ps 89, but as personifying it in some way. So he goes on to give us a summary of the life of Moses, in the context of this Psalm, pointing out the traits that would connect him with Ps 72 and those which show him to be the paradigm of Ps 89. Moses is the visionary who moves in the light (Ps 72), but also the movable human being who manifests God through traits of immutability (Ps 89):

> One who has arrived at this height stands as it were at the border between changeable nature and unchangeable nature. He mediates the extremes [cf. Gal 3, 19-20], offering supplications for those who are alienated by sin and transmitting the mercy of the power from on high to those who have need of mercy, so that we also learn from him that the more we withdraw from what is earthly and base, the more we become like that nature that surpasses all understanding. He imitates the divine nature by his beneficence, and therefore does that which is proper to the divine nature, that is, to shower with good gifts all who are in need of gifts, to the extent that this beneficence is required.

This then is the meaning, as we have understood it, of this Psalm that bears the title: Prayer of Moses, man of God.[41]

It is in this way that Gregory of Nyssa makes us pass from the union with God which crowns the hope-filled vision of the true goods which is the object of Ps 72:28 to a reflection on human mutability as opposed to divine immutability, the object of Ps 89—all within the context of a meditation on Moses. The reasoning is justified: Moses, who was able to approach God in an exceptional manner, was also a man of limitations, a man among men and not only a man of God, a man of human striving as well as a man of epic.

Can we trace the progress from one degree to another? Yes: from Ps 72 to Ps 89 we rise from a vision of the things offered to human choice (the vanity of earthly goods, the beauty of heavenly goods[42]) to a perception of the radical difference of being which separates man from God.

This exegete appears to be faithful, in essential matters, to the obvious sense of the texts. If Gregory takes up the Psalter with the idea, which may initially appear *apriori*, that the structure of the collection, with its division into five parts, furnishes a ladder of the spiritual life in five degrees, he did not attempt to impose on these degrees a predetermined content identical to a scheme found in Origen, which was itself based on

---

[41]*In Inscriptiones Psalmorum*, I, 7, GNO, vol. V, pp. 43-46. Here, as elsewhere in the treatise, Gregory applies his basic idea: "The titles [of the psalms]...would have a meaning aimed at our spiritual profit [chap. 10-25]," observes Quasten (vol. III, p. 379). The response of the Biblical Commission on May 1, 1910, on the titles of the Psalms (DS 3522-3523) certainly does not contradict this position when it states that the titles of the Psalms are more ancient than the Septuagint version and that they derive from Jewish tradition, therefore sustaining their authenticity. When no serious opposition is raised, these titles, which are witnesses of the Judaic tradition, cannot be placed in doubt. The question of the titles of the Psalms had already been resolved in the same way (cf. Lesetre, *Psaumes*, [Paris, 1883], p. L) in the patristic age. St. Thomas Aquinas in his turn acknowledged that they do not go back to the authors of the Psalms themselves, and consequently we cannot regard them as necessarily inspired ("Sciendum est quod tituli ab Esdra facti sunt," *In Ps. VI, Opera Omnia*, [Parma, 1863], vol. XIV, p. 163). The Church has never regarded them as inspired, says E. Pannier (*La Saint Bible*, [Paris: Pirot-Clamer, 1950], vol. V, *Les Psaumes*, pp. 16-18).

[42]Cf. *In Inscriptione Psalmorum*, I, 5-6, GNO, V, 41-42:

He who has lifted up his spirit and whose look reached out far as from an eminent observatory sees in what the difference between vice and virtue consists, and that it is in terms of the final realities [cf. Ps 72:17], and not in terms of the present realities, that the discerning between them is carried out. In fact, it is by means of the soul's visionary and penetrating look that he grasps as present what is reserved to the good in hope [cf. Col 1:5], he goes in spirit beyond the world of appearances, and he penetrates into the celestial sanctuaries [cf. Ps 72:17].

Scripture.[43] Gregory preferred to submit to the text he was commenting on. In contrast to what he did elsewhere (*Homilies on the Song of Songs*), the transitions between the degrees, where Gregory summarizes the preceding degree in view of the next higher grade, do not constitute theological "expositions independent of the text being commented on,"[44] but "adhere" rather well to the Psalms concerned whose basic meaning they genuinely if ingeniously extract.

We must however acknowledge the limits of this exegesis of the Psalms. It is selective in that it extracts and emphasizes only the fundamental theme of the Psalm in question. Gregory comments using broad strokes and ignoring everything that is of less interest to him (the whole of Ps 41 except the first two verses, the first part of Ps 72). But the selection is not purely arbitrary: what he retains is truly the essential. His method seems to consist in looking at the whole in the part (Ps 72 in one word of its first verse, Ps 89 in its title, Ps 106 in its strophic schema).

Another limitation: the Bishop of Nyssa slides easily from the basic meaning of a Psalm into a personal theological development:[45] commenting on Ps 89, e.g., he passes from the precariousness of human existence to the various possibilities offered to human liberty.

Moreover, although the early Fathers[46] mention the division of the Psalter into five sections, this division does not however appear to be original and it already presupposes a long period of usage, as well as later adjustments.[47] No one, to my knowledge, has ever maintained that the very order of the grouping of the Psalms by their final editor came under divine inspiration. Is it possible then to take this division as the basis for an explanation of the goal pursued by the Divine Author of the Psalter?

Above all it would be difficult to retain the orientation toward the apocatastasis of this Gregorian exegesis relative to the purpose of the Psalter. It is in his commentaries on Ps 106 and 150 that Gregory presents

---

[43]Gregory knows and refers in his *Sermons on the Canticle* (*GNO* VI, 17-27) to the distinction that Origen, basing his position on Proverbs, Ecclesiastes, and the Canticle, made among three stages of the spiritual life: ethical, physical, epoptic. See Rondeau, *Epektasis*, p. 520.

[44]According to M. Canévet's expression, *EC*, p. 148.

[45]Rondeau, p. 529: "At Psalm 150 [Gregory] explains the harmony of the universal praise of God as the reunion of men and angels in a single choir." It is interesting to compare Gregory of Nyssa's commentary with the more sober commentary of his contemporary, John Chrysostom (*PG* 55, 495-498).

[46]Such as Jerome, *Ep. XXVI ad Marcellinam, PL* 22, 431.

[47]Cf. E. Pannier, p. 9.

this idea: salvation implies the total disappearance of that which is opposed to the good. For him, the reference to the four points of the compass (Ps 106:3) implies that the entire human race receives the good news of the return to the good. Here, as elsewhere, apocatastasis is the term of Gregory' spiritual anthropology.[48] During his lifetime, the universal Church had not yet clearly rejected this idea that was definitively condemned after his death.[49]

The admission of all these limitations in Gregory' exegesis of the Psalms, while confirming the judgment of M. J. Rondeau, does not in any way imply that it is entirely lacking in value. This "exegesis properly so called" takes place at the level of a "very personal spiritual reading" of the Psalter, "rises to the level of the inspired text and of its fullness, participates in the breath of its inspiration, reveals its power." Gregory of Nyssa's leading idea[50] in *In Inscriptiones Psalmorum*, namely "the strict identity between the dynamic of the Psalter and that of the spiritual life, saves" the work, provided one is willing to prescind from the question of the numerical ordering of the Psalms. Like the risen Christ,[51] Gregory has read the Old Testament in the light of the Paschal Mystery: if the riches of this Gregorian reading remain mixed with shadows, the splendor of these riches disposes us to benefit from the exegesis, often more doctrinal and theological, of the key New Testament texts that we find in the writings of the Bishop of Nyssa: Phil 2,5-11; Jn 20,17; Mt 28,19.

In a great number of his works, but most especially in the *Against Eunomius*, Gregory of Nyssa comments on the Christological hymn of Saint Paul, in his letter to the Philippians, 2,5-11. We will extract the

---

[48]Rondeau, *Epektasis*, p. 528; cf. Daniélou, *L'Être et le Temps*, chap. X, pp. 222-226 for whom "the apocatastasis in Gregory refers essentially to the restoration of human nature to its original state...it is the condition of being revived." This sense is in harmony with Acts 3:21. Quasten, on the other hand, underscores the heterodox character of Gregory's view of the apocastasis (vol. III, pp. 412-413): 'The pains of hell are not eternal but temporary, because they are of a purely medicinal nature." In other words, Gregory sees hell, to which he denies endless eternity, even for the demons, as a simple purgatory. Already in 1890, F. Hilt (*Des hl. Gregor von Nyssa Lehre vom Menschen*, [Cologne]) had shown that the great bishop of Nyssa's authority could not be defended on this point.

[49]See the anathema against Origen published in 543 (*DS* 411: the condemnation of the apocatastasis or restoration of impious demons and men); and the study recommended by the Congregation of the Doctrine of the Faith on "Christian Faith and Demonology," *Doc. Cath.* 72 (1975), pp. 708-718, defining the substance of the text of Lateran IV (1215; *DS* 800) on demons.

[50]Rondeau, p. 530; see also, by the same author, a study in the *Mélanges Puech*, PUF, (Paris, 1974), pp. 263-287.

[51]Cf. Lk 24:25-27.

original point of Gregory's commentary, considering the excellent work of L. F. Mateo-Seco,[52] by considering in turn the divine form, the kenosis and the exaltation of Christ.

"He who was in the form of God" (Phil 2:6): Paul does not say, Gregory insists, "in a form like to that of God (*morphen echon homoian*), as we say of one who was made in the likeness of God (*kath'homoiosin*), but: he who was in the very form of God, for everything that belongs to the Father is in the Son. He says then, by logical consequence, that the Son is eternal, without quantity, matter and body, such that the form of the Father's figure is encountered fully in the Son."[53] For the bishop of Nyssa, Paul here clearly affirms the consubstantiality of the Logos with the Father: "the substance is 'co-signified' (*sussemainetai*) with the form." Paul has "indicated the substance by way of the form."[54]

How does Gregory go about demonstrating this point? By underlining Paul's parallel affirmation: the Son took on the Servant's nature (*ousia*) together with his form and not simply an "empty form or one devoid of substance."[55]

Specifically, this is how the bishop of Nyssa analyzes the following verse (Phil 2:7): "He emptied himself, taking the form of the slave and becoming like unto men." He comments:

> By saying that the Son took on the form of the slave, that is to say the flesh, he is affirming the distinction between the form of God and the form of the slave.... The verb *ekenosen* [emptied] shows clearly that he was not always such as he was seen by us, but that he was in the fullness of the divinity, equal to God, inaccessible to every creature and uncircumscribable by the narrowness of human poverty...and that he was circumscribed by the weak nature of the flesh when he emptied himself, humbling the ineffable glory of his divinity even to the level of our lowliness; thus what he was was great, perfect and incomprehensible; what he assumed was equal to the measure of our nature.[56]

It is clear that "kenosis" is not here understood as an annihilation of the divinity; rather, it is identified with the Incarnation, or better still the Inhumanation,[57] of the Word. The essence of the kenosis does not consist

---

[52]L. F. Mateo-Seco, "Kenosis, Exaltación de Cristo y Apocatastasis en la exegesis a Filipenses 2, 5-11 de Gregorio de Nisa," *Scripta Theologica* 3 (1971), pp. 301-342.

[53]*Adv. Apoll.*, 20, PG 45, 1164A-B.

[54]*Adv. Eunomium*, IV, PG 45, 672A.

[55]*Ibid.*: "*psilèn morphèn.*"

[56]*Adv. Apoll.*, 20, PG 45, 1164C-D.

[57]A common expression in the Fathers: cf. B. de Margerie, *Christ for the World*, XIV.

in the renunciation of external glory, but in the merciful assumption of a created nature, and hence in the renunciation of the total inaccessibility of the divinity,[58] even to the tragic proximity of death on the cross. Even at the moment of death, the Word "did not strip himself of his authentic power, because he said: destroy this temple and in three days I will rebuild it" (Jn 2:19, 21).[59] "He humbled himself, becoming man without any change in himself."[60]

Moreover, by "becoming like unto men" (Phil 2:7), the Son did not become an ordinary man, even if he was a true man:

"Like unto men, recognized *as man* by his appearance" [Phil 2:7], he was man, even if not man in every respect [*ei kai me di holou anthropos*], but *as man*, by reason of the mystery, in accordance with virginity, by means of which, thanks to this mystery, it became manifest that he was not in every respect subject to the laws of nature, but that he made his way into human existence in a divine way [*theikos*], and that, not having needed conjugal activity for the formation of his own body, he might appear not to be an ordinary human being in every respect, because of his unique formation, but rather *as a man*.[61]

In other words, for Gregory, Christ, though truly man and not just apparently so, is nevertheless not an ordinary man but an extraordinary one, Man par excellence. The adverb *theikos*, divinely, underlines the divine manner in which the Incarnation was accomplished. Gregory even speaks—and he is the first to do so—of a virginal generation in God: "It is indeed a paradox that virginity should be found in a Father, who possesses a Son whom he begot without passion.... This virginity shone forth at once with the purity and the impassibility of his generation: still the same paradox which virginity elicits at the thought of a son."[62] It is this virginity of the Father, like that of the Son and that of the Spirit,[63] that Gregory sees as calling for the virginity of Mary, who only in this way was chosen to be the Mother of God.[64]

---

[58]Mateo-Seco, p. 313.

[59]*Adversum Eunomium*, II, PG 45, 532C.

[60]*Adv. Apoll.*, 21, PG 45, 1165A.

[61]*Ibid.*, 1164D-1165A.

[62]*Treatise on Virginity*, II, 1, 2, SC 119; cf. M. Aubineau, p. 151.

[63]Cf. II, 1, 8 in the same treatise: virginity is "contemplated in the essential and incorruptible purity of the Holy Spirit, for in speaking of purity and incorruptibility, virginity is designated by another name."

[64]Cf. M. Gordillo, "La virginidad transcendente de Maria, Madre de Dios, en San Gregorio de Nisa y en la antigua tradición de la Iglesia," *Estudios Marianos* 21 (1960), p. 142.

There is not then, for the Bishop of Nyssa, as exegete of the Epistle to the Philippians, a total parity between Christ and the rest of mortal men. By becoming man, the creator Word did not subject himself to all the laws of human nature of which he is the author.[65]

This brings us to Gregory's commentary on the conclusion of the Christological hymn sent by Paul to the Philippians: "therefore, God exalted him to the highest place and gave him the name that is above every name" (2:9):

> This confirms our previous exegesis. Indeed, everyone knows that the Most High has no need of being lifted up, whereas that which is low, if it becomes what it was not before, has been elevated to the divinity; now what is exalted is that which has gone from a lowly to a sublime state.... And just as the man according to Christ [*ho kata Christon anthropos*][66] had to be called by a proper

---

[65]We could extend this reasoning in the setting of our present problematics and say: the man who comes back from the dead, the man who redeems all mankind is not an ordinary man, but an extraordinary man, the true superman.

[66]Elsewhere (*De perfecta Christiani forma*, PG 44, C-D), Gregory suggests that the name of Christ recapitulates all the titles of Christ and emphasizes that fact that it designates royal power, surpassing all power. In other words, for Gregory, the name of Christ at least implicitly denominates the divine nature of the Incarnate Word. It is for this reason that we did not translate Gregory's commented text here as Mateo-Seco did (p. 325). See also on this expression and others, J. R. Bouchet O.P., "Le vocabulaire de l'union et du rapport des natures chez Saint Grégoire de Nysse," *Rev. Thomiste* 68 (1969), 581. However, we can complete the observations of J. R. Bouchet by noting that Gregory's expression: "the man according to Christ," designating Jesus Christ, is connected with the very thought of Paul himself and the ancient Fathers. On the one hand, Cerfaux remarks: "When we say Jesus, we are thinking of Christ in His mortal life. When we say 'the Lord,' we are thinking of his life as risen and of his presence in the community. To indicate the person who begins his career in eternity and who continues it in his presence in our midst, we will say 'Christ'" (*Le Christ dans la théologie de Saint Paul*, [Paris, 1951], p. 367). Cerfaux insists: "The Old Testament provides Saint Paul the idea of pre-existence, in the sense that the Christ foreseen for Israel had been prepared from all eternity and has been existing from all eternity in God's designs.... The Jewish apocalyptic concretized this idea of pre-existence even to the point of making the Christ, Who became Daniel's Son of Man, into a pre-existing Being...." Then Cerfaux explains the reasons why "it remained for St. Paul to follow the lines of the Old Testament and of the apocalypses and to call *ho Christos* the pre-existent Christ, exercising His salutary activity already from His pre-existence. The Christ will be He Who comes to carry out in the world the work of God" (*ibid.*, p. 374). On the other hand, the first Fathers followed the same line: "With Justin..., the very name *Christos* possesses a mysterious meaning equal to the name *théos* and it designates with a human word, which is not a true name, an inexpressible reality (*II Apol.* 6, 2)," continues Cerfaux (*ibid.*, p. 374, n. 2). We find again, it seems the same way of understanding the word *Christos* in St. Irenæus (*Adversus Hæreses*, III, 18, 3; PG 7, 934AB) and in St. Basil (*On the Holy Spirit*, I, 28; PG 32, 116; RJ 945). The expression *o kata Christon anthropos* therefore indicates not only the singular humanity of the man Jesus, but his divine pre-existence.

name, as was fitting for human nature, so the human was called Jesus in the annunciation of the mystery [*mystagogia*] made by Gabriel to Mary. On the other hand, the divine nature cannot be defined by a Name; now the two natures have become one reality because of the union; this is why God receives a name [understood: Jesus] on the basis of what is human.[67]

Gregory's idea comes through here in spite of a certain obscurity of expression: he gives no consideration at all to the relation between the obedience of Christ and his exaltation, which however is strongly underscored by Paul, but rather attempts to deepen the Pauline reflection on the Name. For him, it is the human form, the human nature which confers on the divine form that which it did not have on its own, namely, the capacity of being called by a name, while the divine form enables the human form to possess a name that is above every name. Gregory comes back to this point elsewhere:

The Divinity endowed Him who had been named in a human fashion with the Name that is above every name.... Because of the exact union [*akribe henoteta*] between the assuming Divinity[68] and the assumed flesh, there is an exchange of names, so that what is human is called by a divine name and what is divine by a human name.[69]

What the exaltation of the Lord in Phil 2:9 evokes for Gregory is then the "communication of idioms" or an exchange of properties, without confusion, between the two natures of Christ.[70] This exaltation consists in the fact that the humanity of Christ participates to the greatest possible

---

[67] *Adv. Apoll.* 21, PG 45, 1165A.

[68] *Tes proslabomenès theotètos*: it would have been more correct to say, "because of the assuming Word-God." Cf. Thomas Aquinas, *Summa Theologiæ*, III, 3, 2.

[69] *Ad Theophilum*, PG 45, 1278A-C.

[70] Cf. Quasten, vol. III, pp. 409-410; Gregory of Nyssa, *Adversus Eunomium* V, 5: "By reason of the contact and the union of natures, the attributes that belong to each belong to both; thus the Lord receives the blows of the Servant, while the Servant is glorified with the honor of the Lord. This is why the cross is said to be the cross of the Lord of glory [Phil 2:2] and every tongue confesses that Jesus Christ is Lord, for the glory of God the Father." In spite of the clumsiness of expression ("the attributes proper to each of the two natures belong to both"), Gregory is not monophysite. He acknowledges in fact ("the Lord...") the true import of the communication of the idioms or properties: "We can attribute to that single subject, the Word, the properties that belong peculiarly to each of the two natures" (cf. G. Rotureau, "Communication des Idiomes," *Catholicisme*, vol. II, [1949], col. 1373-1374; Thomas Aquinas, *Summa Theologiæ*, III, 16; Bartmann, *Theol. Dogmatique*, [1941⁴], pp. 386-387: reciprocal attributions must always be made in relation to the person and never in relation to nature.)

extent in the attributes of his divinity.[71] The Name above every name, before which every knee bends (Phil 2:10), expresses the ineffable character of Jesus' divine being, whose infinity escapes all definition.[72] Every knee will bend before Jesus, "the Man above every name (*anthropos hyper pan onoma*), which is the proper characteristic of divinity."[73]

Every knee, even in the world below, wrote Paul (Phil 2:10): since for Gregory the apocatastasis is the crowning point of anthropology, we are not surprised to see that his commentaries on the Pauline hymn point toward the final reconciliation of the demons and of the unjust, although they do not affirm this explicitly.[74]

We will observe that the Bishop of Nyssa not only does not comment on the link, emphasized by Paul,—"therefore" (Phil 2:9)—between kenosis and exaltation, but even seems to link the exaltation to the Incarnation itself: the name of Jesus symbolizes for him the human nature of Jesus, assumed by the Son who is equal to the Father.

At first sight, we are tempted to say that Gregory is guilty of a misinterpretation. Does not the Name above every name evoke the divine nature of the One who Is?

In reality, however, as the above citations have sufficiently shown, for Gregory the name of Jesus symbolizes the two natures taken in their inseparable union. His reflections help us to better understand what the Pauline text by no means excluded, but rather presupposed: from the time of the Incarnation, the Son, who had received the name of Jesus long before his Resurrection, deserved to see every knee bending before his name. It is Paul's disciple, Luke, the beloved physician[75]—and Gregory recalls this, even reading the hymn to the Philippians in the context of Luke and of other Pauline texts[76]—who shows us the "bestowal" of the Name of Jesus, which was in fact conferred long before the Passion.

If we accept the view that the hymn to the Philippians was in existence prior to its use by Paul and that it was contained in the liturgy which he received together with the tradition of the Mother Church of

---

[71]Mateo-Seco, p. 327.

[72]*Ad Ablabium, PG* 45, 129D.

[73]*Adv. Apoll.*, 21, *PG* 45, 1165D.

[74]Cf. Mateo-Seco, pp. 334-335; *Adv. Eunomium*, II, *PG* 45, 557B-C.

[75]Lk 1:31.

[76]Col. 1:16; 1 Cor 8:6; Gal 4:4; cf. Cerfaux, p. 335.

Jerusalem,[77] we can rightly think that the interpretation of Gregory does agree in a profound way with an idea that emerges from the whole corpus of the Pauline epistles according to which Christ is acknowledged as the pre-existent and creator Son.[78]

In other words, the apparent "telescoping" of Gregory in his reading of Paul arrives at the Pauline understanding, indeed the only possible understanding,[79] of the hymn that the Apostle received from the Mother Church.

Likewise the explanation given us by the Bishop of Nyssa regarding Jn 20:17[80] is not altogether unlike the interpretation of some moderns,[81] whose views are apparently less new than is sometimes believed....

The text reads as follows: "Do not hold on to me, for I have not yet returned to the Father. Go instead to my brothers and tell them, 'I am returning to my Father and your Father, to my God and your God.'"

In his *Apology for an Apology*, Eunomius sets forth his exegesis of Jn 20:17:

> Either the relative signification of the words employed expresses a community of essence between the disciples and the Father, or the words imply that we should not introduce the Lord into a community of nature with the Father. Just

---

[77]The opinion of a good number of exegetes.

[78]Cf. Cerfaux, pp. 385-393, and among other texts, Rm 9:5.

[79]Moreover, it results clearly from Phil 2:6-7 that in Paul's eyes, before Christ's exaltation, he already had the Name above every other name (2:9) since he already possessed the divine form when he assumed that of a slave; it is from the moment of such an assumption that every knee must bend before the God Who has become a slave; from a comparison between the beginning and the end of the Christological hymn, it results that the "this is why" (*dio*) of 2:9 includes a double motive: not only the death on the cross, but also the rank equal to God of him who never ceased being of divine form and condition. In his hymn, Paul never says that the pre-paschal Christ did not merit to have every creature kneel before him, he in no ways denies such an obligation. It is this that, without explaining it with all the clarity we might have wished, Gregory of Nyssa perceived. When all is said and done, we are permitted to think with P. Henry, that relative to that hymn, "Gregory of Nyssa's exegesis is at once one of the most faithful to Paul's thought and one of the most penetrating from the standpoint of speculative theology, nay even philosophy" ("Kénose," *DBS* V, [1957], col. 84).

[80]We take our inspiration for this whole section from M. Van Parys, *EC*, pp. 171-179.

[81]See F. M. Catherinet, "Note sur un verset de l'évangile de saint Jean 20:17," *Mémorial J. Chaine*, (Lyon, 1950), pp. 56-58: Jesus repeats in triumphal chant Ps 21:23 of which he had made verse 19 (*Eloi, Eloi, lama sabachthani*) his own on the Cross. This exegesis is confirmed by Heb 2:12. In the eighteenth century, Dom Calmet had already caught a glimpse of the true sense of Jn 20:17: no doubt it was because he knew the Fathers and their exegesis.... Cf. B. de Margerie, *The Christian Trinity in History*, (Petersham, MA: St. Bede's Publications, 1981), pp. 10-11.

as the servitude of the disciples is proven by the fact that the God of the universe is called their God, so too, by what the text says, the Son is also declared servant of the Father.[82]

The dilemma is obvious: either the Only Begotten is of the same nature as the Father and the disciples also will be of the same nature as the Father, which is absurd, or the Only Begotten is of the same nature as the disciples and the unbegotten God is equally transcendent with respect to both.[83]

How does Gregory reply? His thought is incorporated within a discussion of Rom 8:29 and Christ as first-born among a multitude of brothers: [84]

This first-born then also has brothers, concerning whom he says to Mary: "Go and tell my brothers: I am going to my Father and your Father, to my God and your God." Indeed, by these words, he summarizes the entire design of his wise plan for mankind.

Men have in fact turned away from God and served gods who are not so by nature and, although they were children of God, they attached themselves to an evil father abusing this name.[85]

This is why the "Mediator between God and men" [1 Tim 2:5], having taken on the first-fruits of human nature, in its entirety, sends this message to his brothers, not as God, but as one who shares our human nature and he says: I am going away so that through my mediation[86] the true Father from whom you have been separated may become your Father and the true God whom you have abandoned, your God. For thanks to the first-fruits [the human nature] which I have assumed I am able in my person to lead back all of humanity to Him who is God and Father.

This rich interpretation achieves a veritable synthesis of the earlier attempts at interpreting the passage. Already, in a variety of ways, Origen, Athanasius, Cyril of Jerusalem, Epiphanius of Salamis had interpreted Jn 20:17 regarding the "economy" of salvation. Gregory of Nyssa picks up from Eustachius the distinction between God and man in

---

[82]Quoted by Gregory of Nyssa, *Adversus Eunomium* III, 19, 8; cf. *GNO* II, pp. 291-292.

[83]Van Parys, *EC*, pp. 172-173.

[84]Gregory of Nyssa, *Adversus Eunomium* IV, 82-83; *GNO* II, 346; *PG* 45, 504AB.

[85]We note the allusion to Jn 8:41-44: "You are from your father the devil...."

[86]We depart here from Van Parys' translation in order not to miss Gregory's allusion to the one Mediator (1 Tm 2:5) who was mentioned at the beginning of the sentence and to Whom his expression *di'emautou* no doubt refers us.

Jesus Christ. What is new with Gregory is the combining and the integrating of the economic principle and the Christological principle of the two natures. Gregory shows first of all that it is Christ as man who speaks to Mary Magdalene, and then that this interpretation lies within the *dianoia* or understanding of Scripture which describes for us the salvific economy of Jesus Christ, possible only because He is at once God and man, the only mediator.[87]

In his way, Gregory, in commenting on Jn 20:17, was already explaining what has been pointed out by modern exegesis: in the Gospel of John, Christ never calls human beings his brothers until after he has died and risen to reconcile them with the Father.

From a consideration of the mystery of the economy,[88] Gregory moves us on to a Trinitarian reflection. On the basis of the very formula of Baptism given by the Risen Christ in Mt 28:19, he is able to draw out the *akolouthia* inherent in the command of Jesus: "Make disciples of all nations, baptizing them in the name of the Father and of the Son and of the Holy Spirit." With the help of the notion of relation (*schesis*), he extracts a theological synthesis from Mt 28:19. The name *Father* implies by its very content the relation to a Son, and specifically to the Son mentioned immediately afterward; the Son is co-eternal with the Father because God is immutable. He was called Father by the Word; He was, is, and always will be Father of this Word-Son; and the Son preferred the name Father precisely because this name implies the Son by the very relation that it expresses. Likewise the Spirit is not simply a superfluous new-comer, but rather is inseparably united to the Son, co-eternal to the Son, and to the Father. The mystery of godliness (cf. 1 Tm 3:16), entrusted to the disciples, is the Name of the Father and of the Son and of the Holy Spirit.[89] These designations imply not a difference of natures, but the properties of persons; the Name, mentioned without any complement which would specify its meaning (as the precise name of an animal places him in a species: cf. Gn 2:19-20), reveals the intention—"it seems to me that such was the will of the Word through this statement" (*dia tes ektheseos tautes*)—to persuade us that the divine Essence is ineffa-

---

[87]Van Parys, *EC*, p. 179.

[88]We note that for J. R. Bouchet (*EC*, pp. 194-196, especially p. 196), this term economy designates for Gregory of Nyssa, when it is "used about Christ, exclusively his earthly life." Possibly elsewhere, but this is not the impression of the reader of *Adversus Eunomium*, III, PG 45, 473D and 476A receives, though the matter may be open to question. The interpretation of Van Parys (*EC* p. 190) does not lack probability.

[89]Gregory of Nyssa, *Adversus Eunomium* II, PG 45, 465A-472C. The beautiful comparison between Mt 28:19 and 1 Tm 3:16 comes at the beginning and at the end of this section.

ble, incomprehensible and unspeakable; his Name then surpasses every name, every nomination. This is the case of the one only uncreated nature.[90]

Even if we do not yet have at our disposal a complete treatment of the history of the patristic exegesis of Mt 28:19, we may be allowed to suspect that the interpretation of Gregory of Nyssa, especially in the *Contra Eunomium* to which we have here referred,[91] represents a high-point that would be difficult to surpass.

Conclusions: The Enduring Value of the Exegesis of Gregory of Nyssa

Where precisely does this enduring value lie? Would it lie in his endeavor to employ the method of Origen, that of spiritual allegory, as an extension of a careful study of the literal and historical sense?

Perhaps not. While it is noteworthy that Gregory did, for example, begin his *Life of Moses* by an interpretation which reviewed the events of this life, thus revealing the importance of historical realities in his eyes, it would be a mistake to take this literal exegesis in the modern sense of the term, as though it were inspired by a concern to establish facts in their context and to determine the original meaning of expressions, that intended by the human author of a biblical book.

The exegesis of Gregory is literal, at least in the second part of his life, toward 390-395, when he wrote this *Life of Moses*. Nevertheless, it remains essentially inspired by moral concerns and is basically a continuation of the Jewish *haggada* (edifying literal commentary). Such hagiographical writing is intended as an edifying enlargement on the text of Exodus, with some emphasis on the marvelous, while at the same time engaging in polemic against naturalist interpretations. As an infant, Moses refuses to be nursed by a foreigner.[92] The burning bush, which

---

[90]*Ibid.*, 472D-473C. We will note the distinction made between the Name *onoma* common to the Three and the appellations (*tôn klèseon toutôn*: 472D) of Father, Son and Spirit, without claiming, however, that there is therein, for Gregory, a technical distinction: in this same treatise *Adversus Eunomium*, in book XI (*PG* 45, 880B), Gregory speaks to us of the "confession of the divine Names of the Father, the Son and of the Holy Spirit" (*tôn theiôn onomatôn*). For an attempt at biblico-theological reflection on the reconciliation between the Name and the Names, in the understanding of Mt 28:19, see B. de Margerie, *The Christian Trinity in History*, pp. 142-145.

[91]Mt 28:19 is referred to fourteen times in the *Refutation of Eunomius' Profession of Faith* by the great bishop of Nyssa, we are told by Van Parys (*EC*, p. 186, n. 2).

[92]Gregory of Nyssa, *Life of Moses*, PG 44, 305A.

burns at high noon,[93] dazzles the eyes with the brilliance of its rays and illumines the ears with the incorruptibility of its teachings.[94] Details that are shocking are interpreted in a favorable sense, so much so that Gregory later seems to think—paradoxically—that he should avoid[95] in his *theoria* the interpretation he originally presented as *historia*.[96]

Earlier, around the years 379-380, in the first part of his life, i.e., in the period of his treatises on the *Creation* and the *Hexameron*, the Bishop of Nyssa seems to have been more concerned to arrive at the events themselves and at the meaning of the human author. In particular, he acknowledged that the literal sense can itself be metaphorical.[97] This was precisely, as we have seen, what had escaped the school of Alexandria.[98] At this time in his life, Gregory did not believe that there was a consistently spiritual reading of the creation narrative; he did not view each statement as a sign of an intelligible reality.[99]

Whatever may have been the evolution of Gregory's exegetical practice or theory, it is clear that the enduring value of his work, viewed as a certain type of reading of Scripture, consists rather in helping us to realize the extent to which this reading was conditioned by the liturgy[100] and above all by a theological vision.

---

[93]*Ibid.*, 505C.

[94]*Ibid.*, 505D.

[95]*Ibid.*, 300A-B.

[96]We have taken our inspiration here from Jean Daniélou, "Introduction à la *Vie de Moïse*," (Paris, 1955²), pp. XI ff.: L'exégèse de l'Exode.

[97]See on these two points (the development of Gregorian exegesis and literal metaphorical sense), J. E. Pfister, S.J., *Saint Gregory of Nyssa: Biblical Exegete*, (unpublished thesis, Woodstock, Maryland, 1964), chap. X, pp. 230ff. According to Pfister, pp. 212ff., Gregory evolved from a literal exegesis of the Basilian type toward an allegorical exegesis of the Alexandrian and Origenian type.

[98]Cf. our chapter III on Clement of Alexandria, n. 27, and chapter IV on Origen, n. 22. In his *Adversus Eunomium*, book II, PG 45, 989, Gregory of Nyssa shows himself to have been aware of the figurative and metaphoric character of the literal sense of Gn 1:4, 8:21 and Ps 29: when Scripture tells us that God sees, hears, feels, etc., it is an anthropomorphism used to describe for us the divine (*anthrôpoeides diagrapsei ton theion*). Cf. Pfister, p. 244. There is a very clear progress with respect to Origen and Clement, who seemed to confuse the metaphorical literal sense and the spiritual sense.

[99]On this subject, see M. Alexandre, *EC*, pp. 103-104. Gregory speaks in the same sense of the literary use in the Scriptures (PG 44, 101C) and, according to the rhetorical terminology of his time, he speaks of *catachrèse* or transfer of sense in these cases. Moreover, Philo had preceded him in the same direction (*Congr.* 162).

[100]Cf. R. L. Wilken, "Liturgy, Bible and Theology in the Easter Homilies of Gregory of Nyssa," *EC*, p. 129.

Gregory reminds us, *in actu exercito*, that a reading of Scripture not conditioned by philosophical and theological convictions is difficult if not impossible. If it is sometimes true that the traditional exegesis shapes his theological explanation, the opposite is more frequently the case. The very fact of the Incarnation, carried forward by the consideration, in faith, of the two natures of Christ, becomes the key to the possible explanations of particular texts, notably—as we have seen—to those of John and Paul. Gregory's goal is to extract the theological teaching of the Scriptures.[101]

Such a Christocentric reading of the Scriptures is not, of course, a novelty. Athanasius, as we have seen, had already been its theoretical proponent. More specifically, he read the Scripture in the context of a deeply rooted conviction, namely, that the Bible's purpose is to reveal the two natures of Christ.

Gregory of Nyssa's specific contribution consists in his supporting the same conviction with the principle, not of *sugkatabasis*,[102] which was dear to Chrysostom, his contemporary, as it had been to the minds of Athanasius and Origen, but that of the *akolouthia* of a human logic revelatory of a divine Logic—of a human logic as intensely concerned with an indefinite progress in the biblical knowledge of God within the context of a continual renewal in the exegesis of the finite word of an infinite God as it is intensely propelled by the desire and hope of a ceaselessly renewed beatifying vision of his infinite Essence.

All of this—that is to say, the whole complex of Gregory of Nyssa's convictions regarding the infinite God[103] and man indefinite, whose potential infinitude aspires to the immutable vision[104] of the Infinite in

---

[101]Cf. M. Canévet, *EC*, pp. 164-165.

[102]In the different works of Gregory of Nyssa translated by the *SC*, the indices of the Greek works used by the bishop of Nyssa do not mention *sugkatabasis* even once. From that we can conclude at least that this category was not important in his eyes. But he is not ignorant of the reality that it designates in the divine comportment: cf. nn. 98, 99.

[103]Cf. J. Daniélou, *EC*, 251: "Mühlenberg showed very clearly that Gregory's conception of infinity is not the Platonic indefinite, nor the Aristotelian indeterminate. He has established that Gregory had his own conception of the divine infinity that is an infinity of fullness.... The Gregorian conception of the divine infinite is unthinkable outside of biblical revelation." However, Gregory of Nyssa is not the first Christian theologian to work on the doctrine of divine infinity: Hilary of Poitiers had already spoken of it earlier: cf. on this point J. M. McDermott, *Vig. Christ.*, 27 (1973), pp. 172-202.

[104]There would surely be occasion to examine deeply, in Gregory's writings, the possibility of a synthesis between the two trains of his thought: that which puts the accent on the fixedness in God, already here below, a fortiori in the afterlife (e.g., "It is impossible to lift oneself up toward God other than in always having one's eyes fixed on the goods of on

act wherein ever new aspects will be revealed—conditions the exegesis of the bishop of Nyssa. If finite and indefinite man can always progress in the knowledge of God, his infinite Good, human knowledge and the finite word of the infinite Word and of all the anacoluthons and *"akolouthias"* of this word lead us to an ever renewed *theoria* of this infinite Being, so much so that the earthly and unceasing progress and renewal of exegesis prefigure and anticipate the constant renewal and progress promised, beyond death, in the *theoria* of the One who transcends all *akolouthia*.

Thus we can only view the exegetical act of the Bishop of Nyssa as the search for the *akolouthia* of the finite word of the infinite God, a search that is continuously sustained by a longing for the *theoria* of his Infinity. In the exercise of the exegetical act, the reader of Scripture comes to an ever more profound realization that the word he is examining participates in the *kenosis* of the infinite Word who pronounces that word in eternity. Through it his inaccessible divinity makes itself ever more accessible "to the puny stature of our human nothingness,"[105] revealing to us ever more perfectly, through the *akolouthia* of the particular names of created beings and species, the uncreated and universal Name which is above every name, the Name of Him Who Is.[106]

Thus, exegesis cannot but reach a point that is beyond all exegesis, in the silence of contemplation: "As the apostle says... the only name that is

---

high," [*De Beatitudinibus* 5, PG 44, 1248D]); and that which affirms, in contrast with many other spiritual authors, an "indefinite progress in the vision of God" within the very bosom of beatitude (cf. M. Canévet, "Grégoire de Nysse," *DSAM*, IV, 1 [1960], col. 1008; P. Deseille, *Epectase,*" *DSAM* IV, 1 [1960], col. 785-788). Gregory says explicitly: "the growth of those who share God's goods never ceases to increase during the whole eternity of eternities" (*In Canticum VIII*, 4, 8; pp. 245-246, PG 44, 940D-941A; see also M. Canévet, col. 1005). It remains to be seen if these different aspects can be reconciled in the light of a later distinction between the primordial and immutable object of the beatific vision and its second and variable objects, while remaining faithful to Gregory's thought; in this case, we would be admitting a constant progress in the vision in God of the secondary objects of the beatific vision. It would be good to consider, in this context, the teachings of the Seraphic Doctor, St. Bonaventure, as well as those of Scotus.

[105]Gregory of Nyssa, *Adv. Apoll.*, 21, PG 45, 1164C. Thus does Gregory interpret the *kenosis* in the context of the "human nothingness," in a very satisfying way. His exegesis of Phil 2 is therefore very different from that of a thinker like Serge Boulgakov, as was emphasized by P. Henry, *DBS* 5 (1957), 84.

[106]Gregory of Nyssa, *Adv. Eunom.*, XI, PG 45, 873A. The mystery of the redeeming Incarnation thus reinforces the possibility of human intelligence through sensible things, by analogy, being raised to the contemplation of God's attributes, moving from the consideration of beings to the consideration of the divine Essence, i.e., of He Who Is (cf. Gregory of Nyssa, *Homilies on the Canticle*, 10, PG 44, 979-994).

appropriate for God is to believe that he is above every name. For the fact that he transcends every movement of the mind and that he is beyond the range of any possible grasp by nominal designation constitutes the proof of his grandeur, which no man can express,"[107] not even the exegete.

---

[107]Gregory of Nyssa, *Adv. Eunom.*, XII, PG 45, 1108, 6.

Chapter X
Saint Cyril of Alexandria Develops
a Christocentric Exegesis

Few Fathers or Doctors of the Church have enjoyed the praise and approval of popes and ecumenical councils as did Cyril of Alexandria, who died in 44. Shortly after his death, Chalcedon compares his doctrine to the wisdom of Saint Leo the Great;[1] this pope himself recommended the writings of the Alexandrian doctor precisely because they are fully in harmony with the faith of the holy Fathers;[2] Constantinople II[3] and Constantinople III, in 555 and 681 respectively, render him homage, the latter council clearing his memory of the accusation of monothelitism.[4] The fundamental reason for so many expressions of praise has to do with Cyril's defense of the unity and divinity of Christ the Savior, and no direct mention seems to be made of his exegesis. Nevertheless, this exegesis is scarcely irrelevant to the honor in which Cyril came to be held. The ecumenical councils, beginning with the Council of Ephesus at which Cyril presided,[5] largely retained[6] the christology of Cyril. But by so

---

[1]*Mansi*, VI, 953, 956-957.

[2]Leo the Great, *Epistula ad Imperatorem Theodosium*, PL 54, 891.

[3]*Mansi*, IX, 231 ff.

[4]Cf. *DS* 554, 557; Pius XII, Encycl. *Orientalis Ecclesiae*, April 9, 1944, AAS 36 (1944), 130; on the different evaluations of Cyrillian Christology and its development, the reader can refer to G. M. de Durand, O.P., Introduction to *Deux Dialogues Christologiques*, SC 97, (Paris, 1964), pp. 149-150; and especially A. Grillmeier, *Christ in Christian Tradition*, (London, 1975²), vol. I, pp. 473-483, and J. Liébaert, referred to in note 88.

[5]Cf. Pius XI, Encycl. *Lux Veritatis*, AAS 23 (1931), 493 ff.

doing they also substantially adopted his reading of Scripture, and particularly of the New Testament on a number of fundamental points.

Even today, within a divided Christianity, Cyril of Alexandria is a rallying point not only for the non-Chalcedonian Churches, but also for the Catholic[7] and Orthodox Churches that claim fidelity to the Council of 451.

After presenting some of Cyril's views on exegesis and its method, we will briefly look at how he implements this method in the area of the Old and especially the New Testament, with particular emphasis on his reading of John and Paul in their treatment of the fundamental mysteries of Christianity—the Trinity, the Incarnation, the gift of the Spirit, the Eucharist, the Church—a reading echoed by Vatican II. We will thus have occasion to cite at length from the immortal masterpiece of Cyril of Alexandria, his commentaries on the Gospel of John.[8]

A. Cyril's Method and spiritual Contemplation or Theôria Pneumatike

Cyril inherits the exegetical tradition of the Church of Alexandria; nevertheless, he brings important new nuances to this tradition.

He takes up again the great categories of his predecessors: literal sense, spiritual sense, *skopos* or goal, the "gnosis" of the mysteries, and he does so within the framework of a still more emphatic Christological focus, if that is possible:

> The goal[9] of inspired Scripture is to signify the mystery of Christ through innumerable objects. It may be compared to a magnificent city that possesses not one, but many images of its king, all displayed publicly in many different places. Scripture leaves no stone unturned to achieve this goal.... If the literal sense contains something unsightly, nothing prevents Scripture from employing it elegantly. Its goal [*skopos*] is not to set before us the lives of the patriarchs. Not at all. Its purpose is rather to communicate to us a knowledge

---

[6]Cf. T. Sagi-Bunic, O.F.M. Cap., *Deus perfectus et homo perfectus*, (Rome, 1965); and A. Grillmeier, *Mit Ihm und in Ihm*, (Freiburg, 1975), pp. 379-385, and note 4.

[7]The different diocesan churches within the one and universal Catholic Church.

[8]*PL*, vol., 73, 74; cf. Quasten, *Initiation aux Pères de l'Eglise*, (Paris, 1963), vol. III, pp. 180-186.

[9]Cyril uses the word *skopos*: on the notion of *skopos* in Cyril's exegesis and its background in profane exegesis, see A. Kerrigan, *St. Cyril of Alexandria, Interpreter of the Old Testament*, (Rome, 1952), *Anal. Bibl.*, vol. 2, pp. 87 ff., 224 ff.

of its mystery of salvation by means of which the word that concerns this mystery becomes clear and true.[10]

For Cyril, in this text, the literal sense appears to be totally subservient to the spiritual sense: the sense of the mystery of salvation, which is the Savior, Christ himself.

More precisely—and the works of A. Kerrigan[11]have established this—the distinction between the literal sense and the spiritual sense has to do above all not with the intentions of the subject, the human or the divine author, but with the objects considered: that which is human belongs to the literal sense, that which is divine to the spiritual sense. This point of view not only does not contradict the earlier or subsequent approaches (which distinguish between the respective intentions of the human and divine authors of the text) but even harmonizes with them and complements them: the human author has in mind a sense which one could qualify as human, that is to say the literal sense; the divine Author intends a divine sense, that is to say the spiritual sense. The first is especially concerned with the thoughts of men, the second with those of God. The first considers *ta aistheta*, the realities perceived by the senses, and *ta anthropina*, that is to say the traits and activities characteristic of the human being, whether individually or collectively. In contrast, the spiritual sense relates to the divine dogmas and to the mysteries (to all those things that Pius XII called, in the encyclical *Divino Afflante Spiritu* the "theological literal sense").

Thus for example the Davidic ascendancy of Jesus[12] emerges from the literal sense, as do his declarations to the Samaritan woman: "We worship what we know" (Jn 4:22):[13] Jesus is here expressing himself as a Jew and as a human being, who is obliged by natural law to worship God. In contrast, when he says "Pray the Lord of the harvest to send workers into his harvest" (Lk 10:1-3) Jesus is not presenting himself solely as one who prays, but also as the divine Lord of the harvest.[14]

Later, in the aftermath of the Nestorian crisis, when he will examine the words and the works of Christ, Cyril will distinguish with care three

---

[10]Cyril of Alexandria, *PG* 69, 308 C.

[11]A. Kerrigan, "The objects of the Literal and Spiritual senses of the New Testament according to Cyril of Alexandria," *TU* 63, (1957), pp. 354-374.

[12]Cyril of Alexandria, *PG* 74, 776 A.

[13]*Ibid.* 73, 304 CD.

[14]Cyril of Alexandria, *Homily 60 on the Gospel of St. Luke, CSCO,* vol. 140, (Louvain, 1953), pp. 156-157, the Latin translation of R. M. Tonneau.

categories[15] of expressions: those which relate to his divine attributes (*phonai theoprepeis*), those which described his human traits (*phonai anthropoprepeis*) and finally those which connote his humanity and his divinity simultaneously, the intermediary or mixed expressions (*phonai mesai, ekramenai*). We might mention in passing that a number of modern exegetes, without being aware of it have reached similar distinctions[16] whose remote preparations are undoubtedly found in Cyril's consideration of the literal and spiritual senses.

We see then how Cyril of Alexandria caused the notions of the literal and spiritual sense to evolve: by objectifying these notions, he discovers and presents their living synthesis in the supreme and unique subject, Christ and in the two dimensions of his theandric being. The Christological concentration of the exegetical method matches that of the dogmatic focus.

The point is all the more striking in that Cyril at the same time abandons one of the convictions of Origen: in Cyril's view, certain passages of the Old Testament offer a literal sense but not a spiritual sense. Most notably, Cyril applies this principle to certain legislative aspects of the Scriptures, for example to particular characteristics of the ark of the covenant that he sees as completely devoid of mystical signification.[17] The spiritual sense is always, for Cyril, in one way or another, relative to the mystery of Christ: "all spiritual contemplation (*theoria pneumatike*) focuses on the mystery of Christ."[18] A scriptural sense that has no relation to the mystery of Christ cannot be spiritual; it can only be literal.[19] The admission of the possibility of such a sense, indeed of its actual presence in a number of particular cases, amounts to a radical development regarding Origen.

The key notion of Cyril's exegesis is then that of *theoria-pneumatike* to which he alluded in the words just cited. What is the exact meaning of the term for the Alexandrian patriarch? This expression which Cyril

---

[15]Cyril of Alexandria, *PG* 74, 997 C and 73, 385 CD; cf. Kerrigan, *TU* 63, borrowed from, p. 358 and p. 374; see here below, notes 128 ff. and the texts to which they refer.

[16]Such as D. Mollat, *Introduction à l'etude de la christologie du saint Jean*, (Rome, 1970), pp. 17 ff., 97 ff.

[17]Cyril of Alexandria, *PG* 68, 597 A; cf. Kerrigan, *St. Cyril...*, (see note 9) pp. 367 ff. and 232.

[18]*Cyrilli Alexandrini in Joannis Evang.*, Pusey publ., anastatic reprod., (Brussels, 1965), vol. III, p. 336, fragm. on 2 Cor 3:13.

[19]Kerrigan, *St. Cyril...*, p. 131.

favors more than any other[20] for designating the spiritual sense of Scripture implies a "vision" (*theoria*) that opens the mind to the mystery of Christ (cf. Lk 27:4, 44); but this vision is "pneumatic," spiritual, because in exercising it the human mind is helped by the divine and holy Spirit to transcend "the mask of the letter and the shadow of the things that appear."[21]

This spiritual vision of the spiritual sense of the Scriptures is, for Cyril—who here borrows from the teaching of Clement and Origen—but with his own distinctive nuances—a charism[22] and a gnosis,[23] a revelation[24] which enriches the mind of the exegete by communicating to him the knowledge of the truth,[25] that is to say, of the divine profundities contained in the Scriptures[26] and of the mystery of Christ.[27] The gnosis of *theoria pneumatike* brings us the vision of God or *theoptia*, through which and in which the Inaccessible makes himself accessible to us in the fullness of his condescension. Gnosis, theopsis, pneumatic vision—this gift is given only to the believer who is obedient to Christ, not to the unbelieving Jew. Thus the Alexandrian doctor never tires of asking God for the precious gift of this biblical gnosis, for himself as well as for his audience.[28]

Although Cyril at times tends to enlarge[29] and at times to limit[30] the circle of Christians endowed with gnosis, nevertheless he differs from Clement of Alexandria on an important point: Cyril attributes to priests the role of illuminating the bible which Clement would assign to gnostics alone.[31]

---

[20]*Ibid.* p. 191. See the long list of Cyrillian expressions related to the spiritual sense in Kerrigan, *TU*, 63, pp. 363-364.

[21]Cyril, referred to by Pusey (cf. note 18), vol. III, p. 337: Frag. on 2 Cor 3:17.

[22]Cyril of Alexandria, *PG* 68, 608 AB.

[23]On the gnosis in Cyril, see Kerrigan, *St. Cyril...*, pp. 183 ff.

[24]Cyril of Alexandria, *PG* 68, 489, D; 69, 504 C.

[25]*Ibid.* 68, 489 D; 70, 576 A.

[26]*Ibid.*, Fragm. on 2 Cor. 3,18; Pusey, III, p. 339.

[27]*Ibid.*, *PG* 68, 260 A; 69, 504 C; 70, 1368 D.

[28]*Ibid.*, 70, 885 C; and many of the homilies on Saint Luke, Tonneau edition, *CSCO*, vol. 140, especially *Homily 38* (p. 53).

[29]The gnosis "consists in the reasoning process enabling simple people to know that Christ is God and that He is truly and really the Son of God," Pusey, *op. cit.* II, pp. 494, 9 ff.: commentaries on the Gospel of John). We will note here the anti-Arian point.

[30]It is a question of the *teloi* or those who are perfect, those who have attained to the purity of spirit (*ibid.*, II, pp. 494, 13 ff.).

[31]Cyril, *PG.* 68, 641 D; 69, 424 C; cf. Kerrigan, *St. Cyril...*, p. 181.

B. Cyril, a Christian Reader of the Old Testament

To be sure, Cyril is not unaware that he is himself one of those charismatic priests and that he has received the gift he so ardently prayed for—that of the *theoria pneumatike* of the Old Testament scriptures.

What we have already said shows that his reading of the Old Testament is not *exclusively* Christian, but it is *primarily* such. Not exclusively Christian, because he admits that a certain number of passages do not involve a spiritual sense, nor any allusion to the mystery of Christ. But primarily Christian, because for the Patriarch of Alexandria, the successor of the Apostles, it is his prophetic charism as exegete of the Old Testament that the risen Christ has communicated to him by opening his mind to His own (cf. Lk 24:27, 44). How else are we to understand Cyril when he says:

> Now that the only Son has become incarnate, now that he has died and risen again, now that he has completed the whole economy of his work among us, what further need is there of prophecy and prediction? For us then, prophecy can only mean the capacity to interpret, the hermeneutics for interpreting the prophets.[32]

The Christian prophet is one who has received the charism of recognizing the fulfillment of the Old Testament prophecies in the New.

The Old Law was an illumination accompanied by shadows, in contrast to the unadulterated light radiated by Christ, the Sun of Justice, the Morning Star.[33] It continues to illuminate with a light that may be compared to that of the moon, while the Gospel shines with the radiance of the noon-day sun,[34] thanks to Christ who manifests, in the Spirit, his knowledge of the Law and the Prophets.[35] Following Clement of Alexandria, Cyril employs the term "photagogy" (*photagogia*) to refer to this luminous interpretation of the Old Law by Jesus the Christ. We need this interpretation because the Law of Moses has been darkened by the shadows deriving from the letter. Regarding 2 Cor 3:16, Cyril writes: "The Lord shows the true face of the Law (that which was surrounded with glory) to the wise men sanctified in spirit and rendered illustrious

---

[32]*Ibid.*, *In 1 Cor* 14:2: *PG* 74, 889; a little further (892 A), Cyril adds some shading (*to propheteuein* en toutois *to diermeneuein esti ta ton propheton*) to what was too absolute in his first expression (*to prophesie* is *nothing more* than the faculty of interpreting the prophets).

[33]*Ibid.*, *Commentary on Habakkuk*, Pusey, II, p. 130, 1 ff.

[34]*Ibid.* II, p. 149.

[35]*Ibid.*, *Commentaries on Hosea*, Pusey, I, p. 138, 19 ff. ; on Zec., Pusey, II, 526, 3 ff.

by faith in Christ."[36] The illuminating activity of Christ is inextinguishable, for it is perpetuated in the Church by the apostles, the evangelists, the teachers and the priests of all times who have become bright stars in their turn, capable of illuminating those who live in darkness.[37]

In this context, the way in which Cyril takes up the question of Moses is remarkable for its complexity. On the one hand, the patriarch of Alexandria exalts the prophet Moses:[38] the lawgiver of Israel sees (*blepon*) in advance the glory of Christ, sees "Satan conquered, lepers healed, the sea calmed with a word"; and he even knows that the Law does not justify anyone, that it is Christ who will free the world from its bondage and lead believers into the Church.[39] For Cyril, Moses even understands the symbolism of his actions. Thus, the twelve stones erected for the twelve tribes of Israel were suggestive hints for the people, prophetic of the twelve apostles and the universal Church of Christ.[40]Cyril sees Moses then as a super-prophet of Christ. On the other hand, the same Cyril never tires of underscoring the extent to which Moses needs Christ for his salvation and the extent to which all the prophet's grandeur is eclipsed by that of Christ.[41] There is no contradiction in these different perspectives: it is because of Christ that Moses is endowed with an extraordinary knowledge whose object transcends the knowing subject. Somewhat more paradoxical is the fact that, for Cyril, Moses is endowed with a prophetic knowledge that even the pre-Easter Christ, in his humanity, does not seem so clearly, in his view, to possess.[42]

We cannot enter here into greater detail regarding the Old Testament exegesis of Cyril that was influenced by that of Jerome and which was

---

[36]*Ibid.*, Fragm, on 2 Cor 3:16: Pusey, III, p. 337, 2 ff.

[37]See the texts referred to in note 18 and Kerrigan, *St. Cyril...*, p. 181.

[38]Cf. Kerrigan, *St. Cyril...*, pp. 227-229. Kerrigan shows how Cyril follows Origen here; were they both under the influence of Philo? This is not possible, for Philo exalts the prophet in Moses: cf. B. Botte, "La vie de Moïse par Philon," *Cahiera Sioniens*, 8 (1954), 59 (177).

[39]Cyril, *PG* 69, 673 A.

[40]*Ibid.* 69, 520 C; 517 A.

[41]Cf. L. M. Armendariz, S.J., *El Nuevo Moisés, Dinamica cristocentrica en la tipologia de Cirilo Alejandrino*, (Madrid, 1962), chap. III and IV.

[42]Cf. H. du Manoir, *Dogme et Spiritualité chez saint Cyrille d'Alexandrie*, (Paris, 1944), pp. 150-161: according to this author, there is a real difference between Jesus human knowledge concerning the day of judgment, before and after His resurrection, in Cyril's position.

extensively analyzed, some years ago, by Fr. Kerrigan.[43] We will only remark that if one compares this exegesis with the ancient school of Alexandria (Clement and Origen) it marks a decisive advance on two points: not only does Cyril recognize, as we have already brought out, that certain texts of the Old Testament have no spiritual sense to offer, but he also admits, as had Gregory of Nyssa before him, a necessary corollary of this position, namely, the existence of a metaphorical literal sense.[44] One is tempted to suggest that his method represents a synthesis of the better elements of the two schools of Antioch and Alexandria.

C. Cyril of Alexandria, Doctrinal Exegete of the Fundamental Mysteries of the New Testament

Cyril's exegesis of the New Testament is especially intent on bringing out the revealed doctrine it contains and—at least from 423 on—to expound it in the context of the struggle against Arianism and, later, again Nestorianism. This polemical character that is so often, though not always present, is in line, however, with the polemical character of many New Testament writings themselves—notably of the Pauline Letters that confront the heterodox positions of Judeo-Christianity and of the Johannine literature that confronts pre-Gnostic currents of thought and Pharisaic Judaism. It is precisely on Paul and John that Cyril draws most heavily.

We will examine first his interpretation of the mysteries of Christianity in his great commentary on the Gospel of John, which predates the Nestorian era,[45] and then his insistence on the unity, the eternity and the absolute and universal primacy of Christ.

For Cyril, as he contemplates the continuity of the divine plan of salvation, the Incarnation of the Son is the great means chosen by God to restore to humanity the gift of the Holy Spirit (with the benefits of the divine life)—a gift which it had lost as a consequence of sin. There is

---

[43]See especially the remarkable analytical index of his book, *St. Cyril...*, particularly at the words *Literal sense* (p. 477) and *Spiritual exegesis* (p. 479) as well as the conclusions, pp. 439 ff.

[44]*Ibid.*, p. 477: *metaphorical literal* sense: many references.

[45]Cf. G. Jouassard, "L'activité littéraire de saint Cyrille d'Alexandrie jusqu'à 428, essai de chronologie et de synthese," *Melanges E. Podechard*, (Lyon, 1945), especially pp. 168 ff.: "in 423, probably," there occurred a turning of sorts in the literary activity of Cyril. After that point, his writing would tend toward the dogmatic polemic, with his sword pointed clearly above all against Arianism, and almost exclusively against it...." "There is a mystery as to the why of the new activity Cyril embarked on" (*ibid.*, p. 169).

more: the new Adam is not content to restore lost benefits to humanity; he also takes care, in contrast to the first Adam, to definitively implant the Holy Spirit in that humanity.

Although individual rejections are possible, humanity as a whole will never lose this definitively acquired benefit: the indwelling of the Holy Spirit in the new Adam. This is the theme developed by Cyril in his commentary on John 7:39: "The Only Son became man so that in him the grace of the Spirit might be preserved for the whole of human" nature,[46] in a stable [*ararotos*] manner. Cyril clarifies: "the Only Son...became man to condemn sin in the flesh...and to make us children of God" (cf. Rom 8:3).[47] In other words, the Only Son, by becoming man, pursued not only the goal of the expiation of sins, but also that of founding our divine adoption.

Commenting on Jn 1:32 ff. ("I saw the Spirit come down from heaven as a dove and remain on him"), Cyril is careful to combat the heretical interpretations that deny the equality of the Son with the Spirit and with the Father, in the context of the Baptism of Jesus. He underscores three points: the Spirit does not come to Christ in an extrinsic way, Christ does not participate in the Holy Spirit, and their mutual indwelling is rooted in their common nature and essence. The baptism of Christ does not mean that Christ needed the Holy Spirit for himself, nor does it imply his inferiority concerning this Spirit.[48]

Cyril is then attacking the Arian interpretation[49] of the baptism of Christ seen as an accidental participation in the Spirit received from the outside; if this interpretation were correct, then Christ would be receiving at baptism something that he did not yet have; he would be imperfect; how then could he be God, consubstantial with the Father? Cyril is combating the fundamental assumption that the baptism in the Jordan was for Jesus an absolute beginning in the spiritual domain. For the Arians, the baptism implies that Christ is not holy by nature; hence he is not of the same nature as the Father.

---

[46]Cyril of Alexandria, *In Joh.* 7:39, PG 73, 766 A.

[47]*Ibid.* 74, 273 D; see the following note.

[48]On this whole subject, the reader can consult A. Manzone, *La dottrina dello Spirito Santo nell'In Joannem di San Cirillo d'Allessandria*, an extract of a thesis defended in the Gregorian University, Rome, in 1972, chap. IV.

[49]We have to guess what that interpretation was from Cyril's texts; it would certainly be interesting to be able to quote the Arian authors; but Grillmeier's research (cf. note 4) hardly seems to have clarified this point, judging from the references he invites us to in his index (pp. 200 ff.).

On the contrary, Cyril believes, the true function of the anointing in the Jordan (cf. Acts 10:38) is to reveal that Jesus received the Holy Spirit as being one of our kind, so as to restore to the whole of humanity this Spirit which it had lost: "The Holy Spirit descended on Christ as on the first fruits of a renewed human nature, according to which Christ appeared as a man capable of sanctifying." Cyril insists: "He who is holy by nature, the Word of the Father, has through the Spirit sanctified in himself the temple of his own body."[50] Cyril is alluding here to the first chapter of the Gospel of Luke (1:35). The vision of the descent of the Spirit on Jesus was given to John the Baptist at the Jordan as an external "sign" of an internal and prior sanctification, says Cyril.[51]

Thus the flesh, which by itself is incapable of sanctifying (cf. Jn 6:64), can now do so because it has been assumed by the Word: the incarnate Word possesses the Spirit in fullness, while others merely participate in the Spirit.

It is then by Christ and thanks to Him that the Holy Spirit lives in the believers. But when was this Spirit, which was communicated by the Word to his humanity at the moment of his Incarnation, communicated to other human beings? Cyril replies: after the resurrection of Christ, in two distinct moments—on the evening of Easter, and then on the day of Pentecost. This is how he responds to a problem which exegetes and theologians of our times continue to debate, namely, how to reconcile Jn 20:22 and Acts 2:43? If the Apostles already received the Spirit on the evening of Easter, why did they need to receive this gift again later, on the day of Pentecost?[52] And why did Jesus not give that Spirit, his own Spirit, before Easter, since his whole reason for coming down in the first place was precisely to make that gift?

It is primarily by probing the meaning of Jn 7:37-39 that Cyril discovers the reasons for this divine economy. "For as yet the Spirit had not been given because Jesus was not yet glorified," says the apostle John. Why not? Christ rose from the dead as the first-fruits (cf. 1 Cor 15:20) of renewed human nature. The plant (we human beings) could

---

[50]Cyril of Alexandria, *In Joh.*, comment. on John 17:18-19; *PG* 74, 549 C, D.

[51]*Ibid.*: cf. Pius XII: *Mystici Corporis*, *AAS* 35 (1943), 219: "With that breath of grace and truth the Son of God adorned His soul in the immaculate womb of the virgin." A teaching prepared by Cyril: "the anointed and sanctified Christ...sanctifying Himself, through His Spirit, His temple" (*PG* 74, 560 A).

[52]See on this subject S. Tromp, *De Spiritu Christi anima*, (Rome, 1960), section three, chap. 2-4, pp. 86-106 where different texts of Cyril of Alexandria are examined and compared, both with one another and with the thought of John Chrysostom; and Manzone, pp. 50 ff.

not come up from the earth before the birth of the root, the risen Christ, to immortal life. This is why it was only after his resurrection from the dead that Christ breathed upon us the vivifying Spirit, giving us back our ancient dignity and reforming us in his image.[53] The Alexandrian doctor goes on: "the Spirit proceeds [*proeisi*] in the saints, through the agency of Christ, in a way that is fitting for each, in accordance with the distribution of the Father."[54]

As for the twofold gift of the Spirit, at Easter and at Pentecost, Cyril thinks that the first takes on an exemplary character, one of partial anticipation with respect to the universality of the second: "It was fitting that the Son should appear as co-giver of the Spirit with the Father"[55] in the fulfillment of the universal promise found in Joel (2:28). The breathing of the risen Christ on the Apostles, by way of signifying the donation of the divine Breath of the Spirit, and by its backward reference to the primordial breath of the creator God in Genesis 2:7, reveals for Cyril, at the same time, the unity of the divine plan in the Old and the New Testaments, the Son as dispenser of the Spirit and the proleptic fulfillment, through the agency of the Son, of the promise made by God for the benefit of all and communicated through the prophet Joel.[56]

These remarks on the relations between Christ, his Spirit, the Father and the human race enable us to see, in the light of a concrete example, what Cyril's preoccupations really were: to interpret the Scriptures both in the context of their total unity, divinely preserved from all contradiction, and in that of the Church's tradition, a living tradition which Cyril has received and wishes to transmit intact. In Cyril we frequently find the expression: *hoi Pateres kai he Graphe*, "the Fathers and Scripture." In his theological disputations, as H. du Manoir brings out, he thought of these two as being one.[57] The scriptural argument and the patristic argument cannot be separated, and it is precisely the Fathers who help Cyril to perceive the unity of God's plan as seen through the indivisible unity of the bible, which he refers to as a "vast organism which accommodates some of the greatest human diversities, making them all yield to a single design.[58]

---

[53]Cyril of Alexandria, *In Joh.*, PG 73, 756 B, C.

[54]*Ibid.* PG 73, 753 A.

[55]*Ibid.* PG 74, 713 C.

[56]Manzone, pp. 52 ff.

[57]Cf. H. du Manoir, *Dogme et spiritualité*, pp. 20, 457: such is the expression of the anthology of patristic texts collected at Ephesus during the Council, under the initiative of Cyril.

[58]Cyril of Alexandria, *On Isaiah*, PG 70, 656.

We have just taken a brief look at Cyril's explanation of the baptism of Christ, a scene from the Gospel of John that the Bishop of Alexandria reads considering a Pauline theology of the two Adams. The reader has observed that, even before the Nestorian crisis, Cyril attaches greater importance to the divinity of Christ than to his humanity, although he remains fully convinced of the truth of the latter. He says this plainly himself in his Paschal letter of 423: "[Christ] is man in the visible order, according to the nature of the flesh, perfect as to humanity and nevertheless he is more truly God [than he is man]."[59]

This is the "fundamental intuition"[60] of Cyril in his reading of the New Testament within the context of the Church's tradition; a comprehensive intuition which the Church, and especially that of Alexandria, handed on to him by teaching him to read the whole of Scripture (including the Old Testament) in the light of the Johannine declaration (1:14) regarding the "Word made flesh," an intuition that resounds in all of his interpretations of particular texts. Though not perhaps adequate in this respect to what we would look for today, Cyril fully respects the necessary distinctions in the complex ontological structure of the mystery of Christ. In contrast to Nestorius,[61] he dreads the idea of a strict dualism and goes on to a unifying reading of the multiple Scriptures gathered in a single Bible, to find there the one and only Christ, the unifier of the universe—Christ man, and even more, God.

It is in this context and in this light that he probes some key texts of the New Testament to which he often returns: Jesus Christ is the same yesterday and today and forever (Heb 13:8); he humbled himself in the mystery of his kenosis, while maintaining his divine glory (Phil 2:5-11); thus he is able to be the first- born among many brothers and even of the whole creation (Rom 8:29; Col 1:15), the apostle and high-priest of the faith which we confess (Heb 3:1) and on which we are nourished in our participation in the Eucharist through which we become concorporeal with Him (cf. Eph 3:6). Let us look quickly with him at these major texts, examining each of them in order. Cyril applies to each of them the

---

[59]Cyril of Alexandria, PG 77, 664; cf. PG 70, 1087 A.

[60]Cf. the remarkable article of Msgr. G. Jouassard: "Une intuition fondamentale de saint Cyrille d'Alexandrie en christologie dans les premières années de son épiscopat," Rev. des Et. Byzantines XI (1953), pp. 175-186 (Mélanges Jugie). These are without doubt the most penetrating and thorough pages ever written on the subject.

[61]See especially Rowan A. Greer, The Captain of our Salvation, a Study of the Patristic Exegesis of Hebrews, (Tübingen, 1973), chap. 7: Cyril and Nestorius; Grillmeier, pp. 473-483 and 501-519.

fundamental intuition that was already his before Nestorius appeared and which he had no good reason to renounce considering the segmenting analyses of the Patriarch of Constantinople: the unity of Christ is anterior and superior to any multiplicity in him.

After having commented already a number of times[62] on the affirmation of the author of the Letter to the Hebrews: "Jesus Christ is the same yesterday and today and forever" (13:8), Cyril returns to it in one of his last writings, composed in about 437: *Quod unus sit Christus*, in these terms:

> There is but one Son and Lord, the Word before all ages, who deigned to be born of a woman according to the flesh in the last age of the world. And the fact that the Word did not change once he had become a man like us is what the inspired author tells us when he says: "Jesus Christ is the same yesterday and today and forever." By *yesterday*, he refers to the past time, by *today*, to the present, by *forever*, to the future and all time to come. If they insist on asking us: "How could he who is of yesterday and of today be forever?" we answer by returning the question with its terms inverted: "How can we say that the Word who is forever is of yesterday and of today, because it is just as true that Christ is one and cannot be divided, according to the words of the divine Paul?"[63]

In a commentary devoted *ex professo* to the Letter to the Hebrews[64] and in a letter to Acacius of Melitene,[65] Cyril places Heb 13:8 among the "mean" expressions, those "which reveal that the Son is at one and the same time God and man" (and which differ therefore, as we saw above, both from *divine* expressions and *human* expressions[66]). In another text on Heb 13:8, he again clarified his thought:

> It is of Jesus Christ and not just of the word that the text affirms that he is the same today. Yesterday and forever but how could the human nature possess immutability and unaltered identity when it is subject to movement and above all to that movement that made it pass from nothingness to being and to life?

---

[62]Especially in his eighth paschal letter (*PG* 77, 568 B): "[Christ] was , and will be God according to nature, before and after the flesh" (*èn gar, kai esti kai estai theos kata physin, kai pro sarkos kai meta sarkos*).

[63]*SC* 97, pp. 410-411: Cyril's dialogue on "Christ is one."

[64]Cyril of Alexandria, *PG* 74, 997 C.

[65]Cyril of Alexandria, *Epistle XL to Acacius of Melitenis*, *PG* 77, 196 C.

[66]Cf. note 15; cf. Cyril's letter to John of Antioch, *DS* 273.

...In virtue of the union with flesh that is proper to him, it is still he himself who is described as existing *yesterday* and as pre-existent.[67]

In other words, Cyril is returning here to some of his favorite ideas: the designation "Anointed One," or "Christ" applies to the Word as incarnate, but this incarnate Word does not cease to be the eternal Word, which is what the author of the letter brought out when he said, "Christ is the same today and forever."

It is interesting—and this has been done more than once—to compare the two interpretations of Heb 13:8, that of Cyril and that of the Nestorians. With the Nestorian Andrew of Samosata ("according to what is visible of Christ, *yesterday and today*, according to what is intelligible, *forever*, according to the unity of sonship, *the same*"),[68] the unity is as it were reconstituted after the fact, as is shrewdly noted by G. M. de Durand.[69] With Cyril, on the contrary, the unity is a given from the start. The following text illustrates this with particular clarity:

> The natural properties of the Word who came forth from the Father were maintained even when he became flesh. It is foolish therefore to dare to introduce a breach. For the Lord Jesus Christ is one [1 Cor 8:6] and through him the Father created all things [Jn 1:1-3]. He is composed of human properties and of others that are above the human, yielding a kind of middle term [*anthropinois te au kai tois huper anthropon idiomasin eis hen ti to metaxu sunkeimenos*]. He is in fact a Mediator between God and men, according to the Scriptures (1 Tim 2:5), God by nature even when incarnate, truly, not purely man like us, remaining what he was even when he had become flesh [*anthropos de alethos, kai ou psilos kath'hemas, all'on hoper en kai ei gegone sarx*]. For it is written: "Jesus Christ is the same yesterday and today and forever."[70]

---

[67]Cyril of Alexandria, *Dialogue on the Incarnation*, SC 97, pp. 288-289. It can be said that the response to the objection presented and treated here was completed elsewhere by Cyril himself: alluding to 1 Cor 8:6, the bishop writes in *The Christ is One* (SC 97, p. 401): "Nothing stops us from thinking that through Him everything came into existence, according as we conceive him as God and as co-eternal with the Father." On the names of *Jesus* and *Christ* in the works of Cyril and the earlier Fathers, the reader will profit from reading the wise observation of G. M. de Durand, SC 97, pp. 346-347.

[68]See in the same sense on Heb 13:8 in Cyril's exegesis another wise observation of G. M. de Durand, *op. cit.*, pp. 410-411; it is Cyril who refers us to Andrew of Samosata's text (*ACO*, I, 7, p. 42, 1.9-16). On Nestorius' interpretation concerning Heb 13:8, see Greer, pp. 350 ff.

[69]G. M. de Durand, SC 97, p. 411.

[70]Cyril of Alexandria, *Dialogue on the Incarnation*, SC 97, pp. 286-287. We note the use of the adverb *metaxu*, which is so important in Plato's philosophy.

For Cyril, Christ is a Mediator because he is a Synthesis, a composite being,[71] God and Man, the radical difference between his humanity and our own consists in the fact that Jesus is not only man, rather, he is above all God. Jesus is the Christ today because He is, yesterday and tomorrow, eternally, the Word.

The modern reader might be tempted to object to Cyril's reading of Heb 13:8 that the term "yesterday" does not merely or even necessarily imply eternal preexistence.[72] Perhaps. However, it must be acknowledged that Cyril's interpretation is in perfect harmony with the Letter to the Hebrews as whole that portrays the Son as the eternal creator of the universe (1:2; 7:3).[73]

It is perhaps in connection with the Christological hymn of the Letter to the Philippians that we meet the most striking expression of what Jouassard called Cyril's "fundamental intuition," namely, that even more than true man, Christ is God.

In thirteen of the twenty-nine Easter homilies that he gave from 414 to 442, Cyril cites Phil 2:5.[74] In the very first of these,[75] already engaged in at least an implicit anti-Arian polemic,[76] he links the exposition of the hymn's meaning to a paraphrase of Heb 13:8. Commenting on Phil 2:7 (*morphen doulou labon*, taking on the form of a servant), Cyril explains that

the Son of God, assuming [*anabalon*: taking up from below] our likeness and becoming man, not taking up what he was [i.e., the divine condition], but taking on what he was not [*ouk hoper en analabon, all'hoper ouk en proslabon*], effects our salvation; for he remains, as Paul put it, the same yesterday and

---

[71]The text referred to (*synkeimenos*) paves the way for the doctrine of Constantinople II, in 553: it affirms, in the Person of Christ, unity according to the synthesis (*hè kata synthesin henosis: DS* 425).

[72]Cf. C. Spicq, *L'Epître aux Hébreux*, (Paris, 1953), vol. II, p. 422.

[73]C. Spicq (*ibid.*, pp. 32, 210, 268) emphasizes that, for the author of Hebrews, Christ is the pre-existing Son of God, which suffices for justifying, in spite of him, the traditional exegesis of Heb 13:8.

[74]Cyril of Alexandria, *PG* 77, 401-981; the publication by *SC* of a critical edition and a translation of Cyril's paschal letters has been welcome.

[75]Cyril of Alexandria, *PG* 77, 424.

[76]As P. Henry observes (*DBS*, article "Kenose," [Paris, 1957], vol. V, col., 68), Cyril reconstituted the Arian exegesis of Phil 2:5-11 in the following way: "He possesses the Name which is above every name as payment for His humiliation; He is not by nature God or Son, but He became it through an increase [*ek prosthèkès*]. What requires an increase is imperfect and in need of what belongs to its own nature.... If, therefore, He had been given the Name above all names, he wasn't that by nature, but He became it later by grace. He who is in such a state is not God, for it is recent" (*PG* 75, 328 C-D). In his study already referred to on the kenosis, P. Henry presents us (col. 65-70) an attempt to reconstruct the Arian exegesis beginning with its refutation by the Fathers.

today and forever without undergoing any change in his divinity by reason of his inhumation [*dia tes enanthroposeos*], but remaining what he was and will always be [*on hoper en kai estai dia pantos*].

For Cyril, the process described by Paul to the Philippians is not one of a diminution (in the style of modern kenotic theologies) or one of an (Arian style) increase[77] of divinity as such; it is rather a process of assumption (*proslabon* as he explains Paul's *labon*) of humanity and it is—paradoxically—this assumption itself that constitutes the kenotic stripping. Far from altering the Son, who remains the same yesterday, today and forever (Heb 13:8), such an assumption results in a changing of the human condition, in the Only Son and in all of his brothers. Let us take a closer look at these points.

In perfect harmony with the position already taken in the first Paschal homily of 414, Cyril, in his treatise *Christ is One* written toward the end of his life, defines kenosis as follows:

> The Word of God, subsisting in the form of God the Father, the imprint of his substance, equal in all things to the one who begot him, emptied himself. And in what does this emptying consist? In that he assumes flesh and takes on the form of a slave, in that he who was not like us according to his proper nature, but was far superior to all of creation, becomes like us. Even then he was God, not holding on to as a gift what belonged to him by nature.[78]

The Incarnation is then, for the Word, an assumption which is at the same time a stripping, an emptying: the assumption of a created nature, given that nature's condition of weakness, mortality and ignominy, becomes, for the creator Word, a stripping of the external glory which belongs to Him by right.

Cyril finds countless ways of expressing and defining the mystery of this kenosis, of this humbling through which the Sanctifier is sanctified,[79] he who names everything receives as though by grace, the name which

---

[77]Cf. P. Henry, col. 68: "Like the modern kenoticists, the Arians admit a change in the being and in the characteristics of the Word, but while for the former the change is from the more to the lesser, with the Arians it is from the lesser to the more."

[78]Cyril of Alexandria, *The Christ is One*, SC 97, 395.

[79]*Ibid.* G. M. de Durand quotes two texts of Cyril: "He Who, as God, gives and distributes sanctification to all, in union with God the Father, is sanctifies with us in what He has of human in Him, and that is what we call the kenosis" (*De Adoratione et cultu in spiritu et veritate*, X, PG 68, 692A); "to receive by way of grace the Name above every name, this is what we call the kenosis and the redemptive abasement of the Word" (*Dial. de Tr.*, PG 75, 828B).

is above every name,[80] he who is the giver of everything assumes the posture of one who receives, and then receives the Holy Spirit, glory and the name.[81]

To be precise, if for Cyril the Incarnation is a permanent reality, this kenosis was both permanent and transitory. Permanent regarding the sanctification of one who is holy by essence; transitory regarding the mortality assumed:

> The Only Begotten became man, not to remain always at the depth of his kenosis, of his self-emptying, but rather, while accepting it with all its consequences, to enable himself to be recognized even in that situation for the God by nature that he was and in order to honor human nature in himself, by giving it a share in sacred and divine dignities.[82]

Once again we find here a clear expression, in the context of a discussion of kenosis, and in the course of one of Cyril's last works, of that "fundamental intuition" which haunts his thinking from the very first Paschal homily: "The glory of Christ, which is inseparable from his divinity, remains at the core of the emptying that is the assumption of human nature," as Augustine Dupré La Tour observed in 1960.[83] Such is the magnificent paradox that never ceased to fascinate Cyril throughout his career as an exegete, a preacher and a doctor. But let us listen to Dupré La Tour:

> How can the divine glory subsist in the very kenosis of the Word? To explain this paradox, which he regarded as indispensable to safeguard the integrity of the divinity, Cyril takes the schema of the Christological hymn of the Letter to the Philippians 2:6-11 as his leitmotiv. The very frequency with which he resorts to this refrain underscores his concern. The Word has come down into a condition that is wretched and without glory. But the *doxa* of Christ is to such an extent linked to his *physis*, his glory is to such an extent the adequate expression of his very being, that Cyril will insist on a glorious aspect even down to the very depths of the kenosis and he will underscore all the signs that reveal this.
>
> So much so that the Pauline schema is reversed: the Word made flesh abandons the splendor of the divine glory but even though he has become man he remains God, for divinity is his true nature. Consequently he retains

---

[80]See the last text quoted in the preceding note.

[81]These are expressions of G. M. de Durand, *SC* 97, p. 395, note 2.

[82]Cyril of Alexandria, *The Christ is One, SC* 97, p. 433.

[83]A. Dupré La Tour, "La Doxa du Christ dans les œuvres exégétiques de Saint Cyrille d'Alexandrie," *Rech. de Sc. Relig.*, XLVIII (1960), p. 523.

his glory that he possesses *kata physin*. To deny the divine *doxa* to the Word in his kenotic condition would be tantamount, in Cyril's view, to denying his divine nature. Thus the same "fundamental intuition" continues to guide Cyril's expression, compelling him to maintain the paradox.[84]

Such an interpretation surprising as it may seem, does do full justice to the texts of Cyril as to the deep sense of the Johannine Gospel. The following text of Cyril will illustrate this:

...Although he was in the form of God the Father and in full equality with him, he entered our condition and appeared to those who were on earth [cf. Bar 3:38]; but he was not without glory, even if he became flesh. For he did divine works and performed signs that are worthy of immense admiration.[85]

Cyril's Johannine reading of the Letter to the Philippians enables him then to see this Christological hymn as an affirmation of a glorious kenosis, indeed of a "kenotic theophany," pointing toward that eschatological theophany of Christ," of which Cyril also speaks, though only rarely.[86]

Perceiving the paradox and the need to explain it, the bishop exegete already in one of his first writings insisted:

It is said that he was exalted and that He received the Name that is above every name, according to the expression of the blessed Paul, almost as if his humanity had been deprived of this name and He received it as a favor. The fact is however that it was not a question of a gift that was originally foreign to His nature. Far from it. We would do better to understand it as a return, an upward journey back to what was already inalienably his own, to what belonged to him by essence.[87]

We can conclude then with Dupré La Tour:

While St. Paul was stressing the reality of the Incarnation of the Word and his self-lowering, Cyril, by inverting the statements, places the emphasis on the permanence of the divine nature through the period of the kenosis. The

---

[84]*Ibid.* and p. 524.

[85]Cyril of Alexandria, *In Isaiah* I, *PG* 70, 129B. The exegete of Cyril comments: "Cyril regards the miracles as glimmers lighting the obscurity of the kenosis" (sequence of the same article, 1961, p. 82). For the Christ, Cyril says, "overlooked nothing that might give us full assurance that he is really God and Son of God by nature" (*PG* 70, 1324 B).

[86]Cyril of Alexandria, *In Isaiah* I, *PG* 70, 548 C; cf. 577D; cf. A. Dupré La Tour, p. 70, where the author forged the beautiful expression "theophany of the kenosis," which we have quoted.

[87]Cyril of Alexandria, *Glaphyra* (elegant commentaries), VII, *PG* 69, 376 D-377 A; cf. *PG* 70, 1225-1228.

movement of Paul's thinking can be summarized thus: although God, he became man, Cyril takes up and interprets: although He became man, He remains God.[88]

The observation is fundamentally accurate, It should be noted also that what we have here is really more an inversion of emphasis than of the statements themselves and that Cyril's interpretation is in no way unfaithful to the thinking of Paul: on the contrary it explicates an implicit component of the Apostles thought by affirming the permanence of the divine form within the kenosis itself. There is more: as we have seen,[89] Gregory of Nyssa already perceived the need for such a shift of emphasis to be fully faithful to the thinking of Paul as a whole.

Since he viewed the kenotic Incarnation as already glorious, both invisibly (the divine nature of Christ) and visibly (his miracles), Cyril was particularly disposed to accept and to develop the Pauline message on the absolute and universal primacy of Christ, such as it emerges from the Letter to the Colossians (1:15): He is the "firstborn over all creation." Though Cyril applies this affirmation to the Eternal Word in a number of places,[90] elsewhere, more clearly and expressly, he also applies it to the Word made flesh, to the Man Jesus as man: "The Word is called Only Son because he alone was begotten of the Father alone, but he received the name Firstborn when he became man and part of the world."[91]There is no contradiction here, as the following text shows:

> The same who is Only Son as God is firstborn among us as man, according to the union, economically [*oikonomikos*] among many brethren. Just as being the Only Son has become the property of the humanity in Christ, because of its

---

[88]A. Dupré La Tour, p. 88. As Jouassard says, "between divinity and humanity Cyril discovers an incommensurate distance which will never be made good by the union that was carried out [*PG* 77, 572 A; 569 C, D; 408 A], but beyond this he is convinced that these two realities do not belong to the Savior in the same way. Humanity became His nature, and it is not His "essentially" or by nature [cf. *PG* 77, 568 A].... That he is man represents for the Savior only an aspect and in no way his deep reality" ("A Fundamental Intuition...," p. 182). This does not stop Cyril from professing the reality of the human nature in Christ, a nature he calls by various names (*PG* 77, 664 A; 68, 576 C; 69, 476 A, 477 D, 521.2, 576 B) before the Nestorian period. On this point see J. Liébaert, *La doctrine christologique de Cyrille d'Alexandrie avant la période nestorienne*, (Lille, 1951), pp. 180 ff. The apparent Docetism of certain expressions is a purely verbal Docetism (H. du Manoir, *Dogme et spiritualité...*, p. 156).

[89]Chap. IX, *passim* and especially note 79.

[90]For example, in the dialogue *On the Incarnation*, SC 97, pp. 284-285, etc.

[91]Cyril of Alexandria, *De recta fide ad Theol. Imp.*, 30, PG 76, 1178; written in 430.

economic union with the Word, so also being the firstborn among many brethren is now the property of the Word because of its union with the flesh.[92]

Thus it is well brought out by Cyril, in harmony with the whole of his Christology, that the incarnate Word is firstborn as man, but at the same time that his divine Person is the ultimate subject of attribution (as we would put it today) of this property of his human nature. It is the Only Son who has become man and firstborn, though this does not mean that he has ceased to be the Only Son. This distinction is found throughout the writings of our doctor.[93]

Though we cannot enter here into all the details of Cyril's exegesis of Col 1:15,[94] it appears sufficiently clear that his anti-Arian reading of this verse helped him to see in the firstborn, as man, the principle and foundation of all the ways of the Lord, the first of a series, not in a temporal sense, but predestined as such before the ages.[95] It is therefore with good reason that a number of theologians and exegetes of the Franciscan school[96] have appealed to the testimony of Cyril in support of the doctrine of the absolute and universal primacy of Jesus Christ in the divine Plan of salvation.

Thus we see that Cyril's fundamental intuition (that Christ is even more God than he is man) did not prevent him from drawing attention to the biblical passages which exalt the humanity of Christ, and this, precisely because this basic intuition was itself inseparable from a soteriological perspective: Christ is, not the Man-God, but rather the God-Man Savior.[97] He is the God to whom he himself as man, as Priest in

---

[92]*Ibid.*, A.

[93]*Ibid.*, PG 75, 1159.

[94]See mainly the *Thesaurus de Trinitate*, Assertions XV, XXXII, PG 75.

[95]Cyril reads this verse in the context of Prv 8:22, interpreted as relating to the humanity of Christ: cf. Assertion XV, 159: PG 75, 267.

[96]Such as A. Rosini, "Il primogenito in S. Cirillo Alessadrino," *Studia Patavina*, 12 (1965), 32-64; G. Basetti-Sani, *Kyrilliana*, (Cairo, 1947), pp. 139-196, referring especially to Assertion XXXII of the *Thesaurus*, PG 75, 503: however, their works do not appear always to begin with a thorough knowledge of Cyrillian Christology in its framework and with its own inherent concerns, thus running the risk of anachronistic interpretations; this does not at all mean that there is not much worthwhile in these works.

[97]Cf. Cyril of Alexandria, *The Christ is One*, SC 97, pp. 354-355: "They replace the mystery of the economy in the flesh with its contrary: it is no longer a question of the Word of God lowering Himself, even annihilating Himself by taking the form of a slave...but completely the reverse—a man is raised even to the glory of the divinity" (cf. Thomas Aquinas, *Summa Theologiæ*, III, 34. 1. 1: "In the mystery of the Incarnation, more consideration must be given to the descent of the divine plenitude upon human nature than the raising of a human nature").

his humanity, offers the sacrifice of the salvation of humanity. Let us recall here a number of texts that reveal this direction of thought.

Cyril is a witness not only of the Savior's divine glory but also of his human and "economic weakness in which this divine glory continues to shine":

> He wept in a human manner in order to suppress your tears. He experienced fear in virtue of the economy. at times allowing his flesh to feel what is proper to it in order to fill us with courage.... He slept in order that you might learn not to sleep in times of temptation, but rather to apply yourself to prayer. Offering his life as a model of saintly existence to be used by earthly beings, he took on the weaknesses of humanity, and what was his purpose in doing this? That we might truly believe that he became man, although he remained what he was, namely, God.[98]

These lines enable us better to understand in Cyril's thought—which is not formally and not even materially Monophysite[99]—the importance of the theme of the priestly mediation of Christ which he found in the Letter to the Hebrews (3:1): "Now that the Logos has become man, he is, through his humanity, one who offers sacrifice.... It is the same one who sacrifices as man and as God reigns at the Father's side."[100] This was Cyril's response to the accusation leveled by Andrew of Samosata against one of his anathemas, in which he had declared: "If anyone says that Christ offers the sacrifice for himself and not solely for us—he had no need of sacrifice who knew no sin—let him be anathema."[101]

This anathema allows us to perceive an unexpected consequence of the Nestorian and dualistic exegesis of the Letter to the Hebrews: Christ's self-offering, according to this interpretation, was not only for us but for himself as well. What is implied here is that he had sinned and was in need of salvation. This is where a strictly dualist Christology ultimately leads, and nothing could be more antithetical to the soteriology of Cyril.

---

[98]Cyril of Alexandria, *Apology for the Anathemas against Theodoretus*, written in 431, PG 76, 441.

[99]We are alluding here to the much discussed sense of Cyril's famous formula, unconsciously borrowed from Apollinaris: *mia physis toû Theoû Logoû sesarkômene*: cf. G. M. de Durand, *SC* 97, pp. 134 ff.; Liébaert, *La doctrine christologique...* pp. 174-178; and previously the dissertation of Cardinal Newman, *Tracts Theological and Ecclesiastical*, (London, 1902), pp. 329-382, especially the conclusions, 21, p. 380; Durand coincides with him, in his interpretation of the formula. see also Grillmeier, p. 480 and our note 88. Cyril gave the formula a profoundly different meaning than Apollinaris gave it.

[100]Cyril of Alexandria, PG 76, 368 C.

[101]Cyril of Alexandria, *Third Letter to Nestorius*, DS 251.

The exegesis of the bishop of Alexandria which is always careful to
thus exalt the humanity of Christ without ever ceasing to exalt even
more his divine nature[102] leads to his magnificent vision, which is both
Johannine and Pauline, of the eucharistic concorporeality of human
beings with one another and with respect to the Incarnate Word:

> The only Son worked out, in his wisdom, according to the Father's plan, a way
> to unite us too, to fuse us, into unity with God and with each other, even
> though we are separated into distinct individuals by our souls and by our
> bodies.

> Through a single body, his own, he blesses his faithful, in mystical
> communion, making them concorporeal with Him and with one another. If we
> are all concorporeal with one another in Christ, and not merely with one
> another, but even with Him who comes to us through his flesh, would it not
> then be true to say that we are one, all of us, in one another and in Christ?[103]

There is every indication that for Cyril the Eucharist was the
proximate end of the Incarnation of the Word. It is through it that the
Incarnate Word vivifies human beings and unites them with one another
and with Him.

For him, the Eucharist is the "mystical eulogy, the life-giving body of
the Incarnate Word."[104] If he accords great importance to Christ's sacrifice,
what holds his attention more than anything else—in contrast to so
many theologians of later eras—is the divinizing efficacy of the
Eucharistic communion.[105] He sees it as a source of immortality: "Those
who receive into themselves the bread of life will have immortality as
their recompense."[106] Indeed, it is perhaps on this point that Cyril's
thinking is most profoundly opposed to that of Nestorius, for whom, in
Cyril's view, the life-giving flesh of Christ is reduced to that of an
ordinary human being distinct from the Word, with the result that the
basis of faith in the resurrection of the flesh disappears and communion
is reduced to an act of cannibalism.[107]

---

[102]Such is the sense of the original Greek of Phil 11:2, 9: *hyperypsosen*.

[103]Cyril of Alexandria, *In Joh.* 11, 11: *PG* 74, 560; cf. G. M. de Durand, *SC* 97, p. 82.

[104]Cyril of Alexandria, *PG* 68, 501 B.

[105]Batiffol, *L'Eucharistie*, (Paris, 1905), p. 282.

[106]Saint Cyril, *PG* 73, 560 D; 561 D. Cf. H. du Manoir, *Dogme et Spiritualité*, chap. V.

[107]Cf. H. Chadwick, "Eucharist and Christology in the Nestorian Controversy," *Journal of Theol. Studies*, New Studies, 2 (1951), 156. According to Cyril, Nestorius thinks that it is only a man's body that is lying on the holy table of the churches whence the accusation of anthropophagy; whence also the eleventh anathema, *DS* 262. In fact, Nestorius said:

This is how Cyril understands the teaching of the Savior in his discourse on the Bread of Life.[108]

Our brief survey of how Cyril interprets the fundamental mysteries of the New Covenant should help us to understand why his exegesis has fascinated so many theologians during the centuries. Saint Thomas Aquinas,[109] Petau,[110] Scheeben,[111] Mersch, Tromp[112]—all of these and more have been won over by the views of Cyril and profoundly influenced by him. It might be objected that this influence has above all been at the doctrinal level. This is certainly true. Still it should be observed that the doctrinal exegesis of Cyril is what constitutes the treasure that the theologians have sought out, found and transmitted to posterity It is nearly always when he is commenting on Scriptures that Cyril expounds the doctrines of Christianity and examines them in depth. His merit lies precisely in the fact that he does not stop at secondary affirmations in commenting on the Scriptures, but goes right to their doctrinal marrow. Never would the theologians just mentioned have been so attracted to the thinking of Cyril if he had not been a doctrinal exegete and the same would have to be said of Vatican II that cited him so often.[113]

Conclusions. The limits and the magnitude of the exegetical charism of St. Cyril of Alexandria: What is his special contribution?

It is impossible to deny it: Cyril has an in-depth knowledge and an ardent love of the Scriptures of both the Old and New Testaments. The facility with which he quotes, compares and comments on the texts and employs them in his argumentation against Arians or Nestorians[114]

"What we receive in the Eucharist is not the divinity, but the flesh" (*Nestoriana*, Ed. Loofs, [Halle, 1905], pp. 227-230).

[108]On Cyril's eucharistic theology, see Mahé, *RHE*, 8 (1907), p. 676.

[109]See Renaudin, "La théologie de saint Cyrille d'Alexandrie d'après saint Thomas," *Revue Thomiste* 18 (1910), 171-184; 21 (1913), 129-136, 1934; J. Backes, *Die Christologie des Heiligen Thomas von Aquin und die griechischen Kirchenvätern*, (Paderborn, 1931).

[110]Cf. H. du Manoir, *Dogme et Spiritualité*, p. 36.

[111]Scheeben took much of his inspiration from Cyril s views in *Les Mystères du Christianisme*, (Bruges, 1947).

[112]For Mersch, see his work on *Le Corps mystique du Christ*, (Paris, 1951), vol. I, pp. 505, 516-517; concerning S. Tromp, see note 52.

[113]Especially, four times, in the decree *Ad Gentes* on the missions, in an ecclesiastical perspective, mainly at #7.

[114]Cf. N. Charlier, "Le *Thesaurus de Sancta Trinitate* de saint Cyrille d'Alexandrie," *RHE*, 45 (1950), 66-71: the Cyrillian procedures of argumentation.

shows how literally he possesses the Bible and how marvelously he assimilates its content, thanks especially to his monastic formation[115] and to Saint Isidore of Pelusium.[116] Likewise the ease with which he is able to extract the spiritual, Christocentric sense proves that he meditated on and savored the inspired words at great length.[117] In the words of Hubert du Manoir, the "inspired" books were the true sources of his "inspiration."[118]

There is then something autobiographical in the statement made by Cyril when he describes for us the prophetic charism of the interpretation of the prophets as a gift accorded by the Spirit to those who have resolved to preserve charity toward God and toward their brothers. Let us quote him:

> When we have set ourselves the goal of charity toward God and toward our brothers, that charity that is the fullness of the whole law, may the other charisms then come to us as well. Then indeed, at just the opportune time, we will also be filled with the charisms of God and enriched with the gifts given by the Spirit, I mean with the capacity to prophesy, that is to say, to interpret the prophets.[119]

In short, if we seek first the Kingdom of God and his justice, that is to say, charity, the fullness of the law, all the rest, Cyril seems to be saying all the other charisms, including those which pertain to exegesis will be given to us as well, according to the measure of the gift and of the will of that free Spirit who blows where he wills. Is not true to say that such a charism cannot have been denied to Cyril himself? Is not his exegesis charismatic, especially when he is writing about the New Testament?

The point is generally recognized, and no one would be likely to contradict what Jouassard says: "The bishop of Alexandria made exegesis one of his primary preoccupations as a writer."[120] Jouassard adds: "He has a distinct taste, a sort of passion for Scripture."[121]

---

[115]Cf. H du Manoir, *Dogme et Spiritualité…*, p. 22: "Was Cyril a monk? Did he live amid the cenobites of the desert? The historians have often asked themselves these questions without ever reaching any certain conclusions." On the biblical formation of monks, see our chap. V.

[116]Cf. R. Aigrain, *49 lettres de saint Isidore de Péluse*, (Paris, 1911); PG 78.

[117]Cf. H. du Manoir, article "Cyrille d'Alexandrie," *DSAM* II, 2 (1953), 2673.

[118]H. du Manoir, *Dogme et Spiritualité*, p. 392.

[119]Cyril of Alexandria, *In 1 Cor* 14:2; PG 74, 890.

[120]G. Jouassard, "L'activité littéraire de saint Cyrille d'Alexandrie jusqu'à 428, Essai de chronologie et de synthèse," *Mélanges Podechard*, (Lyon, 1945), p. 173.

[121]*Ibid.*

But the same author who was able with such insight to detect the "fundamental intuition" of Cyril, saw also in the theological character of his exegesis, a trait whose positive aspect we have so far been stressing, a limitation—in fact, if not in principle:

> We would readily admit that if he was an exegete, he was so only very imperfectly since he came with clear doctrinal presuppositions.... It is true that the bishop of Alexandria made a real effort to be attentive to the sacred text; he even managed to succeed in this effort more than some might think, more than a number of early exegetes.[122]

> He did not however believe, any more than did the majority of these exegetes, that the primary function of an authentic commentator should be to begin by explaining every detail of that text, to penetrate in depth into the thinking of the inspired author so as to be able to reach a profound understanding of the meaning intended by God for Scripture.[123] Cyril was a theologian from the first and he always remained one; he cherished Scripture, but as a theologian—to the point where his theology easily intrudes when he claims to be explaining a text. Nevertheless, even as exegete, he is not lacking in ability, particularly because of the fact that he studied St. John and St. Paul with rare penetration, till he truly imbibed their spirit. It is this spirit that he will bring to the study of all parts of the Bible, and even of the Old Testament books themselves. This is why he will often find in these books things that are rather foreign to the text. On the other hand, what he finds is often so beautiful, so scriptural in its inspiration, that it would be difficult to follow his argument without falling in love with Scripture itself.

Jouassard was able then to conclude this evaluation by alluding to "this man of Scripture that Cyril of Alexandria wanted to be and that he always was."[124] Theology, that is to say the use, within a faith context and in the service of the explanation of scripture, of the rational categories of Greek thought did not invade Cyril's pen to the point of

---

[122]Cyril refuses to abandon what he calls *historia*, even in questionable cases, such as that of Hosea, who was pressed by the Lord to marry a woman of bad life: *ibid.*, note 1; *PG* 71, 25B-36C.

[123]A very disputable, even fantastic, position. God alone can penetrate *thoroughly* into the thought of an inspired author and it is to be feared that exegetes hoping to do this will end up neglecting the intention of the supreme Author and Inspirer, as well as the thrust of His teaching through the human author. In short, while there was in the Patristic age the danger of jumping too quickly to the spiritual sense, today there is the opposite danger of never arriving there at all; whence the difficulty for us in gaining a correct appreciation of the efforts of the Fathers.

[124]Jouassard, *Mélanges Podechard*, 173-174.

preventing him from being—like every good theologian—first and above all, formally speaking, a man of Scripture.

If we were to attempt to specify the nature and object of Cyril's special charism regarding his reading of Scripture, we would have to underscore two aspects.

The first—to which we have already alluded—was that his emphasis was always on what Scripture taught regarding the fundamental mysteries of Christianity, whose interrelationships with one another he was also able to bring out. Cyril's is a doctrinal exegesis that flows from a keen awareness of the center and keeps returning to it in concentric waves: from the Trinity to the Trinity.

The second aspect, which was developed thanks to the Nestorian heresy, builds on the discovery of Athanasius and brings it new precision. Cyril's predecessor had proclaimed, as we put it, that "the goal and the distinctive mark of Holy Scripture consists in the two-fold teaching regarding the Savior, namely, that he was God from all eternity and Son and that later, for our sake, he took flesh of Mary and became man."[125] Athanasius was not yet living in times which would oblige him to distinguish, in the words of the Savior, those which were more suited to the eternal God and those which were more suited to the flesh, that is to say, to the human nature of Jesus, if not by way of exception,[126] when confronting the Arian attack. It is precisely the Arian context that will help Cyril, in his *Commentaries on the Gospel of John*,[127] to move toward the elaboration of a distinction that only the Nestorian heresy could force to greater clarity, as we see in the fourth anathema:

> If anyone divides between two persons or hypostases the expressions found in the gospels or in the apostolic writings or those which the saints have employed regarding Christ or those which He used of himself, and if he relates some of these to a human being, viewed as distinct from the Word of God, and others, as worthy of God, to the Word of God the Father alone, let him be anathema.[128]

Before the Nestorian period, Cyril presents the "Savior's words" as "a mixture" (of allusions to the divine and the human in Him), "turned toward both sides," because he "mixes what is composed of two into a

---

[125]Athanasius, *Third Discourse against the Arians*, 29; *PG*, 385.

[126]Athanasius, *Fourth Letter to Serapion*, 19; *PG* 26, 665.

[127]Cyril of Alexandria, *PG* 73, 357 C and 385 CD; the technical idea has not yet been worked out (*phônai theoprepeis, anthrôpoprepeis, kekramenai*).

[128]Cyril of Alexandria, *Epist. III ad Nestorium*, DS 255.

single reality, to which all his words are to be referred."[129] When confronted with the Nestorian attempt to divide Christ into two persons and with the correlative temptation to divide his words in two, attributing some to the "human person" and others to the "divine Person," Cyril, in his anathema of 430, insists that even the words of Christ as man are words of the Word, as he explains, without however fully exiting from the "mixture" idea. But the distinction which Athanasius had already vaguely perceived will become a conscious principle, fully aware of its consequences and of its presuppositions as well as of negations, in the celebrated formula of union of 433. Indeed, this formula includes an important exegetical statement that marks a clear advance over the earlier "mixture" theory:

> We know that theologians have sometimes regarded the words of the Gospels and of the Apostles concerning the Lord as common, as said of a single Person, and sometimes as separated, as said of two natures, some appropriate to God, in accordance with the divinity of Christ, and others, of lowly quality, in accordance with his humanity.[130]

To put it another way, there are words which the Incarnate Word pronounces both as God and as man—the common words; there are also—and this is the novelty in the language of Cyril—words which are not common but which are pronounced by the same Incarnate Word, either as God, or as man. It should be noted too, in the logic of Cyril's statement, that it is always the man Jesus who is speaking when he speaks as God and always the God Jesus speaking when speaks as man.[131]

---

[129]Cyril of Alexandria, *In Joh.*, PG 74, 488 D; cf. Liébaert, *La doctrine christologique...* pp. 168 ff.; G. M. de Durand, *SC 97*, pp. 46-47 and index, p. 545, at the word "mélange."

[130]Cyril of Alexandria, *Epist. Lætentur cœli* to John of Antioch: PG 77, 173; cf. H. du Manoir, p. 142; DS 273. We can call those words *theandric* which Cyril calls common, if we admit that they imply a double operation both of the divine nature and of the human nature (cf. DS 515), with the latter functioning not as principal cause, but as instrumental cause. Incidentally, this view corresponds to an already Athanasian category (the humanity of Christ is the instrument or *organon* of our salvation).

[131]Cyril of Alexandria, PG 76, 413 B, C (*Apol. contra Theodoretum*, written in 430): Since the same Person is at the same time God and man, it will be proper to Him to utter words which are at the same time both divine and human.... His divine and ineffable nature is not diminished by the fact that He speaks humanly. Whether it is a question of what is divine or of what is human, everything belongs to the one Christ." Cyril insists at length (*ibid.*, 416A) As on the necessity of attributing Christ's human words not to another person (*hétero prosôpô*) distinct from the Son, but to the Son Himself in His human nature (*tôis tès anthrôpotètos autoû metrois*).

There is then every reason to believe that the distinction between divine words, human words and mixed (or theandric) words of the Incarnate Word was at least sharpened and perhaps even largely discovered thanks to the Nestorian heresy. By rejecting in his fourth anathema any division of words corresponding to a Nestorian-style division of subjects or persons in Christ, Cyril came not only to see the element of truth which was concealed in the error, but also to recognize more clearly, in the formula of 433, the consequences of the distinction of natures as to the words pronounced by Christ, and, consequently, as to our understanding of those words. Clearly they do not have the same meaning according to whether they are attributed to Christ speaking as man, or as God, or in function of his two natures.

One could safely say that for Cyril the distinction between human words and divine words of the Incarnate Word is the ultimate consequence that he deduces from the Christological hymn of Paul to the Philippians (2:5-11): the human words manifest the form of the servant and the *kenosis* of the Eternal Word whose divine form or condition is reflected by the divine words.[132]

A twofold objection could be raised to the above considerations: first, do they not all pertain more to Cyril's theology than to his exegesis? And then, if we admit their importance for a correct understanding of his exegesis, are they not pertinent to the late exegesis of Cyril rather than describing his exegesis as a whole?

Concerning the first objection, clearly whatever throws critical light on the divinely intended meaning of the Evangelists' words and those of Christ that they report is of the highest concern to exegesis. Now such is surely the case here, and there is therefore no need to insist on this point.

Then, about the second objection, if it is uncertain[133] whether the distinction between human, divine and mixed words had been made before the Nestorian crisis, it is nevertheless clear that the ground work for the distinction had already been laid. This, not only, as Kerrigan brought out, by way of the distinction between the literal, or carnal sense, relative to the humanity of Christ, and the spiritual sense, relative to his divinity, but also, precisely, by way of the distinction between the human nature and works and the divine nature and works of Christ—a

---

[132]*Ibid. PG 76*, 417 C: *kenôsis to Theo Logo to drasai ti kai eipein tôn anthrôpinôn dia tèn pros sarka synodon oikonomikèn.*

[133]There would be every reason to conduct a thorough inquiry to confirm this point.

distinction that was already explicitly present.[134] Now words are works that a person posits through his nature.[135] To be aware of a distinction, even if only in the eyes of faith,[136] between two natures in the one person of Christ is then already to be on the way toward making a distinction between the human and the divine in his works and words as well.

This is so true that the Church, using different terminology, adopted the same distinction, if not in the formula of union of 433 that employed the vocabulary of Cyril, at least, some time later, in a solemn pronouncement drawn up by Pope Saint Leo the Great.

> Each of the two natures, when performing the actions proper to it, does so in communion with the other: the Word does what belongs to the Word and the flesh carries out what belongs to the flesh. The one shines forth with miracles, the other succumbs to human assaults.

---

[134]See the numerous references in this sense presented by Liébaert, pp. 206-208.

[135]Cf. Thomas Aquinas, *Summa Theologiae*, III. 19. 1. 3: "It belongs to the person to act, but according to the nature specifying the operation."

[136]Already in the *Eighth Paschal Letter* (in 420), long before the Nestorian crisis, Cyril, by distinguishing clearly what was carnal in Christ, i.e. what is perfectly man (*to apo gès sarkion, ètoi teleiôs ton athrôpon: PG* 77, 570 D), added: "separate the character proper to each only by thought" (*monais dielontes tais eph'hekastô logon*). What is the meaning of this distinction of the natures only by thought? Lebon thinks, referring to Loofs, that Cyril "wishes to note that after the union, this difference [of natures] is not immediately and experientially verifiable, and that an operation of the intelligence is necessary for distinguishing even the realities that the *henôsis* [union] so tightly grouped together without however destroying the real diversity of natures or essences" (*Das Konzil von Chalkedon*, vol. I, p. 505), like that, Cyril will observe later, between the soul and the body (*Epist. XLVI ad Succensum, PL* 77, 245 A-C). However, there is a difference between the two cases: in that of man, the distinction between soul and body is accessible to unaided reason, even without faith; in the case of Christ, and in connection with His works, the distinction between the two operations of His two natures, human and divine, is accessible to reason and to faith as to their contemplations *monè theôria*," according to the expression, *in substance Cyrillian*, which was canonized by Constantinople II (*DS* 428 *sub fine*: canon 7) in 553. On this subject, see also: G. M. de Durand, *SC* 97, pp. 125-126; Liébaert, pp. 207-208; B. de Margerie, review of J. Meyendorff, *Christ in Eastern Christian Thought. Science and Spirit*, 22 (1970) pp. 252-257; we also note that Leo the Great had repeated, before Constantinople II, Cyril's teaching (*DS* 317). The exegetical significance of the distinction *monè theôria* between natures, operations, and words, whether divine or human, of the one Person of Christ should be underscored in the contemplation of faith, the believing exegete can more easily than the exegete who is only well disposed with respect to the faith, recognize as such the divine words of Christ, the words expressing his divine thoughts (for example: Jn 8:58: "Before Abraham was, I am") which are at the same time part of those "many and admirable divinely disposed exterior signs by which the divine origin of the Christian religion can be demonstrated with certainty by the natural light of reason alone" (Pius XII, *DS* 3876).

Having enunciated the principle of the distinctive and coordinated operations of each of the two natures, Pope Saint Leo hastens to apply it to the words of Christ, which he implicitly views as acts of his natures— of one of the two, or of both:

> It does not belong to the same nature to say on the one hand, "I and the Father are one" [Jn 10:30] and, on the other, "The Father is greater than I," [Jn 14:28].... It is from us that he takes the humanity that is inferior to the Father, and it is from the Father that he receives the divinity by which he is equal with the Father.[137]

Having cited these formulas which Cyril doubtless helped to make possible, it is safe to say that Cyril of Alexandria's contribution to the progress of doctrinal exegesis is secure: he underscored the necessity of distinguishing between the words of Christ which pertain to his humanity, and those which pertain to his divinity, emphasizing as he did the one Person of the Word who pronounced them all, thus developing and focusing the hermeneutic of Word of the Father. All of this clearly justifies the statement of St. Athanasius of Sinai: Cyril is the seal of the Fathers, *sphragis ton pateron*,[138] the seal that crowns and perfects the teaching of the Fathers and especially that of Saint Athanasius,[139] the recapitulator of the biblical exegesis of the earlier Fathers, opening up new horizons for the Fathers of the future. Cyril is and will remain above all the exegete of the glorious divine nature of Christ which shines forth through his humanity: under the action of the Spirit, *theoria penumatike* never ceases to recall the exegete to the vision, in faith, of the glory and the divinity of Christ, who is Son of God even more than he is Son of Man.

---

[137]Leo the Great, *Letter to Flavian*, of June 13, 449, DS 294-295

[138]Athanasius the Sinaite, concerning the Trinitarian doctrine of Cyril, *Hodegos*, chap. 7, PG 89, 113 D.

[139]Cyril praises Athanasius repeatedly in his writings; for an outstanding list of references, see H. du Manoir, *Dogme et Spiritualité...*, p. 18

Epilogue and Suggestions

We have attempted to follow the evolution and progress of Christian exegesis from Justin to Cyril of Alexandria.

A major impression emerges from the route we have traveled, while the fact that we have traveled it helps us not only to grasp the orientation we must have in responding to certain questions of our day, but also to work out this project for the spiritual benefit of the People of God.

The major impression, first of all: the exegesis of the Greek and oriental Fathers is dominated by the Person of Jesus and by an ever more vigorous and complex awareness of the presuppositions and consequences, for an understanding of the divine Word, of the mystery of the Incarnation of the only Son of God, one alone in his two ways of acting, divine and human.

Stimulated by the Arian goad—against which he had no choice but to react—and helped by Origen, Athanasius brings Christian exegesis across its first decisive threshold in recognizing the *skopos* or purpose of Scripture: to declare to men that the only Savior, who is eternally God and Son of God, became flesh, that is, man.

Less than a century after him, Cyril, Athanasius' successor in the patriarchal see of Alexandria, under the goad of Nestorianism, saw that, in the actions of the one Savior, it was necessary to distinguish what belongs to the flesh and what belongs to the divine nature in such a way that one could continue attributing everything to the one and only supreme object, the Word of the Father.[1]

---

[1] We are not unaware of all the difficulties that certain spirits experience today when they are asked, in the contemplation of the mystery of Christ, to "distinguish in order to

273

Standing between those two, and more influenced by Antioch than by Alexandria, Chrysostom stresses that the condescension of God, preparing for the Incarnation of his Word, and then manifesting it and sending it forth for the sake of carnal and limited men, is the reason why the ineffable God accommodated himself to human language when he spoke to them in order to save them by presenting their Savior to them: this is the *sygkatabasis*.

Antioch and Alexandria together show us the Scriptures manifesting first the preparation and the coming of Christ—their historical sense— then they show us the Scriptures manifesting the active presence of Christ in the Church and the sacraments (the allegorical sense). They show us the Scriptures stimulating our ethical effort to attain freedom (the tropological sense) which Christ sets in motion so that we will attain it in the beatific vision, beyond death (the anagogical and eschatological sense). Thus, in a *fourfold sense*, the Scriptures manifest to us Christ past, present, acting, coming, and eternal.

Within the context of this fourfold sense, the genius of Augustine in the Latin West had already[2]—in a way consonant with the West's characteristic bent—given great prominence to the tropological sense by clearly defining the end of all Scripture as the practice of the love for God and love for men.[3] The Christian East perceived the *object* of Scripture, in relation to the Incarnation of the Word, to be the declaration of these two conditions. The Christian West better discerned Scripture's *end*, namely, to facilitate the practice of the twofold charity, toward God and toward men, in order to set out toward the face-to-face vision of the two natures, divine and human, of the incarnate Word, in a final *theoria* that was no less dear to Chrysostom.

Let us not anticipate, however, what we shall have occasion to say in a later work concerning the exegesis of the Latin Fathers and its particular contribution. We would rather emphasize here that the

---

unite," according to Jacques Maritain's formula (in another context). We refer, for example, to the eminent Methodist exegete, Victor Taylor (*The Person of Christ in New Testament Teaching*, [London, 1966]: for him, the distinction between what Jesus does as man and what he does as God is "artificial."). However, this author, a little later (p. 269), states that the doctrine of the two natures in the Person of Christ, if we acknowledge that they are nothing more than what there is of properly human and properly divine in that Person, "is implicit in the New Testament where it constitutes the legitimate development from what is affirmed there." In saying this, Taylor has recovered the great tradition of Cyril of Alexandria and Leo the Great.

[2]Before the end of the fourth century, at the time Augustine was writing the first book of his *De doctrina Christiana*.

[3]*Ibid.*, I, 35, 39ff.; cf. 1 Tm 1:5.

exegesis of the Greek Fathers, at the point where we have stopped our investigation, i.e., with Cyril of Alexandria, tends toward a synthesis of the best that the schools of Antioch and Alexandria offer, analogous to that synthesis whose dogmatic expression was consecrated at Chalcedon. By explicitly rejecting the idea of seeing in every line of the Old Testament a specific announcement of some aspect of the New Testament, and by somehow connecting the literal sense to the humanity of the Savior, the spiritual to his divinity, Cyril keeps his distance from the abuses of Alexandrian allegorism. We have here a legitimate and profound continuation of what St. Paul had in mind when he referred to the distinction between the letter and the spirit.[4]

Thus, there seems to be some deep connection, not immediately seen, between the doctrine of the four senses of Scripture and its two purposes. The literal sense manifests the historical humanity of the Savior and the preparations for his coming, while the spiritual sense manifests in its three dimensions—sacramental, moral, anagogical—the divine nature of the Only Word of the Father. It is interesting that a similar conjunction comes to maturity precisely on the eve of Chalcedon.

Fifteen centuries have passed. In taking up the challenge that the future Cardinal Daniélou issued to us in 1958[5] and in trying to direct the attention of researchers toward the splendors of patristic exegesis (without overlooking its deficiencies), our intention is above all to contribute to the renewal of Catholic theology and to the spiritual

---

[4]In Pauline thought, the letter is connected with the Law, but is abrogated by Christ dying on the cross. Cf. Col 2:14; Rom 8, 1ff.; Gal 2:19-20. Christ suppressed the indictment that was drawn up against us by nailing it to the cross; whence; indirectly, the possibility of seeing the letter of the Old Law as a symbol of the crucified humanity of the Savior.

[5]Cardinal Jean Daniélou: "in the immense work bequeathed to us by the Fathers of the Church, it can be said that the most neglected part of it up to now has been their exegesis. This is even more astonishing in view of the fact that their exegesis represents the largest part of their work" (*DSAM*, vol. IV, [1958], col. 132-133). Previously, in 1934, Bardy had written: "In the present state of research, a complete history of biblical exegesis which would bring out the genealogy of ideas, the influence of ancient commentators on the works of their successors, the development of methods and interpretations, etc. is one of the most urgent and at the same time one of the most difficult undertakings" (*DBS* II, [1934], col. 103: the conclusion of the article is Patristic commentaries on the Bible). It was precisely this urgent and difficult work that Bardy himself undertook at least to begin, in a later volume of the *Dictionary* itself, in 1949: *DBS*, vol. IV, col. 569-591: "Interpretation," *II: Patristic Exegesis*. We also find useful general insights on the exegesis of the Fathers in: Jouassard, "Les Pères devant la Bible," *Etudes de critique et d'histoire religieuses*, Bibliotèque de la Faculté de Théologie de Lyon, vol. 2, (1948), pp. 25-33; L. Leloir, "La lecture de l'Ecriture selon les anciens Pères," *Rev. Asc. Myst.* 47 (1971), pp. 183-200.

progress of the people of God toward the perfect practice of the twofold love toward the God-Man, Christ.

Should it not be easier, in the light of the biblical commentaries of the Fathers, for the Church today to see in the cultures of India and China, ancient rays of the Word as providential preparations for his Gospel?

In fact, the Fathers of the Church were marvelously able to bring the Greek culture, without embracing the errors they encountered there, into the service of the liturgical exposition of the Word of God.

Contact with the exegesis of the Fathers moves us above all to make some concrete proposals for facilitating the study and diffusion of that exegesis.

First, we would hope to see the publication of new annotated editions of each of the Gospels, then of the New Testament as a whole, provided with brief notes inspired by the Fathers and their commentaries. Only those commentaries should be chosen which are in harmony with the exegetical criteria set down in the encyclical *Divino afflante Spiritu* of Pius XII, and in the constitution *Dei Verbum* of Vatican II. Those editions could be prepared in common by Catholics, Anglicans, Orthodox, and other Christians who value the Fathers.

Second, we would like to see patristic collections now existing in various languages (for example, *Sources chrétiennes, Ancient Christian Writers, Fathers of the Church,* etc.) concentrate their efforts in the direction of the biblical commentaries of the Fathers, which up to now constitute only a limited part of their publications.

Then, in the third place, we would like to see the creation, in bilingual editions in each of the principal languages, of a new collection centered on the methodical publication of the patristic commentaries on the Scriptures (unless the collections previously mentioned develop section to this effect). Their purpose would be to place the insights of the Fathers within the reach of contemporary readers.

Why not, in the last place, create an international review having for its proper object the publication of studies on patristic exegesis and the contribution it can bring to the development of the knowledge of the Word of God?

While waiting for these projects to become reality, if that turns out to be possible, we hope that the study here offered to the public will stimulate at least the preparation both of articles on certain particular points of patristic exegesis in presently existing reviews and of theses that follow, in the Fathers, the exegesis of an individual biblical verse or text.

Who knows even if some university theology faculties will not create biblico-patristic institutes, living centers that would enable the projects described above to become realities?

May the reflections and prayers of many readers of this book contribute to these purposes, for the greater glory of Christ Jesus, the only Word of the Father, who became human word and Who reaches us through the Scriptures and through preaching.

Analytical Index

Author Index

Index of Biblical References

10	221
10:3	8
10:1-4	8, 161
10:11	8, 100
11:3	59
13:1	155
13:2, 9-12	131
13:3	89
13:12	104
14:2	264
15:20	250
15:21-16	64
15:22	64
15:24-28	60, 71
15:45-49	8
15:54	64
15:54-57	64

II Corinthians

3:6	9
3:14-15	48
12:10	131
13:5	17

Galatians

2:19-20	275
4:4-6	64
4:21-24	100
4:22-30	8
4:23-24	32, 68, 169

Ephesians

1:10	57-58
3:6	252
4:4	73
4:15-16	76

Philippians

2	158, 216, 238
2:2	230
2:5-11	226, 252, 255, 268
2:6	227
2:6-8	119, 232, 257
2:7	105, 227-228, 255
2:9	229, 230, 231, 232
2:10	231
3:6	147
3:14	131

Colossians

1:15	252, 259-260
1:16	110, 154
2:14	275
2:16-17	100

I Thessalonians

5:23	98

I Timothy

1:5	136, 274
1:6	74
1:9-10	31
2:5	233
2:14-15	61-62
3:16	234
6:11-12	138

Hebrews

1:2	255
1:4	119
1:9	183
1:14	91
2:12	232
3:1	119, 252, 261
5:12-6:1	85
7:3	173, 255
7:18	34
8:5	9, 100, 160
9:11	9
9:23	9
9:24	9, 160
10:1	9, 98, 100, 103, 160
10:20	221
11:7	30
11:13	179
11:17	124
11:19	88
13:8	252-256

James

2:14-16	72
2:19	72

I Peter

1:10	48
3:18-24	30
3:21	8

II Peter

1:4	86
1:6-7	138
3:5-10	29
3:10	29

II John

2:9	19

Revelation

14:6	104
21:5	14

*   *   *

Irenaeus

Is 7:14:	65ff.
Eph 1:10:	57ff.
1 Tm 2:14-15:	62
Luke 1:38:	61ff.
Luke 10 The Good Samaritan:	70ff.
	(cf. 90)

Clement of Alexandria

Luke 10: The Good Samaritan:	90
	(cf. 70)

Origen

Heb 10:1:	102-103 (cf. 160, 173)
Rev 14:6:	104

Athanasius

Gn 22:2-18:	124ff.
Mk 13:32:	122-123
Heb 11:17:	123, 124
Pastoral Letters:	136-139
Psalms:	133-136
Jn 7:37-39:	126-128
Jn 8:56:	124 (cf. 179, 196)

Ephraem

Gn 2:21-23:	144-147
Mt 19, Mk 10 (the rich young man):	147ff., 162
Mt 17 Transfiguration:	152
Mt 27:46 and 50-53:	150-153
Mt 10:12:	162-163
Jn 19:27:	151-152

Antioch

Hos 11:1 and Mt 2:15:	172
Heb 7:3:	173
Ps 16:10 and Acts 2:29-31:	176-180

Chrysostom

Lk 23:43:	202
Lk 10:22:	203

Gregory of Nyssa

Ps 89:	223-225
Phil 2:6:	227-232
Jn 20:17:	232-234
Mt 28:19:	234-235

Cyril of Alexandria

Phil 2:5-11:	255-258, 268-269 (cf. 226-232)
Heb 13:8:	252ff.
Jn 1:32ff:	249-250

182